The Men and Women of Yeshiva

The Men and Women of Yeshiva:

HIGHER EDUCATION, ORTHODOXY, AND AMERICAN JUDAISM

Jeffrey S. Gurock

Columbia University Press   New York   1988

Columbia University Press

New York   Guildford, Surrey

Copyright © 1988 Columbia University Press

Printed in the United States of America

Clothbound editions of Columbia University Press are Smyth-sewn
and printed on permanent and durable acid-free paper

Library of Congress Cataloging-in-Publication Data

Gurock, Jeffrey S., 1949–
The men and women of Yeshiva.

Includes index.
1. Yeshiva University—History.   2. Orthodox
Judaism—United States—History.   I. Title.
LD6371.Y43G87   1988   378.747'1   87-24911
ISBN 0-231-06618-X

To three of Yeshiva's best
Jonathan
Marvin
Shulamith

Contents

Acknowledgments

It is my grateful and pleasurable duty to acknowledge the many groups and individuals who have assisted me in the writing of this book.

I owe my greatest debt to Yeshiva University. My home institution's centennial provided me with the occasion to look back at its history and attempt to place its story within the larger saga of American Jewry and of Orthodoxy in this country. The university's leadership, beginning with Dr. Norman Lamm, president of Yeshiva University, has given me every technical assistance and social support, asking only that I tell my story fairly and completely. This, I believe, I have done. Within the Yeshiva community, the following friends stand out. Dr. Egon Brenner encouraged my efforts from their inception. Sam Hartstein has been my close confidant. I have also gained much from conversations with Dr. Israel Miller. Dr. Roger Kohn directed me through Yeshiva University's Archive. Dean Pearl Berger and her library staff were always there when I needed them. Leonard Brandwein unlocked for me the world of computers. And Yeshiva student Gil Winokur developed the program that I used in collecting my quantitative data. Over at the Albert Einstein College of Medicine Computer Center, Dr. Mark Mizruchi was particularly helpful. Back on the Washington Heights campus, Professor Morris Silverman and Pinhas Friedenberg led me to the registrar's archive. Dr. Yechiel Simon and Toby Weiss put me in touch with literally hundreds of alumni, many of whom I had the pleasure of interviewing. My thanks to all those individuals who opened their homes and recollections to me. Their names are included in the notes of this book. Through all this work at Yeshiva, Arlene Michael has been a special technical assistant. She dutifully and tirelessly transcribed numerous drafts of this manuscript, even becoming a somewhat experienced cryptologist through reading my often illegible handwriting.

I was also most privileged to have my student Shulamith Goldstein work with and for me as research assistant. She enthusias-

tically ran down every lead we developed and worked month after
month in producing the quantitative data which form the core of this
work. Through her dedication to scholarship, to family and commitment and tolerance within Orthodox Jewish life, this Stern College
alumna personifies for me much of what is best in Yeshiva's community. The same can be said for Dr. Jonathan Halpert and Marvin
Hershkowitz, the two men of Yeshiva to whom this book is also dedicated.

A writer is most fortunate when he has colleagues who will
read his work critically, fairly, and sensitively. In my case, I am very
lucky to have had Drs. Benjamin Gampel of the Jewish Theological
Seminary of America, William Helmreich of the City College of New
York, and Marc Lee Raphael of Ohio State University evaluate and
help improve several drafts of this book. All their advice was good.
Any problems with the book are of my doing alone.

I have a nice family. My parents Leah and Jack Gurock are
understandably overimpressed with my achievements. My brother and
his family like reading my books. So does my wife, Pamela. More
importantly, she has built, far more than I have, a loving home for us
and our children. Rosie and Michael do not read yet. Eli does, but
he won't be reading this book for a while. His literary horizons for
now include works for boys on Dave Winfield and Rickey Hender-
son. But then again, isn't that where so many of us began?

Abbreviations Used
in Text and Notes

AECOM   Albert Einstein College of Medicine

AH   *American Hebrew*

AJA   *American Jewish Archives*

AJH   *American Jewish History*

AJHQ   *American Jewish Historical Quarterly*

AJYB   *American Jewish Yearbook*

BTA   Brooklyn Talmudical Academy

CCNY   City College of New York

Comm.   *Commentator* (Yeshiva College undergraduate student newspaper)

CSC   Concerned Students Coalition

EJ   *Encyclopedia Judaica* (Jerusalem, 1972)

EMC   Erna Michael College of Hebraic Studies, (an undergraduate division of Yeshiva University)

Hame   *Hamevaser* (student publication of the Religious Studies Divisions at Yeshiva University)

HILI   Hebrew Institute of Long Island

HS   *Hebrew Standard*

HUC   Hebrew Union College

JE   *Jewish Encyclopedia* (New York, 1906)

JES   Jewish Endeavor Society

JF   *Jewish Forum*

JHLP	Joseph H. Lookstein Papers
JQR	*Jewish Quarterly Review*
JSP	Jewish Studies Program (an undergraduate division of Yeshiva University)
JSS	James Striar School of General Jewish Studies (an undergraduate division of Yeshiva University)
JSWF	*Jewish Social Work Forum*
JTS	Jewish Theological Seminary
MRE	Masters in Religious Education
MZ	*Morgen Zhurnal*
NCSY	National Conference of Synagogue Youth
NFTY	National Federation of Temple Youth
OU	Orthodox Union
PAAJR	*Proceedings of the American Academy for Jewish Research*
PAJHS	*Publications of the American Jewish Historical Society*
RA	Rabbinical Assembly
RCA	Rabbinical Council of America
RIETS	Rabbi Isaac Elchanan Theological Seminary
RIETS-YC Bd.	Minutes of the Board of Directors of the Rabbi Isaac Elchanan Theological Seminary and Yeshiva College
RJJ	Rabbi Jacob Joseph School
ROTC	Reserve Officers Training Corps
SCW	Stern College for Women
SECA	School of Education and Community Administration
TA	Talmudical Academy

TI	Teachers Institute
TIW	Teachers Institute for Women
TLS	Torah Leadership Seminar
UJE	*Universal Jewish Encyclopedia* (New York, 1929)
USY	United Synagogue Youth
YA	Yeshiva University Archive
YC	Yeshiva College
YG	*Yiddishe Gazetten*
YI	Young Israel
YPR	Press Release of the Yeshiva Public Relations Office (circa 1925–46)
YT	*Yiddishes Tageblatt*
YU	Yeshiva University
YUMW	Yeshiva University Men and Women (quantified data derived from the registrar's office at Yeshiva University)
YUNYC	Yeshiva University Neighborhood Youth Corps
YUPR	Press Release of the Yeshiva University Public Relations Office (1946–)
YUSCY	Yeshiva University Synagogue Council Youth

The Men and Women of Yeshiva

Chapter 1

Students at Yeshiva College, 1984

During the winter of 1984, a survey was conducted of Yeshiva College sophomores and freshmen. Members of the classes of June 1986 and 1987—the one hundredth anniversary graduating classes— were asked through a series of 170 scientifically controlled questions to explain "the reasons and influences that led" them to choose this university for their academic training. Students were requested to gauge the relative significance of career, religious, philosophical, personal, and financial considerations in their decision-making. How important, for example, was Yeshiva's "record of getting its graduates into professional schools"? What role did their "own personal desire to lead an Orthodox Jewish life while in college" play in their arrival on Amsterdam Avenue? Did they consider Yeshiva's long-standing "educational philosophy of synthesis" in their college plans? Were they concerned, like many of the students in the generations that had preceded them, in understanding and redefining Yeshiva's effort to effect what can be loosely described as the comfortable and success- ful coexistence of traditional Jewish thought and behavior with the modern scientific and humanistic world? And what of issues common to all American high school seniors—costs of education, family tradi- tions or pressures, campus environment, location, and the like? When these responses were correlated with important background materials on informants a computer-certain profile of the contemporary Ye- shiva male undergraduate emerged of value to university planners plotting the beginnings of Yeshiva University's next one hundred years.[1]

For historians, these data on a university core institution serve as a basis for some informed observations about the role and position of Yeshiva both within the changing world of American Orthodoxy and within the broader American Jewish and American societies at large.

The most typical of today's Yeshiva College students was born in the United States and a middle-class neighborhood, either in New York's outer borough of Queens or in a close suburb, a short commute away from the metropolis. Otherwise, he is likely to have been raised in an outskirt community of some other large North American city. In this regard, he is much different from his father, who, if he attended Yeshiva—and three out of ten 1983–84 freshmen and sophomores had alumni fathers—most commonly grew up in a Brooklyn, New York, Jewish neighborhood. Today only one out of eight come from that now most populous of New York City boroughs. And almost no one comes from Manhattan, certainly not from the Lower East Side, where Yeshiva first began a century ago.

That same parent—Yeshiva man or not—is far more likely than not to be a college graduate. A solid middle-class citizen, he and his wife—in six out of ten cases a college graduate also—have enough money to own their own home in a well-kept neighborhood, a home large enough to allow each of their children a room of his or her own. They and their parents probably did not have such comforts in their Brooklyn or downtown tenements or flats. In only the rarest of cases have these economically successful Americans asked their college-bound youngsters to help finance their higher education by working while at school. No Hebrew school moonlighting or any other part-time jobs for this generation; a potential problem, by the way, for quality Jewish education. Yeshiva students always made excellent bar mitzvah tutors.

The older generation, well-heeled and groomed, may be joined on the weekends by their youngsters, tired only from a week at books or at play, in an architectually and socially modern Orthodox synagogue. Neither *shteibls*—ephemeral old-world synagogues—nor Reform or Conservative temples are for them. Their kitchens are, of course, kept strictly kosher and their Sabbath is a true day of rest as described and prescribed by the Codes of Jewish law. Not surprisingly, they would very much like to have their children continue their traditional Jewish ways. And, as they see it, Yeshiva University's chemistry of the old and revered and the new will help their youngsters follow in the right footsteps. They also have made their desires clearly known to their sons as they reached high school graduation. The freshmen and sophomores of 1983–84 reported in seven out of ten cases that their parents were either a "positive or very positive" influence in their "ultimate decision" to attend the college. Similarly, 43 percent of students noted that their parents' desire that they attend Yeshiva College played either an "important or very important" role in their choice of schools. These strong parental preferences were not cause, however, for much tension around the dinner table. Here youngsters agreed with their parents: some 74 percent of those who enrolled saw their own desire to lead an Orthodox life-style while on campus as "important or very important" in that critical life move.

There are two findings that indicate how students, long before they enrolled, already saw themselves as part of the Yeshiva University community. One in five students never considered another college for advanced training. A full 40 percent applied only to Yeshiva. Significantly, many of the considerations which loom large in the minds of all other college students, such as tuition costs, financial assistance packages, and extracurricular activities, played a comparative limited part in making up the minds of Yeshiva students. Even the vaunted, if sometimes criticized, reputation that Yeshiva students get into medical and law schools in record percentages does not play nearly as strong a part in the individual's decision-making as their desire to remain Orthodox during these youthful years of social and intellectual experimentation. Viewing these statistics, parents, for their part, may feel satisfied that the expense of sending their sons to elementary and secondary day schools—the bicultural educational system that Yeshiva founded, molded, and personifies—had paid off.

Parents may also be pleased that their youngsters, in most cases, did not look at Yeshiva as a place that would alter their religious life styles. At least six out of ten students felt right from the start that they would be able to fit in religiously at the school. They perceived religious observance at Yeshiva as about the same as in their own homes. Meanwhile, only one in four students saw themselves as coming to the school to become more religious. Likewise, in moments of doubt about whether Yeshiva was right for them, only 15 percent felt that the institution might not be religious enough for them. Interestingly enough, almost the same proportion of students were concerned that Yeshiva was too Orthodox for their tastes. More pervasive reservations about Yeshiva included perceptions that the school was situated in a "bad neighborhood"—even though articulated fears about campus security were relatively low—and personal apprehensions alternately about whether they could handle the dual programs of Jewish and general studies or whether Yeshiva's B.A. curriculum was strong enough. It was also more widely feared that life at Yeshiva would be all too boring—not enough campus life and no coeds in attendance at school—even as they were also quick to note that girls and gyms were relatively unimportant factors in their ultimate decision to attend Yeshiva.

One fear that was almost never articulated was the one common to so many freshmen nationwide: Would they know anyone at a strange new school? Almost every freshman and sophomore had known "someone who attended Yeshiva" before enrolling at the school. Moreover, it seems that the desire to continue to be with friends of longest standing for at least four more years loomed large in their choice of this college. In fact, next to their parents and even more than their own siblings—many of whom had attended the college—it was their friends who played the most "positive" role in their deciding upon Yeshiva. And although the survey did not identify friends by gender, it may be supposed that some of those long-standing relationships were with students of the opposite sex.

Though Yeshiva College is an all-male institution, it has always had the closest informal ties with its sister school, Stern College for Women, located since its founding in the early 1950s in midtown Manhattan. Dating between and among students at both schools has always been a fact of life at Yeshiva. For more than a generation, Thursday-night riders on the Broadway subways have observed "spiffed up" young Orthodox gentlemen on the way to meet their girl friends outside West Side ice-skating rinks or at downtown expensive kosher restaurants. Today, the same types of youngsters can also be seen driving down the East Side Drive in their automobiles, although, in truth, relatively few students keep their cars on campus. They belong in suburban driveways. No one can find a parking space in Washington Heights.

Not surprisingly, this close social network within which dating is only a part—they grew up in the same neighborhoods, went together to coed elementary day schools, were split apart during the school year at their single-sex high schools but met regularly at Orthodox summer camps or on teenage trips to Israel—contributes to a very high rate of intramarriage among Yeshiva students. One has only to read the school newspaper's "rings and things" or "who's whose" columns to prove statistically how frequently Yeshiva students find suitable mates among Stern women who share their love and Jewish outlook on life.[2]

But does this outlook on life, specifically at the moment of the students' first formal encounter with Yeshiva, include a conscious commitment to the overarching philosophy of "Torah U'Mada," that synthesis of religious and secular learning defined in passing just a moment ago. For a goodly proportion—four out of ten students—the belief that Yeshiva's generations-old objective to produce students who could live with equal facility and harmony with the world of their fathers and mothers and in the universes of America constituted either "the most important or a very important" factor in their coming to Washington Heights. Others, as we have just begun to see, are in effect living lives that implicitly suggest assent to that mission. Only one in twenty students could say that he enrolled at the school despite this philosophy. One job of the institution would be to bring those dissenters, along with the some one-quarter of the students who felt that coming to grips with the implications of "Torah U'mada" was not important to them, to become conscious of how it was already a part of their being and to make it more fully a part of their lives.

But providing students with a greater appreciation of the challenges of synthesis seems ultimately to stand second among the pressing Jewish agendas facing school leadership. First is the dilemma of how to make Yeshiva students, so confident in their Orthodoxy while so comfortable and so well-integrated into American society, "broaden (their) horizons beyond . . . immediate needs and the concerns of our narrow constituency to embrace all of the Jewish community throughout the world."[3]

For Dr. Norman Lamm, president of Yeshiva University, author of the last few words, the fact that only 7 percent of the students polled were considering the rabbinate as their life's work and even fewer were thinking of teaching (Jewish or general) or of Jewish communal service as their careers might be a cause for some dismay. He would have to be pleased that his youngsters lived in an America where Orthodox Jews could be part of the worlds of science and medicine, of law and high finance without having to surrender their Jewish beliefs or practices. But he would have to be concerned whether this present generation with all its advantages would remain true to one of Yeshiva's oldest goals: the training of rabbis ready and able to devote their lives to the service of the Jewish people.[4]

How different are today's Yeshiva College students from their counterparts fifty years ago? And how removed are they from their last century antecedents, the pupils of the university's root institution, a small school for "poor Hebrew children" called Jesibath Etz Chaiem? These questions are more than rhetorical flourishes. They are sober charges for scholarly investigation. A comparative study of what has brought men, and later women, to Yeshiva over one hundred years not only tells the evolving story of the school they selected, but helps us limn—as we have just outlined for the present day—the evolving social history of Orthodoxy and American Jewry over more than a century.

Though this is the historian's mandate, its achievement is not easily accomplished. The 1984 survey is a first in Yeshiva University history, a commentary in its own right on the level of maturation reached by this American university in its ninety-eighth year. Earlier generations of Yeshiva leadership neither felt the institutional necessity nor possessed the historical sensitivity requisite to bequeath such vital information to us. They certainly did not have, until very recently, the technological tools to interface, integrate, and store such quantitative sources. We will, therefore, never be able to determine with actuarial assurance what or who drove Lower East Side youngsters to attend, beginning in 1886, Etz Chaiem. Nor, for that matter, will we ever fully understand what brought students, beginning in 1897, to the Rabbi Isaac Elchanan Theological Seminary. The backgrounds and proclivities of Dr. Bernard Revel's Rabbinical College of America (circa 1915 +) disciples beg comparison with those of Dr. Samuel Belkin (1943 +) and with those of today's students. But the early sources are simply not there. In fact, for many of the fifty years between Etz Chaiem's founding and the establishment of Yeshiva College in the late 1920s, we do not even know the names and numbers of students attending the changing institution. Such is the partial legacy of a financially unstable immigrant religious institution, born in poverty, settled on shaky legs in storefront locales, too worried about its future to be concerned about whether it would someday have need of a documented past.

And yet all is not lost. When this new American institution entered its second generation and, like the good 1920s Jews who supported it, moved from transient immigrant quarters to better-built and more permanent uptown locales, it began to behave on Washington Heights like the settled American institution it sought to be. That meant, most importantly for us, that, in conformity with state educational rules and regulations, student record files, following individuals from the instant they applied to each of the university's branches and affiliates through their school academic careers and sometimes beyond, were kept and maintained. When these registrar's records are analyzed, both qualitatively and quantitatively, with the help of the computer, answers start to emerge as to Yeshiva's role and position within American Orthodoxy and to the condition of American Jewry over several generations. Yeshiva students speak to us in their own words—through their files and through cognate materials—explaining their choice of Yeshiva and of their expectations from their school. They leave it for us as historians to amplify what these statements mean and what they say about them. Yeshiva University students have always constituted a small, circumscribed group within and without American and Jewish society and have clearly opted for a certain degree of separatism from both worlds. But the typology of Yeshiva student has changed dramatically over time. So has the nature of his, and for the last twenty-five odd years her, separatism from America. Both factors have played an important role in determining the evolving mission of their university.

But before the second and succeeding generations of Yeshiva students speak to us, let us give voice through extant documentation to the inarticulate, the students of Etz Chaiem, early RIETS, and the Teachers Institute (1917 +), the downtown, first components of what became Yeshiva University.[5]

Chapter 2

The Root of a Transplanted
Orthodox Community

By 1887, Rabbi Moses Weinberger had had enough of America. An 1880 migrant to these shores, he had come to despair that this country could ever be home to the Jewish religious world he had known and left behind in his native Hungary. He had arrived hopeful that in this land of religious liberty Jews could build a traditional life comparable to that which had survived centuries of tyranny in Europe. Indeed, he may have dreamed that the United States could become for Jews the ideal diaspora where, free from the fear of pogroms and persecution, Jews would construct great communities and renowned centers of Torah learning. Seven years of living in America had shown him just how unrealisitic his hopes and dreams had been.[1]

He had learned early on in America how freedom of religion also meant freedom from religion. In this land, no earthly power—ecclesiastical or political—could demand religious observance or oblige individuals to build their faith's institutions. He had observed how many of his fellow Jews had chosen to put the synagogue behind them as they tried to make it in a new world. And he had witnessed how freedom of economic opportunity had undermined the faith of so many others who had arrived determined to hold fast to old ways. He understood that those who in this country stopped keeping the Sabbath or who felt it was unnecessary to provide their children with a Jewish education or who turned to Gentile courts and not to rabbis in their business dealings did not seek to separate themselves from their people and their past. They were simply following the road set down by America for its immigrants' integration.

Weinberger also recognized that even as these Jews were not living their lives according to Judaism's traditional tenets, many—particularly those who, like him, were new to these shores—retained a residual affinity for the religious rituals they had followed back in Eastern Europe. The Jew who worked Saturday morning after attending services on Friday night (Sabbath eve) was a common sight in the immigrant neighborhood. This transgressor, as Weinberger would have defined him, participated in the religious life of his downtown community, because going to synagogue gave him the opportunity to communicate with the Almighty while socializing with friends from the old-side. He would remain with the synagogue for the rest of his life or for as long as he needed that comforting way station between the worlds of Europe and America. So disposed, Weinberger was little warmed by the literally thousands of storefront synagogues that constituted Judaism's most visible presence in America's immigrant quarters.

Weinberger would not have denied these fellow Jews entrance into the sanctuary so long as they occupied the back rows of the room. What disturbed him was that in these *landsmanshaft* synagogues that welcomed all Jews, he, as a rabbi, had little to say about who sat where. The power in these ephemeral Orthodox institutions rested with the laity, particularly the more affluent, be they learned or not, observant or not. That was not the way the Jewish life he remembered had been ordered in Europe. He mourned the lack of deference to rabbinic authority that permeated America.

If Weinberger was disturbed that the rabbi's word was not law within the synagogue, he was patently horrified by how little clout he and his colleagues had in all other areas of Jewish religious life. No one, for example, apparently cared who supervised the provision of kosher meats. It seemed as if in America anyone could open a butcher shop, sprinkle sawdust on the floor, paint the words "Baser Kasher" on the window, and declare himself an authorized slaughterer and overseer of meat preparation. And when day was done, that same "kosher" butcher could moonlight performing marriage ceremonies without any rabbinical authorization. The next morning might find him in some other apartment officiating at a circumcision. Weinberger decried those functionaries who always did what their customers wanted, no questions asked. His ultimate dread was that twentieth-century American Jewry would be made up of Jewishly illegitimate children born in a libertine world where those from priestly families married divorcées and where men and women divorced and remarried without securing a rabbinical writ of divorce.[2]

But why focus one's fears upon the poor bastards? As Weinberger saw it, if Jewish parents did not rethink their attitudes toward Jewish education, there would be, within a generation, few Jews around—legitimate or otherwise—still loyal to their ancestral faith.

There were, in his estimation, many skilled teachers in the immigrant neighborhood capable of providing Jewish children with the type of education he had received in Hungary. But there was little support in the community for these pedagogues who prized the continuation of the hallowed European history of learning in America. Few immigrant parents shared Weinberger's dream that their children would become renowned Talmudic scholars. If their progeny were to become famous, it would be through their achievement of the American dream. And the pursuit of economic advancement and social acceptance began with attendance in the American public schools. These temples of Americanization were the places to be, even if there no effort would be made to instill a sense of belonging to Judaism in their children.[3]

Some parents were unperturbed by this gap in their childrens' training. And for them, after-public school hours were for work, play, or whatever endeavors America deemed appropriate for their children. Others were not as accepting of the summons to assimilation and were troubled by their children's ignorance of their people's past. They could see the evidence before them. They could drag their children with them to the *landsmanshaft* synagogue, but they could not sustain the attention of their Jewishly unlettered youngsters to the services. Though disturbed by the toll Americanization was taking, they were nonetheless unwilling to opt for the educational philosophy brought over from the other side. East European style schools, which evinced little interest in developing students' linguistic and social skills as Americans, were simply not for them. So disposed, they looked to the private *heder*, a Jewish one-room "school-house" often situated in a tenement loft, to provide the next generation with the rudiments of Judaism after the public schools let out. That their children would have rather spent their free time in the streets was another matter entirely.[4]

True to form, Weinberger had some nice things to say about the teachers in the Jewish schools who labored without recognition or proper compensation to largely uninterested Jewish youngsters. In fact, he sold copies of his written critique of America, *ha-Yehudim veha-Yahadut be-Nuyork*, to raise funds for the largest and best run *heder,* the Machzike Talmud Torah of the Lower East Side. But the daily struggle of these "submerged scholars," as they would later be called, for economic survival and popular approbation only deepened his gloom about the future of American Judaism. All things considered, he had truly come to rue the day he left Szepes for a country characterized by one later contemporary as "a *treif* land where even the stones are impure."[5]

Weinberger was thus filled with a mixture of pride and wonderment when he learned that Jews in his own immigrant neighborhood had recently founded a school called Jesibath Etz Chaiem (hereinafter called Etz Chaim). He was proud that some 1500 people were committed to backing a school dedicated to providing

> free instruction to poor Hebrew Children in the Hebrew Language and Hebrew Law-Talmud, Bible and Sulchon Aurach [sic] during the whole day from nine in the morning until four in the afternoon. Also from four in the afternoon, two hours shall be devoted to teach the native language, English, and one hour to teach Hebrew-Loshon [sic] Hakodosh and Jargon to read and write.[6]

But he also had to wonder: where had these allies come from? Who were these religious stalwarts who voluntarily supported an institution that publicly articulated a studied separatism from their new environment? They were, after, all, backing a school whose chartered curriculum evidenced little concern with socializing pupils in the culture around them. And what of the immigrant parents who opted to send their children to such an institution? They seemed to be content to see their children mature ill-disposed, if not ill-equipped, to compete in America's market place of ideas and economics. The class schedule allowed for only two hours a day of English language instruction, shared with studies in Yiddish and Hebrew language arts, after a full seven hours of the traditional courses in Talmud, Bible, and Codes. Indeed, the very inclusion of the secular in the study day was more a concession to the letter of an 1874 state law that provided that "all parents . . . shall instruct (their children), or cause them to be instructed in spelling, reading, writing, English grammar, geography and arithmetic" than a primitive attempt at an integrated curriculum. That some students applied themselves with great diligence to the haphazardly taught, rarely monitored secular studies proved only that even the most cloistered were not totally immune to the drive to advance and learn about America. But that was not the mandate of their institution.[7]

Weinberger did not know who these founders and fathers were, although he honored them in print and prayed that their legions would increase. Had he investigated, he would have found that their numbers were far fewer than those reported, but the intensity of their commitment was great indeed. Etz Chaim's people constituted a cadre of resisters to Americanization with whom he could find enduring common cause. They not only shared his educational philosophy, but some were even instrumental in reviving—at least for a while—Weinberger's almost dead dreams.

In 1887, Weinberger called for a concerted last-ditch counterattack against Americanization to be led by a "Chief Rabbi of New York." He argued that if a renowned Eastern European authority would deign to come over and take charge of American religious life, his learning and charisma—if not oratory—would captivate the Jewish masses and direct them back to "respect and dignify" the Torah. At least three of the organizers of Etz Chaim, cap manufacturer Joshua Rothstein and ghetto men of letters Judah David Eisenstein and Kasriel Sarasohn, were either moved by Weinberger's plea or were motivated by similar concerns to work toward just that solution. These three laymen cast their lot with the Association of American Orthodox Congregations which did precisely what Weinberger suggested. Operating out of the Norfolk Street synagogue, Beth Hamidrash Hagodol, where Eisenstein was unofficial congregational historian, they sent letters to European seats of learning asking for guidance and ultimately for candidates. They hoped, as Weinberger did, to find a zealous fighter of uncommon ability who would stop "open and flagrant desecration of the Sabbath, the neglect of dietary laws . . . (while) scrupulously supervising . . . the *shohatim* (ritual slaughterers) and all other matters of holiness." Their search for a leader/saviour ended successfully, or so that association hoped, in 1888 when Rabbi Jacob Joseph of Vilna was brought to this country and began his ministry in the heart of the immigrant quarter.[8]

Thus by the end of the 1880s, Rabbi Weinberger could harbor faint hopes about the future. At least he was not alone. There was Etz Chaim downtown and a chief rabbi in place and there were Jews who willingly surrendered their personal autonomy in religious matters to a higher rabbinical authority. And there were at least twenty-five to thirty immigrant Jewish families who readily kept their children away from the public schools. For these Jews the lures of assimilation in the streets could not be offset by a few hours in the Machzike Talmud Torah and the other afternoon *heders*. Enrollment in Etz Chaim was the only answer. These parents and pupils constituted the most visible element of a community of zealous committed Orthodox Jews who strove to live an East European life-style on the foreign American soil of the 1890s.

But even as these Jews sought to isolate themselves from America, they did not wish to separate themselves from their fellow Jews. The whole point of the Rabbi Jacob Joseph endeavor was not only to bolster those already convinced but to lead others to live in America as they once had in Europe. Similarly, Etz Chaim was established not only to serve the staunchly committed Machzike Talmud Torah families but to stand as a beacon of Torah for the entire wavering community. Equally important, this strictly Orthodox community could not exist without the spiritual and financial encouragement of the larger Jewish polity. They needed the help of other Jews. Hebrew teachers had to be hired, indigent students supported, textbooks purchased, quarters built or rented. And across the street, Rabbi Jacob Joseph had to be paid as did his kashruth inspectors. Such were the myriad of expenses incurred in maintaining a strong religious presence in America. The 1890s showed that, difficult as it was to build European institutions in this country, their perpetuation was even more problematic.

Etz Chaim sought to raise funds by playing on the nostalgic heart strings of the Jewish masses while assuring their more affluent brethren a place in their memory forever. Jews without money were solicited through the ubiquitous charity box as Etz Chaim *pushkes* took their place alongside those of many other shoestring ghetto institutions. Jews on the rise were promised that, in return for a munificent gift in excess of $1,000, a memorial prayer would be recited every Saturday and Holiday of the year after their death. And then "as long as the Academy exists the 'Yahrzeit' shall be held and a chapter of the 'Mishnah' shall be learned on that day." Of course, "the names of the donors would be inscribed on a tablet of the Academy to be remembered forever."[9]

Undoubtedly to the dismay of Etz Chaim's organizers, the next-worldly offering netted few takers. Penuriousness only partially explains the lack of response. Poverty endemic to the newly arrived immigrants may be closer to the point; nouveau-riche immigrants were only beginning to emerge from the neighborhood. And they, like their poorer brethren, found themselves bombarded from all sides with legitimate requests from deserving charities. Here again American voluntarism took its toll on religious life. There was no legally constituted authority that could direct and set priorities for the flow of charity.[10]

Rabbi Jacob Joseph would have been glad to serve in that capacity. But he was having problems fulfilling his own responsibilities. Fund-raising for the Chief Rabbi was accomplished through him, not by him. And meeting the Norfolk Street rabbinate's payroll severely undermined the rabbi's community-wide reputation and authority. Rabbi Jacob Joseph was charged with overseeing the proper provision of kosher meat. In fulfilling that role, the Rabbi dictated that a tag certifying kashruth be placed on every chicken slaughtered in his domain. Rabbi Jacob Joseph wanted this monitoring done gratis as a service to the Jewish consumer. However, the association that hired Rabbi Jacob Joseph had very different ideas. They assigned a one-half cent tariff on every slaughtered chicken and used the revenues to offset chief rabbinate expenses. This levy, which raised cries of corruption if not of "korobka" (an infamous czarist tax) from the Socialists and other unsympathetic downtown groups, did much to alienate the wider immigrant Jewish community from the Chief Rabbi.[11]

Though beset by this and other challenges to his authority and authenticity, Rabbi Jacob Joseph labored to bring the immigrants and their children back to the Torah of Europe. But his counterattack against Americanization never got off the ground. His fiery Yiddish exhortations to Jewish masses demanding that they observe the Sabbath did not halt his flock's march to their work on Saturday as he preached from his pulpit. He threw his weight behind the need to invigorate Jewish education, but he could not stop parents from sending their children to the public schools. He did not come close to engaging the younger generation. He spoke warmly about that past civilization which his youthful listeners were curtly told by their public school teachers to forget. The only parents and children who heeded his words were those already dedicated to him and his world.

It is thus not surprising that Etz Chaim grew ever so slowly in the 1890s, drawing its student body from those committed from the outset to its philosophy. Eisenstein estimated that as late as 1905, after almost twenty years of service, Etz Chaim's student body numbered but 150-175 boys. If anything, the 1890s witnessed not the efflorescence of the yeshiva's ideas but rather the first incursions of America into the philosophy and practice of the school.[12]

The founders, fathers, and faculty of the yeshiva seemed to be united in their expectations for the school and students. The teachers, for one, were resolved to instruct and have students learn as they had previously in Poland and Lithuania. Students, on the other hand, while sharing—or at least respecting—their benefactors', parents', and teachers' goals, also wanted to learn about America. For them, the state-mandated afternoon hours for secular studies were more than a formal concession to the Gentile government or a respite from the core religious subjects. That was the time when they would gain the skills their friends were obtaining in the public schools to advance in this new country. Moreover, in showing enthusiasm for the study of "grammar, arithmetic, reading and spelling," students were implying that they wanted to be *more* than *just* a Talmudic scholar.[13]

The older generation could not easily relate to this different perspective, but they were aware of the dangers it posed to their way of life. Like it or not, America was seeping through the walls. Decisions would have to be made: How much of the outside culture might be admitted and what had to be censored? And for now most importantly: Who would be chosen to open the windows for the boys? On that basic question a tentative but suggestive decision was made early on. Anyone clearly identified with ideologies and practices inimical to "God-fearing Jews" would not be allowed to teach even the most neutral of subjects in the yeshiva. So demanded Kasriel Sarasohn's *Yiddishe Gazetten* when it called for the ouster of Socialist writer and journalist Abraham Cahan, who was in 1887 teaching general subjects to twelve- to fourteen-year-olds. Joshua Rothstein followed his colleague's suggestion and Cahan was let go. But the broader question of finding qualified teachers acceptable both academically and effectively remained an enduring dilemma.[14]

Meanwhile, as the twentieth century opened, school leaders faced up to another American reality. Beginning in 1901, they had to accept that their's was no longer the only institutional option and educational philosophy available to the most observant parents on the Lower East Side. In that year, Samuel Y. Andron and his son Jacob, true members of the strictly Orthodox community and closely connected with the Etz Chaim board, broke slightly with their fellows in presenting a new way of coping with the lures of America and the threats posed by public education. Responding apparently to a crisis within their own family—the younger Andron's brother had been sent to public school only to return "one afternoon in late December asking . . . for money towards a Christmas party"—the Androns raised funds from among friends and associates to start their own alternative to the public schools. At the Beth Sefer Tifereth Jerusalem, later renamed the Rabbi Jacob Joseph School, an attempt was made from the very outset to offer a quality secular education—approximating that which was taught at the religiously unreliable public school—while maintaining the curriculum of the traditional Jewish school. This departure, which later arrogated to itself the description the "first Yeshiva in America where students receive a synthesized program," undeniably cut into Etz Chaim's modest financial pool and may well have made it reexamine its own approaches and philosophy.[15] In fact, during these same years Etz Chaim's leaders went so far as to acknowledge that while the education they offered was the ideal form of Jewish teaching, it was clearly not the first choice of even most religiously observant immigrant Jews. That understatement was expressed institutionally in 1904 when Etz Chaim opened an after-public-school program. From 4 to 7 p.m., children were exposed to the Talmud and the world of East European Judaism after the full day spent in the temple of Americanization.[16]

This tacit recognition of the impossibility of complete resistance to the public schools broadened the base of Etz Chaim's student body and helped insure its survival. It attracted to its ranks families that approved of the Eastern European methods of study but who felt that American education came first, at least by day. Though these scholars and their parents were clearly more committed to traditional Jewish education than those who sent their children to disorganized, ephemeral *heders,* they still brought a new heterodoxy to Etz Chaim. How these "public school boys" were appreciated by their European teachers is not known. Nor can it be determined how well they integrated with the pupils who were at Etz Chaim all day. What they may have suggested to contemporary and later leaders is that for the school to survive, it would have to accommodate a more broadly defined American Orthodox community. But more than a generation would pass before that perception would become an institutional policy.

Chapter 3

An East European Yeshiva
in American Soil

Rabbi Moses Meyer Matlin must have wondered whether his trek to America had really been worth the effort as the century drew to a close. He had come from Kovno early in the 1890s to serve as a judge on Rabbi Jacob Joseph's rabbinical court. He wanted to contribute to the great crusade of his times: the return of straying immigrant families to old-world religious ways. Only things had not worked out as he had hoped.[1]

As a rabbi he observed daily how Jews blithely ignored and some even actively opposed his attempts to monitor kashruth. And as a parent of a school child attending Etz Chaim, he witnessed how his son and his son's classmates remained anomalies among the youth of the immigrant quarter even as the school slightly amended its policies in order to attract more pupils. For all his efforts and for all those of Rabbi Jacob Joseph and others of his committed community of zealous Orthodox Jews, the hoped for revival of East European religious life in America simply had not taken place.

But even as he feared that the immigrant masses might never harken to the words of Rabbi Jacob Joseph, he remained totally convinced that the holy labor of reconstituting East European institutions in America had to continue. A Torah civilization had to be built, even if it served only the few surviving unassimilated Jews. He would do whatever he could to encourage that "saving remnant to hold fast to the past."

So disposed, when his son Akiba and two of his Etz Chaim classmates, Hillel Rogoff and Aaron Abramowitz, decided upon completion of their studies at school to continue their learning of the Torah informally, Rabbi Matlin opened his home to their study circle and served as their teacher. Not long thereafter, when the number of students desirous of advanced European-style learning reached a dozen, Matlin joined with Abramowitz's father, David, Rabbi Yehudah David Bernstein, a founder of Etz Chaim, and eight lay members of that

Orthodox community in formalizing their study program. Classes were moved from Matlin's Clinton Street home to a synagogue on East Broadway as the school assumed the incorporated name Rabbi Isaac Elchanan Theological Seminary (RIETS) in memory of the recently deceased and renowned Rabbi of Kovno, I. E. Spektor.[2]

These teenage students were the pride of Rabbi Jacob Joseph's community. Whatever their interests in the world around them, they were committing themselves to the world of the European cloister upon American soil. Although the Certificate of Incorporation indicated that the purposes of the seminary included the preparation of "students of the Hebrew faith for the Hebrew Orthodox Ministry" and the public newspaper announcements of the school's programs indicated—albeit obliquely—that instructors would include a "teacher (who) would give instruction in the language of the land," RIETS' founders in actuality planned their school as an American counterpart of the finest yeshivas of Eastern Europe. They hoped to build a school where disciples would study the Talmud and its commentaries intensively "for their own sake," for the merit, satisfaction, and intrinsic intellectual value inherent in religious scholarship. No practical ministerial training would be offered. And vernacular language studies, though ruled permissible, would not be encouraged. If the school was to have an ultimate practical or professional goal, it would be the production of scholars who would write talmudic treatises, thereby raising the prestige of the Torah among those who in America were still interested and garnering respect for their American Torah enclave in the estimate of the religious community worldwide. In any event, those committed to the old ways were making sure that, whatever their numbers, their approach to Jewish life would have a future in America.[3]

As RIETS struggled to maintain its foothold in the immigrant quarter—it moved five times during its first seven years from synagogues to storefronts and back before securing a semi permanent location at 156 Henry Street—it became more than just a school for the children of Rabbi Jacob Joseph's court. New immigrants were constantly coming to this country, among them a goodly number of already ordained rabbis and ritual slaughterers who saw in RIETS a close facsimile of the European yeshivas they had left behind. These arrivals heartened the Matlins and the Abramowitzes, for their presence suggested that, if their community of believers could not easily grow from among those already settled in America, at least some support for their point of view and efforts could be found among the newest Americans, those still not captured by the acculturation process. Of course, these scholars could do nothing to support their fledgling institution financially. If anything, they looked to RIETS to help them as they sought to continue their studies in this strange new land. Unfortunately for all concerned, RIETS people were in no position to really help their students. Like Etz Chaim before it, RIETS relied on the contributions of an immigrant community possessed of the most limited resources.[4]

RIETS' prospects for institutional survival were improved dramatically in 1903 when it became the favored charity of the newly constituted Agudat ha-Rabbanim (Union of Orthodox Rabbis of the United States and Canada). This continent-wide organization of some sixty East European rabbis from immigrant centers as geographically diverse as New York, Bangor, Denver, Montreal, and Toronto represented a fresh approach to solving the problems which had frustrated Rabbi Weinberger and defeated Rabbi Jacob Joseph. Formed in New York on July 29, 1902, the very day of Rabbi Jacob Joseph's funeral—delegates had been summoned to a summertime rabbinic conclave only to find that their senior colleague had expired on the day of their arrival—this alliance pledged that it would not make the mistakes that had undone poor Rabbi Jacob Joseph's efforts. These rabbis tacitly admitted that Americanization and voluntarism were forces too powerful for any one rabbi or disorganized group of leaders to combat effectively. But maybe together they could bring the kashruth industry under control, curb the calamitous state of divorce and marriage practice, and, most importantly, regenerate widespread interest in old-world religious ways. Time would tell how well the rabbis would stick together and whether the Jewish community at large would respond to their collective voice. But in the meantime, steps would have to be taken immediately to insure the survival of their own natural constituencies: in this case, RIETS.[5]

RIETS *Rosh Yeshiva* (Talmud instructor) and Agudat ha-Rabbanim member Rabbi Yehudah David Bernstein placed the school's survival high on the list of the rabbis' priorities when, at their second annual conference in 1903, Bernstein proposed formal rabbinic recognition of RIETS as an advanced center of Torah learning and the pledging to it of financial support from delegates coast to coast. Bernstein was joined in his appeal by fellow Rosh Yeshivas Matlin, Alperstein, and Kaplan, who also impressed upon the East European rabbis the dimensions of their needs. But the point did not have to be pressed. Charity boxes and appeals in support of RIETS would be carried from New York to other American immigrant enclaves through the Agudat ha-Rabbanim's collegial network. A year later, in 1904, the relationship between the school, its teachers, and supporters was solidified further when a four-man *Semicha* (ordination) Board was created at RIETS under the control of the Agudat ha-Rabbanim. Now another piece of the East European yeshiva system was put in place. When a young man in the course of learning Torah for its own sake desired for financial or personal reasons to be ordained a rabbi, he could present himself to the Semicha Board, just as young men then in Russia could appear before their leading seniors to be examined and, if qualified, ordained. Through this, the shadow of the East European civilization lengthened ever so slightly in this country.[6]

But even as the RIETS' instructors were gaining the well-earned approbation of their colleagues and soliciting important financial support for their institution, certain of their assumptions and practices were being challenged from within the yeshiva itself. As early as 1901, voices were heard within RIETS' student body suggesting that their school provide "the instruction in the language of the land" set down in its charter.

The pressure to systematically introduce nonreligious studies into the advanced yeshiva emanated from several different quarters and for a number of reasons. As the yeshiva grew from little more than a minyan in 1897 to as many as fifty students in the early years of the century, it attracted, among others, young men, most probably from Etz Chaim, who "regarded the yeshiva simply as a stopover before they pursued secular studies." Or, as one contemporary student saw it, "they (who) were seeking a way in the American labyrinth of life, stopped for provisions at the yeshiva, which they viewed as a kind of stocking-up point on the way to Americanization." These students may have attended RIETS out of respect for, or some residual interest in, their parents' world. They may have been compelled to attend by their elders. Or they may have simply attended in the hope of receiving the benefits of their school's meager student stipend. In any event, like the students at Etz Chaim—and remember that that school too was fighting over curricula—their career horizons and social outlooks were clearly American. Those whose "ultimate objectives were medicine, law, engineering, journalism, and similar rewarding careers—not the rabbinate"—needed to be able to compete with their less observant co-religionists and with Gentiles. And RIETS was slow to provide a teacher of general studies. Accordingly, while students pressed for change, those seeking to prepare themselves for college looked to a secular high school to get them ready for CCNY. Others were autodidacts. One student learned his English by comparing the texts of his Hebrew Bible with the King James version, with humorous results: When annoyed that his landlord had not provided light in a darkened tenement stairwell he declared, "My anger is kindled against the lord of the house for hastening to extinguish the small luminary."[7]

Ultimately, however, it was those individuals who desired to remain permanently in the yeshiva's orbit who articulated the more troubling complaints. They wondered whether the school's noninclusion of English subjects in the curriculum was ironically making it impossible for them to advance the Agudat ha-Rabbanim's ultimate ends. More optimistic than Rabbi Matlin, they were not content to remain the cloistered few, learning as their counterparts did in Eastern Europe. They expected that no matter how long their stay at school, gaining expertise in the ways and methods of the past, at some point—again like their yeshiva fellows in Russia—they too would leave to teach and to lead the Jewish people. But they were also more realistic than Rabbis Weinberger, Jacob Joseph, and even their own Agudat ha-Rabbanim about the society they hoped to serve. Unlike Eastern Europe, where a student would study in a yeshiva for many years and at some moment would decide it was time to work as a rabbi, travel to Kovno and sit for an exam before Rabbi Spektor, then take a position as a community's rabbi, in America fellows were more severely tested. They would emerge from the yeshiva and would be asked to participate immediately in a religious renaissance. And while not doubting for a moment—at least not publicly for now—the hallowed assumptions concerning what makes one a qualified rabbi, they still had nagging doubts as to their abilities to communicate to their fellow Jews their commitment to East European ways. In their opinion, if they could preach their most traditional teachings only in Yiddish, they would be doomed like Rabbi Jacob Joseph before them to reach only those already convinced or of the older generation. In fact, RIETS disciples were beginning to suggest that their yeshiva needed to do more than just promote rabbinical scholarship:

> Being a rabbi in America is not like being a rabbi in the Old World. In America a rabbi must know the English language to be able to preach to the younger, American born and bred generation, for whom Yiddish is an alien tongue. Look at the humiliating and embarrassing position of Rabbi Dan [Nachum Dan Baron was an early RIETS Rosh Yeshiva] when important guests who don't know Yiddish visit the yeshiva.[8]

This student call for English for the rabbis represented, moreover, a significant statement by a younger generation of rabbis to the elders that if they desired to keep alive the dream of transplanting European life-styles to America a major shift in strategy was called for. Until now, from Weinberger to Jacob Joseph to the Agudat ha-Rabbanim, the marching orders had always been: draw the parents back to the Torah and their children would fall in line. The new plan of action stemmed from the understanding that even if parents were persuaded to re-adopt old ways they would be no more able than the Yiddish-speaking rabbis to get their message across to their youngsters. By 1900 the "rising generation in Israel," as the Anglo-Jewish newspapers began to call the rapidly maturing children of 1881, were striking out on their own. And if they were to be reached at all, it would have to be through their own language, English.[9]

To be sure, the teachers, leaders, and benefactors of RIETS were not of one mind in response to these challenges. Rabbi Baron, for one, understood and respected those who looked beyond the cloister at ivy-covered walls. And, although he was powerless to affect what they wanted within the yeshiva, he did assent to his prize student Hillel Rogoff attending high school and later college. The rabbi may have surmised that if he stood in Rogoff's way, he might lose this best of his community's young people to even worse "evil cultures."[10]

RIETS' directors were alternately heavy-handed and less than candid in their reactions. In the fall of 1901, coinciding with the start of the public school year, the "yeshiva supervisory board" ordered that students devote all their time to yeshiva studies under pain of revocation of their stipends. Several months later, however, the board's perspective seemed to change when they installed Rabbi Dr. Philip

Hillel Klein, a man who, as we will see, sympathized with the students' demands. But no substantive curricular changes were effected. Then, in 1904, with students' concerns still unaddressed, a sixteen-year-old high school student, David Harry Barash, was engaged to be the long awaited "teacher in the language of the land." But his later afternoon and Friday classes lasted only a few weeks. After a recess for the High Holidays, Barash was not rehired. And from then on, into 1906, the threat of forfeiture of stipend was held over the students' heads.

The Agudat ha-Rabbanim, for its part, was on record from its very start in support of maintaining America's yeshiva just like the ones most remembered from Eastern Europe. And always prepared to aggressively stand for reconstituting old ways, it arrogated to itself the privilege of supervising "the subjects taught in the yeshiva" lest students fall into Americanized ways.[11]

Saddened by their elders' attitude, some students, who dreamed of secular careers, packed their bags and left the yeshiva. Others "submitted" and meekly "devoted the entire day to their yeshiva studies." One student, who hoped someday to be a rabbi, came to realize, through his attempt to come to grips with the anti-English stance, that what he really wanted out of life was not the pulpit but the university. "Sadly and dejectedly" this future American Hebrew poet "sailed back to Boston." Others looked to an already established uptown rabbinic training school, the Jewish Theological Seminary of America, for assistance in preparing them for careers of service to the Jewish people. Still others remained on Henry Street and environs and fought their directors for the systematic study of the secular and, more basically, for a broader definition of the Yeshiva's mission.[12]

Their fight took the form of a student strike in the winter of 1906. Angered specifically by the withholding of stipends from those who had violated the decree against secular studies, students took to the streets to dramatize what they described as their "battle with fanatics." In their strike manifestos, RIETS students clearly indicated that they did not conceive of their school as a transplanted Volozhin yeshiva. In fact, as they retold the brief history of RIETS, such had not been the original intention of the school. As they described it, RIETS was "formed . . . to produce great rabbinic scholars who would be acceptable to the people and know the language of the land." But it had yet to live up to its character. They read that document as emphasizing "educating and preparing students . . . for the Hebrew Orthodox Ministry."

The protestors pointedly declared that they and their colleagues had been tragically misled. Students had enrolled in RIETS expecting someday to serve an American congregation. They were assured that they would "be given the best teachers" to prepare them for that high calling. But after months of double-talk from the directors they came to realize they "lacked the opportunity to better themselves." Frustrated and embittered, many of the "best young men . . . drifted from the stream because the Yeshiva did not given them the opportunity to study the English language."[13]

In calling upon their yeshiva to be the true theological seminary they believed it should be, students articulated a new, concrete vision of what they believed an Orthodox rabbi in America needed to know to serve the larger Jewish community effectively. Their list of requirements was quite different from that of their teachers and directors. Rabbinical qualifications, in their opinion, only began with knowledge of the Talmud and Codes. The English-speaking rabbi also had to be a preacher, trained in the art of public speaking. He would, of course, be a teacher, but he would teach not only the traditional texts but also Jewish culture and history. He was to instill a sense of Jewish identity in a new American generation.

To be sure, this new vision of a rabbi was not entirely of their own creation. If anything, RIETS' men of Henry Street were most immediately influenced by the religious foment then taking place around them on the streets of East Broadway, instigated by a very different contingent of Orthodox elders, the rabbis and lay leaders of the Orthodox Union.

This national association of nineteenth-century German and the earlier Sephardic Orthodox congregations of America was founded in 1897, ostensibly to "protest against declarations of Reform rabbis not in accord with the teachings of our Torah." But as Union policies developed around the turn of the century, it became clear that the primary thrust of this organization would be the defense of "Orthodox Judaism whenever occasions arise in civic and social matters"; principally to help immigrants adjust religiously. Or as its critics, most from within the Agudat ha-Rabbanim, would later put it uncharitably: They were a group of undertrained American clerics bereft of their

own constituencies uptown and elsewhere, where Reform, if not assimilation, predominated, who were now sweeping into the ghetto in
search of East Europeans to convert to their untraditional mixture of
Jewish and American ways.[14]

Putting the Eastern European rabbis' vitriol aside for a moment, there was more than an element of truth in their assessment of
the Orthodox Union. Men like Bernard Drachman, Henry Schnee-
berger, and to a lesser extent Henry P. Mendes were men without
large-scale constituencies, fired with programs for the survival of Judaism under freedom, in search of those who needed and would
heed their preachings. Bernard Drachman, long-term president of the
Orthodox Union, was a prime example. This American-born, English-
speaking, university-trained rabbi received his advanced Torah training not at an East European yeshiva but at a Western European theological seminary in Breslau, Germany. There he came to believe that
Jews could live as integrated citizens in the modern world without
abandoning their essential traditions. Indeed, he would later argue
that unless Jewish leaders showed their flocks how to manage this
synthesis of cultures, Judaism would not survive its encounter with
the troubling freedoms of the modern age. His problem, by his own
admission, was that when he returned to America in the late 1880s
to begin his ministry there were few people willing to follow his lead.

Reform Jews comfortable with a Judaism radically redefined
to meet contemporary conditions found him too traditional for their
liking. Most East European religious Jews—as we have seen—were
working to transplant a civilization, not to refashion the old to fit the
future. Even those Americanized Jews of German descent who called
themselves Orthodox were for Drachman sources of little satisfaction.
They, who reportedly "do not lead a Jewish life but read the olden
prayers," were also not attuned to the nuances of his message.
Drachman did, however, feel that there was a constituency interested
in his synthesis of cultures. The future resided with the children of
the Russian immigrants. And the constitutency lived on the Lower
East Side and in similar immigrant neighborhoods in Philadelphia and
elsewhere.[15]

That at least was the message Drachman offered his own
rabbinical students at the Jewish Theological Seminary of America,
where he served as professor of Bible, Hebrew, and Philosophy from
its inception in 1887. The Seminary, from whose faculty and lay board

arose the original leadership of the Orthodox Union, during the first
generation of its service led an existence quite parallel to that of its
daughter congregational organization. It was founded as a coalition
of American Orthodox rabbis and those of more liberal persuasion
who were united in their opposition to what they saw as the aberra-
tions of a burgeoning Reform movement. But it slowly moved toward
becoming a rabbinical training school dedicated to preparing rabbis
who could minister to the second generation East European. Practically that meant that students recruited from the downtown neighborhoods were taught to go back into the immigrant enclaves and,
utilizing the most contemporary progressive social work methods and
approaches, talk to their own kind, address their religious problems,
and promote American-style plans for bringing them back to the Jewish religious fold. This new type of rabbi spoke English, was a trained
preacher, addressed audiences on historical and general Jewish cultural topics, and confronted the issues of identification and assimilation. The institutional framework for these efforts was the Jewish Endeavor Society (JES), sponsored by the Orthodox Union, blessed by
Bernard Drachman, and manned by Seminary rabbinical students.[16]

The Endeavorers inaugurated their campaign to bring an
"indifferent generation back to ancestral faith" in 1901 when they
organized their first "young people's synagogues" on the Lower East
Side. Borrowing or renting space from some of the same large downtown congregations that RIETS had called home, Drachman's disciples conducted "dignified services" with the American social needs
and values of their clients foremost in their minds. Society organizers,
to be sure, characterized their services as Orthodox and backed up
their assertion by utilizing the traditional *siddur* and insisting upon
the separation of sexes during prayer. But in many dramatic ways,
these services differed from those in the *landsmanshaft* synagogue.
Endeavorers admitted America into the Orthodox service as much as
Jewish law would permit and took out those European customs that
would disillusion acculturating worshipers. They recognized the
growing unfamiliarity of Jews with Hebrew and instituted supplementary English language prayers. A weekly English sermon on American
Jewish culture and historical topics was standard as was congregational singing in English and in Hebrew. And all overt signs of com-
mercialism were eliminated from synagogue life.[17]

This prototype of the twentieth-century American Orthodox

and Conservative synagogue was, however, by no means immediately or universally accepted. Many immigrant parents could not understand how a synagogue could be decorous, utilize English, and still be called Orthodox. Agudat ha-Rabbanim stalwarts not only questioned JES ritual but also the qualifications and Orthodox authenticity of its leaders. If Endeavorer rabbis were students of Drachman, they were, at best, disciples of a master who could not pass muster at an East European yeshiva. And if they were students of the post-1902 Seminary, they were implicated as the heretical followers of Rabbi Solomon Schechter, the man who reorganized the uptown institution and slowly moved it from its original moorings as an American Orthodox rabbinical seminary to its latter position as the flagship organization of what would become the American Conservative movement. Most importantly, many downtown youths simply were uninterested in expressing their Jewishness through synagogue life, whether it was their father's *landsmanshaft* or Endeavorer modern services. Still, the Endeavorers, the Orthodox Union, and the Seminary were forces to be reckoned with downtown. Moreover, the students running JES programs—they preached, they taught talmud torah classes, they fought against conversionist efforts to capitalize upon assimilation, they counseled other Jews—gained invaluable experience which they would draw upon in their careers of service to American Jewry for the next fifty years.[18]

RIETS men must have been impressed with the vitality of these efforts around them. And if they had taken careful note of the activists' tactics, they could have learned much that would help them in their own struggles. Their contemporaries made effective use of the Anglo-Jewish and Yiddish press to publicize their causes. And when they identified a foe, they were frequently ready to use those most American of means—boycotts, strikes, and the like—to achieve their goals. Actually, students in the Yeshiva did not have to pick up the newspapers to learn of these actions. Many knew, if they were not the personal friends of, the Endeavorers. Akiba Matlin was a contemporary of Seminary graduate Mordecai M. Kaplan. Both of their fathers had served on Rabbi Jacob Joseph's rabbinical court and the younger Kaplan had been a student for a while at Etz Chaim before going off to private tutoring, public schooling, City College, and then the Seminary. Clearly RIETS men, too, wanted to make their mark in their community, to be participants in this very new religious renaissance. And they must have felt that they had much to offer. To begin with, they had greater basic training in the world of the traditional past than did their Seminary counterparts, making them a logical bridge between Jewish generations. But they also understood that they could not get the message of reconciliation across to youngsters if they could not preach and teach in English.[19]

Fortunately for them, there was a significant segment of the downtown community—literate, influential, and in some cases newly affluent—who shared their point of view. Men like Kasriel Sarasohn and builder Harry Fischel led a coterie of East European laymen who through word and deed pressured RIETS' directors to make meaningful changes. That Sarasohn, through his newspaper editorials, backed the student demands shows how a generation of living in America had changed his social-religious perspective. He had come to America committed to transplanting European Judaism to America. As editor of the *Yiddishes Tageblatt*, it will be recalled, he was an organizer of Etz Chaim and a member of the Association of Orthodox Congregations that had hired Rabbi Jacob Joseph. This pillar of the strictly Orthodox community had also called for, through his weekly *Yiddishe Gazetten*, the firing of Abraham Cahan. But the experiences of the 1890s had shown him the impossibility of maintaining the old ways unchanged. Still he remained loyal to the faith, while becoming himself quite Americanized, and perceived that that was the direction many other, younger Jews might successfully take. Accordingly, even as he remained personally loyal to the declining Rabbi Jacob Joseph until the latter's passing, as early as 1902 Sarasohn was on record in support of both the Seminary's efforts—Schechter's theological bent notwithstanding—and of the first student rumblings for change at RIETS. Not surprisingly, he was also by that date a member of the Orthodox Union. And he provided the Endeavorers with newspaper coverage— most notably in the back (English) page of his daily—giving them and the parent Orthodox Union important entree into the immigrant neighborhood. Thus, when RIETS men took to the streets, they were, for him, merely dramatizing what he had said four years earlier: "The days have gone when it was a virtue for a rabbi to be alien to all other cultures . . . It is the duty of the leaders [RIETS directors] to bring more enlightenment into this institution and not go against the spirit of the times."[20]

For Fischel, an early member too of the Orthodox Union,

support for the strikers through the promise of financial contributions
to the school, if and when it changed, reflected his own long-standing view that American realities had to be addressed and accommodated by Orthodox institutions. For example, as early as 1892 he had
been instrumental in providing religious classes for girls in the Machzike Talmud Torah, a dramatic step at that time. And as an early
leader of the Orthodox Union, he had stood shoulder to shoulder
with the young Seminary students supporting their endeavors on behalf of the youth of the Lower East Side.[21]

The demands of RIETS students were advanced even further
by the rallying to the cause of three well-known ghetto-based rabbis:
Philip Hillel Klein, Zvi Hirsch Masliansky, and, probably most significantly, Moses Sebulun Margolies (Ramaz). Klein's support for the
concept of an American Orthodox seminary was not that surprising.
He had a model before him of what RIETS might become that coin-
cided directly with what the protestors wanted; RIETS could grow to
resemble Azriel Hildesheimer's Rabbiner Seminar in Berlin, where
Klein had received his own ordination while he simultaneously earned
a Ph.D. from the University of Jena.

While studying under Hildesheimer for six years, Klein had
been exposed to Hebrew language studies, Jewish and general philosophy and history, and such esoterica as Arabic and folklore while
attending regular Talmud classes. His learning of the Talmud, Codes,
and Commentaries was tested at regular intervals each semester. And
he had there been obliged to demonstrate what he had learned of
public speaking by preaching either in the Seminar's synagogue or in
Hildesheimer's own home congregation, Adass Israel of Berlin. This
well-ordered program—a model of structure, which was another of
the RIETS student demands—reflected the world view of its founder.
Israel Hildesheimer consistently spoke out not only about the need
for worldly rabbis who could appeal to the disaffected, but also of
the value of knowing about the modern secular world in order to
comprehend more fully the traditions of the past.[22]

Klein's feel for the justice of student demands also grew out
of his own respect for the activities of the Endeavorers. As a founder
of the Orthodox Union, he had encouraged Seminary students to work
downtown. As rabbi of the First Hungarian Congregation Ohab Zedek on Norfolk Street, he had opened that synagogue's doors to Endeavor activities, even as he was simultaneously a leader of the Agu-

dat ha-Rabbanim which was on record as opposing all these assumptions and activities. If RIETS students were confused by this rabbi's welter of affiliations, they were unperturbed. They welcomed his support for their efforts.[23]

They were also warmed by Masliansky's backing, although they had probably assumed all along that this rabbinic gadfly would stand with them. A graduate of the Volozhin yeshiva, he did not share his school's orientation toward the study of the secular. (This famous East European yeshiva, it should be noted, closed down in 1892 rather than give in to czarist government demands that it admit secular studies and Hebrew language training to its curriculum.) Ordained by Rabbi Spektor, he chose not to join with those similarly trained and ordained by that East European luminary. Reverend Masliansky, as he was apt to refer to himself, never joined the Agudat ha-Rabbanim. Masliansky's sympathies were with those who understood that this country's social realities had to be addressed and accommodated by Jewish religious leaders.

Masliansky found common cause with the founders of the Orthodox Union and was an early supporter of the JES. Most interestingly, he backed the Endeavorers home institution, the Jewish Theological Seminary, and remained its supporter even after Solomon Schechter took over its helm in 1902. Masliansky was not moved by downtown rabbinic admonitions that the appointment of Schechter, "an exponent of the Higher Criticism," made the Seminary "anything but Orthodox." As late as 1904, Masliansky was confident that young Orthodox men could attend the Seminary, garner there the training requisite to serve an American Jewish community without falling prey to philosophies and traditions inimical to Orthodoxy. In fact, he may have felt that Seminary Bible classes would become a battleground of interpretations, if the Orthodox students stood for their principles against the teachings of their professors. He also knew that Drachman was at the Seminary (at least until 1908) serving as a role model, if not an inspiration, for the Orthodox youngsters studying uptown. And if Masliansky was afraid that the rabbis emerging were not skilled Talmudists, as some downtowners charged, he understood that greater facility with the ancient texts might not be as important as more profound understanding of American society in meeting the needs of this upcoming generation of Jews. Of course, Masliansky had also to admit that it would be better if students could have a better grounding in the ancient—without modern critical amendment—while gaining knowledge of the here and now. But in its early years, RIETS did not provide that necessary multifaceted training. That was what the strike was all about. So when students spoke out for what he believed was right and needed, Masliansky was on their side.[24]

There he found a unexpected colleague. Ramaz was not a graduate of a Western European seminary with a Ph.D. like Klein, nor was he a nonconformist like Masliansky with a close working relationship with Jews of all identities and allegiances. Ramaz was bedrock East European. Born in Kroza, Russia, he attended yeshivas in Kovno and Bialystock before serving for more than twenty years as a rabbi in Slabodka. Like Rabbi Jacob Joseph before him, he was the recipient of little formal secular education when he migrated to the United States in 1899 and became unofficial chief rabbi of Boston, fighting there the good battle for effective kosher meat supervision and troubled by the rampant nonobservance that surrounded him. Moreover, Ramaz was president of the Agudat ha-Rabbanim almost from its inception. In fact, it was in Ramaz's home in the spring of 1902 that the organizational plans which led to the founding of the rabbinical association were first composed. For this "High Priest of American Jewry," as he would later be called, to back the demands of students rebelling against policies most dear to his organization certainly heartened the protestors. Ramaz's decision may also have astounded them and the community around them.[25]

But Harry Fischel was not surprised. From his vantage point in the pews of Congregation Kehilath Jeshurun, an uptown synagogue attended by newly affluent East European Jews, Fischel witnessed how Ramaz had come down from Boston a year before the strike and shared a pulpit with the young former Etz Chaim student and JTS graduate Mordecai M. Kaplan. Margolies appealed to the older generation who still wanted to be ministered to by an East European rabbi. At Kehilath Jeshurun, Kaplan began building his career of youth-centered activities among the second generation.[26]

Ramaz's implicit validation of seminary style rabbinic training and Endeavorer activities may have reflected the results of the senior rabbi's own six years experience with the problems of American Jewish life. Like Sarasohn, he may have come to realize that an unaccommodated America would ultimately destroy Judaism, and thus Ramaz cast his lot with those careful in making the necessary alteration. And, of course, the ardor of some of his major Kehilath Jeshurun trustees for a reformed RIETS may have helped confirm him in his beliefs. How Ramaz remained head of the Agudat ha-Rabbanim while espousing these pro-Americanization sentiments is another matter entirely.

RIETS' leaders could not ignore all the voices arguing for change, but they were not prepared to immediately institute meaningful reforms either. To bring a quick end to open hostilities and to unfavorable publicity injurious to RIETS' limited charity pool, Ramaz was elected president of RIETS and Klein accepted the honorary presidency. But the basic curricular concerns were not addressed. Contemporary observers, like Kasriel Sarasohn, knew very well that this uneasy truce among students and faculty and directors would not long hold unless Ramaz, Klein, and their supporters were allowed to rule as well as to reign.[27]

The "temporarily postponed" student strike resumed once more in May 1908. The immediate cause of this second walk-out was the unexpected expulsion of fifteen student "protestors" by the school's directors. According to strike leaders, a committee of students had gone to their seniors in the early spring of 1908 demanding that the yeshiva make good on its two-year-old promises. The now familiar list of demands was articulated: organized Talmud classes, secular studies in the curriculum, and training "in the art of the sermon so that graduates might compete against the graduates of Schechter's Seminary." Angered by what they perceived as the "effrontery" (literally, chutzpah) of the committeemen whom they accused of being "tainted by Socialism," the directors decided "to make an example" of the protestors. Hoping to intimidate the students who would remain and thus quell all movements for change, the fifteen were expelled on the spot. To be sure, student voices continued, and the directors publicly disavowed the capriciousness of their act. They allowed only that the yeshiva's severe financial problems required unfortunate reductions in the student body. Unmoved by this apologia and clearly unintimidated, students took to the streets both for the reinstatement of their fellows and for the institution of the long-anticipated reforms. There they found the Tageblatt and other downtown organs and groups ready to support and publicize their cause.[28]

This time strikers were not content with promises and gestures. Heartened by the backing of the Sarasohn and Fischel people, they stayed out for three weeks, until the directors sued for peace. When the school's elders assessed the financial damage the adverse publicity was doing to RIETS, the directors had no choice but to call all those concerned to a reconciliation conference, fittingly enough at Congregation Kehilath Jeshurun, Ramaz's home synagogue. There under the chairmanship of the congregation's senior rabbi, RIETS' leaders acceded to student demands, while promises were made by some of the newly affluent to help improve RIETS' long-standing financial difficulties. A deal seemed to have been struck: The yeshiva would become "an institution of Torah and *hakhma,* secular knowledge . . . according to the spirit of the times." Its survival would be insured by the Fischels and A-Z Lewin-Epsteins (he of the Carmel Wine Co.) of the community who would try to be for the Yeshiva what the German philanthropists Jacob Schiff, Louis Marshall, and Felix Warburg et al. were for the Seminary—committed philanthropists who would provide a safety-net for the school in confronting its financial crises. Under this arrangement, students returned victoriously to their classes.[29]

Student confidence that true reforms and stability would now come to the yeshiva was heightened further by the selection a month later of Bernard Levinthal as president of the RIETS faculty. Students believed that Levinthal, an outspoken apostle of the possibility of coexistence of Jewish tradition with American life, was the perfect man "to maintain the yeshiva on the principles of the reorganization and keep it on a firm footing so that it will no longer be in constant danger of being closed down." Like Ramaz, this Vilna- and Kovno-trained leader, the so-called Chief Rabbi of Philadelphia, was a revered spokesman for the Agudat ha-Rabbanim. Also, like his New York colleague, Levinthal had come to recognize in the course of his some seventeen years in America the unique problems caused by this land of freedom. Committing himself to the refashioning of Orthodoxy he earned a reputation as "the most Americanized of the strictly Orthodox rabbis in this country." In fact, Levinthal stood for American Orthodox ideas and principles not even advanced by the students themselves. He consistently argued the possibility of cooperation with Seminary rabbis on the nondenominational issues of concern to all Jews. In any event, for RIETS students such a man could indeed be the teacher they awaited. He would help produce rabbis "devout and observant . . . who are equipped with knowledge in the spirit of the times." And he would help disciples step out into the real Jewish world. After all, more than anyone else around, he knew the strengths and weaknesses of the competition.[30]

The drift by RIETS, as slow and tortuous as it was, toward becoming the modern Orthodox theological seminary the students desired could not have sat well with many members of the Agudat ha-Rabbanim. After all, at the very outset of the troubles, the organization had made clear that it wanted RIETS to remain an East European yeshiva in America. Moreover, they had arrogated the right to oversee the yeshiva's curriculum "lest students fall toward Americanized ways." To be sure, the support of Klein, Ramaz, and Levinthal for changes within RIETS could not be overlooked. Certainly no one could question their training or religiosity, though some privately might have questioned their judgment. But still, RIETS and its students as an institution were moving toward accepting the approaches and outlook of the Orthodox Union, an organization it did not recognize.

The rabbis of the Orthodox Union, at least those trained in Western Europe or at JTS before Schechter's arrival, were viewed by the Agudat ha-Rabbanim as sincere Orthodox Jews "full hearted for the faith of Israel and its Torah." But to these East Europeans, the Drachmans and others were not *really* rabbis and their organizational mandates were inimical to the survival of Judaism. And now, the very men who were not invited to join the Agudat ha-Rabbanim were to be the role models for the graduates of RIETS. How could they, the rabbis of Poland and Lithuania, remain the ordaining body of the American seminary? Or maybe more properly put: they feared that the students who would soon appear before them for ordination would be unworthy of the title rabbi. And yet when the Margolies-led conclave announced its recommendations, the yeshiva committee of the Agudat ha-Rabbanim fell into line. It now averred that students be given their withheld stipends and offered its blessing to students studying the secular outside the yeshiva pending the creation of an ordered program at RIETS. It also redoubled its fund-raising commitment to the institution.[31]

Several factors contributed to the Agudat ha-Rabbanim's change of heart. To begin with, the power and influence, not to mention the money of Klein, Margolies, and Levinthal, must not be overlooked. Each was a rabbi of a newly affluent congregation or substantial group of synagogues capable of using charity dollars at their

disposal to influence the rabbinic body. But there were other ideological and practical considerations which contributed even more to
the strengthening of the triumvirate's hand.

Those who stood for change could legitimately point out
that, although the study of the secular was not a hallowed tradition
in the East European yeshiva, the making of that cloistered world
more responsive to its environment was not without precedent in their
own generation. As early as 1882 Rabbi Isaac Jacob Reines had argued at a rabbinic conference in St. Petersburg, Russia, that the yeshivas under their jurisdiction introduce the study of Russian and the
secular sciences into their curricula. Future Agudat ha-Rabbanim
members then living in Russia may have witnessed the furor which
arose when Reines reasoned that the yeshiva world could not afford
to ignore the impact of Enlightenment, both Jewish and general, and
the other modern movements and ideologies were making both upon
their student bodies and the larger Jewish community. Reines could
see that yeshiva students were reading Abraham Mapu, the father of
the modern Hebrew novel, and Y. L. Gordon, he of the famous motto
"be a man when you go out and a Jew in your home," by candlelight
under their beds. They were also reading Tolstoy and Marx surrepti-
tiously when time allowed. Segments of the more affluent laity were
flirting with ideologies which spoke of a new Russia where religious
identities would be voluntary, if not unnecessary. Even the poorer
folk, Reines could not help but notice, were not totally immune to
the secular and revolutionary currents around them. Reines thus reasoned that for the yeshiva to remain a force in the lives of its students
and for its graduates in turn to be able to communicate with their
changing community accommodations would have to be made. Those
students, who also dreamed of some day taking their places as religious Jews in a more tolerant general society, had to be reassured
that they could learn at the yeshiva and not lose out on the future.
Those who planned to emerge as rabbis and communal leaders would
have to be prepared to address the crucial concerns of the day in the
idioms of their times.

These far-reaching ideas, to be sure, did not receive the approbation of the majority of the Russian rabbinate. "Secular learning," they countered "detract(ed) from the study of Torah and Talmud and may even lead the student away from traditional observance."
Reines' conference suggestions were, consequently, tabled; his early

attempt in 1882 to create a yeshiva in Shwenvan, Lithuania, was pilloried and undercut financially. Still Reines and others of his opinion persevered and some twenty years later, in 1905, at the same time that battles were raging in New York over the place of the secular at RIETS, Reines succeeded in establishing a modern yeshiva in Lida, Belorussia. There students were trained in "Hebrew language and literature, the language of the country (Russian) and in general disciplines as taught in the secondary schools." Public speaking was not part of the new style of study. But faith in the power of the well-addressed homiletic message was not lost upon the students at Lida. Reines was a master preacher who emphasized the role sermons could play in inspiring their listeners.[32]

This minority opinion made it theoretically possible for good Agudat ha-Rabbanim men to go along with change at their own yeshiva without abandoning their hope of transplanting Europe to America. If anything, the Lida experiment, evolving as it did as RIETS struggled along, may have helped some New York-based rabbis come to grips both with their own presence in this "treif land" and with their possibly idealized view of the old-side. Some rabbis may have mused that if Torah-strong Eastern Europe perforce produced a Lida yeshiva in response to the modern world could one expect less from an American Orthodox institution. Moreover, the Agudat ha-Rabbanim's tacit accession to what they characterized as the "transplantation" of Lida to America was eased greatly by the respect many members had for Reines himself.

In the years between his failed first attempt at Shwenvan and his success at Lida, Reines had emerged as a leading ideologue and practical tactician for the Religious Zionist movement. Most importantly, in 1902 he had founded the Mizrachi movement, an independent body within the Zionist cause dedicated to promoting the wishes of religious Jews and serving as a watchdog organization against the pervasiveness of secular ideas within the Jewish National movement. Agudat ha-Rabbanim men were themselves Mizrachiites. And their respect for their teacher of Zionism may have carried over to other aspects of his creed. They could ultimately admit that movements and ideas clearly inimical to the survival of Judaism had to be fought on their own ground, even as they recognized that in so doing they were supporting a yeshiva that no longer resembled in toto the schools they remembered in Europe.[33]

Those willing to be thus convinced were able to make their own equations out of Reines' apologia for change. If concessions were not made and made quickly to meet student demands, disciples would not only be lost to the wide secular world and to the movements to save the world, but some of the best and brightest would end up as students at the hated Jewish Theological Seminary of America.

This fear was rooted in the unavoidable reality that almost from the moment of Solomon Schechter's arrival in America, RIETS students had been presenting themselves to him seeking admission to the Seminary. For these defectors, the hegira uptown was not so much an act of faith as an attempt to avail themselves of the American rabbinic training they had so long awaited on East Broadway. Need-less to say, every time RIETS dragged its feet in making meaningful change, the decision to move on became more reasonable and jus-tifiable. The men who made the break saw the Seminary as a school with a logical, progressive curriculum. Disorganization was the rule in RIETS classes. The Seminary delivered its stipends without delay or investigation. Yeshiva men ofttimes found themselves put out on the streets. The Seminary was in the process of building a magnificent Jewish library, a wonder of the Western Jewish world. The Yeshiva library, as one visitor uncharitably put it, was a dark room with empty walls, devoid of even the most basic books for advanced Torah learn-ing. The Seminary provided students with on-the-job training while Endeavor activities were not on the agenda of Yeshiva's directors. Most importantly, RIETS men on the move could join the Seminary without leaving the Orthodox fold; at least not the American vari-ety.[34]

After all, the popular and respected Masliansky was not afraid of the Seminary's new direction. Nor, it seemed, was the venerable Ramaz, who not only cooperated with Seminary leaders in commu-nity-wide efforts but also shared a pulpit with a Seminary graduate. Moreover, Drachman was at the Seminary. And that principled man was long on record as refusing to countenance tampering with the essences of Orthodoxy. For example, when it came to religious ser-vices he was unequivocally opposed to mixed seating—even as he encouraged many social reforms in American synagogue life. He was also a voice within the Seminary opposed to the more liberal theo-logical bent identified with Schechter, and he remained there a less than loyal opponent for almost the entire first decade of Schechter's tenure. Finally, upon arrival uptown, students were not pressured to change their belief system. Schechter, by his very nature and philosophical orientation, did not demand strict ideological conformity from his disciples. He was intent on building American traditional Judaism. He required only that students be united in their comprehension of what were America's and American Jewry's unalterable demands.[35]

Initially, the Agudat ha-Rabbanim sought to slow down the Seminary simply by excoriating their opponents before the eyes of the downtown public. In 1904, it "branded" the Seminary as "non-Orthodox since Professors Schechter and (Louis) Ginzburg, the leaders of that institution, are exponents of the Higher Criticism which is anything but Orthodox." Three years later it called upon downtown newspapers to refrain from designating JTS graduates as "rabbis." The term "Reverend, Doctor, or even Professor," they declared, would be more appropriate for men who were "not authorized to make decisions in Jewish law." But even as these periodic denunciations continued, Agudat ha-Rabbanim men came to understand that at least some portion of the Seminary's methods would have to be adopted at RIETS to keep the boys down on the Lower East Side. They grudgingly acknowledged that condemnations were not enough when, as one Agudat ha-Rabbanim worthy put it, "sons of our own member rabbis attended and graduated from that institution." Fear of the Seminary clinched their decision to stay with RIETS as its "rabbis"—as its rebbes, its instructors, its Semicha Board—working from within, serving as a bulwark against the implementation of all but the most necessary changes.[36]

But as it turned out, the Agudat ha-Rabbanim's moment of practical acquiescence had not yet arrived. While Levinthal, who was sympathetic to the students, was officially in charge, it is clear that, like Klein and Ramaz before him, he was little more than a figurehead who was not involved in the day-to-day management of the school. Only a half-hearted attempt was made to upgrade the English language curriculum. An instructor was hired who taught English by reading Dickens' *David Copperfield* to the students and translating it line by line into Yiddish. With no text before them, such education was totally (as one contemporary described it) "Torah she'al peh" (the oral law), albeit of the most primitive form. Frustrated, feeling that a double-cross was in the making, RIETS students were once again talking strike in the late spring and early summer of 1908.[37]

This time, however, yeshiva directors were way ahead of the protesters. Citing their real financial difficulties, RIETS officials closed their school in the summer of 1908. The activists were, in effect, locked out of RIETS before they could mount a campaign and garner, once again, popular support. Put out on the streets, some students took the next available elevated railroad to Morningside Heights and the Seminary. Others turned for help, interestingly enough, to Zvi Hirsch Masliansky and Agudat ha-Rabbanim members Shalom Elchanon Jaffee and Shalom Rabinowitz. Together they hatched plans to found their own new yeshiva, the Yeshiva le-Rabbanim of East Broadway. This new school was to produce "rabbis who are well-grounded in Torah and secular subjects (in a program which includes) Jewish history, Jewish philosophy, and full-course university curriculum."[38]

This external challenge caused the leaders of RIETS to immediately discharge its defecting students from their now temporarily closed institution. And when RIETS reopened several weeks later, a condition of reinstatement was imposed: students had to stand for an examination before a committee of directors. There they were probably given a loyalty test as part of the checkup on their learning of Talmud and Commentaries while they were away.

The students on their own had other problems on their minds. Their new yeshiva was encountering the same affliction that plagued RIETS itself. It could not raise funds. One contemporary allowed that "charity collectors were sent but returned empty handed primarily because most people could not understand why a new yeshiva had to be opened." Wiser from this experience but no less determined to see modern rabbinic education become part of the downtown Orthodox scene, some of the protesters sought to return to RIETS.

But RIETS' leaders were not in the mood to forgive and forget. The defectors were deemed persona non grata. In fact, at one point, an angered treasurer of the board threatened to call in the police to forcibly remove former Yeshiva le-Rabbanim students who were still using RIETS facilities without permission. One protester egged on the directors by declaring that he would prefer "dying by the sword (i.e., the police) than by famine (i.e., expulsion and absence of stipend)" and planned to await the arrival of the authorities. Other students of his crowd hoped that a confrontation would put RIETS back on the front pages of the Yiddish press and bring public censure down upon their elders. But ultimately cooler heads prevailed. The threat was withdrawn, students dispersed, and the yeshiva was spared the unseemly sight of Gentile authorities settling an internal Jewish conflict.[39]

Still all was not well or happy at RIETS. Director intrigues continued and no real redress of grievances was immediately undertaken. In the aftermath of the open turmoil, school officials agreed to replace the seemingly insensitive old faculty. But to student dismay, the first of the old timers to go was their friend Rabbi Nachum Dan Baron. Students believed that their supporter was made a "Judas goat" by the directors; an unconscionable retaliation against them for forcing their yeshiva toward the twentieth century. But there was another reason why school leaders were against Rabbi Baron. He was the one who permitted Hillel Rogoff, that budding Talmudist in RIETS' original student body, to go off and study the secular. And everytime these directors saw Rogoff's name on the masthead of the *Jewish Daily Forward,* the Socialist newspaper, it reminded them of how right they were about the dangers of the secular and how appropriate it was to keep students apart from it. Rabbi Abraham Aaron Yudelewitz was hired to replace the beloved Rabbi Baron. But his "dry, boring" classes that put his listeners "to sleep" did little to improve student morale. To be sure, Rabbi Yudelevitz made some faltering gestures toward instituting modern training for his disciples. He arranged for students to preach Friday evenings in downtown synagogues. But he did not know how to teach the art of sermonizing. His advice to students was to read a book of sermons and then stand before their audiences. Most of the students gained little from these unprofessional exercises.[40]

While those who ran RIETS, and the others who influenced it from within and without, remained of several minds about the direction the school should take, students voted with their feet against their yeshiva. The RIETS student body fell by more than one-half (to approximately 55 students) between 1908 and 1913, as many young men disgusted by the infighting, by the frequent leadership changes, and by their school's concommitant financial instability looked to the Seminary and elsewhere for their educational and professional training. These students would not wait to see whether those committed to an American Orthodox seminary would succeed or whether they would continue to be foiled by their European-looking opponents. In the meantime, they were unimpressed by still-born efforts to unite RIETS with its little brother yeshivas, Etz Chaim and Rabbi Jacob Joseph School, into a rationalized Jewish parochial school system. And they were also unmoved by announcements by RIETS that their school would resettle in Harlem, then the home of many of the most Americanized of the yeshiva's supporters, just a mile or so away from JTSA. For students to return, RIETS would have to make its institutional mandate unequivocally clear and put its financial house in order. Most importantly, it would have to find a leader who would stand foursquare for the synthesis of America and Jewish tradition they so desired, while earning for himself, and for them, the approbation of all segments of New York's Orthodox community.[41]

Chapter 4

Bernard Revel and an Identity
for American Orthodoxy

The changes student protesters so vociferously demanded finally became permanent parts of their institution's life in the mid-
1910s. The school's new elite East European patrons made every effort to strengthen RIETS' financial position. A new dynamic president
was brought on the scene and, after a brief but significant hiatus early
in that career, he would remain in power for more than a generation.
He would, more than anyone else, insure that the ideal RIETS student
could be both a renowned Talmudic scholar and a man well versed
and comfortable in the American and modern Jewish world around
him. And the president would be there to see his disciples take their
places in this country alongside of and in competition with JTS graduates as ministers to American Jewish communities. But he would
find that in his success and in putting the struggles of the prior decade
behind RIETS, new questions and dilemmas were raised. Once he
effectively moved the school away from the world of Volozhin and
from the perspective of the early directors, he would find that elements outside his own still limited religious and intellectual circle
would frequently ask him to explain how his Jewish perspective was
also Orthodox and how his American approach differed from that of
the other Jewish rabbinical seminary in town, the JTS. Out of his
experiences and answers, an enduring identity for American Orthodoxy would begin to emerge.

The beginning of a real peace at RIETS dates from 1912
when an agreement in principle was reached between the directors
of Etz Chaim and RIETS to merge their respective institutions. This
deal, engineered by Harry Fischel, among others with substantial links
to both schools, aimed at legally transferring charity dollars from the
older, more solvent yeshiva to its financially plagued brother school.
This move toward amalgamation also constituted a major step in the
creation of an enduring Jewish parochial school system in the city.

Etz Chaim was to become a "feeder school" sending its best boys on to the advanced Torah center.

But these moves—as important and warranted as they were— could not alone insure the survival of RIETS. The yeshiva could move in with Etz Chaim on Henry Street, saving it the burden of renting a school building. Ultimately both could move together to more modern quarters on Montgomery Street. And there young scholars could be persuaded to continue with higher Jewish education at the yeshiva. But unless and until RIETS made up its mind and articulated once and for all where it stood on long outstanding ideological demands, it could neither expect older scholars to return nor the next generation of American-born rabbis, not to mention those with ultimate secular career goals, to enroll at RIETS.

By 1913 the Fischel crowd clearly had the votes to dictate institutional policy. And they were certain of ongoing support for their efforts from the Klein-Ramaz-Levinthal faction of the Agudat ha-Rabbanim. But they also understood that to make their revolution truly permanent they would have to address the legitimate fears and concerns of the now minority of directors who still advocated the old ways. Failure to do so would leave the yeshiva open to a continuation of those subversions from within which had waylaid all earlier modernization efforts. A search was thus undertaken for a new, decisive leader for RIETS. They sought a man of Torah and secular knowledge; a lover of Torah for its own sake, who, while committed to the evolution of an American Orthodox seminary, would be on the spot to see that their mandate was carried out. He would have to be sensitive and appeal to those who still pined for the yeshivas of Europe; they had to be mollified if harmony were ever to return to their institution. RIETS' search for the impossible ended successfully in 1915 with the appointment of Rabbi and Dr. Bernard Revel as president of the faculty of a reorganized RIETS, temporarily renamed the Rabbinical College of America.[1]

Revel was, first of all, a man of Torah. According to family tradition, while still very young, this son of the rabbi of Pren, born in that suburb of the great Torah center at Kovno, was identified as a budding Talmudic prodigy by none other than Rabbi Isaac E. Spektor. Young Revel proved the namesake of the American yeshiva right at the yeshivas in Kovno and Telshe where he earned ordination at age sixteen. True to the European tradition of Torah study for its own sake, Revel, upon arrival in this country in 1906, sought out RIETS as a base for his continued study of the most sacred of texts. He was the type of student the school's earliest supporters really wanted.[2]

Subsequently, and totally in keeping with Old World traditions and the earliest goals of RIETS, Revel began publishing pilpulistic Talmudic treatises. In 1915, the year of his appointment to the RIETS presidency, Revel published his first discourse, a consideration of the permissability of men from priestly families performing or being witnesses to an autopsy, an issue which, interestingly enough, his school four decades later would have to consider. While RIETS president, he wrote on questions of Jewish civil law, on rules regarding purity and impurity, and a host of other theoretical Talmudic issues. Revel's impressive rabbinic pedigree and his ongoing commitment to traditional Torah studies held him in the greatest stead as he emerged as the advocate of change in RIETS. As a respected Talmudic scholar, he could speak to those who would not accept that RIETS had to change in their own language. He could try to mollify them; he had earned the right with his erudition, even if his listeners would not subscribe to this new perspective.[3]

But it was Revel's knowledge of and comfort with the general world around him which captivated the students and their older lay and rabbinic supporters. All had to be impressed that Revel had achieved through his own initiative and perseverance that which the yeshiva-as-seminary advocates wanted for all American Orthodox rabbis. He was the true prototype of the talmudic scholar comfortable both in his parents' world and in the universe of America. He would teach those who would teach America's Jews to harmonize conflicting cultural and traditional values.

Significantly, and unlike many of his rabbinic contemporaries, Revel's own affinity for the new predated and transcended his encounter with America. While still a student in the East European yeshiva, he began living a life that argued the intrinsic merit of knowing vernacular and secular ways and of intimacy with wider Judaic disciplines also, as it were, "for their own sake." This rabbinic *maskil* (son of the Jewish Enlightenment) did not acquaint himself with the world of the Eastern Enlightenment or with the universe of the Western *Wissenshaft des Judenthums* (Science of Judaism) primarily to defend the faith, in Reines-like terms, against the onslaught of unsympathetic modern ideologies. Nor was there a Jewish communal agenda for his association with Bundists (Jewish Socialists possessed of a most unorthodox modern expression of Judaism) during the 1905 Russian Revolution, a move which led to his arrest and hastened his departure to America. He was clearly captivated by these novel ideas, even as he personally and intellectually remained true to a strict religious definition of Jewish existence.[4]

Upon his arrival in America and while attending RIETS, he continued to study secular teachings not only, or primarily, because the Endeavorers were showing the way to reach other Jews, but because he personally desired university training. He had no American rabbinic career goal in mind when he studied law for two years at Temple University. Nor was he thinking of pulpits and of Americanizing Jews when he entered New York University in 1909 to study comparative religion, philosophy, and Semitic languages, earning himself an M.A. degree for work on a medieval Spanish Jewish philosopher. To be sure, he may have agreed, through his studies there and later at Dropsie College, America's first nontheological Jewish academic institution, that modern Jewish studies were not the sole province of those with liberal conceptions of Judaism. Significantly, Revel's doctoral thesis on "Karaitic Tradition and Its Relation to Sadducean, Samaritan and Philonian Halakah" addressed scholarly contentions made by Reform Jewish thinker Abraham Geiger about the uniformity of Jewish legal traditions. But his studies in this area were not primarily designed as a polemic to belittle liberalizers and to strengthen the faith of the many who may have heard that holy traditions were under attack. Rather, his *Wissenshaft* work reflected his own desire to set the record straight for himself, as he defined it, and to satisfy his own needs for wide-ranging study.[5]

Revel did serve during his school years in Philadelphia as secretary to Rabbi Levinthal—it was Levinthal who facilitated his young protegé's attendance at Temple University in the first place—and worked with his senior rabbi on a myriad of communal and educational projects. But the practical rabbinate, a life of service to the Jewish people, was not at that movement Revel's ultimate career objective. In fact, upon graduation from Dropsie in 1911, the recently married Revel entered his in-law's prosperous petroleum business. He moved to Tulsa, Oklahoma, and helped run oil plants owned by the Travis family's Oklahoma Petroleum and Gas Company. Revel family tradition has it that the young rabbi spent all his spare time engaged in Torah study. But during his sojourn in the American Southwest his Jewish horizons were totally personal ones: his ongoing quest to be the best possible scholar he could be.[6]

Still, when a committee from RIETS approached this man, whom Ramaz had characterized decisively as "one of the great Torah giants of our generation and perhaps the only one in general knowledge and science," to help them permanently establish secular study and diversified Jewish learning at their school, in the service of the Orthodox Jewish community, they hoped that he might agree. For Revel, during his pre-Oklahoma days, was well aware of and concerned about the trials of his Jewish alma mater. During the strike years he had written to his friend Rabbi David Rackman, himself an ordained rabbi, who upon arrival in America had sought out RIETS for study, that the protesters' demands accurately reflected American realities. Striking at both the ideological and financial heart of the matter, Revel argued that if American Jewry had not sufficient resources to support both a Torah center for immigrant rabbis and an American Orthodox seminary, first attention must be granted to that school which would raise men able to serve the masses of disaffected Jews.[7]

In essence, Revel rejected Rabbi Matlin's earliest assumptions about the yeshiva and Orthodoxy's role in American Jewish life. The younger rabbi believed that those who remained true to the old ways could not serenely isolate themselves from the majority of American Jews who could not be brought to rebuild the European life. Provisions had to be made to reach out to those drifting away. The first priority was American Jewish survival under Orthodox auspices and under the conditions of freedom.

Revel was also on the record as offering practical suggestions to those who would change RIETS. In a letter to Masliansky at approximately the same time that he was offering his critique to Rackman, Revel declared that the "salvation of the yeshiva is possible only in a new building—new from top to bottom"—reflecting the necessary internal curricular transformation students demanded. He also let Masliansky know that he and the senior Levinthal were thinking about establishing their own rabbinical seminary in Philadelphia. This school, to be run "along the new principles," would be offered "as a prototype" for—if not competitor to—RIETS. Thus almost a decade before answering RIETS' call, Revel was clear in his own mind about what an American Orthodox rabbinical college should look like.[8]

Once ensconced on Montgomery Street (Revel began his RIETS administration in a new building), the head of the yeshiva and president of the Rabbinical College made clear early on the directions the Orthodox seminary would take. Ever the man of Torah, he assigned himself the teaching of Talmud and Codes at the yeshiva. He kept on as colleagues Volozhin graduate Rabbi Joseph Levine and Rabbi Benjamin Aronowitz, formerly an instructor at the yeshiva in Telshe, Revel's own old home institution. And, in 1916, he added Hungarian-born and trained Rabbi Samuel Gerstenfeld to the Talmud faculty.[9] Although some may have read a subtle move toward change in the appointment of the English-speaking Gerstenfeld who had learned his English during a short turn-of-the-century sojourn in London, such was not the case. Revel's efforts here were to project continuity and commitment to the old in the yeshiva. Torah for its own sake would remain a byword even as he fashioned the desired broader orientation for the school. He hoped that his expansion of the Talmud faculty would help keep the Agudat ha-Rabbanim aligned with his school.

Revel was also both careful and politic through his choice of faculty and in designing aspects of the new RIETS curriculum. The study of Bible, which included analyses of the texts with medieval and modern commentaries and, in some cases, the study of ancient Palestinian geography, was put in the steady hands of Rabbi and Dr. Moses Seidel.

Revel was confident that Seidel could lead his disciples through this most difficult of modern Jewish disciplines, teaching them, minimally, how to answer those biblical critics who challenged the authenticity of the most dearly held texts. His faith in Seidel may have grown out of the fact that his background, training, and orientation closely paralleled Revel's own. For the Bible scholar, appointment to the RIETS faculty represented a first milestone in a career dedicated from its outset toward articulating the Orthodox perspective on scientific Jewish studies.

Moses Seidel was born in Bursky, Lithuania, in 1886. A year younger than Revel, like his future dean he had studied in the yeshiva in Telshe. Revel and Seidel may have been classmates in that school's informal learning setting. There they would have heard the lectures of Rabbi Eliezer Gordon, the noted Talmudist, and they may have spent time under the tutelage of Rabbi Aronowitz, later their colleague in New York. Also like Revel, and critically so, Seidel's intellectual interests transcended the world of the yeshiva. He wanted to study *Wissenshaft*. But here, unlike Revel, Seidel from the very start sought such advanced training to be of service to Orthodox Jewry in answering its critics. So disposed, he turned to the rabbi of his home community, the famous Religious Zionist thinker Abraham Isaac Kook, for advice on how to proceed and what precisely to study. Kook counseled Seidel to choose among "philosophy, Semitic languages, and national economics" to prepare himself "to elucidate the ideas that now confuse our generation . . . to bring spiritual benefits to our people." [10]

Seidel left Telshe in search of just that kind of training in 1905, the year of Revel's departure for the United States, and studied for two years in Germany before moving on to Switzerland. While Revel studied Semitica in New York and Philadelphia, Seidel did the same in Bern, earning his Ph.D. in 1913, the year of his arrival in America. For Revel, Seidel was clearly a man who would not only teach his students what they had to know, but would also be around to engage them personally on scholarly issues of mutual concern.

Revel was also most comfortable with his choice to teach Jewish history to rabbinical students. Dr. Nahum Slousch was a second generation Orthodox *maskil*. His father, Volozhin graduate Rabbi David Slousch, was a rabbi in the modernist and revolutionary city of Odessa. There he too was caught up in the wide-ranging Jewish Enlightenment of his times and transferred these interests to his son. The younger Slousch was taught to live in two cultures. He was "educated at the common school of his native city and in rabbinics by his father." An early devotée of the Zionist cause openly espoused in Odessa, he was sent at age nineteen (1891) to Palestine to investigate the establishment of an Odessan colony in the Holy Land.

Footloose, he spent the next few years traveling through Palestine, Egypt, and, back in Europe, through Austria and Lithuania and attended the Second Zionist Congress in Switzerland before studying literature and philosophy at the University of Geneva. In 1900 he enrolled at the Sorbonne, where, in 1903, he earned his Ph.D. in Neo-Hebraic literature. While a student, he corresponded regularly with *Ha-Zefirah* and *Ha-Melitz*, two important Russian Jewish journals. And in the years prior to his arrival in America, he lectured in his discipline at the Sorbonne. Here, for Revel and for whoever else was looking, was another example of an Orthodox Jew who trod successfully through the modern world of study without violating his most basic faiths. A rabbi was not teaching Jewish history but the discipline was in reliable hands.[11]

One year later, Slousch was joined on the RIETS faculty by a man close to his own heart—and close to Revel's too—Rabbi and Dr. Solomon Zeitlin. Zeitlin was born in Russia in 1892 and studied in Dvinsk where he was influenced by Rabbis Joseph Rozin and Meir Simhah Ha-Cohen. Like so many of the men in Revel's circle, while at the yeshiva Zeitlin became enamored with the Jewish Enlightenment and ultimately looked elsewhere for wide-range training. His quest led him to St. Petersburg, where, in 1908, he enrolled in Baron David Guenzberg's Academy of Jewish Studies. There among other "former students of the traditional Beth Midrash and some who were already leaders of Zionist and revolutionary movements," Zeitlin studied philology, Arabic, history, and Hebrew literature" in the first and only "advanced school for Oriental Studies" established in Czarist Russia. Zeitlin counted among his teachers the famous historian and Jewish communal leader Simon Dubnow. Zalman Shazar, who a half century later became Israel's third President, was one of his schoolmates.

Zeitlin's desire to learn more in an integrated world of rabbis and larger Jewish culture took him from Russia to the Ecole Rabbinique in Paris. There, at this Western European rabbinical seminary sponsored by the traditional but liberal-leaning French Chief Rabbinate, Zeitlin earned his ordination and Ph.D. in theology and published his first scholarly piece. For Revel, Zeitlin, like Slousch, was an example of an Orthodox Jew who lived successfully within the modern world of study without surrendering fundamental religious beliefs.[12]

When it came to the teaching of philology, Revel offered his students and the Jewish community a very different Orthodox role model. Dr. Solomon T. H. Hurwitz was American-trained. Brought by his parents to America at age nine in 1896, Hurwitz was enrolled immediately in the public schools. A clear exception for his generation, he retained a strong interest in Talmud and Bible even as he "managed to keep at the head of his class" in public school. This truly uncommon youngster acquired in high school a profound interest in classical languages which he pursued at New York University where he may have made his first acquaintance with Revel. An M.A. and Ph.D. from Columbia followed several years later, and by 1915 he had already served as a librarian of the Judaica department of the New York Public Library and as an instructor in Semitic languages at Columbia. Revel had great plans for this earliest of American Orthodox Jewish academicians. He would soon draw upon his familiarity with the public school world and with the wide general academic scene. But first Hurwitz would teach what he loved most, philology, while personifying for all the successul harmonizing of cultures and traditions.[13]

With the teaching of *Wissenshaft* at RIETS secured, Revel turned his attention to the practical aspects of an American Orthodox rabbi's professional training. Through the appointment of Orthodox Union worthies Bernard Drachman and soon thereafter his colleague H. P. Mendes as teachers of pedagogy and homiletics respectively, significant political statements were made. The Endeavorers—or at least their methods—were finally at home at RIETS. American Orthodoxy, a movement that had earlier been belittled by the Agudat ha-Rabbanim, RIETS' oldest patron, was now a partner in the mutual battle against the disintegration of American Judaism.

Drachman must have been moved by this new appointment. For him, the reorganization of RIETS undeniably constituted a new start for the American Orthodox "seminary idea of 1887" which he believed had been waylaid by the liberalizing innovations of Schechter. Personally, he was now being given a second chance to produce true advocates of traditional Judaism in America, theologically prepared and socially comfortable in the marketplace of American ideas and theological expressions. He had been unceremoniously let go by Schechter some years earlier because of their irreconcilable theological differences, even as the Orthodox Union leader and his Conservative opponent retained their abiding beliefs in the ways of Judaizing American youngsters.[14]

Mendes had to wait for RIETS students themselves to point out to their new leader that he had omitted a significant part of their training from his reorganization plan. Apparently soon after his arrival at RIETS, a notice was posted in Revel's name admonishing students "not to spend precious time on the study of Midrash and Sermonics." Older students were aghast, and younger students were confounded by this denial of possibly the oldest and most basic of student demands. Student meetings were held and deputations were sent to Revel demanding the teaching of this key to the modern pulpit. Apocryphally, when informed of a student comment that "Dr. Revel forbids us the study of Midrash and quotes a Midrash to prove his point," Revel moved quickly to rectify this oversight.[15]

Mendes was appointed first professor of homiletics at RIETS. Interestingly enough, he was joined in that "department" by Revel's own patron, Levinthal, who was appointed nonresident lecturer of Midrash, and by Judah David Eisenstein, lecturer of Midrash. In assuming his post, Eisenstein demonstrated that he had come a long way in his attitude toward Americanization from the days in the 1890s when he backed Rabbi Jacob Joseph and early Etz Chaim and from his turn-of-the-century days when he opposed the Orthodox Union.

The third phase in Revel's reorganization plan revolved around the founding in 1916 of the Talmudical Academy, a "High School Department of the Rabbinical College." Here Revel built upon the feeder school idea implicit in the Etz Chaim-RIETS merger, while addressing a dilemma that had challenged all yeshiva leaders from the days of Abraham Cahan's brief teaching stint. Once having recognized that students would not long attend a school that did not offer training in the ways of the new world, the question became one of who would supervise secular instruction. In its relatively brief history, RIETS had come up with two equally unsatisfactory solutions. The Nachum Dan Baron policy of letting a budding talmudist learn about America in a secular high school ended with that youngster's being lured away from the Jewish religious fold. And the director's plan of hiring someone from the neighborhood who was but a chapter ahead of his students had led to strikes, and walkouts, with the possibility that other students would follow in the footsteps of Hillel Rogoff.

Revel opted for a third solution. He extended the road first paved by Etz Chaim and its competitor sibling school, the Rabbi Jacob Joseph School. Talmud and mathematics, Bible and American history, Hebrew language instruction and English literature would be studied under the same roof. In the early morning students would prepare independently or in groups for their daily Talmud class (Sunday-Thursday). From 11 a.m. to 1 p.m. they would encounter the world of East European learning directly from their rabbis. After a brief hour for lunch, the early afternoon would be devoted to round-ing out their Judaic expertise. Bible, Prophets and Writings, Jewish history and Hebrew were the order of the hour. After three in the afternoon, a full four hours were devoted to general education. Their instructors were Jewish licensed teachers recruited from the neigh-boring public schools. (During the early 1920s, a whole contingent of teachers from Stuyvesant High School, one of the elite New York schools, made their way to RIETS). To be sure, not all of these in-structors were themselves Orthodox Jews and no formal loyalty test was administered. Still, in recruiting his faculty, Hurwitz and his suc-cessor, Shelley Safire—Hurwitz died while still in his thirties during the influenza epidemic of 1919—looked for men who could teach with sensitivity toward their students' uncommon personal and reli-gious commitments. Hurwitz and Safire found them primarily at CCNY and NYU, the schools they, and most Jewish children of immigrants, knew best. Advertisements for teachers sometimes appeared in the *Tageblatt,* but Cahan and Rogoff were never approached at the *For-ward* for help-wanted ad space.[16]

The emergence of the Talmudical Academy made it possi-ble for the next generation of Orthodox youngsters to learn about America under religious auspices from first to twelfth grade. This great incipient Jewish parochial school system had, on the elementary school level, six New York neighborhood schools. By 1917, students were learning the Torah and about America at Etz Chaim and at Rabbi Jacob Joseph downtown, at Yeshiva Toras Chaim and at the Harlem Yeshiva in that second largest New York Jewish community, and in Brooklyn at the Yeshiva Rabbi Chaim Berlin and at Yeshiva Torah Vodaath, then the youngest of American yeshivas. Now with a high school in place, potential rabbis could be identified early on and directed toward RIETS. All others would be prepared for other profes-sional and trade careers while maintaining the strongest possible links to the Jewish past then available in America.[17]

Revel's blueprint for his American Torah center also called for the establishment through RIETS of a "Society of Jewish Acade-micians of America." Here Revel again articulated, in the broadest possible terms, the compatibility of the yeshiva with the world of modern Jewish scholarship when the latter is explored "from the point of view of traditional Judaism." Under his plan, a highly heteroge-neous American Jewish intelligentsia, including professors at "Jewish or secular higher institutions of learning," men with doctorates in the sciences, arts and theology, physicians and lawyers among others would sit together

> to further the ideals of traditional Judaism; to promote, encourage and advance constructive Jewish scholarship; to study current questions and problems from the point of view of traditional Judaism; to elucidate the truths and principles of Judaism in the light of modern thought; to determine the place of Judaism in human progress; and to apply the methods and results of modern science towards the solution of ritual problems.

Not surprisingly, the members of Revel's own *Wissenshaft* and high school faculties were charter members of the organization. Solomon T. H. Hurwitz, that paragon of American Orthodox academicians, was designated secretary as the society made plans to hold an inaugural conference in the winter of 1916. But most significantly, invitations were also sent to, among others, Cyrus Adler, Mordecai M. Kaplan, Henry Malter, and Joseph Reider, leaders of either Dropsie College or RIETS' arch-competitor, JTS. In Revel's opinion, each of these men was Orthodox, conforming to "the usages and practices of Judaism as expressed in the Torah, Talmud and authoritative codes;" the "unalterable *sine qua non* . . . for membership."

The wider world of Jewish scholarship did not, however, look favorably upon Revel's proposal. As they saw it, it was a "piece of chutzpah" for this upstart leader to invite them, scholars senior to him, to join a society connected with his home school. They may also have seen Revel's endeavor as a poorly veiled attempt to coopt the JTS faculty and to promote his own seminary as the bastion of American traditional rabbinic learning. Moreover, many of his invitees did not appreciate having Revel determine whether they were Orthodox or not. Nor did they like the planned exclusion of more liberal colleagues from his proposed discussion circle. All but one of the Dropsie Seminary crowd stayed clear of the plan. (Interestingly enough and ironically, Mordecai M. Kaplan, soon to be seen as the most controversial of the religious thinkers invited, was the only member of the Seminary family to join the Orthodox circle of Jewish Scientists). In fact, those who opposed Revel's plan did more than just boycott. They moved to define Revel's own attitude and contributions to modern Jewish scholarship as outside the elite scholarly pale. When, four years later, many of these same men organized what came to be known as the American Academy for Jewish Research, Bernard Revel's name was left off the list of invitees.[18]

Still, this early experiment helped Revel make several significant points for future reference. The ideas that the study of Jewish Science—not unlike the study of Torah itself—was a lifelong pursuit of the yeshiva man, that the Orthodox perspective on these weighty modern problems had to be heard, and that Orthodox Jewish scholarship could have a wide range of professors both from within and without the yeshiva itself were institutionalized a generation later when, in 1936, Revel organized a "Graduate School for Jewish Studies" at RIETS. This school, which later bore his name, provided, on one level, "the facilities for ordained rabbis to carry on with their formal education" (in the world of modern Jewish scholarship) "for some years beyond their ordination." The school also, not insignificantly, addressed the personal religious problems experienced by RIETS rabbis who tried to live up to their congregation's expectations that their rabbi possess an advanced academic degree. As Dr. Samuel Belkin, who headed the school from its inception, pointed out:

> Young men who graduated from the Yeshiva . . . were often forced to take courses in Jewish history, Semitic languages and correlated fields in institutions whose approach to these subjects was not in harmony and often contrary to the teachings and religious philosophy which they received in the four walls of the yeshiva . . . Since the day of its founding, over 50 rabbis have availed themselves of the courses in historical fields from the *Jewish* [emphasis his] point of view.[19]

Revel's failure, in 1916, to broaden the purview of his institution beyond the RIETS community hardly damaged his reputation among those Orthodox families attracted to his reorganized yeshiva. By 1917, after two years of his administration, when the Rabbinical College of America stopped to take public stock of its achievements through a register or school bulletin—the first of its kind in RIETS' history—it was clear that Revel's mixture of traditional learning and modern professional training had touched a responsive chord. There were 170 students at the yeshiva, approximately ninety studying beyond the elementary level. Notably, some fourteen of the fifty most advanced students had come from outside New York and thirteen of these fifty were either graduates of, or were then students at, North American universities. That meant, in the first instance, that Revel's school was coming into contact with—possibly under the aegis of the Agudat ha-Rabbanim's long-standing charity connections—the scions of Orthodox families from Baltimore to Denver, to Montreal, Toronto, and nine other cities in between. RIETS was no longer—if it had ever truly been—only a New York institution. The presence of college men and recent graduates in the student body highlighted the fact that some fellows, possessed of that prestigious sine qua non for admission to JTS, were finding their way to Montgomery Street.[20]

By 1919, when Revel's first administration abruptly ended— he was called back to Tulsa to help save his family's now faltering oil business—RIETS could celebrate the ordination of the first five rabbis trained under the new curriculum. Of almost equal importance, six boys were then graduated from the Talmudical Academy: two of them were to become RIETS rabbis. Clearly, Revel's system was in place and working. Student cries of the prior generation had been answered. RIETS men were now on the road: in the case of the first five, three went to Savannah, Georgia; Pittsburgh, Pennsylvania; and Pittsfield, Massachusetts; only two stayed home in New York and Brooklyn. They were taking Revel's messages to second-generation Jews on America's religious frontiers, clearly in competition with JTS graduates, but united with their liberal counterparts in their commitment to assist their fellows in reconciling American and Jewish identities.[21]

But had Revel moved too fast and too precipitously in his reorganization of RIETS? There must have been times during his long second administration (1923 until his death in 1940) when Revel himself wondered if he had made all the right moves. There were so many people who did not grasp the subtlety of that mixture of tradition and change, of commitment to Torah study and to Jewish communal service, that constituted the rationale for his American Orthodox institution. Revel was frequently forced to define, through word and deed, how similar his yeshiva was to the Torah centers of Europe and how different his rabbinical college was from the Seminary in New York.

Upon his return from Tulsa in 1923 and his resumption of the formal reins of the school, Revel was confronted with the now minority opinion that argued that the new RIETS was no longer a true yeshiva. There were those within his yeshiva faculty itself who informed his students that the early afternoon Bible, history, and cognate subjects were a waste of time, and that the hours might better be spent reviewing the morning's Talmud lecture. And there were those who, both within and without the yeshiva, raised their eyebrows over the religious reliability of some of his appointees. Drs. Seidel and Zeitlin were particular objects of concern. Revel "appreciated the sincere and effective opposition of those who feared consequences disastrous for the supremacy of the Torah . . . without, of course, sharing" their apprehensions. Moreover, he understood that politically he could not simply ignore their concerns. He needed to have these colleagues—and within the larger American Orthodox milieu, the Agudat ha-Rabbanim itself—stay with the school and to have his rabbis continue to be recognized as authentic "teachers in Israel."[22]

Revel did not confront his critics head-on. In fact, in one particular instance, he actually accommodated the opposition's wishes. In 1926 Revel invited Professor Samuel Krauss of the Vienna Jewish Theological Seminary to lecture on Jewish history at the yeshiva. But when some faculty objected to having this renowned practitioner of Jewish Science address their students, Revel disinvited his guest. Revel did not care for a public symposium on the value of modern Jewish scholarship at the yeshiva or for a forum on the question of the Orthodoxy of its adherents. He rather believed that, in the long run, the best way to validate the curriculum he instituted was to appoint to his core Talmud faculty men of impeccable rabbinic pedigree whose very presence at the yeshiva would attest to the rightness of what he was doing. Talmudists like Rabbi Solomon Polachek, the so-called "Meitsheter Illui," and, later, Rabbi Moses Soloveitchik were offered to students as additional personifications of Torah and wider Jewish knowledge and were presented to the Orthodox public as tangible evidence that Revel's yeshiva had arrived.[23]

Rabbi Polachek was recruited by Revel to RIETS in 1922, just a few months before the latter's official return to the institution. Polachek came to New York after a career of more than thirty years as a student, scholar, and teacher at some of the most famous Torah centers of Lithuania. Born in 1877, this renowned scholar had been enrolled at the Volozhin yeshiva where he reportedly became the most exceptional student of Rabbi Chaim Soloveitchik of Brisk. When

Volozhin closed in 1892, the "Meitsheter" continued private study with Soloveitchik in his Rosh Yeshiva's home. Ultimately, Polachek also would count among those who influenced him Rabbi Chaim Ozer Grodzenski of Vilna and, probably as important for Revel, Rabbi Jacob Reines of Lida. Indeed, it was the latter who invited Polachek to teach at his modern yeshiva when it opened in 1905. Polachek also had an affinity for the Haskalah. He had dabbled in that world of new thoughts and letters while in Vilna. The "Meitsheter" taught at Reines' school for a decade before moving to a similar Mizrachi school, the Tachkemoni, in Bialystock. He then accepted Revel's call to upgrade what one might call Lida's sister school across the Atlantic. Rabbi Polachek was destined to teach at RIETS but six years. He died in 1929 at age fifty-one, a victim of complications arising from apparently minor oral surgery.[24]

Fortunately for Revel, fifteen months later Polachek's "younger brother," Rabbi Moses Soloveitchik, joined the RIETS faculty. Only two years younger than Polachek, he had followed the latter's diversified learning and teaching career. He too had studied at the knee of Reb Chaim Brisker before becoming head of the Talmud department at the Tachkemoni Rabbinical Seminary in Warsaw, a school quite similar to Reines' Lida. A man blessed with a wide Torah purview, he brought luster to RIETS' reputation in both Europe and America. Moreover, his willingness—like Polachek's before him—to be associated with faculty members of a variety of Orthodox types and backgrounds bespoke much in favor of Revel's American experiment.[25]

None of these faculty moves, nor Revel's ongoing policy of inviting famous men of Torah to guest lecture at RIETS, ever convinced all segments of the Orthodox community that all was well with RIETS. But as the 1920s drew to a close, the need to prove that his yeshiva still stood for the study of Torah "for its own sake," even as it addressed broader communal agendas, was not Revel's most pressing problem. By then a storm was brewing on Revel's ideological left among those Orthodox lay supporters who, having backed plans for the Americanization of RIETS, could not understand why the institution could not modernize more and ultimately join forces with yet another traditional American Jewish group, the people of the Jewish Theological Seminary.

Revel may have sensed that trouble was ahead when, in

1926, a committee of lay leaders planning a music festival to raise funds for the then proposed Yeshiva College decided to invite a female vocalist to participate in the program. In his letter to Revel requesting his go-ahead, Harris Selig acknowledged that some people might raise questions about the permissibility under Jewish law of a woman's voice being heard by men in a public gathering. Selig, who was RIETS' first professional fund-raiser, also surmised that, since their American Jewish institution had already done so many things that were unheard of in the East European past, there was no reason why liberalization could not be taken a step further. "You sanctioned dinners and other affairs," Selig pointed out, "where men and women mixed freely, a thing that my grandfather and your grandfather could not and would not allow." Why not accede to this present unprecedented move? It was left to Revel to overrule Selig and his associates and to establish the fine line that separated permissable sociological accommodation from unacceptable changes in Jewish law.

It was true, Revel would argue, that in the traditional Jewish community, men and women lived very different and separate existences. Social mores dictated that at public occasions men and women sat apart. Men sat and ate. The women were likely to congregate near the kitchen. But there was no legal proscription per se against men and women dining together in public. Moreover, who ever heard about fund-raising testimonials in Eastern Europe? Thus, if American values and procedures called a new social relationship into existence and the details of that interaction did not do violence to the Jewish legal tradition, there was no reason why a flexible Orthodoxy could not put its best American foot forward.

But a woman singing before an audience was, for Revel, another matter entirely. Here was a practice clearly in line with American ways. But it violated an articulated rabbinic teaching that "the voice of a singing women is indecent." There was thus no room for sociological accommodation. The committee would have to search for other more acceptable devices.[26]

In rendering his decision, Revel must have felt that he was on strong Jewish legal ground. But he must also have been troubled by the question itself. He knew that no one would have asked that question of the leader of a yeshiva in Telshe. Nor for that matter would anyone on RIETS' early board have conceived of such a fund-raising tactic. But these questions could be and were asked of an institution that had itself made significant accommodations to the American way of life.

Less than a year later, Revel was forced to reemphasize that RIETS was a yeshiva still, albeit with a unique American Orthodox mission to perform, when Selig and other trustees entertained the notion of merging RIETS with the JTS. The intertwined economic and ideological rationale for considering consolidation was their understanding that American Jewry had neither the resources nor the need to support two institutions, both apparently dedicated to basically the same objective—the perpetuation of Jewish tradition through social accommodation to America. Revel was to find himself hard-pressed to explain where and how RIETS stood apart.

How could Yeshiva's lay leaders have countenanced an institutional coalition with United Synagogue schoolmen whose scholarship and vision on Jewish legal matters deviated from their own? Those sympathetic to merger overtures would have responded that there were several working relationships already in place between respected Orthodox luminaries and younger Seminary counterparts. Moreover, Orthodox practices and viewpoints were still very much alive in the Seminary itself while some Seminary people were part of RIETS' wider family. If anything, they would have argued, the Seminary was merely the representation of the liberal wing of the amorphous American Traditional movement. The Yeshiva was the flagship of its moderate branch. And since their social agenda were so similar and their legal disagreements were more theoretical than practical, why not get together to advance Judaism in the United States? Who could not help but notice, they would have argued, that none other than the venerable Ramaz had shared his uptown pulpit for more than two decades with no fewer than three Seminary graduates. And whereas the first two associates, Kaplan and Herbert S. Goldstein, had received Orthodox ordination before or during their tenure at Kehilath Jeshurun, the most recent of his juniors bore no such distinction. Elias L. Solomon, a Seminary graduate during the early Schechter years, served from 1918–1921 at Kehilath Jeshurun before moving on to a Conservative pulpit on the West Side of Manhattan. Ramaz and Solomon could work together and put their theological differences aside because they shared a common dedication to the social reform of American Judaism. Certainly, RIETS board member and merger supporter Sam Levy was aware of the implications of this relationship. He was among the Kehilath Jeshurun trustees who had elected that "Conservative" rabbi to their Orthodox pulpit.[27]

When Levy and all other American Orthodox lay leaders looked a few blocks uptown or crosstown, they saw their own rabbis in the Seminary itself. Although Drachman had long been gone from JTS, his colleague and spiritual brother within the Orthodox rabbinate of Upper Manhattan, Moses Hyamson, still held sway there. And had they known of Hyamson's private responsum while working within the Seminary's walls, they would have been convinced more than ever that Orthodox views were alive and well on Morningside Heights. When approached by a young rabbinical colleague for advice as to whether he could serve a mixed seating congregation and still be seen as within Jewish law, Hyamson as late as 1926 replied, as decisively as had Drachman a generation earlier, that such behavior was impermissible. And this was at a time when this colleague and many other RIETS men—no less than Seminary graduates—were confronted by these questions and frequently acquiesced in congregant demands. For a young RIETS graduate to turn for guidance to an Orthodox rabbi at the Seminary raised suggestive questions as to where that movement's institutional purview ended and Conservative Judaism's began. It certainly did not begin and end at the line of a synagogue's mechitza.[28]

The Rabbis Levinthal, father and son, contributed their own share to perceptions of a complex and perplexing ongoing Yeshiva-Seminary liaison. Bernard Levinthal, it must be noted, was, during the earliest decades of this century, an outspoken critic of the Seminary who still demonstrated understandable pride in the achievements of at least one of Schechter's pathfinding graduates. It was Levinthal who, in 1905, led the Agudat ha-Rabbanim in its nonrecognition of the JTS. Ten years later, Levinthal orchestrated his organization's reiteration of that decree, which was then coupled with condemnation of the recently founded United Synagogue of the Seminary. The latter denunciation, it will be recalled, prompted one Agudat ha-Rabbanim member to remind his organization "that sons of our own member rabbis attended and graduated from that institution."

Levinthal, of course, did not have to be reminded. His own son, Israel Levinthal, was ordained by Schechter in 1910. And the younger Levinthal soon became one of the outstanding early Conservative rabbis. He served, beginning in 1919, in the prestigious and mixed-seating Brooklyn Jewish Center pulpit. But neither Bernard Levinthal, who upbraided the Seminary, nor RIETS, the Agudat ha-Rabbanim's historically most favored institution, put distance between themselves and the younger Levinthal. On the contrary, Bernard Levinthal often occupied a seat of honor when he visited his son's liberal-leaning congregation. And the Yeshiva, in 1925, held a fund-raising dinner at the Brooklyn Jewish Center where Israel and Bernard Levinthal were the featured speakers. Merger advocates were able to wade through this welter of affiliations and attitudes and determine that Bernard Levinthal, a consistent supporter of social accommodations, was an Orthodox rabbi who could be approached for a favorable recommendation. In his earliest communications with the committee, he reportedly gave indications that under certain circumstances some sort of merger or formal association was not an impossibility. So encouraged, and not put off by what one might perceive as Levinthal double-talk, Orthodox lay leaders and their Seminary friends carried on.[29]

Finally, those sympathetic to merger possibilities must have known—as emphasized previously—that RIETS men for more than a generation had been part of the Seminary's orbit without necessarily abandoning their personal Orthodoxy. The availability of regular stipends and sometimes just the general greater organizational sophistication of the Seminary, more than distinct ideological commitment to Conservative Judaism, had long turned Yeshiva men into Seminary students. For these students and the others who might follow them, a merger would assure greater availability of funds and contribute mightily to their feeling at home in an overarching American traditional seminary.

When JTS major benefactor Louis Marshall floated "cooperation if not consolidation" ideas to some RIETS board members, he found them ready to talk. Yeshiva worthies and "warm friends of Dr. (Mordecai) Kaplan," Judge Otto Rosalsky and Samuel C. Lamport, Sam Levy and the omnipresent Harris Selig did have their reservations about merger. But their concerns were primarily in the areas of curricula and staffing, not with the concept itself. They favored "a more comprehensive course of study in the Talmud and Codes than that which is now pursued in the Seminary." And they were troubled over what "is to be done with members of the faculty of the Yeshiva and especially with Dr. Revel" in the event of consolidation. In addition, they understood that they would have no easy time convincing their more conservative board colleagues that merger was in the yeshiva's best interests. Interestingly enough, very early on, they identified Ramaz and Levinthal and, of course, Revel as probable opponents of the plan. They clearly recognized that no matter how great their affection for Kaplan—he was Lamport's former rabbi at New York's Jewish Center—if the presence of this most dogmatic of Conservative ideologues "were to operate as an insuperable objection, some way would have to be found to deal with that problem which would permit consolidation." Still, the Yeshiva-Seminary merger was a goal worth at least considering in the best interests of American Jewry.

So disposed, Levy and his allies and their new-found Seminary colleagues hoped to draft the rough outlines of an agreement. In the winter of 1926 deputations were made to bring Bernard Levinthal to their side. After a meeting with Levinthal in February, Seminary head Cyrus Adler allowed that he believed that his Orthodox contemporary "was favorably inclined if some measure of autonomy were granted to the units within the larger organization." Levinthal also intended to look at the Seminary's requirements for ordination and expressed "the opinion that (the Seminary) devoted proportionately too little time to Bible and Talmud and far too much to what he considered nonessential History, Poetry, etc." But the door to merger still seemed to be open.

Ultimately, however, Levinthal did not fall in line. And Ramaz never evinced any enthusiasm for the merger. Indeed, during the spring and summer of 1926, RIETS' most famous rabbis stayed clear of any subsequent meetings with Seminary leaders. And in the fall of that year they rallied their Talmud faculty and the most traditional of RIETS' inner circle of lay leaders—the so-called Committee of Eleven—to squelch all heretical talk. In December, a now-confident triumvirate of Levinthal, Ramaz, and Revel agreed to meet with Adler, Marshall, and Louis Ginzburg to determine "whether it will be possible for Yeshiva and the Seminary to work together for the benefit of Judaism and for the advance of Jewish learning." But before sitting down, they made it clear that the RIETS board "cannot at present see a basis for cooperation."[30]

It remained, however, for Revel to explain to all concerned in his own home why the merger was ideologically impossible. In a paper "Seminary and Yeshiva" distributed to Yeshiva's leaders, he helped delineate where American Orthodoxy and his American Orthodox institution ultimately stood in the spectrum of social accommodation and dedication to past ways.

Revel began his apologia for what he had wrought by acknowledging that "to the casual observer, the Seminary and the Yeshiva are sister institutions serving the same purposes and working towards the same ends." Both have students committed to Torah study, both hope that its graduates will serve the Jewish people, and graduates of both institutions deal in their careers with the fallout from the assimilation of their laity. But that, he averred, was where the similarities ended. For the yeshiva man, he continued, the strength of his appeal was rooted in his great facility with the teachings of the past which have properly prepared him to confront and remedy Judaism's social problems in the here and now.

In Revel's opinion, his disciples came to their calling better prepared than Seminarians. "Many of the Yeshiva students" gained their earliest training at "Palestinian and European yeshivot where Torah is the only study." The American boys emerged out of the committed, strictly Orthodox community and through Revel's own parochial school system and were now looking to preserve the identities of their fellow Jews. Moreover, they received their advanced training, said Revel, choosing his words carefully, "at a yeshiva," "in a house of learning . . . *not* [emphasis his] in a professional school."

Practically that meant that "the center of the Yeshiva study is in Rabbinics, the Talmud and Codes"—Revel was always quick to link RIETS with its European past—"all the rest is complementary." What his revolution had brought, Revel argued more implicitly, was a greater sensitivity within his own community to those complementary studies which related immediately to American situations. For Revel, the ideal American rabbi was the man who could identify contemporary communal perplexities and understand what solutions to teach those around him, because of his immersion in the ways of the past and his training in the most modern of methodologies.

Revel also argued mightily that his yeshiva "movement" or "ideal" did more than just prepare American rabbis. It provided them with an attuned and concerned laity to encourage them in their work. It trained committed teachers who would assist them in their labors.

A good proportion of RIETS' students, Revel continued, then resident in their "house of learning" were not there for professional training. They were the products of the Torah system started by Etz Chaim, modified by the Rabbi Jacob Joseph School, and expanded by the Talmudical Academy. They, who would make careers in all walks of American life, were the essential "portion of our laity . . . intensively trained in the knowledge of the Torah" who would back the rabbis in refashioning American Jewry.

Revel also made it clear that his institution's own Teachers Institute (a wing of Yeshiva whose history will be discussed below) was providing the instructors for the day school and supplementary school systems coming under the control of the RIETS graduates. All things considered, Revel proudly spoke of his creation of a new Jewish civilization in America, with RIETS as traditional Judaism's flagship institution.

The Seminary, on the other hand, was denigrated by Revel as merely a rabbinical training school. And these rabbis were ill-equipped, as Revel saw them, to do anything other than accommodate their laity's wishes, whether or not their desires were in conformity with Jewish tradition. Moreover, Revel pointedly suggested that Seminary men often did not know that their liberalizations in response to congregant calls were outside the pale of Jewish law because they knew so little of the tradition.

But what could one expect, Revel contemptuously argued, from students who came to Torah late in life, after public school and college work and through a rabbinical school curriculum which "outlined" but did not "consider directly" Judaism's hallowed sources. "The best that can be acquired by such study," Revel haughtily suggested, "is knowledge *about* [emphasis his], not knowledge of the Talmud and Codes." Such men, Revel disdainfully predicted, certainly could be "good fellow(s) whose social values are appreciated; but (they) can in no wise be a spiritual influence to be followed, a force for uncompromising Judaism."

Finally, Revel argued that, unlike his men, Conservative rabbis were on their own. The Seminary—its own Teachers Institute notwithstanding—was not, he believed, building the support systems his school had in place. And although the Seminary's "most influential faculty member" (Mordecai M. Kaplan) was already speaking of a

new American Jewish civilization, it was the true American Orthodox, as Revel had described them, who were out there reconstructing
contemporary Judaism under RIETS' banner.[31]

To be sure, though this apologia ended merger considerations, it did not inaugurate a period during which JTS and Yeshiva
men stayed apart from one another. Nor did Revel's remarks accurately presage the relative success of Orthodox vs. Conservative rabbis in promoting differing versions of "civilization" to Jewish masses.
Revel's system, as we will later see, worked better in theory than in
practice. Still, Revel's remarks, along with the reorganization of RIETS
and the battle that attended his response constituted major milestones
for the American Orthodox. It helped them set goals through institutions for themselves and definitions for their movement as they moved
from their European roots toward a rapprochement with America.

Chapter 5

The Teachers Institute and the Trials of Orthodox Men of Hebrew Letters

By the time Bernard Revel spoke glowingly, in his anti-Seminary apologia, of the Teachers Institute (TI) contribution toward "a revival of a true and intensive Jewish education for at least 'a saving remnant' of our children in this land," that school was already an integral component of what he called his Yeshiva "ideal" or "movement." But Hebrew teacher training was not originally part of Revel's reorganization plan at RIETS. The Teachers Institute was rather the creation of a small group of immigrant Orthodox Jews who, though quite different from Rabbi Jacob Joseph's community, were, like their fellows, fired with the dream of transplanting an East European ideal to America. Theirs was the vision of the effloresence upon these shores of the ideology of the Mizrachi (Religious Zionism) as a basis for a new identity for America's Jews. They prayed that their Russian-born mixture of modern Jewish nationalism, its vitality tempered by the traditions of their people as expressed in a revived Hebrew language, would prove attractive to the younger American generation. But they were to find early on and quicker than the Etz Chaim people before them that without money, concrete institutional supports, and a clear rationalized American plan of action, their European-born movement would never be popular here.[1]

Mizrachi men, of course, should have been inured to rejection. Back in Europe, even most Zionists, themselves a minority group within the Jewish community, did not share their point of view. This "distinct group within the Zionist organization" was founded in Vilna in 1902 by the most religiously traditional members of that nationalist camp. Though professing and practicing Orthodoxy, Mizrachiites were often viewed by their religious contemporaries as out of line with the old teachings. After all, they were part of a modern national movement which preached an end to Jewish passivity and which, in the minds of opponents, violated daily the rabbinic dicta which prohibited attempting to reestablish Jewish sovereignty in the Holy Land. Others, who were more ambivalent about whether such activities were truly prohibited, were no less critical of the Mizrachi men's involvement with a movement whose majority routinely ignored Jewish religious practices. Religious Zionists were marginal in their own traditional communities.

They were also clearly a minority in the Zionist camp, but Mizrachiites could live with that predicament. Their theologians would later argue that the promised redemption was slowly coming and Jews were permitted, if not obliged, to participate in the redemption. They would also explain their affiliation with secular leadership by suggesting that even free thinkers were unwitting agents of the Divine plan. What Mizrachiites could not accept—and what called their organization into existence—was what they deemed, beginning in 1902, was the larger movement's total insensitivity to Judaism's religious heritage.

At that year's Zionist Congress the delegates turned their attention from purely political agendas—"a legally secured home for the Jew"—to the fear that "unless Zionism widens its program to include cultural activity . . . among the Jewish masses, it may always remain a party movement but not a national striving." High on the list of cultural activities was the promotion of secular Hebrew-language educational programs wherever Zionism had gained a foothold. Mizrachiites broke with the political movement when the Fifth Zionist Congress' proposal made no reference to a religious component in educational programs. The Orthodox were also seemingly threatened by the tacit "sanctioning by the Zionists of such forms of culture which are not in agreement with the traditions of the Jewish spirit."

The concerns of Religious Zionists crystallized a few months later in Vilna, when a Mizrachi manifesto was adopted pledging to "protect the Zionist movement from being influenced by antitraditional tendencies." More importantly, it redefined the Congress' proposal to mean that Religious Zionism must work "towards regenerating Jewish life in the Diaspora" by inculcating youngsters with the enthusiasm of Zionism, instilling in them a love for the Hebrew language while holding true to Jewish traditions. Without these youngsters, they argued, there would be no future for Zionism. And in the lands of assimilation, there might be no future for Judaism.

Religious Zionism was officially brought to America in 1914 after a decade or so of relatively undistinguished achievements in Eastern and Central Europe. Following the lead of the World Zionist Organization, the Mizrachi moved its office to the United States, then a neutral country, when hostilities began on the European continent. Here the movement met with the Orthodox rabbis and laity who had followed Mizrachi activities from afar. And under its leader, Rabbi Meir Berlin, a central bureau was set up in New York, ostensibly to serve the more than one hundred ephemeral societies situated in twenty three states.[2]

Acting upon their commitment, the Mizrachiites were quick to address what they perceived as the calamitous state of Jewish education in America. Rabbi Jacob Levinson, Berlin's second in command, would later recall that, as late as World War I, "anyone who wanted to, became a Hebrew teacher without any study, without experience in teaching and without preparation. All he needed was a *Siddur* in his pocket." There was no one, argued Berlin in his party organ *Ha-Ivri*, "educating people in the way of the Torah, in observance of the mitzvoth (commandments), in knowledge of the Hebrew language . . . and in love of the land of Israel." The way was clear and the time was at hand, cried the ideologue, for Mizrachi to step in and provide those "properly trained teachers" so essential to the survival of "American Judaism."[3]

According to their plan, the Mizrachi Teachers Institute would be a tuition-free school offering high-school-age boys a diversified program of traditional Jewish subjects (Torah, Talmud, etc.) along with the modern skills and disciplines of educational psychology, art, music, physical training, and speech. The hallmark of this nineteen-hour-a-week program, running weekday afternoons and Sundays, was that all courses, with the possible exception of educational psychology, were to be taught in Hebrew. As such, it would be the only school in America where Talmud was taught in Hebrew, a development surely to be applauded by Mizrachi followers. Nine students answered Berlin's call and the Teachers Institute opened its doors in May 1917 in a private house on Orchard Street on the Lower East Side.[4]

Finding qualified instructors to train these prospective teachers was a relatively simple problem for the fledgling institution. Finding money to pay these motivated professors was another matter entirely. There were in New York, and to a lesser extent elsewhere, groups of Hebrew-speaking intellectuals who might be coopted for the job at hand. In fact, by World War I, Jewish culturally poor America had been home for more than fifty years to transplanted *maskilim* who had earned themselves respectable reputations back in Europe for their accounts of immigrant life in this land. Men like the footloose Leon Horowitz, the eccentric Henry Gersoni, and Etz Chaim people Judah David Eisenstein and Kasriel Sarasohn were known as contributors to such journals as *Ha-Melitz* and *Ha-Maggid* in Russia. And when Hebrew newspapers appeared in New York, they contributed their talents there too. But in America they had to write quickly: most of these journals folded in rapid order.

These same men, and their even more anonymous colleagues, also constituted whatever rank and file existed in the earliest Zionist organizations in this country. In 1881 some of them may have joined the *Hevrat Shoharei Seat Ever* whose aim was "to spread the knowledge of Hebrew and Hebrew literature amongst the Jews in America." Later, around the turn of the century, they and the younger intellectuals who shared their dream about the efflorescence of Hebrew in America made up the membership of the Hebrew-speaking clubs which came under the banner of the Federation of American Zionists beginning in 1897. This elite cadre of thinkers and writers, particularly those who were religiously traditional, could be used effectively in the service of the Mizrachi splinter of their ephemeral community. In addition, how many teachers were required to instruct nine students?[5]

Rabbi Levinson, who moved from Chicago to Brooklyn to help set up the school, chose himself to teach Talmud law and lore. For music instruction, Mizrachiites turned to the famous cantor Jacob Beimel. Significantly, at the time of school's opening, this Minsk-born virtuoso, who had trained and served in Berlin and Copenhagen, had just been appointed cantor at Kaplan's uptown Orthodox Jewish Center. He may have brought traditional musical training and a modern Jewish socioreligious orientation to the Teachers Institute.[6]

But the key men in the Teachers Institute, the individuals who did most of the actual instruction, were two young religious *maskilim*, Mizrachiites and partners also in other early twentieth-century American religious endeavors. Rabbi Meyer Waxman was appointed to be the school's principal. Born in Slutzk in 1887, Waxman attended yeshivas in his home town and later in Mir, earning ordination before migrating to America in 1905. Like Revel, Seidel, Zeitlin, and so many others, Waxman's intellectual horizons transcended the yeshiva's walls. Upon arrival in America, he looked first to New York University and later to Columbia University for secular and higher Hebraic training. He learned about the crises of American Judaism at the JTS where he was ordained as a rabbi in 1913, two years before Revel's arrival at RIETS. While still a student in American schools, he earned his first stripes as a budding man of Hebrew letters with his articles to the Vilna-based *Ha-Zeman* and the short-lived New York journals *Ha-Le'Om* and *Ha-Yom*. He also contributed to *Ha-Ibri* and wrote Mizrachi English-language pamphlets when the movement made it to these shores.

For this leader of the next generation of literari to cast his lot with the Teachers Institute over the Seminary—Schechter's school, had its own effective teacher-training arm—had to be seen as a coup for the Orthodox Zionist organization. Practically, he could bring not only his linguistic skills but also his knowledge of educational psychology, gained at New York University and Columbia, to the school. For Waxman, the promise of building a totally Hebraic school may have touched a deeply felt ideological chord. In any event, once on the staff he taught Torah, Jewish history, pedagogy, and Hebrew literature.[7]

Rabbi Yechiel (Julius) Kaplan was Waxman's main colleague. He too was a traditionally minded immigrant *maskil*. Born in 1885 in Russia, he studied in East European yeshivas before coming to the United States in 1909. Following the now familiar pattern, he attended Columbia University, earning a B.A. there in 1913 and his M.A. in 1915, the year of his ordination at JTS.[8] A man destined to contribute much to modern Jewish scholarship in this country, in 1933, he would write *The Redaction of the Babylonian Talmud,* a major scientific work for its day. Kaplan taught his specialty at the Teachers Institute for more than a generation.

Three years later, Waxman and Kaplan were joined on the faculty by Rabbi Joseph S. Zuckerbraum, a man with almost identical credentials and convictions. Born in Raigrod, Russo-Poland, a year after Waxman, he studied in Mir and Minsk, earning ordination in

1905. Another apparent refugee from the pogroms of that year, he came to RIETS upon arrival in America. But he soon departed from that still disorganized yeshiva for New York University and then the Seminary, graduating from the latter institution in 1917. This contributor to the *Ha-Ibri* and to Anglo-Jewish journals was engaged to teach the Bible.[9]

The pride Mizrach leaders felt in the quality of the men they had selected was greatly tempered, however, by the harsh reality of the fact that they could hardly afford to keep this vanguard of the next generation of American *maskilim* on the staff. With organizational finances the way they were, faculty members often did not receive their meager salaries on time. Waxman himself would later recall that "the first years were full of difficulties. The small budget was covered by the Mizrachi and from time to time, the teacher's salary was late." To be sure, the immigrant organization did look beyond its struggling community for succor. Philip Hillel Klein was a New-York-based rabbi who threw in his lot with the Teachers Institute, one of six Orthodox rabbis in this country to do so. And a group of seven lay leaders, including Solomon Travis of Tulsa, Revel's brother-in-law, pledged support for the group. But the most famous of the East European Orthodox philanthropists, Harry Fischel and his crowd and their rabbinic confidant Ramaz, a Mizrachi man himself, did not adopt the school as their own.[10]

It is possible that these new elite forces believed that the Teachers Institute was unnecessarily duplicating existing efforts that they had long supported. They had heavily backed the Bureau of Jewish Education since its inception in 1910 as part of the New York Kehillah, that far-reaching experiment in communal cooperation. That parent organization had brought together the Schiffs with the Fischels of the metropolis' Jewry to find solutions to the pressing needs of their mutual constituencies. The dilemmas of crime, unemployment, poverty, and, most importantly for us, Jewish education were all addressed. There, under the supervision of a paid professional, Palestine-born educator Dr. Samson Benderly, and his "boys," as they were called, who were recruited and trained at Columbia University's Teachers College, important strides were made in rationalizing Jewish curricula and in upgrading the existing Orthodox Talmud Torahs. Naturally, these men and their philanthropic friends were drawn into close partnership with the Teachers Institute of the JTS, founded the same year as the Bureau. In fact, the Schechter school classes were first held in the Uptown Talmud Torah's building, a school closely aligned with the Bureau supported by the Fischel crowd. Together, uptown and new elite money men, Orthodox and Seminary people alike, aspired to inculcate, through their modern schools, an enduring American Jewish identity in this country's youngsters. They were already doing in large measure what the Mizrachi was only promising to do.

The subtle differences that separated the two institutions were lost upon all but the closest observers. Bureau schools like the Uptown Talmud Torah utilized the "Ivrith-b'Ivrith" system, the so-called natural method in their language instruction. The Mizracht promised to go further: all its Jewish subjects would be taught in Hebrew. Bureau schools had a Zionist orientation. They taught Palestinian geography and modern Hebrew literature and their teachers were members of the fledgling Hebrew-speaking societies. Undoubtedly Benderly boys Alexander Dushkin, Emanuel Gamoran, and Albert Schoolman knew Waxman, Kaplan, and Zuckerbraum from these societies, from Columbia classes, or simply from encounters on Morningside Heights. Certainly, the Mizrachi approach was more specific and ideological, but that made it less appealing. In addition, the Bureau with all its problems was already a vibrant communal reality and the Mizrachi Teachers Institute was in its infancy. And the older institution seemed to have a more pragmatic approach toward recruiting students. The JTS school recruited men and women who were high-school graduates. Their only other entrance requirement was that their sixteen-year and older pupils have a "knowledge of elementary Hebrew" upon entering. They would provide them with all the Teachers College pedagogic skills and Judaic knowledge they needed. Upon graduation, their more mature students would be ready to enter the field. The Mizrachi program, on the other hand, was directed at the outset toward fourteen- to eighteen- year-old youngsters. Although possessed of better Jewish educational backgrounds, for that was their school's major entrance requirement, they would not on the whole be as mature as their uptown counterparts. All things considered, there was little communal enthusiasm for the avowedly Orthodox institution beyond the poor ranks of the Mizrachi itself.[11]

Ultimately, however, the absence of a solid financial base was not the Mizrachi's most undermining problem. Those who were so committed to their Hebrew letters and to their specific view of Jewish life had known poverty before and had a long history of being ignored by their fellow Jews. Their most troubling dilemma was rather one of finding youngsters ready to share their life of poverty with them.

Orthodox men of letters were a group of loosely linked individuals; they were not a community. In comparison, the committed group that had supported Rabbi Jacob Joseph and founded RIETS had much more in common to keep them together. To begin with, the old-line Orthodox could at least look back to Europe, where they had a long history of being united and in the majority, and hope to emulate it here. These writers and poets could not even do that. They and the movement that supported them were marginal even back in Russia. In New York, among the many transplanted Yiddish and religious and emerging American Jewish civilizations, there was little chance that the few practicing Hebraicists could find others on precisely the same Jewish wavelength.

How many families were there like the Halkins in the immigrant quarter? The father, Hillel Halkin, a ritual slaughterer by profession, was born in Minsk in 1866. He received his religious, educational, and career training in the Hasidic school run by Rabbi Shmaryahu N. Schneersohn in Bobruysk. But it was that Russian city's Jewish Enlightenment atmosphere which captivated Halkin and influenced his entire life. He became "a veritable concordance" when it came to knowledge of the Bible. He read Hebrew literature and Jewish philosophy. He acquired a facility with Russian and German. His personal synthesis of love of Torah and affinity for general culture could be seen graphically "when at night he would sit and learn a page of the Talmud while on his table there was also a copy of *War and Peace*." Hillel Halkin had three sons, two of whom made a life of their father's avocation. Simon Halkin, destined to become a major twentieth-century Hebrew poet, received his training while the family was still in Russia. His younger brother Abraham, the future Hebraicist and Semiticist, was enrolled in the Mizrachi Teachers Institute's first class, three years after his family's arrival in the United States. For youngsters like Halkin, advanced study with the Waxmans and Kaplans was more than simply teacher training. It was an exercise in a somewhat secularized "Torah for its own sake."[12]

The only other conceivable major constituencies that could

be tapped were the local yeshiva boys, who were already planning to enter the Talmudical Academy, and the best students emerging from the Bureau Talmud Torahs. But in these cases, basic ideological considerations or the low esteem and low salaries that came with Hebrew-school teaching limited the number of aspirants.

Talmudical Academy boys came from homes that were attracted to Revel's mix of old-line Talmudic learning spiced with the modern Jewish disciplines and complemented by the secular high school course of study. Their ultimate career goals were either the practicing Orthodox rabbinate or, more generally, the wide range of professions and trades desired by the fellow children of immigrants. For these youngsters to consider careers as Hebrew teachers—a calling related to but clearly different from and less prestigious than the rabbinate—required a significant reorientation of goals. Moreover, the very training for this profession required a significant change in attitude toward their learning. At the Teachers Institute, Talmud, the cornerstone of the yeshiva education, was but one of many Judaic disciplines. And that may have disturbed many students and their parents. One could not become a great Talmudic scholar—even an American Talmudic scholar—at the TI. And the title of Man of Hebrew Letters did not carry much weight in the yeshiva's community. There was, finally, a very basic logistical problem that kept down enrollment. TI classes were held in the late afternoon, at the very time public school teachers were offering their all-important classes at the Talmudical Academy. One early observer of the teachers' school would later recall that "very few of the students came from yeshiva homes." [13]

The best of the Bureau Talmud Torahs' graduates had no problems with the emphases of the Teachers Institute curriculum. For them, it would be an advanced version of what they had learned in late afternoons on the elementary level. Their lack of interest was based simply on the fact that so few of these graduates had any interest in a Hebrew teaching career. And those who were inspired to pursue that most financially unrewarding of occupations were not impressed by the availability, through Mizrachi, of training and "certification" at a tender age. It made more sense for aspiring teachers to bank the fires of their enthusiasm for two more years, and, if upon graduation from high school their interests still burned, to look to the stipends and placement advantages offered by the Seminary.

Nonetheless, some students did find their way to the "dreary surroundings, equipment-poor" house on Orchard Street. One student was recruited by an itinerant fund-raiser sent out by the Rabbi Jacob Joseph School to New London, Connecticut. This son of immigrants, who received his religious training at home and in a local heder, moved to New York in 1918 at the age of fifteen and lived with the fund-raiser himself. He attended public school and the Teachers Institute. Interestingly enough, in 1922 this now more mature student moved on to the JTS program. He was attracted from downtown by the offer of a substantial $800 student loan. Others, however, stayed on, and in 1921 a graduating class of five emerged from the TI. Still, the school's future remained seriously in doubt.[14]

It was then that Meir Berlin turned to RIETS for assistance. Financial backing and concrete institutional grounding were on his mind when, in 1920–21, he entered into long-distance negotiations with Bernard Revel. Berlin's appeal for funds was coupled with the request that the yeshiva's secular afternoon classes be opened to Teachers Institute students. This latter move, it was hoped, would significantly aid recruitment efforts. Hebrew teacher training could now become a component in Revel's incipient Orthodox parochial school movement. At least, the logistical barriers for yeshiva boys, who studied with Waxman and his colleagues would be overcome. Presumably Berlin had here offered his colleague the opportunity to be master of an even broader "Yeshiva ideal" system. Whatever the reasons, Revel agreed to accept Berlin's overtures. With the backing of some of his Mizrachi-affiliated backers, an agreement was reached wherein RIETS and Mizrachi would jointly administer the TI teacher-training courses would be moved from the late afternoons to the morning. TI students would move from their storefront school to the RIETS building. Berlin was also happy to add RIETS *Wissenshaft* men Seidel and Zeitlin to his staff. That same year, 1921, on Revel's suggestion, Pinkhos Churgin, a man destined to play a key role in TI's future, came down from Yale, where he was then a student of Semitics, to join the education school's faculty.[15]

Most unfortunately for Berlin, however, his own organization did not live up to its end of the bargain. By 1922, Mizrachi, which only five years earlier had been stirred to solve Judaism's problems in America, had now turned its attention elsewhere. The new thrust of the movement, in these early years of the British mandate over Palestine, was the establishment of their own broader institutional presence in the Holy Land. There was no budget available for the American school. And when the Zionist ideologues withdrew their support from their own Teachers Institute, RIETS followed suit. Berlin, his school, and his faculty were back out on the street and their leader spent a goodly part of 1922 desperately trying to raise moneys to keep the Teachers Institute alive.[16]

Happily for Berlin, a leadership crisis at RIETS peaked that same year. Out of the latter institution's difficulties came a new job for Berlin and a new life for his TI. As noted previously, Revel's first administration ended abruptly in 1919, when he was called back to Tulsa by the Travis family to help them out of impending bankruptcy. For the next three years Revel was on the road between New York and Oklahoma trying to keep both a school and a business afloat. The Travis' difficulties had specific financial ramifications for RIETS. Until this crisis, their oil-rich yeshiva president was an unpaid official and his tycoon family helped support the school. It might even be suggested that Revel's power of the purse, or his financial independence, had gone a long way toward insuring the success of his transformation of RIETS. In any event, now neither the Travis family nor their son-in-law could be counted on economically.

During his frequent sabbaticals, Revel placed the day-to-day operations of the school in the capable hands of Rabbi Samuel Sar. "Mr." Sar, as he was called, a 1914 migrant to America and an ordained rabbi from Revel's home yeshiva at Telshe, would become Revel's majordomo and supreme confident throughout the latter's entire subsequent career. But now he was the conduit through which the traveling president learned about incipient crises at his school. It was from Sar's reports that Revel kept abreast of RIETS' troubled financial profile. Talmud Department faculty complaints about the influence the "secular" Zeitlin and Seidel had upon their students were also funneled through Sar. Sar was also on the scene when, in 1921, RIETS directors moved haltingly toward providing a larger facility for the school on East Broadway. It was Sar who let all parties know how disturbed Revel was with the foot-dragging of some directors. By that time, however, Revel himself realized that an absentee president was of little value to his school and he reluctantly tendered his resignation.[17]

After much consternation and some differences of opinion—Revel for one had his own candidate in mind—RIETS directors turned

to Meir Berlin to head the school. Though some might have questioned Berlin's administrative abilities and knowledge of the American scene—his Mizrachi school had clearly gone nowhere financially
during its brief history—others argued convincingly that he was the
most dynamic modern and European-trained Orthodox leader on the
horizon. In accepting his post, Berlin probably made it clear that his
administration would quickly integrate the TI into RIETS. That amalgamation took place in 1922.

As it turned out, Berlin's school became a permanent fixture
at RIETS, although its founder did not last for a year. During his brief
tenure there were staff disputes and rivalries. Mizrachi directors clashed
with anti-Mizrachi men. The financial picture did not improve. Berlin
simply did not have Revel's uncanny mix of talmudic erudition,
knowledge of the ways of this country, and the political savvy to
work with all the cliques and fragments that made up RIETS' world.
By the end of 1923, a troubled Yeshiva looked back to Revel. Deputations implored Revel to return permanently to work for "Judaism,
Torah study, and scientific Jewish study in the United States." After
some additional cajoling, Revel agreed to return and, armed with an
ironclad financial and programmatic mandate from his directors, left
Tulsa to begin what turned out to be a seventeen-year second administration.[18]

Though Revel had objected to Berlin's appointment, he did
not move to undo what his colleague had done. Revel recognized
the validity of Berlin's original 1920–21 arguments. Well-trained Orthodox teachers were a sine qua non if the envisioned great Yeshiva
system was to produce the "Torah-informed Jew . . . as well as to
prepare the exceptional student to continue his intensive studies at
the Yeshiva Rabbi Isaac Elchanan." Moreover, he felt that for Orthodoxy to remain competitive with a growing Seminary movement, it
too would have to maintain its own teacher-training programs. However, Berlin's program, even as modified in 1921, had to become
more pragmatic, attractive, and attuned to existing realities. That was
precisely the message Revel gave to Pinkhos Churgin when he installed this uncommon educator and organizer as the TI's new principal in 1923.

Churgin began by setting aside Mizrachi's utopian hopes that
the school would project a new Religious Zionist identity for large
numbers of ambivalent American Jews. Rather, he spent his time among

those of the most committed American Orthodox Jews. He spoke to the families that sent their boys to the few elementary yeshivas and to the leaders of these schools. Churgin hoped to produce a symbiotic relationship between this institution and that circumscribed constituency.

He needed these children to be his future teachers. He understood that there were not that many families devoted to the efflorescence of Jewish letters who could be tapped for students. By his own admission he "began a public relations campaign" to acquaint "parents with the aims and objectives of the Teachers Institute." He struggled with their irrefutable perception that "surely little glory could be accorded an institution which was preparing its students for an 'undesirable' profession—teaching Hebrew." Churgin did what he could about the job placement issue by turning to the principals of the elementary yeshivas. He discussed with them their curriculum and staffing concerns. These schools, he suggested, had to become "American" yeshivas. They had to emulate the Talmudical Academy and RIETS by mixing the study of Talmud with a diversified Judaic studies curriculum and the state-mandated general studies. The TI's American-skilled teachers would be their future faculty, covering all Jewish subjects, including Talmud, and all in Hebrew. Instruction in that latter discipline, he averred, was no longer the exclusive province of rabbis, at least not on the basic level.[19]

Churgin also had thoughts about how his own disciples were to be trained. He recognized early on that eighteen-year-olds were not really ready to manage a classroom. He also believed that those who emerged prematurely lacked an enduring commitment to the hard life in the field. He restructured the curriculum to extend the course of study two more years. Of course, this move to increase the time students spent in school would limit the numbers considering the Teachers Institute. But in the long run, he would be prouder of the disciples he would raise.[20]

These new TI plans did not immediately increase the school's enrollment figures dramatically. But it did stir once more a healthy debate within RIETS and its community over Orthodoxy's relationship with new conditions. Some familiar refrains were heard. Some said the TI was a "strange branch" grafted on to yeshiva's "tree of life." It was a financial burden. In addition, teacher-training schools had never been part of the historical yeshiva, they were only modern seminary creations. Moreover, Churgin's recruitment plans, if successful, would take part of the next generation of Torah elite away from pristine study. And ultimately it would create a new image of the American man of Torah, a scholar immersed in a variety of disciplines not solely committed to the study of the Talmud and its Commentaries. Mizrachi people, American Orthodox men of letters, and possibly Revel himself would have called that outcome a success. But they were a minority in the Orthodox camp on that issue.

Hostility toward the Teachers Institute manifested itself in the halls of RIETS. Churgin would later recall that, when his school moved in with its parent institution, opponents "denied it use of any rooms for its classes and it had to conduct its classes in different parts of the large hall downstairs." One contemporary student remembered that "students of RIETS looked down upon the students of the new school and showered them with derogatory epithets." More sophisticated critics—some of the rabbis themselves—reiterated their reservations about the Zeitlins and Seidels and added questions about the Churgins and Kaplans.[21]

Ignoring these complaints, Churgin went about his plans to expand the scope of the Teachers Institute program. By 1924 he had changed enrollment policy to admit only "students sixteen years old and older (who) . . . have completed at least two years of high school." And by that year he had surrounded himself—as had Waxman previously—with additional promising men of Hebrew letters. He gave his boys the best his coterie could offer. Churgin brought in Russian-born, Palestine-educated Rabbi Samuel K. Mirsky to teach Talmud. Mirsky, who later was to edit several Hebrew rabbinical journals while teaching in several divisions of Revel's enterprise, came to Yeshiva after having taught in the Mizrachi's Tachkemoni, its Orthodox gymnasium in Palestine. At the TI, Mirsky found common cause with his indigenous colleagues and with, among other newcomers, Solomon Gandz, and Nathan Klotz. The younger twosome, both of East European heritage, came to the TI after receiving advanced Jewish educations in the Vienna and Breslau theological seminaries respectively. Gandz taught Hebrew and later became Yeshiva's librarian. Klotz' field was Bible, and he published a study of Samuel David Luzzatto as a Bible scholar the same year that he was appointed to the TI. Revel and Churgin were themselves undeniably more than pleased when RIETS graduate Hyman Kaplan, Julius Kaplan's brother, joined the TI faculty in 1923. Though family pressure here may have helped immensely, Kaplan's arrival meant that the TI was not defined as off limits to the RIETS community. Subsequently, Kaplan's RIETS school-mate Solomon Wind joined his colleague on the Talmud faculty.[22]

If, by the end of the 1920s, Churgin and his *maskilim* had yet to gain the widespread approbation they desired, they still must have felt that progress had been made. They were grounded now in a permanent and promising institutional setting. And they would soon be part of their president Bernard Revel's most dramatic departure yet. The building of a liberal arts college under Orthodox Jewish auspices was now on the agenda. The Teachers Institute would grow with "The House of God on the Hilltop," the college to be built on New York's Washington Heights.

Chapter 6

The Men of "The House of God on the Hilltop"

Bernard Revel called them "the few, the saving remnant," and prayed that they "remain in our camp to qualify for the leadership that we lack." One contemporary referred to them as "the select few . . . who were devoted by their parents, their love, and years of training to the intensive study of Jewish culture." Others within the Orthodox community in America may have named them "the lucky ones" or described them, with more than a bit of envy, as "the sheltered ones." They were youths, who because of where they lived or their parents' extraordinary commitment to Jewish education, were earmarked for future service to their own and to the larger Jewish community. They were the success stories of the first generation of Jewish parochial school education. These youngsters were the beneficiaries of the implicit agreement struck between their community and American society through the long years of Etz Chaim-RIETS' first generation. The Orthodox had agreed to abandon forever Moses Weinberger's dead dream. Their children would be taught about America and would learn to compete in its marketplaces. In return, these privileged few would be permitted to acquire these skills in splendid isolation from other Americans and from less observant Jews, while devoting equal time to the study of their hallowed past.[1]

These children were spared their fellow Jews' problems with America's public schools. They never heard their people's social mores or their parents' modes of speech belittled by unsympathetic school teachers. They never heard their religious traditions denigrated as mythologies compared to seemingly omniscient scientific truths. And they were not marked absent when they stayed home on the Jewish holidays. Nor were they forced to give silent assent to another's religion, when Christianity was paraded as America's faith in the schools at Yuletide and Eastertime. They also did not have to absorb the verbal and physical assaults of their Christian schoolmates who, outside the classroom, practiced what their elders and teachers all too often preached. The only times yeshiva boys had connections with the public school world were when the yeshiva brought in sympathetic Jewish teachers to teach general studies. Of course, they did meet public school children in the playgrounds and on the street corners where, like all other Jewish children, they fought to hold their own.

Still, this splendid isolation was simply not of interest to the overwhelming majority of Jews, not even for most of those who readily identified with Orthodox teachings and practices. Solomon T. H. Hurwitz's father, himself a good Eastern European rabbi, may have kept his son in the public schools because he believed that only there could he receive the training he needed to advance in his chosen field. He may also have thought that Hebrew lessons at home could counteract the negative influences of school. Shelley Safire's parents may have felt the same way and thought, too, that the public school crucible was essential preparation for the Jews' future interaction with Gentiles. As far as Christianity in the schools was concerned, Jews could either silently ignore its observances or, if they were more militant, boycott classes on those days. In any event, it was, in the opinion of many, better to receive bad marks for staying away on Jewish holidays or when the class celebrated Christian festivals than to be described as un-American for attending a Jewish school.[2]

Interestingly enough, the great benefactors of Orthodox education dealt differently with the problem of where and how to educate their own children. While they were unhappy with the harsh assimilation and social rowdiness that characterized the public schools, they turned down even the Americanized yeshiva as still too foreign and clearly too déclassé for their children. Private schools like New York's Dalton or Fieldston were often the places to be. And if Jews and Judaism were criticized there even more than at public institutions, it was at least done in a more genteel manner. Jewish education for these children began and ended at home, if they were trained in their faith at all. In the meantime, they worked assiduously to integrate with their Gentile peers. With these "silk-stocking" youngsters out of the picture it is not too surprising that Revel's own "select few" numbered no more than 1,000 students in the early interwar days.[3]

These numbers might have been increased several-fold if all the Orthodox Jews living outside New York had had access to yeshiva education. But as late as 1929 there were only two elementary and secondary yeshivas in North America situated away from the metropolis; one in Baltimore and the other in Montreal. So while the Bronx-based rabbi could send his son to the Yeshiva Rabbi Israel Salanter and then on to the Talmudical Academy, his Brockton, Massachusetts, brother could not. And while the Brooklyn ritual slaughterer could choose between the Yeshiva Chaim Berlin or the Hebrew Institute of Borough Park for his son's elementary training and then look to the TA or to its then parallel school Yeshiva Torah Vodaath of Williamsburg, his Des Moines colleague had no such options. Those in the hinterlands seemed to have no choice but to send their children to the local public schools and then hope, as Rabbi Hurwitz did, that private tutoring or Talmud Torah training would offset what was wrong at school. Parents did have the option of sending their sons to learn in the metropolis, where they might live with relatives, strangers, or in primitive dormitories. Such a move, in one case, did free a "small town" young Jew from "the bullying during public school days . . . (from the) physical beatings and mental anguishes that made many of those days unbearable." But it required a forced separation from one's family at a tender age, a move that at that time few families were ready to make.[4]

Elementary school enrollment day was, thus, the moment of truth for many out-of-town families. Would it be public school problems or big-city loneliness for their sons? Whatever the decision, high school graduation day was the ultimate turning point in their boys' lives as it was in those of the privileged New York Orthodox. For the Orthodox parochial system protected its students from the widest American world only until the end of high school. College loomed on the horizon. There the loyalties of Orthodox Jewry's future lay and rabbinic leaders would be severely tested. If they attended CCNY—the goal of so many aspiring Jews of all religious stripes—they would find a socially and politically heterogeneous student body awaiting them. There was also a teaching staff ready to challenge their religious sensibilities. If they chose to attend New York University, Revel's alma mater, similar crises awaited them. And if they went anyplace else, the social and educational circumstances were even more threatening. By the early 1920s, commentators were already speaking of the "mental dualism" that afflicted the former yeshiva student on his own for the first time in the foreign world of academe.[5]

To be sure, CCNY in the 1920s was seen by many—friends and enemies alike—as a Jewish college. By some estimates, close to

80 percent of the student body was of Eastern European origin. And New York University was often referred to in the most uncomplimentary terms as "NY Jew." Jewish men flocked to these institutions during a time in American history when this country's more prestigious universities were, more often than not, off limits to them. Briefly put, a second-generation Jew from the Bronx could change his name from "Schwartz" to "Black" and consciously dissociate himself from anything that smacked of Jewishness. But his Grand Concourse address and his transcript from that borough's Morris High School would still have labeled him in the perceptive eyes of Harvard admissions officers. So rebuffed, these youngsters enrolled in "Proletarian Harvard," a more affectionate, if value-laden, nickname for CCNY.[6]

The large Jewish presence at CCNY did not make the school very Jewish in its orientation, at least not as Orthodox Jews would have defined Jewishness. For observant students, "City" was not a "cheder on the hill" (St. Nicholas Heights). They did not feel that there "the Jewish student feels at home" and is able to "be himself . . . without fear of any effectively contemptuous criticism." Orthodox youngsters rather felt very much alone and unwanted in "an academic environment generally unfavorable to and often intolerant of the religious Jew."

There was the vexing problem of reconciling Judaism's calendar and clock with that of the college community. Although the preponderance of Jews at City caused the college to all but close on the Jewish High Holidays allowing students either to "pay homage to . . . God in the synagogue or to Babe Ruth at Yankee Stadium," no such unwritten rule applied to all other Jewish holidays or, most importantly, to the Sabbath. That meant that in organizing one's program, a major objective was selecting those courses that met at times that were religiously convenient. Failure to do so would open one to penalties for nonattendance. In those days, a student who missed more than one-third of his classes could receive no more than a "C" in a course, unless he found a sympathetic faculty member. And what about those unsympathetic faculty colleagues who inadvertently or purposefully scheduled exams on Jewish holidays and made no provision for makeup tests? That same professor might also "poke fun" at the Orthodox student's "antiquated" religious beliefs. Fear of failure and public scorn haunted many students.

The Orthodox collegian's constant looking at his watch and

at his date book had a marked deleterious effect on his social life at City. Of course, no one knew at first glance whether a student was observant or not. At CCNY, surnames gave no one away. And yarmulkes were almost always left at home. Caps and hats were the order of the day—worn indoors and out, but not in class. That would be ungentlemanly. Problems arose in the after-school hours. So much of college life, even at CCNY, where career-training and after-school work came first, was tied up in extracurricular activities. Debating and literary societies, student government and student journalism, athletics and the like all helped round out the man's education. The Orthodox student simply could not keep up with the clubs' schedules if he desired to remain loyal to his faith. There were identifiably "Jewish" groups and societies on the campus. However, the secular Jewish Menorah Society was really not for the Orthodox student and Jewish left-wing groups were totally outside these students' interests.

Even those Orthodox students who found the right teachers and who cared less about student activities found life at CCNY difficult. For some the demands of college study and career training conflicted daily with their own desire to continue their intensive Jewish education. If they studied at the university full time by day and prepared their lessons by night, when would they have time for Torah learning? A world without much Torah had not been their lot in the past. And they, like all other TA students, had "never been given any direction, or training, or guidance on how to adjust to problems they might face." Moreover, what was true about the Orthodox Jew at CCNY was even more true at those colleges where Orthodox students constituted a minority of observant Jews on a campus where Jews were generally the smallest of minorities.[7]

To be sure, there were Orthodox Jews who clearly withstood these "excessive strains," "antagonistic forces," "pangs of readjustment," or "the dark abyss . . . of unending conflict," as one TA-CCNY man dramatically described college life. Bernard Revel, Meyer Waxman, and Nathan Isaacs of Harvard University, and Solomon T. H. Hurwitz and Shelley Safire only head the list of those who found time for Torah and science and lived harmoniously with both. Although it is noteworthy that in almost all of these cases, these "survivors came to college socially and psychologically prepared," they did not encounter this heterogeneous environment for the first time directly from the sheltered Jewish parochial school system. Others deflected the impact of college by studying at RIETS by day and attending night school on a part-time basis.[8]

Those students committed to that "moonlight program" would leave Yeshiva en masse after three o'clock to take courses either on St. Nicholas Heights or in one of CCNY's extension schools held in public high school buildings. One popular center was in Queens' Bryant High School. Yeshiva students learned early that there new students were allowed to take three courses their first semester rather than the two mandated by college policy. Other oral traditions about that Queens college further increased its popularity. It was "known" which instructors possessed a liberal attitude toward Orthodox Jewish students and which ones were antagonistic. And once that word spread it attracted a large enough Orthodox constituency to create almost a home away from the yeshiva. Such networking helped students both within and without the classroom. One student recalled that one particular instructor of a required economics course agreed to excuse Orthodox students from Friday night classes, so long as they kept up with class assignments. But he required that they make up the missed work "by reading 1,000-page books every weekend."

> But we were just as smart as he. There were quite a few fellows from Yeshiva in the class. We divided up the work and we wrote very similar looking essays. By the way, I don't think he ever read them anyway.[9]

Orthodox students were also aided by the ephemeral nature of these institutions. Faculty members were adjunct appointees. Instructors came and went; few harbored overriding loyalties to CCNY's protocols. In addition, a goodly number of these marginal professors were Jewish. There were certainly more Jews teaching at night than in the regular day sessions on the hill.

Yeshiva students also experienced fewer social difficulties in Queens. Night school students rarely had time for extracurricular activities. They had little affinity for "college spirit." They took their courses and dreamt of careers on the way home. Yeshiva students fit well into this campusless world. They too were always on the move. After they left home, there was time to stop with other yeshiva men for evening prayers. At services or on the subway from RIETS to Queens, they created a sense of community and a forum for news about courses and professors.

The major problem with this system was endemic to all night school education. It seemed to take forever to earn one's degree. At three courses per semester, assuming that the courses one needed were being offered in the right sequence, it took students "five-six-seven years to get out." That meant that students ultimately had to choose between continued Torah study coupled with the warmer night school environment or more rapid career advancement with all its problems at the day schools. As Bernard Revel reviewed the record of his first generation of Talmudical Academy graduates, it was quite apparent that all too many were drifting toward the day sessions.[10]

There were 280 youngsters in the TA's first eight graduating classes (1919–1926). Fifty-three of them chose to remain solidly within the RIETS orbit: thirty attended CCNY in the evenings after morning-afternoon Talmud classes; twenty-three other RIETS men avoided college completely, another, albeit less popular way, of dealing with the problems posed by college. These students probably spent their afternoons preparing the next day's Talmud lessons or were out working in part-time jobs. Those RIETS men at work were joined in the labor force by forty-seven other TA graduates who pursued neither Jewish nor secular higher education. But these Jews were not Yeshiva's foremost concern. It may be assumed that most of these young men worked in Jewish industrial or commercial lines and had the opportunity to keep close to the way of life of their youth. In any event, they did not have to confront the problems which faced the more than one hundred students who enrolled in CCNY (72), NYU (12), or other secular universities (20). These students had "either to make a secret of religious practice and live up to it as circumstances will permit or shed their Jewishness, religiously speaking." And truth be told, many resolved the "divided personality" problem by choosing the path of least resistance. "At college, they acted the part of the un-Jewish American and at home that of the almost un-American Jew."[11]

There were, of course, exceptions to the rule. In 1927, Emanuel Rackman, son of Revel's friend Rabbi David Rackman, left Yeshiva for Columbia University, only to return to RIETS with his B.A. to pursue ordination, which he received in 1932. Norman Abrams (TA, 1926) returned to a career at his alma mater and in the Teachers Institute after a sojourn at NYU. And there were others. But for every one of these, there were more who seemed to follow in Hillel Rogoff's footsteps, becoming foot soldiers lost in Revel's campaign for

American Orthodoxy. In addition RIETS officials must have been dismayed that some fourteen TA graduates who had completed their degrees at CCNY applied for admission to JTS. And Revel's people may well have become apoplectic over the defection of Samuel Wolk (TA, 1920). This young man received his B.A. from the University of Cincinnati and his M.A. at Columbia, then devoted himself to Jewish education. But his institutional base was the Reform Hebrew Union College where he became an instructor in that seminary's college for teachers.[12]

For Bernard Revel, the only solution to the dilemmas posed by college was to bring the best of CCNY into his yeshiva. Adopting a now familiar American Orthodox methodology, this man of two worlds argued that his disciples' desire to acquire a higher secular education was both understandable and warranted. There was much of value to be learned "of the beauties of Greece" (modern culture). Separatism from American education even on this level was not the way to proceed. But the pursuit of advanced training had to be done with respect for Jewish tradition. As Revel saw it, the experiences of his disciples within and without CCNY classrooms proved unequivocally that such general training could only be done right in "the tents of Shem," in Yeshiva's own liberal arts college. But he also knew that to keep students at the yeshiva, they would have to be convinced that they were not losing out by staying with their own group. Yeshiva College (YC) had to be more than simply convenient and religiously supportive, it had to look like and rival existing academic institutions.[13]

So disposed, Revel devoted the better part of the 1920s to fashioning what he would later triumphantly call "The House of God on the Hilltop." This Orthodox alternative to the "cheder on the Hill" would look down at CCNY from Washington Heights. Its campus overlooking the Harlem River would house five modern structures. Classroom, library, synagogue, and dormitory buildings done in Moorish-style architecture would rival in grandeur CCNY's Gothic great halls. And if the "sturdy sons" on St. Nicholas Heights had their own Lewisohn Stadium, YC would have a competitive "stadium, playground, and athletic field."[14]

YC students were promised that they would also be competitive with City men in the classroom. Under Revel's plan, CCNY faculty and other reputable professors would come into Orthodoxy's home in the late afternoon, rather than have his students cope with taking the subway to outlying campuses. The CCNY-YC connection was created in 1926 when Safire and fellow TA faculty member Joseph Shipley, both CCNY men, brought Revel into alliance with Dr. Paul Klapper, the former's professor of education at CCNY. Together the foursome set out to recruit faculty for their basic liberal arts curriculum.[15]

First priority in appointment was given to men in the Solomon T. H. Hurwitz model. Chemist M. L. Isaacs, mathematician Jekutiel Ginsburg, and Safire himself were all committed Orthodox Jews who had earned advanced degrees at America's best universities and coped effectively with the social-religious rigors of college life. Ginsburg, the scion of Orthodox *maskilim,* came to the United States in 1912, trained at Columbia University where he was undoubtedly friendly with future TI faculty members, and taught for a decade at his alma mater's Teachers College before joining the YC faculty. In his spare time, he wrote Hebrew feuilletons for *Ha-Doar* under the pen name J. C. Gog. His Cincinnati-born colleague M. L. Isaacs received his college and postgraduate training at that city's university. He and his brother Nathan Isaacs, an economist and law professor at Harvard University, gained their Jewish training from private tutors hired by their Orthodox parents.[16]

Ginsburg, Safire, and Isaacs were joined on the faculty by Bernard Drachman, who taught German, and Solomon Gandz, who came from the TI to put together the college's fledgling library. But allegiance to Orthodoxy or Jewishness itself was not a sine qua non for appointment. In fact, when the founding of YC was announced, Revel was inundated with inquiries from prospective and apparently unemployed Jewish academics from all over the country, who often remarked that anti-Semitism had denied them their chosen careers. Revel, however, looked past religious and ethnic lines in his appointments and in many cases brought in Gentiles and nonobservant Jews if they were the best available candidates.

Four of Klapper's colleagues, Gentiles all, were associated with YC at its outset. History department head Nelson P. Mead was joined by English professor Charles P. Horne. Gustav F. Schulz taught Oral English and George M. Fallion was the instructor of Latin. And as far as the long-standing question (from Etz Chaim days) of whether individuals identified with ideologies and practices inimical to "God-fearing Jews" should be allowed to teach at the yeshiva, Revel set down the following policy. It was hoped the professors coming to the yeshiva would respect the religious practices of the school and its students. Some Gentile faculty members wore yarmulkes on campus as a sign of respect and affinity for those with whom they associated. But when it came to what and how to teach in the classroom, the faculty was left alone. Revel's complaint had always been that everywhere else religious teachings had never been given equal time with the secular sciences and humanities. He hoped that at his school both would be taught with equal sophistication. Revel prayed that Orthodoxy could survive scrutiny by the Jewishly knowledgeable student, "possessed of a full education in modern thought and culture." "Harmonization" or "synthesis" of cultures was stressed, but the details were left to evolve.[17]

This most ambitious of Revel's dreams required more than the combined efforts of a community of scholars. Millions of dollars were needed to build a college, the very commodity the Orthodox community had the least. Revel was, however, more than pleasantly surprised by how forthcoming RIETS' core trustees were to this new departure. At a Chanukah dinner in 1924, hallowed in Yeshiva University's annals for obvious reasons, $800,000 was pledged by only a handful of trustees to the Washington Heights building plan.

The ardor of the Fischels, Lamports, and others who rose to pledge their $100,000 contributions may have reflected their personal desire to be trustees of a college at a time when college leadership was off limits to their kind. Certainly, they were aware of collegiate prejudice all around them. Harris Selig, who masterminded this banquet—an American college certainly needed a professional fund-raiser—cast the YC idea as, in part, a haven for Jewish students stonewalled by prejudicial collegiate admissions officers. And at that same dinner, Herbert S. Goldstein, then the Orthodox Union's head, spoke of Jewish higher education as the "best response to all those maligners, those 100 percent Americans . . . to the Ku Klux Klan . . . to our defamers." Revel rejected emphatically this appeal to ethnic anger, pride, and defensiveness. The anti-Semitism he was most alarmed about was the subtle and almost inadvertent kind that arose from the harsh integration of his disciples into the secular world around them.

But he also knew that, in the opinion of many, his concern

for his disciples' tender souls smacked of unwarranted and dangerous separatism which threatened the integration of all American Jews. Louis Marshall, for one, feared that if the Jews were identified with their own institution, unsympathetic exclusionary colleges could say to Jewish aspirants: go to your own, which "would be apt to lead to the introduction on a large scale of the infamous *numerus clausus* which now prevails in German, Polish, Austrian and Hungarian schools." Revel understood that these and other more ungentlemanly attacks—the Reform *American Israelite* referred to the Yeshiva campaign as "the Hyper-Orthodox Menace"—would have to be parried if Yeshiva hoped to broaden its Jewish appeal.[18]

Revel's plans for the yeshiva were made during the peak of the debate within the country over what made one a good and true American. Revel adroitly centered his form of Orthodoxy within American thought and society, a position it would comfortably occupy for more than a quarter century thereafter. Exclusionary colleges, Revel implied, were standard-bearers of the nativist, ofttimes racist belief in Anglo-Saxon conformity; all newcomers must attempt to emulate the behavior and accept the values of the first and real Americans, the so-called WASP elite. In their opinion, America's greatness lay in its ability to remain as homogeneous as possible. And although all tried to be like the families that came here on the Mayflower, few could really succeed. The majority who could not should not be allowed to pollute this country. They should be stopped from settling here. And if they were already here, they should be restricted in their interaction with those who would make America great. Applying this view of America to college life, Anglo-Saxon conformists argued that it was understandable that Jews would strive to be Harvardians, Princetonians, and the like. But the ungentlemanly-like Semite could never really be an Ivy Leaguer. He could not fit in socially and culturally with true American college students. And to those who argued that the good grades Jews earned at school merited a place at college, it was said that intellect alone did not make one the ideal academic citizen.[19]

Critics of Anglo-Saxon conformity, both within and without the Jewish community, constantly argued that if given a chance the Jewish student who scored high academically could be as refined as the Gentile. And with his acknowledged scholarly acumen, the Jew could make a substantial contribution to American society. Harboring a philosophy not unlike melting pot advocates, these Jews argued that there was a lot to be said for all Americans being very much alike. It would further assimilation of the best kind and the muting of points of group conflict. Moreover the Jew, and for that matter all other groups, had an inherent capacity to be an ideal American. The negative fallout from this assimilation might be family and generational crises within groups and individuals. But that was ultimately not America's concern or problem. When it came to the college question, people like Louis Marshall opposed all forms of separatism, whether it came from WASPS or, as tragically for him, from Orthodox Jews.[20]

The Yeshiva president did not, at this time, directly address what the acceptance of the assimilating Jew on campus would mean for the wider Jewish community's survival, although the implications of his remarks are quite apparent. He did pointedly argue that integration at that price for his "saving remnant" or "chosen few" would not be in America's best interests. Drawing from the philosophy of cultural pluralism identified with thinker Horace Kallen, Revel suggested that "the true exponents of American culture agree that the enrichment of America would not be fostered by the submerging of all the cultural and spiritual phases and heritages." To make a contribution to America—to be a good American—required that immigrants, or in this case their children, be aware of their ancestral roots. This was particularly true of his Orthodox students who, until college, adhered close to their families' codes. "Thrust into an environment," Revel wrote, "that is not altogether sympathetic, these students fail to respond. And their loss of talents is on no level America's gain." However, he continued, if his disciples were given "a congenial home, unhampered by restrictions, real and psychological, which stifle the spirit . . . they will be able to realize their energies and mental endowments for the enrichment of general and Jewish culture." Here Revel argued the legitimacy of limited Orthodox separatism within the best spirit of America's emerging spirit.[21]

Revel's definitions did not still his critics. Neither did the publication of his remarks bring an avalanche of outside contributions. As in all previous eras of its history, Yeshiva relied on its own community's limited resources. Agudat ha-Rabbanim worthies solicited nickels and dimes while the new elite contributed dollars. Still, by 1928 there was enough enthusiasm and sufficient moneys in the coffers to begin classes in the West Side Jewish Center's rented quarters while the Yeshiva campus' first building was under construction.[22]

Revel's hopes that his "saving remnant" would now stay with Yeshiva were, however, only partially realized during the first years of the college. To be sure, at least half of his inaugural class of students came from the TA. In fact, TA high-school graduates constituted roughly 45-50 percent of the college student body throughout Revel's lifetime (through 1940); a proportion that would remain constant for almost the entire history of his school. However, at least in the early years of the college, only half of his high school graduates responded to his initiative. In 1929, for example, of the TA students known to be attending college, eleven stayed with the yeshiva while ten moved on to CCNY, NYU, and Columbia. This defection, which presaged a continuing dilemma for college officials, may have reflected dwindling interest on the part of students in continuing to accept the yolk of a yeshiva program while at college. Equally important, it may have reflected concern about the academic reputation of the fledgling institution. One TA student, who did attend YC in its earliest days, recalled that upon graduation he and a classmate presented themselves to graduate school officials at Columbia only to be told that they could be admitted there solely on a "trial basis, since Yeshiva had yet to be considered a college among colleges." Others may have feared this eventuality early on and sought a better pedigree of sheepskin.

On the other hand, some of their classmates were more than responsive to Revel's plans. Probably the happiest were those already beyond high school and enrolled in RIETS' advanced Talmud classes. They were glad to abandon the subways, the night schools, and the like for a Jewish campus. When Shelley Safire approached one such student and told him of Revel's plans, that student "jumped at the opportunity."[23]

But even as Revel may have worried about the fate of the TA boys who looked elsewhere, he must have been pleased to see how diversified his "saving remnant" turned out to be. In truth, even before the opening of YC, Revel had told Board member Samuel Levy that although the chief purpose of the college department is . . . to afford . . . those continuing their studies in an atmosphere of love and loyalty to Torah and Jewish ideals an opportunity to acquire the culture of the modern world, other (Jewish) students who desire the knowledge of the Torah and Hebrew culture . . . and such non-Jews as may seek to add to their own, the knowledge of Judaism may also come.[24]

However, this statement only begins to indicate how widely—although the real numbers were small—Revel's harmonization plans were appreciated within the New York and the larger American Jewish communities. No Gentiles came to Yeshiva. But a variety of Jews with different backgrounds and goals in mind sought out this mixture of separatism and integration. The stories of the men who sought out Washington Heights show how wide the social experiences and attitudinal ranges were among those calling themselves Orthodox Jews during the interwar years.

There were, to begin with, students from Orthodox homes geographically far removed from Yeshiva who came to the school from a world quite different from that of their metropolitan counterparts. One member of the College's first graduating class was from Nashville, Tennessee. He could count among his classmates men from Los Angeles, St. Louis, a variety of upstate New York communities, and Canada. Soon thereafter, the son of a cattle dealer from Manitoba would sit in a class with a rabbi's son from Houston, Texas. In fact, during Revel's time, close to one-fifth of the student body came from cities smaller than the twenty-five largest Jewish communities on the North American continent.[25]

Orthodox life on these Jewish frontiers was not easy. If the student's father was a rabbi, a ritual slaughterer, or kosher overseer, he was probably the only Jewish clerical jack-of-all-trades in the area. Most Agudat ha-Rabbanim members, for example, were either based in New York or served along the Baltimore-Boston corridor, in Chicago's midwest environs, or in western Pennsylvania. The isolated rabbi's family was most likely the only observant one in the area. If not, there may have been one other Orthodox family in town with a son whom the rabbi encouraged to go off to the Yeshiva in New York.[26]

These students were graduates of the local public school system. Some may have experienced all the noted anxieties. But their files indicate that they were remarkable youngsters. They were boys who grew up quickly and took leading places early on in their talent-poor Jewish communities. Take, for example, the case of the student who came to Yeshiva College and Teachers Institute in 1937 from Utica, New York, a moderate-size Jewish community. (The TI, as we will see, had by this time expanded its program well beyond the high school level.) The son of a Polish-born merchant, he attended a local rabbi's heder from age seven until his bar mitzvah, then continued in the community's Hebrew Free School until graduation after the junior year of high school. At age sixteen, the young man, who claimed the ability to "read and write modern Hebrew fluently . . . to carry on Hebrew conversation—translate Bible and Rashi, Early Prophets, Jeremiah, Ezekiel, Isaiah, and minor prophets" was already teaching Hebrew School at the local Conservative Temple Beth El. This star of the local Talmud Torah may have been, apart from the city's rabbis, one of the most learned men in town by the time he turned to New York for advanced training.[27]

In a somewhat larger Jewish community, Portland, Oregon, the local community not only made every effort to send its leading young light to Yeshiva College, but prayed that he would come back as a rabbi to serve his children's generation. In 1936, the heads of the Portland Jewish Education Association tapped funds originally earmarked for indigent Jewish scholars attending Oregon colleges to send their best student to "the Teachers Seminary and the College for a period of four years." A local businessman put up sixty dollars yearly to cover the student's personal expenses. It was hoped that following his TI training the young man would move on to RIETS for rabbinical preparation, then return to a career in Portland.[28]

That same year a rabbi in Houston sent his Hebrew school's best student, his son, to Yeshiva, expecting he would return home a rabbi. This San Jacinto High School honor student prepared for Yeshiva by studying privately with his father. The student claimed in his application the knowledge of "Choomush [sic] earlier prophets and 50 blatt Gemorah [sic]." But this Texan did not leave his hometown a remote, isolated lad. A busy boy, he had found time to be on his school's debate team and in his remaining leisure hours affiliated with the local B'nai B'rith youth organization. He came to New York having navigated well through the public school world.[29]

On the train to New York the Texan met other youngsters

from larger Jewish communities who often had different stories to tell. They boarded the B&O Railroad after years of less than satisfactory experiences with public education. But these youths—take, for example, the boys from Baltimore—had made up for their marginality at school by immersing themselves in a highly advanced supplementary Torah program and the Orthodox Jewish youth activities then available in their hometowns.

Baltimore, in the 1930s, was close to New York both geographically and in its wealth of Orthodox Jewish organizations. In 1917, it housed the Hebrew Parochial School, later renamed Yeshiva Chofetz Chaim, the first elementary day school to be built outside the metropolis. Although it did not receive widespread communal support, it did attract some eighty students in the early years of classes under the direction of Rabbi Eliezer Samson. From that time on, Orthodox parents had an option other than the public schools for their children's elementary education. The yeshiva maintained six grades until it built a high school in the 1940s. [30]

The great crunch for families clearly came during the junior high and high school years. Parents could either keep their boys in a yeshiva by sending them to New York or they could enroll them in public schools like the Baltimore City College (a secondary school). On the latter campus Jewish students were not harangued at Christmas time. And, although they had to recite the Lord's Prayer daily and participate periodically in schoolroom Bible readings, they were not overly perturbed. One Orthodox student remembered that he was not threatened by the denominational offering. "After all, what was wrong," he thought, "with thanking God for our daily bread." As for Bible instruction, he recalled thinking, "who could object to studying the Bible out loud." Discomfort was felt, however—and significantly—in the school's social settings. Students were inured to attending school with their heads uncovered. But what did one do when it came to eating lunch? The same student recalled that he brought lunch from home, sat in a corner, placed a cap on his head, and ate in secret. One day he risked eating with his hat on in the school's cafeteria, only to be told in no uncertain terms by a teacher that caps were not worn in school. For this boy and his fellows, school days were filled with hours of social tension.

After school these students retreated to their Jewish environment. Intensive Talmud classes for high school boys were held year round at their local yeshiva. Four hours of classes were held daily, and during the summer, sessions ran all morning. There they received instruction comparable to what fellows were gaining at the TA in New York. They were also encouraged to continue their Jewish education at YC/RIETS after high school. (Rabbi Samson, who sent his own son to YC went so far as to check with Revel about the placement of his boys in college Talmud classes.) Whatever time was left for recreation and socializing was often spent by these boys at local Orthodox and Mizrachi youth groups initiated by neighborhood synagogues. For many of these Orthodox families, the first time they saw the yeshiva in New York was after high school. Until that time, they dealt at home with whatever problems arose from their children's not being "the privileged few."[31]

Upon arrival at Yeshiva, they met youngsters who had just entered the world of advanced Jewish education. These students were not considered in Revel's original master plan. They came out of New York's well-established modern Talmud Torah system, an institution which until the 1930s had very few connections with the RIETS community.

New York's modern Talmud Torahs, as noted, were born during the last decade of the nineteenth century, but showed their first signs of real maturity only during the 1910s when they became the favored project of the New York Kehillah. RIETS benefactor Harry Fischel and his new elite associates supported these endeavors. However, the major figures in innovative supplementary Jewish education were men and women associated with Columbia University and the JTS. Samson Benderly and his students and the Teachers Institute of the Seminary were, it will be recalled, the Jewish education establishment against which the Mizrachi attempted to compete. The Kehillah died after World War I, but Benderly's Bureau and his men in the field worked on. In fact, the 1920s witnessed an efflorescence of progressive supplementary education even as Jews moved from immigrant quarters to second generation neighborhoods. Jewish educators capitalized, for example, on state law which mandated that students had to remain in the public schools until their sixteenth birthday—fourteen had been the age limit until 1918. They made good use of those two additional years before teenagers could go off to work.

By the mid-1930s, graduates of communal and congregational Talmud Torahs could continue their after-school education in Hebrew High School. These sessions, which soon bore the name Marshaliah, combined weekday afternoon lessons with informal social and cultural activities on Sundays. Heavily influenced by Mordecai Kaplan's then emerging Reconstructionist philosophy, these schools essayed to reach beyond book learning to create a sense of community among students. They attempted to fashion a "civilization" composed of youngsters who were Hebraic-speaking and Jewishly knowledgeable, comfortable by day in their public school's American environment and at home in the afternoon and on Sabbath and Sunday in a wide-ranging Jewish world. The best among these students could look forward to even more intensive Jewish living during the summer months at Benderly's Camp Achvah, where they were immersed in a totally Hebrew-speaking environment with a distinctive Zionist flavor. Dance, drama, and song, sports and recreation were all conducted in the modernized holy tongue. Hebrew newspapers and plays were produced by Achvah's children, while gardening projects were designed to remind all of the Palestinian Jew's return to the soil. All these experiential activities were complemented by formal classroom sessions where Jewish history and literature were taught. Upon return to the city, campers were encouraged to join or lead Hebrew-speaking clubs both within and without their Hebrew schools. Benderly prayed that these youngsters would be the vanguard for the next generation of Jewish educators and communal leaders.[32]

Orthodox leaders did not contribute to the evolution of these plans. But Orthodox Jews played important, if unacclaimed, roles in Benderly's operation. Orthodoxy provided many of the teachers for the neighborhood Talmud Torahs which fed the elite Hebrew high schools. And more often than not, the students who went on were youngsters from Orthodox homes. Where did the rabbi of the Conservative Adath Israel synagogue on the Bronx's Grand Concourse look for his Hebrew School faculty? The same places to which his Orthodox counterpart at Brooklyn's Pre Eitz Chaim congregation looked: the Teachers Institutes of the JTS and Yeshiva. These congregational schools frequently provided the entry-level jobs for the 1920s and 1930s fledgling Jewish educators. These Talmud Torahs also provided indigent prerabbinical students from both the Seminary and

Yeshiva with all important moonlighting opportunities. In all events, these young educators were probably the first modern Hebrew teachers to whom the next generation of Benderly's boys were exposed.[33]

Many of the youngsters they instructed also came from Orthodox homes. But they were Orthodox homes somewhat different from those which produced many Seminary men and nearly all of RIETS' graduates. It was noted that, from Etz Chaim's earliest days, those families that kept their children apart from the public schools were a minority even in their own limited Orthodox community. As late as the interwar period the majority of families known to be Orthodox—those who kept the Sabbath, observed kashruth laws carefully, pledged allegiance daily to the traditional ways of life—kept their children in the public schools. All the modernization efforts, first in the elementary yeshiva and then in the establishment of the TA, did not significantly change the proportions. One present-day Orthodox leader has written that "when I was a youngster, it was very possible for someone to be an Orthodox Jew without continuing (yeshiva) past elementary school." Many who remained in the fold did not have that intensive early training. The place for them had always been the large communal or congregational Talmud Torah in their neighborhood's leading Orthodox or Conservative synagogue.[34]

The students attending the Benderly advanced classes and summer sessions were recruited directly from these local schools. And a portion of these youngsters heard the call for more advanced training and leadership in the Jewish community. In this regard Benderly's goals and objectives were not that different from those of Bernard Revel and, for that matter, JTS head Cyrus Adler. All were seeking to produce a leadership cadre for American Jewry and beneath them a constituency of involved laymen. And all were drawing many of their disciples from the same limited congregation of religiously minded second-generation Jews.[35]

The moment of truth for these students, as for all traditionally minded fellows, came with public high school graduation. Then they had to decide whether their mentors' expectations would be their goals. And even if Jewish education or continued Jewish study at the advanced level was not for them, they had to think through the problems of being a traditional Jew on a college campus. For some, Jewish education was to be their career and the Seminary was the place. They came from and remained in their Orthodox homes, and, for at least their first two years at college, they went to CCNY or New York University or Columbia by day and found the Seminary's evening TI classes educationally and socially productive. Many went on to careers in the Conservative rabbinate; others became Talmud Torah educators. Some of their classmates disappointed Benderly's men in the field. They left Jewish education behind after high school and possibly also jettisoned their traditional Jewish leanings. Whatever residual feeling that remained may have found expression in Menorah Society activities. A final segment of this elite of Talmud Torah students looked to Yeshiva for either advanced Jewish education or for careers as Hebrew teachers.[36]

The choice of Yeshiva may have been influenced by its convenient combination of Hebraic training and general education under one roof. It may also have been caused by a belief that it was preferable to study Torah at an Orthodox institution. Some perceived the Yeshiva program as being superior to that of the JTS, while many others did not feel that way at all. One student, who ultimately matriculated on Amsterdam Avenue, also felt that the Benderly supplementary education was not all it purported to be. Yeshiva training was the only answer. This youngster attended the Bronx's Congregation Kehilath Israel Talmud Torah and then Marshaliah. But he left Hebrew high school because "my father did not think I learned enough." After private lessons with a Yeshiva student, he left James Monroe High School and entered the TA's Teachers Institute program as a high school junior.[37]

The TI, for its part, had been ready for him and his fellows since 1928. All through the 1920s, Churgin had endeavored to expand his program into the college years. He, no less than RIETS' instructors, did not approve of high school boys leaving Torah learning behind after graduation. He also felt, as noted previously, that eighteen-year-olds did not make mature teachers. But until the start of the college, he had little success in holding his students to Torah. TI graduates departed for secular surroundings in far greater numbers than RIETS rabbinical students. Those who desired to be Hebrew teachers while in college found that jobs in local Talmud Torahs, Churgin's concerns notwithstanding, were often available.[38]

The start of the College altered TI's fortunes dramatically. Churgin found support for what became a six-year program running from high school through college. There was a natural progression for TI high school students into their college careers. They were joined in a most heterogeneous student body by those special youngsters from out of town and by New York Talmud Torah graduates of different sorts. All Yeshiva collegians, RIETS men included, sat together in the secular department classes. Their placement in the TI was a bit more complicated. Although 75 percent of the student body boasted of ten to twelve years of Hebrew education and less than 5 percent came to Yeshiva with only four to six years of Jewish study, Churgin's interviews always showed that levels of proficiency ran the gamut. Ofttimes TA boys outstripped the out-of-towners. But every so often, a prize from Portland or a local New York Talmud Torah lad made all take notice.[39]

During the mid 1930s, Churgin admitted both to the advanced and middle-level classes of the TI a group of New York Talmud Torah students—some twenty in all from 1935 to 1939—whose interest in Yeshiva emanated from an additional unanticipated source. They came out of the New York City public school system's own Hebrew language and Jewish culture programs.

All along, from Etz Chaim days forward—and we have noted each step along the way—the yeshiva's world had struggled mightily to protect its children and those of any other Jews from the harsh assimilation of the public schools. But in the 1930s, Yeshiva became allied with its former adversary—at least affiliated with some significant Jews in the school system—toward the perpetuation of Jewish identity.

The movement toward rapprochement did not begin within the halls of RIETS. It came out of successful efforts on the part of the Benderly people, Jewish public school teachers, and leading Metropolitan area Zionists and their local neighborhood Jewish allies in Brooklyn and later the Bronx. They had two intersecting goals. They sought to use the public school's precincts to reach a significant segment of public school children growing up with no contact with Jewish education. Equally important, they wanted the public schools to end their generations-long attacks against their students' cultural heritage. The institution of Hebrew, cast as the language of the vibrant modern Jewish nationalist movement, was a definitive statement that Jewish culture was alive and respected in the city's schools. They were able to achieve their goals in specific school districts because, in Bushwick, in Soundview, and elsewhere, not only were Jewish children predominant but increasingly large numbers of sympathetic Jewish teachers influenced and supported the campaign. Most importantly, out on the streets in the heavily Jewish areas of Brooklyn and the Bronx, Jews had significant political clout, a reality not lost upon City Hall and the Board of Education. Not surprisingly, the rhetoric of the Hebrew in the schools campaign was the same as that used by Revel in justifying Yeshiva separatism, the philosophy of cultural pluralism. One memorandum to the school board rings particularly familiar:

> The Jewish child has been given a new set of values . . . and has frequently grown up not only to misunderstand his parents and the people from whence he sprung, but to dislike them and consider them a burden . . . The teaching of Hebrew may reestablish for the Jewish child a harmonious relationship between psychological and social complexes . . . It may develop in him a sense of "noblesse oblige" and a desire through further study to contribute to the cultural values of America.[40]

Under this campaign banner and after some struggle, Hebrew came to Brooklyn's Thomas Jefferson and Abraham Lincoln High Schools in 1930. In the next half-decade the movement extended to Brooklyn's Tilden, New Utrecht, James Madison, and Boys High School. In the Bronx, the same courses were offered at James Monroe High School. And just a few years later, a Boys High School student could take a two-semester "Survey of Jewish History" course as part of his regular academic program.[41]

Yeshiva College received a small segment of the best students from these programs. They were the youngsters who not only did well in their courses but also were out in the hallways recruiting others for these classes. There was a Hebrew Culture Council in each of these schools which worked along with its Jewish faculty adviser to stimulate student interest in Hebrew; the Board of Education required lists of prospective students before it would approve these ethnic courses. Out of this work arose, in some cases, a desire on students' parts not only to learn more but to emulate professionally the teachers with whom they labored and studied so closely.

Take, for example, the case of a 1937 entrant into Yeshiva College and Teachers Institute. This graduate of Monroe High School was a leader of the school's Akiba Society. As a freshman and soph-

omore, while his family resided in Brooklyn, he had attended Boys
High and had been active in that school's Ivriah Society. During his
senior year he was a delegate to the Jewish Culture Council, a city-
wide amalgam of the heads of school Hebrew clubs. Significantly,
this youngster did not begin his Hebrew training at Boys High. He
had previously graduated from two Brooklyn Talmud Torahs and, while
a high school boy, had a private tutor for advanced Bible, Talmud,
and Code instruction. In fact, he, like all other indentifiable public
school leaders who ultimately enrolled at Yeshiva College, had a much
better than average Jewish education and was very involved with Jewish
activities outside of school. Hebrew in the public schools provided
these youngsters with an outlet for their energies and offered them
greater prospects if they considered a career in Jewish life. A number
of these students stated upon enrollment at Yeshiva that their career
interests were to teach Hebrew within and without the public schools
along with English on the secondary level. For Churgin, they were an
unanticipated but welcome addition to the student body and, potentially, to the Jewish teaching profession.[42]

        During this time the TI also took in New York public school
graduates who had once attended local elementary yeshivas. These
hybrids grew out of the modernization of Jewish parochial education
in the late 1910s and the changes in the city's system a decade later.
The former transformation had opened up the yeshiva world to a
wider American Jewish constituency. And the new atmosphere within
the public schools had made these schools less and less forbidding
for Orthodox parents. Together these circumstances produced collegians who returned to intensive Jewish education after a four-year or
more hiatus. In some cases it produced students who ended up on
Amsterdam Avenue as reluctant Yeshiva men. They looked at the TI
as a "half-way house out of Orthodoxy."

        Take, for example, the experiences of students who entered
Yeshiva College in the mid-1930s from the elementary Yeshiva Etz
Hayim (aka the Hebrew Institute of Borough Park) by way of their
neighborhood's James Madison High School. They received their primary education at a school founded in 1916, almost at the same time
that the Mizrachi's TI was entering RIETS' orbit. The latter relationship may be helpful in understanding Etz Chaim's position within the
Orthodox educational spectrum. The Brooklyn elementary yeshiva—
call it now a day school—may be effectively contrasted with already

existing institutions like Manhattan's Rabbi Jacob Joseph School. Yeshiva Etz Hayim has been characterized both as the first "Hebraic all-day school—a modernized version of the old yeshiva"—and as a "synthesis of the old type yeshiva and the modern Hebrew school." It was certainly "the first yeshiva to introduce Hebrew as the sole language of instruction in the religious studies department." Most rabbis at RJJ taught the holy subjects in Yiddish. Equally important, the teachers in Brooklyn offered their students a consciously diversified Jewish studies program consisting of "an elementary knowledge of Torah . . . the Prophets, Mishnah, Talmud, Jewish History, and Hebrew Literature," a primary school version of the TI curriculum often taught by TI men. It was an approach to study quite different from the core of Talmud learning at RJJ that had led students toward the TA and ultimately to RIETS.[43]

Etz Hayim attracted a somewhat religiously heterogeneous student body. There were, of course, those families central to the yeshiva world, who, if they had lived in Manhattan would undoubtedly have sent their youngsters to the Rabbi Jacob Joseph School. But at least until the mid-1930s those destined to attend the TA, RIETS, and YC or alternately—as we will soon see—Brooklyn's Yeshiva Torah Vodaath, were the minority in the school. Those who would have preferred Yiddish-language instruction and greater emphasis on Talmud were outnumbered in the early days of Etz Hayim by more marginally Orthodox elements. This latter group, which reportedly included "cultural Hebraists"—the TI's own core group—not to mention "the children of *balabatim* (lay leaders) from the neighborhoods' Orthodox synagogues" gave the school the reputation of being "orthodox in character (but) somewhat less than uncompromising in observance than the older traditional yeshivot."[44]

For some parents, the decision to send children to a day school reflected Jewish realities quite different from those that energized Orthodox families a generation earlier. These second-generation Jews, living in the new neighborhoods of the 1920s, were not opposed to American values. In fact, they were so comfortable with their acculturation that they did not feel obliged to send their children to the public schools, at least not on the elementary level. These families—America's first day school parents—looked to Etz Hayim "to engender in (students) a love for their people and its cultural heritage and a strong attachment to the Zionist way of life." Their affinity for Judaism through Zionism was also a product of efflorescence during the 1920s of the Jewish national movement as a positive cultural phenomenon in this country. Families like these, whose religious practices were more traditional than not, saw their day school as in partnership with Zionist youth groups and other active Jewish communal organizations. On a minor scale, they were the American Jews Meir Berlin had hoped to produce at the start of World War I.[45]

When it came to high school training, Etz Hayim parents could, and many did, send their boys into Manhattan and the TI's high school age program. Others, however, found the now changing public schools acceptable for their youngsters. They could be active in James Madison's Junior Menorah Society while taking Hebrew language courses in school. After school, they could take special classes offered in the late afternoons either by their home day school or other Brooklyn-based primary schools. One such student attended Etz Hayim's sister school, the Yeshiva of Flatbush (established in 1927 with a similar orientation and constituency) for eight years before moving on to James Madison. A son of a Hebrew teacher, he spent some of his afternoons tutoring in his Reverend father's small talmud torah. On other days, he attended high school classes run by his alma mater. Significantly, some of his Hebrew teachers were Yeshiva TI men moonlighting in Brooklyn. For this student, the high school hiatus from yeshiva education ended without difficulty with his enrollment in Yeshiva College. Family desires, his own predisposition, and his early contact with some of the TI's best made it a foregone conclusion that he would attend YC. It was the only school to which he applied.[46]

There were others in his generation at Teachers Institute who were not as satisfied with their choice of college. Yeshiva University lore has it that during these years, numbers of TI students did not adhere strictly to Orthodox traditions and practices. For them, like so many other more observant fellow TI men, Jewish education was not their career objective. Moreover, they were the fellows who "traveled from their homes in the Bronx bareheaded and only put their yarmulkes on when they approached the school." They were clearly most unlike the Baltimore young man who ate his lunch Marrano-like in the public school and the RIETS-CCNY men of the 1920s who felt so uncomfortable standing without a hat in the halls of academe.

Though it is impossible to determine exactly how many TI "inverted Marranos" sneaked away from the dormitory on the Sabbath or practiced what they pleased in their homes—student files did not ask about personal observance and college disciplinary reports are very sketchy and speak only of those who were caught—certain informed judgments can be made about what brought these youngsters to and kept them at Yeshiva.[47]

They may have been children from Orthodox homes who went to the Yeshiva D'Bronx and then to the TI's high school department. Upon graduation from high school they, or more likely their parents, were concerned that they stay within the Yeshiva's environment. The highly secularized world at other colleges was not for their elders. The youngsters, for their part, may have been ambivalent about the universe beyond the yeshiva's pale. They may have been afraid of CCNY even as they questioned and grew decreasingly committed to Orthodoxy. One contemporary has suggested that the TI was the place where Orthodox adolescents "could rebel against their parents within their own environment." Another has asserted that Churgin's school served as a "half-way house between their parents' Orthodoxy and the secular world around them." That disaffection with the old might have expressed itself publicly in absence from mandatory attendance at prayers and through harsh words with "knockers" (RIETS students practicing the beadle's task of rousing their community for morning prayers). Mr. and Mrs. Purvis were far more respected and less controversial monitors. This Scottish-Gentile couple administered the dormitory from the late 1920s to the early 1960s. In any event, some of those estranged from the yeshiva while on campus remained permanantly separated from the school. Others, of course, ultimately made their peace with the yeshiva.[48]

"The children of *balabatim*" (lay congregational leaders) from elementary yeshivas who arrived at Yeshiva College by way of public high schools also may have contributed members to the crowd of "TI bums," as they were uncharitably called, within and without the college. These reluctant yeshivamen enrolled uptown because their parents felt that, while the public schools were now kosher for their sons, secular universities were another matter entirely. These students also may have been of two minds about leaving their Jewish cocoons for the wider world of education. They could delay that decision while remaining on Yeshiva's campus.

Public school children from Talmud Torah and Marshaliah backgrounds who, as we have noted, were only beginning to gravitate toward more intensive Jewish education may also have contributed to the heterogeneity of religious practice at YC. Whatever the origin and the numbers of these problem students, it is clear that their presence was well known and discussed within the Orthodox community, particularly within those segments that had little good to say about Revel's grand experiments.

From its earliest days, eyebrows had been raised about the place of a Teachers Institute in a yeshiva community. And remarks had always been made about the religiosity of TI instructors. Similar criticisms were directed at the idea of integrating a liberal arts college where, according to one critic, "philosophy, the humanities and all other meaningless matters are taught" in a house of Torah. Here the Orthodox reliability of Revel's school was once again challenged. A yeshiva, it was argued, should be a homogeneous community of believers, free of heretical influences, whether they came from the classroom or the dormitory.[49]

That viewpoint was one of the factors that Mesivta Torah Vodaath, Mesivta Chaim Berlin, and Mesivta Tifereth Jerusalem students had to consider when they sought out Washington Heights in the 1930s. During Revel's leadership at the college, approximately 20 percent of the student body, enrolling almost exclusively in YC and RIETS, came from yeshiva high schools other than the Talmudical Academy. These students were, in their own right, defectors from a predominantly Brooklyn-based Orthodoxy that, as alluded to above, had serious misgivings about Revel's assumption about Jewish and general education.[50]

Interestingly enough, Mesivta Torah Vodaath's founders had not been critical of the direction in which Revel had taken RIETS. If anything, they had been part of his wider constituency. When organized in 1918, the then elementary yeshiva augured to become a prime feeder school for the newly born Mizrachi Teachers Institute. It also held promise of employment to Waxman's and later Churgin's best early students. At that point, Torah Vodaath was, in outlook, curriculum, and constituency very much like its neighboring Hebrew Institute of Borough Park, founded just two years earlier. Rabbi Wolf Gold, one of the school's pioneers, and Rabbi Eliyahu Mordecai Finkelstein, the yeshiva's first principal, were tried and true Mizrachi men. Their curriculum emphasized Hebrew language arts, and the study of Bible, Jewish history, and Hebrew literature took an honored place alongside the most traditional Talmudic subjects. This course of study, they hoped, would be attractive to the Americanized and second generation Jewish families of a variety of Orthodox stripes then resettled in Williamsburg from the Lower East Side. Their work might also have been seen as essentially another wing of Revel's great Orthodox parochial school system. It was to be a school devoted to effecting a viable mixture of general studies, the most Jewish of learning, and a multifaceted Hebraic curriculum under one roof.[51]

Rabbi Shraga Feivel Mendlowitz clearly didn't share their educational goals. And when, in 1921, this Hungarian-born and trained educator was elected principal of Mesivta Torah Vodaath, he acted quickly to remove his yeshiva from the RIETS orbit. The early working relationship was ended and the Mesivta Torah Vodaath soon emerged as Yeshiva's foremost competitor within the American Orthodox community.

The selection of Mendlowitz reflected the significant changes then occurring in the socioreligious composition of Williamsburg's Orthodox community. Right after World War I the neighborhood began to absorb more recent immigrants and families from downtown who had never totally accepted the formulas Revel promoted for Americanization. They were the last remnants, if you will, of the old-line Etz Chaim community. In short order, albeit over the protest of indigenous Orthodox maskilim, they demanded and made changes in the neighborhood school's orientation. Mendlowitz shared their desire to resist accommodating their new environment. Although he had become keenly aware of American Jewish realities during his first years in this country—a principalship in a Hebrew school in Scranton, Pennsylvania, was very helpful in that regard—he remained unconvinced that RIETS' "splendid isolation" was separate enough and the best possible solution to Jewish educational dilemmas.[52]

To be sure, Mendlowitz and the community that first supported him and later coalesced around him understood what his Hungarian-born predecessor Weinberger had had to learn: state law and American Jewish sensibilities would not permit complete separatism from America. The first Etz Chaim experience had taught all that secular subjects had to be taught in the yeshiva on the primary level. And the early RIETS students had shown that American boys would largely want to continue their secular pursuits. These givens could not be ignored. Where Mendlowitz differed with Revel was on the critical questions of with whom should Orthodox children study Torah, what constituted a Torah curriculum, and from whom should secular subjects be learned.

The Mesivta Torah Vodaath formula emerged as follows: On the elementary level, general studies would be taught on the premises by the same type of sympathetic Jewish public school teachers who showed up in the late afternoon at Rabbi Jacob Joseph School in Manhattan. Jewish studies, even on this basic level, would be geared toward preparing students for lives devoted to examining the most traditional sources. The oldest Etz Chaim agenda was redoubled, as voices were heard speaking of raising great Talmudic scholars—at least more learned lay people—on American soil. A variegated Jewish studies curriculum was not for them. And if that orientation meant that only those families central to the American yeshiva community would seek out their Mesivta, so be it. As it turned out, the Mesivta ended up with a more heterogeneous student body than might be supposed. At one point in its early history, approximately one quarter of the student body was made up of transfers from public schools. But, of course, when these youngsters arrived they were obliged to conform closely to school strictures and the curriculum was not modified to attract them.[53]

An intentional downgrading of the secular began in the high school years. In 1926 Mendlowitz took a big step when he organized his own Parochial High School. That move surely deterred many youngsters from traveling across the East River to the more heterogeneous TA, then still on the Lower East Side. But Mendlowitz's school, during at least the first decade of its existence, ran only through the sophomore year (maybe it was established only to keep faith with State law?). Mendlowitz's sixteen year olds were encouraged to continue their advanced Torah learning by day and, if they wanted more secular training, to attend public evening high school. East District High School literally across the street from their school was the most popular choice. Commuters to Torah Vodaath from adjoining Brownsville attended the New Lots Evening School held on the premises of Thomas Jefferson High School in Brooklyn. Some enterprising youngsters combined these four-nights-a-week classes with attendance at a Manhattan-based continuation school on Friday mornings.

These schools instituted primarily for former dropouts willing to take a course here and there one morning a week were perfect for Torah Vodaath boys ready to spend their own one morning free a week to speed their way through high school.

School officials did not seem to be concerned with the possible deleterious effects of their disciples' attending public school. Like evening college, night high school was a place where students took courses, not a challenging new academic environment. The workmen and mature adults who sat in with yeshiva students took their lessons and went home. For Mendlowitz, these schools were institutions that his Jews could do without. But if yeshiva boys desired their diplomas, night school really posed no danger.[54]

College training was another matter entirely. Here Mendlowitz, no more than Revel, was concerned with the impact the university might make on the Orthodox student. His answer was to actively discourage students from entering that foreign world. His fall-back position was to close his eyes to boys going off to Brooklyn College at night after a full day of intensive Torah learning. At those late hours, he thought, college was an evil that could be managed and somewhat controlled.[55]

Yeshiva College, on the other hand, was entirely the wrong place to be. For Mendlowitz and his community, any move toward Washington Heights constituted a step away from the world of Torah. There, it was argued, Revel had made a separate and unreliable peace with the secular and wider Jewish worlds around them which threatened the integrity of Orthodoxy. Revel had told his disciples that there was value in familiarity with modern Jewish scholarship; Torah Vodaath officials would not hear of curricular changes that would turn their good Eastern European yeshiva into an American Orthodox seminary. A Rabbi Adler, an early leader at the school, prophesized a bitter end to Revel's effort: ultimately RIETS would share the fate of the JTS. "Schechter's Seminary," he suggested, "also started as a strict orthodox school, but when they got rich . . . they lost their direction." But concern over how Revel "made rabbis" and produced Jewish scholars was only part of their critique. Brooklyn people were even more concerned with what the college department said to the next generation of lay leaders which they and RIETS competed to produce.[56]

Revel, in their opinion, had done much more than just open

a college to solve a commuting problem and to spare the wavering from CCNY day sessions. By teaching secular science and foreign languages and literature in the same classrooms where in the morning the Torah of Moses was taught, he had tacitly declared that Gentile learning was not only compatible but comparable with Jewish teaching. That was a struggle far worse than the individual student's dilemma over how to make up a missed CCNY physics class.

Yeshiva College was seen, moreover, as having altered the balance between what students had to know of the world around them to succeed in America and what they might learn to satisfy their general intellectual curiousity and the limits set down in the Torah about what one could not study to insure that the sacred remain supreme in the student's mind and heart. Revel was seen as having sent a dangerous mixed message to the next generation of Orthodox leaders.

And what sort of Orthodox leaders were they anyway? It might have been said that sharing a lectern in the morning with an "inferior" TA graduate might be injurious to one's enthusiasm for learning. Yeshiva men were often viewed as "amoratzim" (unknowledgeable ones) who did not study "lishmah" (Torah for its own sake). But working in the afternoon at the same laboratory table with a "heretical" TI boy was seen as a distinct danger to one's spirit and Jewish commitment—and it didn't take many boys to prove the point. Everyone knew a Yeshiva student who was a "stickle shaigetz" (tainted by free thinking or less than punctilious in observing mitzvoths). The college classes were seen by those within Yeshiva as the great levelers. Sons of rabbis sat with sons of cattle dealers and with sons of Hebrew poets. But to those outside Washington Heights, yeshiva student interaction with those whose commitment to overriding Orthodoxy was defined by the four walls of the House on 185th Street was a great cause for concern.[57]

As the 1930s drew to a close, these anti-Yeshiva canards were reiterated within the halls of Torah Vodaath's two advanced sister yeshivas. For the first generation and a half of its existence Mesivta Chaim Berlin was an elementary school, not unlike its contemporary the Rabbi Jacob Joseph School and the by then long-gone Yeshiva D'Harlem. Its Brownsville-based graduates seemed to end up in the TA, at Torah Vodaath, or in public schools. In 1935, however,

under the influence of Rabbi Isaac Hutner, one of the first of a cru-
cially important generation of Lithuanian-trained rabbis—albeit by way
of the University of Berlin—to find refuge in America, a high school
was established. A year later an advanced rabbinical department was
added. Here again, students who truly wanted college training were
advised to attend Brooklyn College at night, so long as it did not
interfere with their Torah learning. The same message—including the
admonition that YC was no answer—was preached at the Mesivta
Tifereth Jerusalem established in 1938 on the Lower East Side. Rabbi
Moses Feinstein, likewise a Lithuanian Torah great, then of recent
import, might have found some of his students by night at the East
Side High School but they were monitored closely by day.[58]

Significantly, these yeshivas did more than just rule out Revel's school for those within their orbit. They actively proselytized in
Revel's own Brooklyn backyard for the most traditional of his students to come home to their world of European Torah. One present-
day sociologist has captured well the keenness of the competition
between RIETS and Torah Vodaath in the following interview:

> I went to Torah Vodaas [sic] for elementary school and then to
> Yitzchak Elchanan [RIETS] for high school. I was there for two and
> a half years when Rabbi Mendlowitz asked me to come back to
> Torah Vodaas along with eight or nine of my friends. We were all
> in RIETS. At that time, you learned *Gemora* [Talmud] until 3:00
> p.m. and then English. Rav Mendlowitz wanted to break this tradi-
> tion and have us go to high school at night and learn all day. Then
> Dr. Revel and Dr. Safir, he was principal, called us in and they said:
> "What do you want to leave us for? There's no need for a new
> yeshiva in New York. Torah Vodaas won't last. Stay with us." And
> they tried to induce us to remain. You know, to offer a young boy
> five dollars a month in those days was a lot of money. Dr. Revel
> also said: "We have the Meitsheter Illui (Rabbi Shlomo Polachek)
> here. Little did they know that he used to come to us (at Torah
> Vodaath) once a month. I think he wanted to leave YU, but the
> Agudas haRabbonim [sic] prevailed upon him not to.
>
> But we left and went to Eastern District High School at
> night. Go to school at night? You can't imagine what a disgrace it
> was for our parents. Only immigrants and the very poor did that.
> But we went because we wanted to learn and Rav Mendlowitz gave
> us that feeling. He was the most unique personality in the last 100
> years.[59]

To be sure, there were others with similar sentiments toward their rabbis and schools. But the New York subways ran in both directions. Significant numbers of Brooklyn and Lower East Side mesivta boys "checked out," as the term went, for uptown during these years. Some clearly believed that "RIETS was the place to be to be trained as a modern Orthodox rabbi." They, and many others, did not share their community's misgivings and welcomed Yeshiva's conveniences. One Mesivta Tifereth Jerusalem student said it for many when he explained:

> During the past year and a half I have been attending classes in City College during the evening while learning in a yeshiva during the day. At present I feel that I would no longer like to continue in evening school because I am convinced that I would appreciate my college courses more if I attended the day school. I would also be able to complete my college courses in approximately half the time. (At) Yeshiva College . . . I would be able to continue both my religious and secular studies without having to sacrifice any one for the sake of the other. At the same I know . . . that the seminary and the college is not in any way inferior to any other school or yeshiva.[60]

Other students were apprehensive and even somewhat guilt-ridden about their decision. One such aspirant expressed his marked ambivalence this way:

> I want to go to Yeshiva College because that's what it is, a yeshiva and a college. I have no reason to believe that the yeshiva is superior to others in the city. For four years, I studied at the Mesivta Rabbi Chaim Berlin and I have no complaints to make. It is well nigh impossible for me to imagine a school which features a more superior and thorough Jewish education than the aforementioned institution . . . Most of the reports I have heard about your seminary were derogatory, to say the least. Then why do I want to go to Yeshiva College? . . . .
>
> There comes a time in every young man's life when he has to consider attending college. I've decided to continue my Jewish education. To do so effectively entails considerable study during the day. Night college holds no appeal for me. In other words, I wanted both my religious and secular training during the day. I had no other choice but to apply to Yeshiva College . . . I wish to add that I trust that I shall enter my new school with unprejudiced thoughts

and an unbiased mind. I have not let preconceived notions influence what I consider a correct choice.[61]

Revel's heterogeneous student body was also favored by the presence of a small but significant number of advanced rabbinical students who came to Yeshiva directly from German, East European, and Palestinian seats of learning. Some of these nineteen young men accepted by Revel—all of 3 percent of the Yeshiva College community—were themselves already ordained rabbis. They were very much like RIETS' first students, who came from lands of oppression and found RIETS a congenial place to continue their learning even as they adapted to America. Clearly the most famous of these men was the young Rabbi Samuel Belkin, an ordainee at seventeen at the yeshiva of Rabbi Israel Meir Ha-Kohen Kagan in Radun, Russia, who had studied at Yeshiva on the road to more advanced training in modern Jewish scholarship and the humanities at Brown University. Others, particularly Palestinian Jews, found the TI program more suitable linguistically and ideationally for their needs. The Jaffa-based Tachkemoni, the Mizrachi gymnasium, was the feeder school, an institution with which Churgin and men like Samuel K. Mirsky were well acquainted.[62]

Revel was most anxious to accept "these ready-made products" from abroad. Those who chose RIETS added luster to his yeshiva's reputation as an American Torah institution. Churgin was undoubtedly pleased to have these more advanced Hebrew language students in his division of the school. Of course, there were questions about whether the foreign-trained youngsters could keep up with the secular studies. In some cases, Revel addressed that problem by inducing the best of his college students to tutor the newcomers in English subjects. The European/Palestinian may have also, in turn, worked with his classmate in their religious studies.[63]

These mutual tutoring arrangements were but one of the subtle, if not advertent, ways integration was achieved among these disparate groups of students. Maintaining harmony within a small but heterogeneous student body was no mean feat. There were clearly tensions between RIETS and TI boys, between the more and less religious over such issues as regular attendance at daily services and public punctiliousness in observance of Jewish law. In the late 1930s, an imaginative attempt was undertaken by a group of RIETS student leaders to address their concern over some TI boys' conduct. Concerned because their fellow students kept their heads covered only when they approached school and while on campus, they suggested that the entire student body begin wearing college beanies with the year of their graduation emblazened on the cap while on the way to and from Yeshiva. This appeal to the "collegiate spirit" among their fellows, they hoped, would lead to greater observance of a tradition. Interestingly enough Revel was not impressed with this plan. He was unhappy with this measure, because it would make Yeshiva men look like all other college students.[64]

It was left to other, more ephemeral forces, to bring students closer together. To the extent that a sense of community was achieved in Washington Heights, one must look to Brooklyn for its origins. For all the remarkable accounts of Jews from Portland, Manitoba, and Texas finding their way to New York—there were over one hundred such stories during Revel's lifetime—the fact remains that during those years the majority of yeshiva men came from New York. More specifically, they grew up in the Brooklyn neighborhoods of Williamsburg, Flatbush, Brownsville, Crown Heights, and Borough Park, the key second-generation Jewish areas of the time. At some time during the 1930s, three out of four students came to the still small school from New York's three most populous boroughs. In 1935 more than four out of ten came from Brooklyn alone. In these Brooklyn neighborhoods there were at least two central and critically important Jewish institutions, overlapping in membership and in orientation, both frequented by students in significant numbers. Both played a role in directing students to Yeshiva and in creating a community uptown.[65]

The first and most important of these was the Young Israel (YI) synagogue. This major American Orthodox congregational movement was born in 1913 on the Lower East Side. A worthy successor to that community's Jewish Endeavor Society, it was founded by a combination of young Seminary students and some of the immigrant quarter's "young business and professional people." It set as its goal "a revival of Judaism among the thousands of young Jews and Jewesses . . . whose Judaism is at present dormant." Hebrew classes, educational forums and lectures, and Americanized Orthodox religious services were the calling cards of this movement. Equally important, the YI defined its synagogue as an American Jewish social center where young men and women could meet. Dancing, boat rides, athletics, all standard fare at settlement houses, were included as part of synagogue life. As such, it aspired to do more than just "return the hearts of the fathers unto their sons and the hearts of sons unto their fathers" (Malachi 3:24), an ambitious objective in itself. It hoped to make all Jews welcome and comfortable with American Orthodoxy and make Orthodoxy compatible with America, sentiments that Bernard Revel could appreciate.

During the 1920s, concomitant with the movement of the maturing second-generation Jews from the Lower East Side and co-incidental with Yeshiva's first thoughts of moving uptown, the YI spread beyond the Lower East Side. By the mid-1930s, it could boast of some thirty-two affiliates coast to coast, in places as remote from New York as Los Angeles, Toronto, and Akron. But the hub of the movement was Brooklyn, where fourteen of New York City's own twenty-four YI synagogues were situated. There the movement became permanently fixed within the Orthodox orbit and the Seminary connection ended. Under the leadership of its lay officialdom, it began, neighborhood by neighborhood, living a history which closely parallels that of RIETS. It emerged as an institution primarily for Americanized second-generation Jews. It struggled to establish its own identity, distinct from that of the competing American Jewish religious movement in the community, the Conservative Temple, even as both dealt with the wider questions of Jewish affiliation. Unlike Revel's initiative, however, YI activities and ideas received almost total support within the Brooklyn Orthodox community. By that time in American Jewish history, all Orthodox elements were agreed that America, when strictly controlled, could be admitted to the social realms of synagogue life.[66]

Brooklyn-based Orthodox youngsters and their friends elsewhere in the city were surely unaware of the historical significance of that movement. They knew only that it was their central meeting place. It was their afternoon center and their weekend home. Many congregations had their own junior congregations and youth services within the YI itself as youngsters moved through the ranks toward the adult service. The YI was also a place where they played ball in the courtyard until the beadle called them in for afternoon weekday prayers or where they held club meetings until nightfall. It was likewise a mecca for meeting members of the opposite sex at socials and parties, all within the approved parameters of synagogue life. Most importantly, it was a locus where different types of Jewish young people who saw themselves as Orthodox met and shared common social experiences.[67]

An estimated one out of every four or five YC students hailing from Brooklyn belonged to the Young Israel. Their connections with the institution ranged from leadership of, or participation in, teenage services to simply playing basketball on the YI basketball team. Some students clearly planned their week's social activities around their synagogue's functions. One Torah Vodaath and Mesivta Tifereth Jerusalem high schooler who found his way to Yeshiva believed that his work as an officer in the Young Israel of East New York was "harder than work I do during the rest of the week." His labors, typical of many YC-Young Israelites began "at the synagogue at 9:00 a.m. The synagogue I attended is part of a large building, most of which is used by a large organization of young men and women, of which I am an active member. During the services, I helped in keeping order and quiet . . . and I'm also responsible for the direction of the services . . . After the afternoon meal I return to this synagogue and often I give classes to various groups of young boys and girls . . . Saturday night my duties again return me to this organization where I help in planning and organizing the various activites and functions of the organization." Through all these endeavors, this young man could be "constantly in the company of young men who share with me the same *general* convictions"—the same type of men he would study with at Yeshiva College.[68]

Significantly, the Young Israel did more than provide a warranted outlet for the energies of those already central to the Orthodox community. It drew the marginally Orthodox toward the synagogue some of whom moved on to more formal Jewish training at Yeshiva College. One public school Talmud Torah student, who went to Washington Heights with the expressed goal of becoming a rabbi, identified the YI as the major influence in his religious life. Born on the East Side, he followed his family in their peregrinations from Manhattan to the Bronx and ultimately to Brooklyn—a not uncommon hegira at that time—before settling in Borough Park prior to his bar mitzvah. His Hebrew educational transcript ultimately read: "various Talmud Torahs, Hebrew Institute of Borough Park (for a few months), and Marshaliah and private tutoring while attending New Utrecht and Abraham Lincoln High Schools" where he took their Hebrew-language courses and participated in the Hebrew Culture Club.

But the activities that made these studies all worthwhile and directed him toward the Yeshiva were those at the YI of Borough Park. Positive experiences in the synagogue drew him toward Orthodoxy, the rabbinate, and "to work in Palestine for and under the Mizrachi ideals."[69]

He would share that final sentiment with a significant proportion of Yeshiva collegians. During the 1930s Yeshiva, in fact, became much like the Mizrachi school Meir Berlin first hoped it would be. One out of every four or five students—most from the Bronx or Brooklyn—belonged to a Zionist club or society, the majority affiliated with Ha-Shomer Ha-Dati, the Mizrachi Youth movement and the second critically important Jewish institution. Now not only were many of Yeshiva's teachers and some of the rabbis devotees of the cause, but clearly students too were talking about Zionism outside the classroom. Some had even sought out the Yeshiva to prepare for careers in the movement. A few also talked aliyah.[70]

To be sure, Mizrachi activities drew to its ranks both potential RIETS and TI students. And more often than not these clubs, which emphasized Hebrew-speaking and awareness about events in a rapidly growing Palestine at the height of the Mandate period, held their meetings in Young Israel buildings. This nexus among neighborhood, synagogue, and youth group provided an additional basis for community in the college. Moreover, Ha-Shomer Ha-Dati ideology also closely approximated the Young Israel's open-door policy. The Mizrachi spoke passionately about the need to see all Jews involved in the Zionist endeavor as partners in a holy cause, though they emphasized that the holy work of building must be done according to the Law of Moses. Like the YI, they were comfortable with the wide range of ideas and commitments harbored by their members, raising the possibility that these sentiments could be carried over to the group leaders and members who chose advanced Jewish training at Yeshiva College in the 1930s.[71]

Ultimately, however, the greatest force for integration was Revel's system itself. Whereas Torah Vodaath men learned the secular and encountered all others on the fly and on the sly, at Yeshiva, even those least tolerant of difference were obliged to meet and live with others who were subtly different in the classroom and in the dorm. Although the student newspaper would speak with some regularity of the need to "revive Judaism in the college," an equally strong case could have been made for the harmony which arose from the close propinquity among segments of the Orthodox community.[72]

Bernard Revel may have seen one other commonality. Whether they were born to their calling, trained for it early, or were unaware of the significance of their acts, YC students of that generation were united as ambassadors of a slowly emerging American Orthodoxy to a wider American Jewish world. In the interwar period, which witnessed the maturation of American-born children of East European immigrants, their migration from their immigrant homes, and their concomitant drifting away from even the residual forms of their parents' European Orthodoxy, these Yeshiva men were a minority that stood apart. For all their differences and internal squabbles, they were united in their concern with Jewish survival. They were among the most committed—Torah Vodaath and JTS men must be included here too—to the perpetuation of Jewish tradition, to the promotion of Hebrew letters, and ultimately to the continuation of Jewish life in America. They made their mark while still in college in a subtle almost inadvertent way. They were the teachers in the congregational and communal Hebrew schools, who encountered and tried to teach Judaism to so many of their second-generation brethren who would have preferred to be any place else. Later on, their efforts would be more consciously directed and possibly more decisive. They would lead congregations and direct Jewish schools or simply be the most active lay leaders in all parts of this country. Revel, of course, hoped that his graduates would "remain in our camp" once having qualified "for the leadership that we lack." That aspiration would be only partially fulfilled. Many YC graduates would find their ultimate calling in non-Orthodox pulpits, schools, and communities. More liberal forms of Judaism would prove for some to be more philosophically appealing and financially remunerative. But in all cases, they too would be undaunted advocates of Judaism in an era when assimilation made tremendous strides among America's Jews.[73]

9–11 Montgomery Street, home of the Rabbi Isaac Elchanan
Theological Seminary (1915–1921)

Dr. Bernard Revel, President, Rabbi Isaac Elchanan
Theological Seminary and Yeshiva College (1915–1919, 1923–
1940).

Rabbi Benjamin Aronowitz, an early Rosh Yeshiva at the
Rabbi Isaac Elchahan Theological Seminary, and his disciples

Yeshiva College Faculty, 1928

Artist's conception of Dr. Revel's vision of "The House of God on the Hilltop"▶

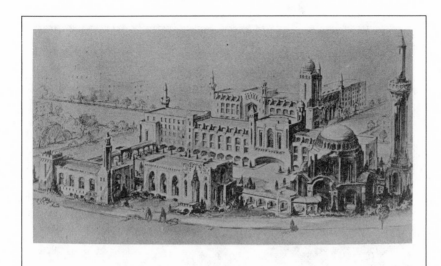

Yeshiva College students, circa 1940

Yeshiva College students, late 1940s▶

Dr. Samuel Belkin, President, Yeshiva University (1943–1975)▶

The Faculty of the Rabbi Isaac Elchanan Theological Seminary, 1945

Rabbi Joseph B. Soloveitchik and his disciples, early 1950s

Early home of the Community Service Division, Yeshiva University, early 1950s

Medical School named for Albert Einstein on his seventy-fourth birthday. L to R: Mr. Max J. Etra, Dr. Samuel Belkin, Dr. Albert Einstein, Mr. Nathaniel L. Goldstein, Dr. Marcus D. Kogel, Mr. Max Stern, March 14, 1953

Yeshiva College basketball team, "Skull Session," in a New York subway, mid-1950s

Chapter 7

Interregnum

Bernard Revel died on December 2, 1940, at the age of fifty-five. His closest disciples claimed with an equal degree of sadness and anger that the jobs of reorganizing RIETS, integrating the Teachers Institute and building Yeshiva College, then defending these initiatives on many fronts had proved too much for his "fragile frame, hardly strong enough to bear the burden of his lofty spirit." In the aftermath of his death from a cerebral hemorrhage, RIETS' students cried out against those in the Orthodox camp who had "stopped their ears to his call." As they saw it, their teacher had been "a lone prophet crying in the wilderness." Where, they asked, "was the aid that had been promised him? Where was the friendship and the shouldering of a common task?" Important factions in both the rabbinical and lay sections of Orthodox Jewry had paid only "lip service to his ideals while secretly damning both himself and his plans for the future." "Their destructive jealousy and fatal shortsightedness," Yeshiva men argued, had not only "endangered the financial basis of the Yeshiva but jeopardized forever his vision of a religious unity of all factions of Orthodox Judaism in America." In the meantime, they continued, "a camp of religious appeasers cloaked in the mantle of traditionalism who were 'conserving' Orthodox Judaism by undermining it" were carrying the day.[1]

The lamentations expressed much that was undeniably true. Revel had succeeded in articulating a viable American Orthodox approach to confronting and living within the secular civilization around them. He had set his sights straight on producing a generation of rabbis and learned lay leaders comfortable in two worlds and capable of convincing their fellow second-generation American Jews of the compatibility of their ancient traditions with their growing identities as Americans. Certainly he must have been proud of his flagship institutions which were educating the rabbis, teachers, and concerned lay leaders he believed American Jewry so desperately needed.

But the truth be told—Revel no less than his students must have known this—Yeshiva activities invariably found more than their share of vocal, and sometimes more subtle and insidious, detractors. Revel, equally the man of Torah and the Americanizer, constantly perceived by his variegated army of critics as either more of one or less of another, was forever obliged to reiterate where he and his institution stood within the evolving interwar Jewish religious spectrum. In the 1920s the trials of the Yeshiva-Seminary controversy had put Revel on the defensive within his home institution. During the next decade, related questions reemerged both from the Agudat ha-Rabbanim and his students, leaving their colleague and teacher misunderstood and decidely unappreciated.

Back in 1915 the Agudat ha-Rabbanim had gone along with Revel's reorganization efforts. Approbation for American seminary-style programs within a yeshiva was not a problem for the Klein-Ramaz-Levinthal constituency within the rabbinical organization. For others in this loose confederation, however, acquiescence to change was predicated in part upon their sad recognition that, if concessions were not made, good students would be lost not to the wide secular world but some of the best would end as the rabbis of the hated JTS. Agudat ha-Rabbanim support for Talmudical Academy and Revel's incipient Orthodox parochial school system was a relatively simple issue. Etz Chaim people had shown the way as early as 1900. Rabbinical support for the incorporation of Teachers Institute and its small legion of Orthodox *maskilim* was not as forthcoming. Some colleagues had significant reservations about Revel's Yeshiva College initiative. But despite articulated concerns about the directions Yeshiva and its men were taking, most Agudat ha-Rabbanim members remained supporters of the expanding school. They stayed with Yeshiva because they trusted Bernard Revel.

For all his affinities for Americanization, Agudat ha-Rabbanim members countenanced their colleague Revel as a man of impeccable rabbinic pedigree and sensitivity to the feelings of his colleagues. That, of course, did not mean that Revel and his school were left alone. When it came to RIETS, for example, the rabbinic body's policy from Revel's earliest days was to work from within to meet their group's ultimate goals. They would be the traditional teachers of the next generation of rabbis, bulwarks against all but the most needed changes. They would raise colleagues whose loyalty they hoped to retain. When disciples showed signs of deviating from their seniors' plans, they turned to Revel with serious complaints.

The Agudat ha-Rabbanim camped at Revel's door more often than not to protest the alleged invasion by RIETS graduates of their members' home communities. To be sure, most of the thirty or more rabbis produced by Revel's school in the first generation after the reorganization (1915–1935) stayed close to home. They found positions in metropolitan area pulpits or as heads of large communal Talmud Torahs or smaller elementary yeshivas. A few ventured outside to Jewish communities previously served by only one or two Agudat ha-Rabbanim members. And RIETS' graduates surely increased in the last years of Revel's life. Their arrival evoked anxieties among the indigenous rabbis, and their subsequent activities caused many of their senior, European-born colleagues to call for help.[2]

Parsonage was at stake, cried a rabbi in Portland, Maine, during the Passover season in 1931. There a young RIETS graduate brought north by a local congregation for the holiday reportedly began "buying his community's *chometz*" (leavens) and accepted payment for his services. The senior European rabbi, who counted on such holiday honoraria for financial survival in that wilderness, was beside himself. Under "attack," the rabbi appealed to Rabbi Eliezer Silver, since 1923 the head of the Agudat ha-Rabbanim, to stop "this young chick whose eyes have not yet opened" by publishing a ban on the interloper in the *Morgen Zhurnal*, New York's most religiously oriented Yiddish daily.

Insolence was the charge in New Bedford, Massachusetts, that same year when another RIETS man publicly characterized his senior's decision in a matter of kashruth as "foolish." This young man's effrontery was again manifest when, subsequent to that statement, he "acted as if the (Agudat ha-Rabbanim's) chairman was not worth knowing and . . . boasted that he had no desire to be a member of an organization such as the Agudat ha-Rabbanim."[3]

When Revel's men joined more liberal rabbinical colleagues on interdenominational rabbinic boards they were accused of treachery against Orthodox unity. Agudat ha-Rabbanim members, who would not recognize clerical organizations which included Reform or Conservative rabbis, were aghast when RIETS men discussed with these transgressors issues of common Jewish social and communal concern.[4]

But then again, transgression of Jewish law and tradition was one of the attacks leveled by the Europeans against their American-born Orthodox juniors. Agudat ha-Rabbanim members counted as deviations from the Jewish way all such common practices as the too low *mechitza* and the sponsoring by synagogues of weekday evening mixed social dancing. Even such seemingly innocuous events as the Friday night lecture forum sometimes came under fire. The latter activity was deemed inappropriate because late after-dinner activities seemed to emulate the practices of the Conservative and Reform temples.[5]

These critiques of his men in the field surely pained Bernard Revel. He could sympathize with the economic predicament of European colleagues in the Depression era—he was having his own financial difficulties at the time. He hoped that his disciples would treat elders with the utmost respect. But he also understood that Yeshiva men were playing a major pioneering role in these communities. He had in his files letters from lay people pointedly informing him that old-style rabbis had little appeal to their younger generation. As one representative letter stated unequivocally:

> If we do not get one of the Yeshiva men, I am quite sure that there will be a (JTS) Seminary man. I am not saying this in the nature of a threat, but I feel that the spirit aroused among the younger men is such that they feel the need for an English-speaking Rabbi and they will want it satisfied.[6]

Moreover, while Agudat ha-Rabbanim were exercised over the exact height of a *mechitza*, Revel had to deal with the reality that some of his men, over his objections, were accepting employment in non-*mechitza* and mixed seating congregations. Some were even joining the nascent Conservative Rabbinical Assembly. It was clear to Revel that Yeshiva had to understand the needs of the rabbi looking for employment in the field and the desires of the congregations they sought to serve. At the same time he knew that mere lip-service to Agudat ha-Rabbanim complaints would be disastrous for his yeshiva. What made RIETS more than a seminary was the continued approbation of his labors by the rabbis from Europe. Revel adopted what must be described as a fence-straddling approach. He was officially sensitive toward Agudat ha-Rabbanim positions and complaints and he did his best to sensitize his young men to respect their elders.

Simultaneously he encouraged the Europeans to understand the youngsters and their problems.[7]

In this same spirit Revel moved to link up more closely with the Agudat ha-Rabbanim when, in the mid-1930s, it seemed to extend an olive branch toward RIETS men. Even the most "imperiled" Agudat ha-Rabbanim member—like that Portland, Maine, colleague—had to admit in his heart of hearts that Yeshiva men had much to say to the younger generation. Their point was that these young men had to be controlled and monitored and better trained to be true rabbis in Israel; an implied critique, to be sure, of the yeshiva they had long supported in this country. To soften existing conflict and to head off any future disputes, Rabbi Silver inaugurated a program to recruit RIETS men into the Agudat ha-Rabbanim's fold, offering them organizational collegiality and mutual aid, with the provisio that the American-trained pass the more stringent rabbinic ordination (yadin yadin) required of European members. Revel accepted this plan: membership for his graduates would lend additional all-important legitimacy to his institution. Revel took steps during that decade to expand RIETS rabbinical curriculum to ready his students for that advanced degree.[8]

Revel's students and graduates were, however, unmoved by this initiative. For many of them the Agudat ha-Rabbanim was an organization out of touch with American realities. Membership there had little to do with one's success or failure within the American Jewish community. If anything, young rabbis may have felt that Revel spent too much time accommodating those who still pined for Europe and not enough of his energies aiding them in their American careers. They placed their own pressure upon the Yeshiva president. In March 1932, for example, the Rabbinical Association of Yeshiva, since 1928 the alumni society of RIETS graduates, issued an angry "final appeal" to their alma mater. They demanded the appointment of a "Field Secretary" in cooperation with the Rabbinical Association "for the purpose of placing our graduates in rabbinic positions." Here they were, they undoubtedly argued, prepared to fight the good battle for Orthodoxy out in America's early Jewish suburban frontiers against the forces of liberal Judaism and assimilation, and their yeshiva was doing little on their behalf. And all along the JTS was doing its level best to place its men. Accusing their school of "neglecting its ideals and . . . becom(ing) simply a money collecting agency," they threatened "that if no immediate satisfactory response will be forthcoming, the Rabbinical Association . . . will be forced . . . to abstain from and even obstruct by all means the making of appeals for the Yeshiva."[9]

Once again Revel found himself sympathetic to the demands of a critic, although he may have been put off by the harsh tones on a letterhead bearing his name as honorary president of the association. Tragically for him, there was little he could do for his graduates save offer consistent vocal support for their fraternal and mutual aid organization and its successor, the Rabbinical Council of America. (His words, of course, did little to raise his or Yeshiva's currency within the Agudat ha-Rabbanim as their rabbis and his graduates continued to find a myriad of issues upon which they could not agree.) The financially strapped school simply had no money during those Great Depression days. And although the board of directors promised repeatedly to help young graduates, a rabbinical placement service was just one of many necessities Yeshiva did without. College lore has it that Revel "stood at the window and watched with agony" as apartment houses were built on lots sold off to meet mortgage payments on the "One House" on Washington Heights. Gone was the dream of a Yeshiva College campus and five-building academic complex, a calamity that Revel said struck "a blow at my heart."[10]

The depression also affected Revel's daily routine, even his mode of dress. One former student has recalled that before 1929 Revel was accustomed to come to Yeshiva by taxi. (It should be recalled that when Revel first came to RIETS in 1915 he received no salary: his financial needs and many of Yeshiva's were then met by the Travis family.) However, by the 1930s Revel could be seen riding to school on the subway, Talmud tractates spread out on his lap, oblivious to the uncomprehending stares of fellow passengers. He was also probably unaware of the sad glances of his students who observed the Yeshiva president wearing a suit torn under the shoulder.[11]

These minor personal indignities were nothing in comparison to the shame Revel felt for his institution. During the 1930s students were starving in their unkempt, deteriorating dormitories. Students frequently appealed directly to Revel for assistance. Many could not look to their own homes for help. In 1932, 1935, and 1937, close to one out of every ten students was recorded as having an unemployed or disabled parent. These numbers do not include the more than one-fourth of the student body whose fathers were skilled or semi-skilled workers—the majority in needle trades—and who struggled for employment and were often out of work in that often depressed industry.[12]

Faculty members could empathize with these parents. They, too, missed paychecks month after month. In 1935 Shelley Safire informed one student's father that the current academic year had opened with Yeshiva owing its professors and rabbis "upwards of $34,000 and it was a most difficult and unpleasant task to induce the members of the faculty to return to their teaching assignments." "The task," he continued:

> became increasingly difficult as the teachers began to lose faith in the promise which Dr. Revel and I were forced to make from time to time—promises which unfortunately were not kept because of lack of funds. We lost some very valuable members of the faculty as a result of our financial stringency, but each time we were able to replace them, although at great expense of time and trouble.[13]

The financial picture was so bad, Safire reported, that in 1934 Revel personally "secured a loan of $4,000 which enabled us to reopen the college. Otherwise we should have been compelled to allow it to remain closed, to the everlasting humiliation of the Jews of this country." Yeshiva tradition has it—Safire's remarks and his own departure in 1936 notwithstanding—that despite all the difficulties Yeshiva faculty remained on board. But it was agreed that teacher strikes were threatened. Financial worries and jealousies coupled with long-standing ideological concerns sometimes splintered the College-RIETS-TI community. There was, for example, the Moetzet Roshei Yeshiva, a rump alliance of RIETS faculty that during the 1930s complained to Revel about the directions the yeshiva was taking and alleged that Revel favored the TI and YC over their school. Revel denied outright their accusation that teachers and professors were paid more at the expense of Talmud instructors. Moreover, he pointed out to his critics that the evolution of Yeshiva's newer wings helped keep RIETS afloat. He wondered "if there aren't people in America who contribute to the Yeshiva solely because they know that we also conduct an institution for the training of teachers . . . I also want you to know that even though the College does not add a penny to the

Yeshiva's budget, it aids greatly when collecting funds for the Yeshiva." [14]

    This explanation of the economic significance of YC and TI
may have quieted some critics within Yeshiva's community itself. It
did nothing to enhance these schools' reputations within the larger
Torah community. Even the presence of acknowledged Torah greats
like Rabbi Polachek and then Rabbi Moses Soloveitchik did little to
stop the whispering. They were perceived as European "window
dressing" in this American school "not far removed from right-wing
Conservatism." These "Gedolim" (great Talmudic sages), it was admitted, "were able to learn with the best," but it was clearly noted
that "these rabbis did not go to College and that is what made Gedolim." Revel must also have been stung to the quick when in the
early 1930s a placard appeared in Orthodox synagogues calling his
school "a nest of atheism and apikursus (heresy)." And he was truly
saddened when later in the 1930s Rabbi Elchanan Wasserman, head
of the famous Yeshiva in Baranowitz, Poland, published a responsum
criticizing Revel's approach to studying the secular. His sadness was
intensified when in 1938 this same great European rabbi on tour in
this country refused to speak at RIETS, preferring to support the Mesivta Torah Vodaath instead. But by then it was just another part of
the unhappy fate of a man who sought, through dint of his personality
and intellect, to accomplish what proved to be impossible: the uni-
fication of Orthodox Jews in America under Yeshiva's banner and the
projection of his view of Judaism and the world to all American Jews
as an answer to the problems of modern times and to the liberal
Jewish solutions around him. [15]

    Revel's death left Yeshiva College without a leader, bereft
of its compass and rudder. The passing just two months later of its
foremost Talmudist, Rabbi Moses Soloveitchik, threatened to deprive
the institution of its most essential anchor. Not since the days of the
troubles of the 1910s was Yeshiva's destiny and direction so decidely
imperiled. Revel had sculptured a delicate, nuanced identity for
American Orthodoxy. Rabbi Soloveitchik had joined Revel in legitim-
izing his work for those who were willing to be moved. And now, as
the 1940s opened, it appeared that all Revel had done might quickly
unravel. At least those were the fears of the students who eulogized
their teacher. To a great extent the forces challenging the center position Revel had tried to define and occupy were much stronger than

they had been twenty-five years earlier in a more structured organized world of Jewish denominations.[16]

On one side, the Agudat ha-Rabbanim stood and quickly
flexed its muscles. Soon after Revel's death, they moved decisively to
return the yeshiva to its original moorings and to control better than
Revel the men RIETS sent out into the field. Now under the leadership of Rabbi Eliezer Silver (Klein and Ramaz had predeceased Revel;
Levinthal alone remained from the old triumvirate), the Agudat ha-
Rabbanim telegraphed Yeshiva announcing that they had reclaimed
the authority invested in Revel and were now prepared to run RIETS.
They would reset the priorities of Yeshiva. No mention was made of
what they would do to or about the Teachers Institute and the College.

The Yeshiva board disagreed politely but unequivocally with
Silver's reading of RIETS' history. Led by Chairman Sam Levy, the
board members strongly averred that it was they and their Americanized rabbinic supporters who had chosen Revel and would select his
successor. But, like the board in 1915, they knew that they would
have to select a candidate who could coexist with the older European
rabbis. They clearly understood that the Agudat ha-Rabbanim would
watch their every step and would never abandon their desire to influence the final decision.[17]

In the meantime, Yeshiva was quietly but profoundly under
attack on its other flank. Some rabbinical students were hopping on
the subway and when they emerged on Morningside Heights were
presenting themselves to Rabbi Louis Finkelstein, the youthful chancellor of JTS, requesting admission. Harking back to a tradition which
began in Yeshiva's earliest days of crisis, students sought to separate
themselves from the disarray and looked to the better organized and
more stable and substantial school to finish preparation for the American rabbinate. To some it may have seemed as if Yeshiva's days
were truly numbered. The transplanted Orthodox rabbis from Europe
would not let RIETS flourish unencumbered. The future for traditional
Judaism in America seemed out in the field with Conservatism then
on the verge of great expansion.[18]

It was thus the old story of defining a coherent middle ground
for Yeshiva's form of Orthodoxy and finding men who could articulate their synthesis of American and Jewish cultures and the difference between themselves and other Jewish religious groups that oc-

cupied Yeshiva's board in the early 1940s. They turned their attention first to selecting a successor to Rabbi Soloveitchik. Here the prime concern was the acquisition of an outstanding Talmudic scholar who understood the realities of America and approved of RIETS' approach to solving this country's dilemmas. Two names were offered early on. Rabbi Leo Jung of Manhattan's Jewish Center, a man destined to play a key role in this and all interregnum deliberations, nominated Dr. Chaim Heller. Jung's neighbor, Rabbi Herbert S. Goldstein of the West Side Institutional Synagogue, then also Professor of Homiletics at the Yeshiva, brought up the name of the late Rabbi Soloveitchik's son, Rabbi Joseph B. Soloveitchik, who, since his arrival in the United States in 1932, had been the unofficial Chief Rabbi of Boston.[19]

Dr. Revel would have been most comfortable with Dr. Heller. But it is questionable whether he would have deemed his colleague appropriate for the most traditional of Yeshiva's posts. Certainly, Revel had long seen this Bialystok-born, Warsaw-trained talmudic scholar—as a youth he was called "the Warsaw Illui"—as a kindred spirit. Like the Yeshiva president, he was a master of Torah and Orthodox modern Jewish scholarship; a remarkable autodidact, he reportedly studied the Talmud alone from the age of four. His only other intellectual companions were *Wissenshaft* writers whose works he voraciously absorbed. While a rabbi for close to a decade in Lomza, Poland, he expanded his self-motivated training in the wide worlds of Semitics, linguistics, and the humanities before moving to Berlin after World War I for more extensive training in these areas. Comparable to the Seidels and the others Revel brought into RIETS after 1915—he became an outspoken defender of the traditional understanding of biblical and rabbinic texts against liberal Jewish critics. He also did much, while still in Western Europe, to spark interest within the Orthodox rabbinate of his time for his combined modern and traditional approach to learning. In 1922 he opened, in Berlin, the Bet ha-Midrash ha-Elyon. Rabbi Joseph Soloveitchik, then a young student of philosophy at the University of Berlin and fresh from a decade of intensive close talmudic study with his father, was one of Heller's students in the mid-1920s. How close Heller was in his attitudes and sympathies to those of Revel may have been best expressed by a New York Yiddish newpaper that described the Berlin Yeshiva as "trying to do for Europe what the Rabbi Isaac Elchanan Theological Seminary is doing in America."[20]

Not surprisingly, Revel made every effort to bring his illustrious confrere to the United States and to Yeshiva. His efforts were rewarded in 1929 when Heller accepted appointment to RIETS' Bible faculty. Interestingly enough, however, Revel did not ask his colleague to teach Talmud. In fact, that same year witnessed the appointment of Rabbi Moses Soloveitchik to do precisely that: to head the Talmud faculty. Revel may have thought that Heller might strike some elements within the Orthodox community as too modern to be the yeshiva's standard-bearer Rosh Yeshiva. That feeling about Heller may have entered into the deliberations almost a generation later, in 1941. For his part, Rabbi Jung, a product of Hungarian yeshivas and the Hildesheimer Berlin Seminary, had no problems with the seminary-like aspects of Heller's resumé.[21]

In any event, there was far more interest in Heller's student, Rabbi Joseph Soloveitchik, within and without the yeshiva community. Goldstein and the other insiders may have early recognized his "great(er) talents both in Talmudic erudition and knowledge of general philosophy." They moved directly in 1941 to have him continue his father's works and those of Revel. Remarkably, he was also the candidate of "Grand Rabbi Schneirson of Lebovitz and his son-in-law Rabbi Guraryeh" and of the Agudat ha-Rabbanim.[22]

The Eastern European rabbis apparently were either unaware of or unperturbed by the young Soloveitchik's links to the wider worlds of scholarship. No concerns were expressed over his following in the footsteps of his teacher in Berlin. In 1931 he had earned a Ph.D. from that city's university for a dissertation on the philosophy of Hermann Cohen. Possible ideological misgivings were set aside because the Agudat ha-Rabbanim apparently saw in the appointment of the son of Rabbi Moses Soloveitchik as the school's new leading talmudist an opportunity to make a significant political statement. In their letter to Samuel Levy and his colleagues, they had asserted the right to lecture board members on how the "election" should proceed. They unilaterally declared Soloveitchik elected as "the Rosh Yeshiva and on a permanent basis . . . as a matter of *Chazokah* (i.e., in this case right of succession), which is Jewish law." Furthermore, they "set a time limit within which the Board was to act" and held strongly that "Yeshiva cannot secure any (other talmud instructors) before that matter is settled."[23]

Board members were clearly torn by this move. They very

much wanted Soloveitchik and what he stood for. But they also feared the ramifications if they appeared to be "subservient" to the European rabbis. Board ambivalence was shared by the Yeshiva student body. On the one side stood those fifty-eight students who petitioned the board immediately after Rabbi Moses Soloveitchik's death asking that the young Soloveitchik be appointed. Simultaneously, a different point of view was expressed by the College's undergraduate newspaper, which editorialized about their fear that this new man might be the pawn of the Agudat ha-Rabbanim, "diabolically" attempting "to penetrate the Yeshiva organism" for the first time "in twenty five years."[24]

Operating under their own clouds of suspicion, the Yeshiva board moved cautiously in their selection of Soloveitchik. They tendered him an offer in the winter of 1941 to serve in his father's stead "for one year, during which time he was to prove his usefulness," but only if he agreed to "waive his right of *Chazokah*." Would Soloveitchik accept such a half-hearted invitation? Rabbi Goldstein felt he would. He reported to the board that he discussed just such a possibility with the young scholar and had been moved by Soloveitchik's reply: "if he could not be useful, he would not want to stay there." One month later a board subcommittee announced that Joseph B. Soloveitchik had accepted the nontenured post.[25]

No subsequent contract renewal discussions were ever held. As it turned out, Rabbi Soloveitchik, over the next four decades, would exceed the expectations of even his strongest early supporters at Yeshiva and make his initial detractors look most unnecessarily troubled, even as he presented problems for those who would turn Yeshiva's clock back or challenge its subsequent initiatives.

The "Rov," as he came to be known to his disciples—even more than Revel and his father and certainly more than the Ramaz-Klein-Levinthal triumvirate before them—underscored the permissibility and possibilities of Yeshiva's creed. He would soon be seen as the man among men possessed of the highest Eastern European rabbinical credentials and yet philosophically and psychologically capable of relating " the ideal *halakhic* system to the basic realities of human life" and able to formulate "a creative philosophy, conservative and progressive, keeping intact . . . Jewish tradition even as he was developing it further." He became, and remains, the ultimate spiritual guide and legal mentor for Yeshiva men both within the home institution and beyond it.[26]

Practically that meant that Rabbi Soloveitchik stood up for RIETS men as they made appropriate social accommodations within the rabbinic field, while setting distinct parameters to their efforts. From the 1940s on, Yeshiva rabbis knew that his approval carried the greatest Jewish legal weight, and that the issues and stances he disapproved of could not be countenanced if they wanted to remain respected members of the Orthodox rabbinate. For those at Yeshiva, he has been a constant reminder not only that it is permissible to undertake secular studies, but also that it is possible to integrate them into a total Jewish Life. The positions he has taken have not always endeared him to those who would have moved the institution toward stricter Orthodox grounds. But what could these critics do? Such, they might have noted sadly, were the prerogatives that come with prodigious erudition. Of course, the same things had been said about Bernard Revel.[27]

But Rabbi Soloveitchik ultimately was not hired to replace Dr. Revel. The directions the institution would take and the priorities it would set in its next generation were to be set by another, even as the Rov, by his influence, approbation, and very presence, anchored the Orthodoxy of the institution. That, at least, was the position of the Committee of Seven, the executive board of Yeshiva, set up in June 1941, by the larger Board of Directors to identify the school's foremost problems and manage the affairs of Yeshiva while "the proper survey of the field" is undertaken "in order to find either in Europe or in Palestine a person who shall properly succeed the universally recognized Bernard Revel."[28]

This all-powerful presidium was made up, first, by Dean Moses Isaacs, TI head Churgin, Dr. Samuel Belkin, then dean of the Graduate School, and long-time Yeshiva operative, newly named Dean of Men, Samuel Sar. They were joined by Rabbi Jung, Sam Levy, ex-officio chairman, and Levy's rabbi from Congregation Kehilath Jeshurun, Yeshiva's long-standing sponsoring synagogue. Joseph H. Lookstein, Ramaz' grandson by marriage and a force within the nascent Rabbinical Council of America, was named vice-chairman. These leaders, who largely controlled Yeshiva's academic life from within and greatly influenced its financial destiny from without, had no difficulty in articulating what was wrong with the yeshiva, and they had some definite ideas about where the school should be going. The question of who would lead them into the interwar period would prove to be another matter entirely.[29]

As they assessed the scene during the first year of their deliberations, the committee recognized that certain of Yeshiva's longest enduring headaches still plagued the school. It must have seemed to some that they were back in 1908, when they acknowledged that student unrest, academic disorganization, and financial instability engendered "rumors and disturbances from within and without." To silence the voices that whispered and sometimes shouted that Yeshiva did nothing for its graduates, leaving them with "bitterness and resentment" in their competition with Seminary men, the committee instructed their colleague Mr. Sar to focus his attention on appointing "more senior students to High Holiday positions" and on placing "graduates in permanent rabbinical positions throughout the country." He was also told to respond to the needs of the students for "more attention, happier surroundings, more pleasant attitudes and more friendly relationships" while on campus.

The committee was also sure to want it known that the school's Talmudic Department—the core of its existence and its calling card to the Orthodox world—was both stable and certain in its direction. Toward that end, they appointed their own Dr. Belkin as the administrative head of the Yeshiva program. Rabbi Soloveitchik, of course, had just taken up residence as Yeshiva's leading Talmudist. Arrangements were made to have Rabbis Levinthal and Aronowitz— two of Yeshiva's oldest old-timers—serve with Rabbi Soloveitchik on the RIETS ordination board. And promises were made that soon "several additional appointments" to the Yeshiva rabbinical school staff would be made. These moves, they averred, would end perceptions that at Yeshiva "there was no one to make appointments to the faculty and supervise those in service and (that) there was no one to arrange for the senior students of Yeshiva who where ready for their ordination examinations."

But as always, it was clear that these academic moves could never be completely effectuated without improvement in Yeshiva's financial portfolio. Here the committee's inauguration of an audacious departure in fund-raising policies carried with it significant ideological ramifications for the school's future. In Yeshiva's earliest days, funds came in through student-held charity boxes or from appeals conducted by Agudat ha-Rabbanim members in their small synagogues. During Dr. Revel's era, small halting steps were taken toward professionalizing Yeshiva's campaign. Early on, a fund-raiser from outside Yeshiva, Harris Selig had been hired. But his differences with his bosses over Yeshiva's goals and image lead to his resignation in 1928. From then on, through the depression years, the responsibility for fund-raising fell upon Samuel Sar's broad shoulders. Mr. Sar, acting in most instances alone—but sometimes with assistance—solicited moneys from Orthodox synagogues across the nation even as he worked to place RIETS men in pulpits in the same synagogues. Of course, Sar did not abandon the older forms of fund-raising: itinerant fund-raisers traveled the country, raised dollars, and were compensated on a small commission basis. Sometimes illustrious rabbis from the East Coast hit the road for Yeshiva, performing a mitzvah for no financial compensation but receiving valued Jewish communal exposure.

The Committee of Seven detached fund-raising from Sar's responsibilities, a move which conceivably freed him to be more objective and detached in his negotiations on behalf of students. In his stead, a bureau devoted exclusively to raising money was established. One of Sar's assistants worked in the well-trod area of synagogue appeals. But a new colleague was designated "Director of Dinners, Federations, Welfare Chests, and work in various trades." With this appointment, Yeshiva embarked on a different path. For the first time in its history, the school was looking directly at non-Orthodox and even non-Jewish sources of income. This move did not sit well with some of Yeshiva's constituents. Fears were expressed about the "pressure" these foreign elements would bring to bear upon the Orthodox establishment.

The bureaucratization of fund-raising was completed by two final, suggestive moves. The business office of the institution was moved from "the Yeshiva building . . . to a suite of offices in the mid-town area of the city." This removal would, it was argued, facilitate the "layman's supervision of the financial aspects" of the school. Moreover, it was said, "it is common practice among educational institutions to completely separate their business departments from the academic department." Yeshiva also began to look more like other universities when it hired a publicity director. Here, it was noted, that the people they now hoped to reach "do not read the Yiddish press" where most notices about the school were posted.

Having defined Yeshiva's problems and taken the first steps toward their amelioration, the Committee of Seven paused to offer a tentative suggestion about a new direction the institution could take. Possibly in keeping with their new fund-raising approach, a proposal was offered to establish "with the aid of the Young Israel . . . an adult school around the Yeshiva." The "continuing education program"—to use an anachronistic term—would prove to be but a modest first step toward involving Yeshiva both financially and intellectually with the larger Jewish community in the postwar years.[30]

It was not until the spring of 1943 that the committee discharged its ultimate responsibility: the identification and recruitment for the larger board and for Yeshiva itself of a successor to Bernard Revel. Indeed, as the board seemed to procrastinate, impatient voices emanated from a variety of quarters. Probably the voice that was taken most to heart was that of the New York Department of State, which "wonder(ed) why no president has been elected" and made clear "that it was contrary to accepted academic policy not to have an accredited head for an institution like (Yeshiva)." It is not known what caused the delay or how far and wide the committee looked for a "focus of the eyes of the Jewish and general community upon (that) one single personality symbolic of the synthesis that Yeshiva . . . represents." Did the committee look overseas at the Chief Rabbi of Palestine, Dr. Isaac Herzog, who, one Anglo-American Orthodox newspaper suggested, was the "only one who can succeed (Revel) in the leadership of this institution and maintain the standards . . . established"? Was Rabbi J. B. Soloveitchik, the favorite son of the Agudat ha-Rabbanim for this post as well, given any consideration? Or did the board's fear of and antipathy toward the European rabbis disqualify the Rov from the very start? And what about the possibilities of Jung's candidate for Rosh Yeshiva, Dr. Chaim Heller? Heller himself had made it known as early as 1941 that he would be willing to assume Yeshiva's highest post. What is known is that the committee did select a man from its inner governing circle, but a relative unknown outside the Yeshiva itself. On June 24, 1943, the Committee of Seven offered Dr. Samuel Belkin as their choice for president of Yeshiva.[31]

In arguing for Belkin's election, committeeman Lookstein claimed that his candidate possessed many of the qualities that had made Revel great. He was "first and foremost . . . a confirmed and widely recognized *talmid chochum,* (Talmudic scholar) in the oldest and most traditional sense of the word . . . and he possess(ed) secular knowledge." He typified "the philosophy of integration that is the soul of Yeshiva College; the fusing of piety, torah, and secular learning in one talented individual."

Like Revel, the candidate had been identified while still a child as a potentially, prodigious talmudic sage. He was ordained at age seventeen after studies in the yeshivas of Radun and Mir. And again like Revel, but even more so, Belkin manifested a voracious appetite for secular, humanistic learning. His quest for worldly scholarly training had brought him to the United States and to American universities where he mastered the English language and earned a Ph.D. in classics from Brown University. Lookstein would also note that, although Belkin was still in his early thirties, he had already written two major books, *The Alexandrian Halakah in Apologetic Literature,* published by the Jewish Publication Society in 1939, and *Philo and the Oral Law,* noted for its quality and published in 1940 by Harvard University Press. Yeshiva's president would clearly have important academic and personal ties to the wider world of scholarship, even as he was a student of Jewish traditions.

Lookstein also emphasized that Belkin possessed other qualities which the committee clearly rated highly and which Revel did not always have: executive ability and administrative skill. In fact, Lookstein noted that it was Revel himself who first recognized these skills. He appointed Belkin in 1937 "executive head . . . of the Graduate School for Semitics which now bears his (Revel's) sainted name, because of the confidence he had in him." And in the last year of his life, Revel appointed Belkin along with Churgin and Isaacs to serve "as the executive committee in full charge of Yeshiva College." And of course, they, the Committee of Seven, had selected their fellow as administrative head of the Talmud Department.

The committee clinched its effort to link their man with his predecessors by noting that Revel had appointed Belkin professor of Talmud in 1936 and "simultaneously as instructor of Greek in Yeshiva College." And Revel had been richly rewarded. Belkin was "revered by faculty and loved by his students." And if that was not enough, they brought in letters of support for Belkin from the Rabbinical Council of America, a group close to Lookstein's heart and within his power, and from the TI Alumni Association, a rump organization of those students most devoted to Dr. Churgin.[32]

As it turned out, the committee's recommendation, the letters of support, and the power behind both provided just enough leverage to elect Belkin. Support for the future president, a man even his backers said "they did not really know," was by no means overwhelming. Other factions within the Board had fears about Belkin as well as having preferred candidates of their own. As divergent views were articulated, all were reminded that there still remained different visions of what Yeshiva should be and who should project its image.[33]

There were those, for example, who wanted a different member of the Committee of Seven, Leo Jung, to succeed Revel. Support for the rabbi of the Jewish Center came primarily from the members of the board who were his leading congregants. They saw in their spiritual leader the quintessence of the modern Orthodox rabbi. He was a philosopher who would write and edit more than a dozen books during his long career. He was a master homiletician; his sermons would receive wide dissemination. He was a trained academician; he believed in the good that could come from secular studies. He would be ideal for Yeshiva because he was intimately attuned to the changed sociology of the American and world Jewish scene and unqualifiably committed to Revel's stand that RIETS and its men were the ones to show all how to live as Jews most loyal to their faith within the contemporary world. And, of course, he was their man, their rabbi.

Leo Jung was, moreover, known for his stands and loved for himself and for his teaching by RIETS men in the field. He had taught the first generation of post-1915 RIETS rabbis ethics and philosophy from the time they were all on the Lower East Side. He had followed many of them in their careers, giving them advice and assistance in their pulpits. And he had backed wholeheartedly their RCA. He would be sure to champion their cause and that of Yeshiva within the wider Jewish community that each sought to serve.

Significantly, his links to Yeshiva had long transcended the classroom and pulpit. He was a major fund-raiser for the school. He was proud of his trips around the country to solicit funds for Yeshiva. He would later write of a semi-miraculous adventure which led to a donation to the financially strapped Yeshiva of a then magnificent gift of $25,000 from a most unlikely source, Mussolini's ambassador to the United States, a mid-twentieth-century secret Jew. Of course, Leo Jung's congregation had also done more than its fair share in keeping Yeshiva going over the generations. It was felt that he and his followers, with their multiplicity of organizational and business affiliations within and without the yeshiva world, could and would do more in succeeding years.[34]

To be sure, there was one significant deficiency in Jung's candidacy. His vita did not include ordination from a leading yeshiva in Eastern Europe. This graduate of the Berlin Orthodox rabbinical seminary was not a Talmudic scholar in the conventional sense of the word. The Agudat ha-Rabbanim and its legions would surely be heard from on that count.

But that possibility was not in the forefront of board and Jewish Center member Max Stern's mind when he moved at the June 26 meeting to have the election of the president postponed for two months "so that every member of the Board has an opportunity to study the qualifications of the nominee." Rumors that a pro-Jung faction was about to gather steam were strengthened further when Board and Jewish Center worthy William Feinberg jumped to second Stern's motion. And when Jung, himself member of the committee which seemed to have nominated Belkin unanimously, did not rush to block Stern's motion, it became clear to Levy and many others in the room that the board was definitely not of one mind on the presidency issue.[35]

The troubling perception was confirmed when Yeshiva and Jewish Center Board member Abraham Mazer asked that Stern's motion be voted on by a secret ballot and then refused to withdraw his procedural motion when personally asked to do so by Levy "in the interests of amity . . . and especially on the fact that a letter had been circulated, signed by Mr. Joseph Kaminetsky, president of the College Alumni, in which it asked that the election be postponed." Levy prayed that the board stick together, vote immediately and for the one candidate in nomination, so as "not to yield to outside pressure which was not advisable."[36]

But the Alumni Association—not to mention the Stern group—

had significant support within a divided board and its recommendations were taken seriously. Samuel C. Feuerstein, the father of alumni
leader Moses Feuerstein, for one, shared the young men's point of
view. These outspoken young graduates had grave concerns over the
election. They were not so much troubled by Belkin's background
and putative abilities as they were about those who were promoting
him. They frankly feared that the thirty-three-year-old Belkin would
be Churgin's and Lookstein's man and not his own.[37]

The association's problems with Churgin reflected long-
standing Depression-era concerns within Yeshiva over its religious
image. For all his pedagogic efforts and the quality of the many Orthodox laymen and future rabbis he produced, Churgin and his school
were always suspect. Certain quarters within Yeshiva would not believe that the TI was anything more than "at heart a school for minimally observant *maskilim*." Although alumni leaders would never
suggest that the TI not have a role in Revel's overall construct—they
would never articulate strident Torah Vodaath canards against their
alma mater—they feared that if not monitored closely the more sec-
ular-leaning TI might come to rule Yeshiva now in flux. It seemed to
them that Belkin would be unable to effectively keep Yeshiva's priorities straight.

To Joseph Lookstein alumni leaders projected a very different anxiety; the fear of outside influence. They respected Lookstein's
rabbinic and family pedigree. He was arguably the most articulate of
RIETS' post-1915 group of rabbis. He was leader of Ramaz' congregation which had the longest legacy of support for Yeshiva. And he
was an outspoken proponent of the RCA and had led the battle in
1941 to keep the Agudat ha-Rabbanim from taking over the school.
(The return of Sam Levy to board leadership was just one of his moves.)
It was acknowledged that he had wide connections with the larger
Jewish community and with American Jewry's greatest philanthropists, and was skilled in bringing those with resources to support Yeshiva.

But it was precisely his connections with outside forces that
troubled his fellow alumni. Kaminetsky, the young Feuerstein, and
others were unconvinced that the money-people Lookstein might approach to shore up Yeshiva would have the best interests of Orthodoxy at heart. They were not certain that Lookstein would have the
utmost concern in bringing them into line. Their worst possible sce-

nario was that this new wave of benefactors might push Yeshiva toward altering its stand on graduate rabbis tarrying in mixed seating congregations. (The protocol at the time was that a new ordainee could accept a liberal-practicing congregation on a trial basis if it seemed willing to fall into line or had the potential for doing so.) Alumni may have known that Revel—clearly his own man—had long struggled with the mixed blessing of money from outside his camp. They were afraid that a young, weak successor would not come up with the right answers and, under Lookstein's influential hand, might be led to accommodate new lay powers at the expense of Yeshiva.[38]

In the end, Belkin was elected on the first ballot and no other names were officially entered in nomination. The idea in some quarters that since no one man could replace Revel a presidium consisting of both a general and a religious scholar should be elected was never formally entertained. The test vote over whether the selection of president should be done by secret ballot was close but resulted favorably for the Levy forces. Fifteen members voted for an open ballot, against eight—six from the Jewish Center, including Rabbi Jung—who voted for a secret ballot. With that issue resolved, an unsurprising 15-10 vote favored the Levy group in opposing the postponement motion. The final vote was a formality. Jewish Center men, Feurstein and others, joined with their fellows in unanimously electing Dr. Samuel Belkin as Yeshiva's second president. Only time would tell whose dreams, visions, or apprehensions would be fulfilled or confirmed by the youthful university executive.[39]

Chapter 8

Samuel Belkin and the Mission of an American Jewish University

Broadening their constituency beyond those already on board was a commitment first harbored at Yeshiva in the minds of Etz Chaim people. But those strictly Orthodox Jews made absolutely no progress in making it a reality. They could do nothing to effectively lead the masses away from the road toward assimilation because the solution they offered to the pressures of Americanization was unacceptable to almost all Jewish immigrants. They had to be content to do their best to keep their own kind in the fold: a challenge to which they responded, but with a limited degree of success (see chapter 2).

Bernard Revel committed his life to expanding Orthodoxy's battle against assimilation. But he did not succeed in making the Yeshiva a prime factor in wider American Jewish life. He did lay down a coherent ideology for an American Orthodox response to American society. And he raised a generation of rabbis charged with spreading his messages to the unaffiliated, the disaffected, or, more often, to the wavering, in the United States and Canada. Practically, Revel did whatever he could to help his men in the field and the synagogues aligned with them. In 1935, for example, a Yeshiva Synagogue Council was established at Washington Heights which provided both leadership and educational materials to fledgling, troubled congregations all over America. And there was intermittent talk from the RIETS Alumni Association and other quarters of adult education programs and lecture series that would bring the wisdom of the Heights to the hinterlands. However Revel's attempts to reach beyond Amsterdam Avenue were marked more frequently by failure than by success.[1]

An indication of the shortness of Yeshiva's reach during the Depression was that the school's most exciting outreach was an extension school created in conjunction with Young Israel. This alliance brought Jewish studies courses to teenagers and adults, but the school operated only in the New York area and lasted but a few years. In the meantime, rabbis from Danville, Virginia, to St. Louis, Missouri, to Los Angeles, California, cried aloud about the decline in their areas of Judaism in general and Orthodoxy in particular. They complained that all they ever got from New York Orthodoxy was frequent calls for financial assistance for metropolitan-area based institutions.[2]

We know that the old demon, lack of money, scuttled even the best intentions of Revel and his cohorts. As we review Revel's administration, it is clear that Yeshiva circles had barely enough money to educate and motivate those already strongly committed to American Orthodoxy. Yeshiva College, Revel's crowning achievement, was perforce for "the select few," and the school had a difficult time keeping body and soul together to support them. Missions to the unattached would have to wait for another day, but the mandate was not forgotten. Indeed, the Committee of Seven that nominated Dr. Belkin was keenly aware of that need as it outlined basic priorities for Revel's successor (see chapter 7).

Some favorable demographics during Revel's days partially assuaged Yeshiva's guilt over its community-wide ineffectiveness. Assimilation was still mitigated in the interwar era by the continued geographical propinquity of Jews in so-called Jewish neighborhoods. What was said about the disaffecting Jew on New York's Delancey Street in 1900 could still be said in 1920 about his son or daughter on that city's Grand Concourse or in similar neighborhoods in other major cities. In each instance, the Jew could publicly renounce his Jewish identity, but he would have to associate with his own kind on his predominantly Jewish block. For those who lived away from the large Jewish concentrations and wanted to stay that way, there too assimilation was stymied by social anti-Semitism.[3]

After the war, those who were increasingly concerned could no longer count upon neighborhoods or anti-Semitism to help maintain group allegiance on the largest scale. Jews were caught up in the march toward the "crabgrass frontier," as suburbanization became a critical part of the postwar American social and cultural scene. In these new settlements the lines of ethnic demarcation and long-standing tensions were blurred or overlooked, as everyone, Jew and Gentile alike, made an effort to "get along." Although most Jews remained somewhat loyal to their intangible "special relationship" with other Jews, assimilation accelerated as Jews got to know Gentiles across picket fences, on library committees, school boards, and the like.[4]

The Jews' fitting in was facilitated further by the perceptible drop in anti-Semitism in those heady days. "Chaim and Irving came marching home" and found the prejudice against Jews had lost its social status as it came to be associated in the popular mind with the enemy the United States fought and defeated in World War II. Social anti-Semitism in hotels and resorts took a particularly precipitous nose dive. The "business" of exclusion became unprofitable as all competed for America's entertainment dollar. Colleges and universities were somewhat slower in changing their attitudes. But government pressure, through the "G.I. Bill," which opened doors for the veteran, led to progress in this area. A more egalitarian America no longer directed the Jew to stay with his own kind.[5]

Yeshiva's keen renewed interest in the battle against assimilation was intensified further by the reality that other Jewish groups were caught up in the struggle to save those who were drifting and the Conservatives especially were doing a better job.

By 1945 almost a half century had elapsed since American Orthodoxy and those later called Conservatives first offered themselves and their programs to second-generation Jews as alternative answers to the dilemmas of assimilation. In the early decades (until 1920), Orthodoxy was particularly effective. Its popularity certainly had something to do with the geographical and social closeness of its clients to their European Orthodox parents. During the interwar days, Orthodoxy still held its own, even as the second generation matured and moved away from immigrant quarters. But in postwar suburban days, when the break with the European past was complete, Conservatism emerged as the way of the future for those native-born Jews who wanted to be American, to have a sense of tradition, and to be comfortable with both.[6]

Standing not far behind the Conservatives, both in numbers and orientation, was a changing, growing Neo-Reform element. They too took their places in suburbia and offered their line of Judaism, far more traditional than Classical Reform and still attuned to the American world around them, as an institutional focus for Jewish life. Given these competitors, Orthodoxy could concern itself only with the already committed, leaving the vast majority of Jews either to assimilation or to other forms of Jewish religious identification. Or they could compete: address the disaffected and debate their more liberal counterparts. Under Samuel Belkin, the decision was made to reach

beyond Washington Heights and attempt to make American Orthodoxy the prime beacon against assimilation Bernard Revel thought it
should be.[7]

Information bulletins describing new approaches to synagogue programming "mailed regularly to individuals in small Jewish
communities . . . that are not able to retain a rabbi" and "share-the-
rabbi" circuits, permitting "several small communities in the same
area . . . to engage one rabbi to serve them all," were just two of
the early initiatives developed by the Yeshiva's Community Service
Bureau created in December 1944. Bureau Director Rabbi Morris Finer
knew well many of the problems of the isolated community. Before
being recalled to New York by his close friend Belkin, Finer had
served in pulpits in Haverstraw, New York, and Tulsa. Just a few
years later he was joined in the Bureau by a colleague who knew
frontier Jewish life even better. Rabbi Irwin Gordon, formerly Hillel
(Jewish College Students Association) Director at a university in Sas-
katchewan, was brought in to head the Bureau's Program Office.[8]

As the Bureau grew, Finer more often came to address concerns closer to home. He was particularly interested that those urban
and early suburban congregations, then served by an Orthodox rabbi,
European-trained or a RIETS man, maintain that religious outlook and
not look for a Seminary man when the senior rabbi died, retired, or
moved on. Toward that end, Finer made every effort to reform Yeshiva's placement policies. Meanwhile, Gordon, for his part, endeavored to steer Jews away from disaffection and their congregations
from the Seminary by providing his Orthodox men with in-service
field training and their synagogues with social programs and educational services. Finer and Gordon understood that the long-standing
list of what Yeshiva rabbis had to know to succeed with American
communities, first articulated by Revel himself, had to be broadened
significantly. They argued that for an American Orthodox rabbi to be
effective and competitive, away from his academy, his study, and his
East Coast home, he had to be more than a Talmudic scholar, an
effective sermonizer, and a synthesizer of cultures. He also had to be
a model pastor to a new generation, a trained social group worker,
and a professional administrator. That meant that if those skills were
not learned at Yeshiva itself, they would have to be learned on the
job. They recognized that it was often the most basic ancillary abili-

ties that mattered most in the pulpit. Teaching rabbis how to edit their synagogues' bulletins was just one of the mundane but essential services provided by the Bureau.

By the mid-1950s, however, it became clear that the greatest struggles and competition would be fought on another front, in America's new communities. Battle lines would ultimately be drawn most closely in those emerging suburban synagogues that had yet to decide whether to identify with Orthodoxy or with the Conservative movement. The story was repeated in literally hundreds of congregations coast to coast. Jews asked both Yeshiva and Seminary men— sometimes in great formal debates in the same room and on the same night—to explain why and how their movement could best help them live as Jews and see their children grow up Jewishly and still fit in with their new affluent and accepting surroundings. At these battle royals in living rooms, rec rooms, and basements each side explicated its perceptions of Jewish culture and society and the demands and flexibilities of Jewish tradition.[9]

The highly successful Conservatives offered potential congregants a myriad of social and educational services and institutions. Men's clubs and women's leagues for the adults, recreational and youth groups for the youngsters, and large-scale Talmud Torah programs for boys and girls alike provided second- and third-generation Jews with positive links to each other and to their faith. And if and when they came to pray, they could do so in an architecturally pleasing synagogue center and participate in a service that remained all of the "best" of the ancestral tradition. Moreover, this American Jewish religious movement uniquely suited to the suburban life-style took a major step forward in the 1950s when it officially countenanced driving an automobile to services on the Sabbath. And if many Jews failed to comprehend the subtle caveats to this rabbinic legislation, that failure had no negative effect on the movement's popularity. Finally, Conservative spokesmen were effective in projecting their Orthodox opponents as out of touch socially as well as theologically. They evoked images of "the smell of herring and the sight of spitoons," to remind all of the "worst" of the old customs.[10]

The Community Service Bureau—reclassified as a Division in 1954—spoke up for Orthodoxy in these public forums. Their representatives, "All-American boys" all, wore ties and jackets and used the same sociological terminology as the Conservatives in advocating their cause. They noted the comparable cluster of age-group activities available to congregations affiliating with their movement. Probably these Division people were most proud of their Youth Service wing. They promised to send staff people into member synagogues to run Sabbath programs and to organize retreats. Beginning in 1955 they offered the Torah Leadership Seminar which brought the best and most motivated congregational youngsters first to Yeshiva in New York, then to resort localities for intensive one- and two-week experiential programs. Yeshiva's public line of argumentation was that their educational and less than dogmatic Orthodox activities paralleled what the Conservative United Synagogue Youth and Training Leadership Fellowship groups were then doing. Youth work, they averred, was also part and parcel of their movement.

Significantly, although youth work was a major part of the Division's affiliation pitch, these activities were offered also to those synagogues which ultimately voted against aligning with Orthodoxy. United Synagogue congregations led by RIETS or YC graduates and mixed seating synagogues with no national affiliation whatsoever often welcomed the Yeshiva operatives' educational programs. The Washington Heights crew, for its part, relished the second chance "to turn a congregation around." Not unlike the Endeavorers fifty years earlier and the first Young Israelites a generation before them, Division people felt that if a small number of youngsters from the "marginal congregations" could be moved toward Orthodoxy, they could have a dramatic impact on their home institutions.[11]

But the promise of youth work even at its best and even better than that offered by the Seminary could not easily offset the great psychological edge that Conservatism's approbation of the practice of Jews driving to Temple on the Sabbath provided that movement. Congregants no longer needed to feel guilty on the road to services as the Conservative rendering of Jewish law legitimized what most laymen were doing. Orthodoxy, on the other hand, could not officially sanction something which it saw as a clear deviation from Jewish tradition. What Division people could and did say was that how one got to synagogue was the individual's business. As one articulate spokesmen put it: "Jewish tradition does not gain strength from what you do and does not lose its validity from what you do not do." Defining their potential suburban followers as either "Orthodox or confused Jews," they let it be known that all would be welcomed in the synagogue and no questions would be asked as to how they arrived there. However, when they got to the synagogue, it was essential that they follow the most traditional paths.

Conservative synagogues, they counterattacked, with their family pews, late Friday night services, and instrumental music on the Sabbath, only reflected "the strengths and weaknesses of it founders, a mirror of people who built them." The desire to sit with their families grew out of the American ideal that "the family that prays together, stays together." Suburban highway billboards preached this message. The 8 p.m. Friday night service corresponded to present-day work schedules and ethics. And their form of service looked like that of all other American religious groups. The Orthodox synagogue, on the other hand, "stood for something bigger." It was not a mirror of its members but "a model, an ideal toward which all could strive." Although it was agreed that not all its practices fit totally with American mores, its deviation from some conventional norms was seen as giving it its strength. As that same Orthodox spokesman put it: "The synagogue represents Torah. Whatever you do is unimportant, but the shul should stand for Torah."[12]

Through these subtle but dramatic statements, a major ideological shift in American Orthodoxy was articulated. The quintessence of the early postwar movement would no longer lie in its overriding concern with the individual's performance of the mitzvoth—though Orthodoxy prayed that more would do more. Rather, its interest would be that, when Jews chose to pray and participate in the public arena of congregational life, they do so in the most appropriate traditional manner.

To be sure, most suburban congregational groups were ultimately unmoved by this new approach. The 1950s turned out to be Conservatism's halcyon days. Still the Division was proud of the some one hundred or more congregations that it brought under its wing nationwide. Looking back on that era, Division people have spoken with pride of their success in Riverdale, Bronx, New York, which was destined in the next generation to become a hotbed of new metropolitan area Orthodoxy. One former debator for Orthodoxy could talk of the time they won in Glenwood, Queens, where after competition with the Conservatives, the vote was left exclusively to the women of the congregation and they voted for Orthodoxy. Of course, sometimes it was the eloquence of the presentation that won the day.

Other times it was good old-fashioned practical politics that produced results. Once, in Flatbush Park, Brooklyn, those in favor of separate seating within the sanctuary organized a neighborhood-wide babysitting service for those families ready to vote with Orthodoxy.[13]

Whatever the success-failure ratio in these debates, the implications of Belkin's people's efforts were not lost on Yeshiva's home constituency. As with so many prior initiatives, departures, and shifts, the many who applauded these activities were counterbalanced by those who harbored serious misgivings over what Orthodox outreach work to a wider community and its subtle redefinitions of Orthodoxy would mean to a Torah institution.

One early critic from within the RIETS student body, preparing himself to enter the field, spoke for his group when he submitted that the best way Yeshiva could counteract the problems of disaffection from Orthodoxy was to intensify the core Talmudic learning component in the rabbinical curriculum. In his opinion, there was certainly no denying the explosive problem of postwar assimilation. In a poignant observation, written at the very end of the Holocaust period, he noted that:

> Hitler has . . . greatly hastened the coming of age of American Jewry. Until our day . . . American Jewish communal life has been given shape by the explosive pressure of immigrant European Jews, (Accordingly), if one Jew was lost to the synagogue, through assimilation and lack of interest, then Jews in Warsaw were training to take his place. Today there are no more Jews in Warsaw. The American Jewish community is on its own.

But the "adjustment of the Yeshiva" was not the answer to America's religious dilemmas. Harkening back to arguments more representative of Revel's early era than his own, he argued that the "Yeshiva in America has gradually taken on a duality of function, trying at one and the same time to be a professional training school and a school of pure study," a mixture that cannot survive. For him there was but "one road open in this dilemma . . . become once again a true Yeshiva." As far as meeting the calls of the unaffiliated was concerned, Belkin's critic argued: "we must be veritable missionaries among our own people and bring Jewish youths to Judaism in large numbers if we expect Judaism to live. This can never be done if the Yeshiva will become a professional training school."[14]

Dr. Belkin, for his part, was little concerned with debating whether these new measures and attitudes were appropriate for a yeshiva. He was more engaged in projecting these anti-assimilation activities as consistent with the mission of an American university, his own Yeshiva University, chartered in 1945. In announcing, in May 1945, his plans to establish graduate schools of community administration and social research, Jewish education, adult education, and a summer graduate school for higher Jewish education and community leadership—the original components of his university structure—Belkin allowed that his school's agenda was expanding "to serve the communal, educational and religious needs of American Jewry." Practically speaking, it was envisioned that the educational administrators and social workers produced by SECA (School of Education and Community Administration, founded 1948) would find their ways into secular and non-Orthodox Jewish institutions like Jewish community centers and YMHA's where suburban Jewish youngsters often congregated. There, it was assumed that these workers would use their combination of professional training and "deep appreciation of spiritual values" learned at Yeshiva to promote positive Jewish identity among their clients. An unspoken but implicit additional agenda was that these social workers would promote, with the lightest touch, interest in Orthodoxy.[15]

As with the Community Service Division's activities, competition with the liberal Jewish denominations was a spur to these efforts. In the late 1940s, the JTS had supplementary training programs for "rabbis, educators and executive directors of synagogue centers." HUC for its part had a non-degree bearing program for communal workers and educators. Belkin hoped the aura of university status would induce some of his own TI men to go into Jewish communal life. He figured that others already in the field—Orthodox or not—might look at his university-affiliated structures and see value in his degrees for their professional development. In any event, the key was getting his men, and now for the first time women, out there in the fields and into the lives of the next generation of Jewish children.[16]

Dr. Belkin was, once again, occupying the highest ground in Jewish communal life. He was accentuating and expanding upon the long held American Orthodox teaching that called upon those who were comfortably observant and secure in their integration within American culture to assist the disaffected, the assimilated, feel tied once more to their faith and community. But was Yeshiva's overwhelming concern, however lofty, with the problems of survival of their particular religious or ethnic group, appropriate for an American university? It was, Yeshiva people, would argue, if the creation of a better America was a major pursuit of the country's centers of higher education. Drawing from the source utilized by his predecessor during the great debate over Yeshiva sponsoring a college and tapping into Revel's own rhetoric, Belkin argued that the philosophy of cultural pluralism mandated that such steps be taken. Service to the Jewish community, he argued, would assist his clients in "the creation of a harmonious blending between the cultural heritage of our American democracy and the ancient spiritual traditions of Israel," making them better Jews and better Americans. Borrowing lines from his own mentors—Revel and Kallen—he averred that his school and its students would make their "unique contribution to the cultural pluralities of the great democractic way of life."[17]

A decade later Belkin took his argument one step further and suggested that what Yeshiva was doing for its own ethnic group was not only legitimate and justifiable, but should in certain educational contexts, be a model for all other schools and the groups they serve to emulate in making a better America. The founding in 1957 of a separate social work school under Yeshiva's auspices (named Wurzweiler School of Social Work in 1962) provided the opportunity for Belkin to essay just that. Ethnicity must be addressed head on by all who work in American communities.

The Wurzweiler approach constituted the first conscious infusion of the teachings and values of cultural pluralism into American social work training and practice. For several generations social workers had labored among the immigrant, the poor, and the ethnic groups, often selflessly, helping them meet their needs, but always projecting their solutions from the preconceived notion of the American melting pot. Solving the problems of families and youngsters was to be done the way Americans did it. Now the goal was—as an era of renewed ethnicity was about to begin—that all social work must consider the ethnicity of its clients. A redefinition of what constituted appropriate American social norms was argued. Yeshiva's model, which would be emulated by others, suggested that "social work as a profession could never overlook the cultural heritage and influence" of those it would serve.[18]

This approach to social work at Yeshiva grew out of Belkin's reorganization of SECA in the mid-1950s. After close to a decade of activity all could see that the school had contributed as much as it possibly could to its community. There were some people with Yeshiva ties in Jewish communal and institutional life. Rabbis were being given advanced ancillary training of all kinds through summer programs. But the school seemed to attract only those already in Jewish lines of work and enrollment figures were not increasing. Two interlocking factors contributed to SECA's inability to recruit widely. Its curriculum did not qualify graduates for degrees in social work (M.S.W.) accredited with the Council on Social Work Education. The university's M.R.E. was no attraction for those looking beyond the parochial precincts of specific Jewish institutional services. The transparent parochial nature of the school's environment also dissuaded potential students. Of course, the latter factor, when coupled with the absence of a permanent full-time faculty for the school, made gaining the prestigious accreditation impossible.

Significantly, nonexistent or insufficient professional accreditation along with the old standby, lack of funds had destroyed all prior efforts over two generations to teach social work under Jewish auspices. Of course, Cincinnati's School of Jewish Social Service (1913), the Kehillah's School of Jewish Communal Work (1913–World War II), the National Conference of Jewish Charities' Graduate School for Jewish Social Work (1925–1940), and the most recent, Training Bureau for Jewish Communal Service, backed by five international Jewish boards, all were doomed almost from the start because they were not university affiliated. Jews who wanted social work training and degrees during these two generations went to New York University, Columbia, and elsewhere for their education. Maybe, when in the field, they would stop for Jewish training in these non-degree bearing institutions, assuming, of course, that these schools were in business when they felt the need. SECA, on the other hand, did not attract "true" social work students because, though a university school in the eyes of the New York Board of Regents, it was not run appropriately enough for the Council on Social Work Education.[19]

Belkin addressed the deficiencies in his program by splitting his graduate school into two. Jewish education and administration, along with educational psychology—the more parochial elements of the school—would eventually bear the name Ferkauf Graduate School of Humanities and Social Science (named in 1965). The Social Work School was clearly nonsectarian, proudly nonparochial but intensely ethnic in its disposition. Possessed of a rationalized and appropriate curriculum, it was hoped it would attract Jewish and Gentile students alike.[20]

Wurzweiler fearlessly walked its own thinly stretched tight-rope between being like all other schools and limiting its Jewish mission and still being intensely Jewish, thus threatening its popularity and legitimacy. The school aggressively addressed this dilemma by making sure that the core of its curriculum was identical in scope and, it was hoped, in quality to what was available at New York University and Columbia. At the same time, it unabashedly introduced courses in "Jewish Social Philosophy" and "The American Jew and His Society," courses previously unseen in American university schools of social work. Wurzweiler's other significant deviation from the norm was its attention, in its early years, exclusively to social group work. As a Jewish institution, dedicated to dealing with its own group's social problems, group work sequences seemed more appropriate than the casework models most popular at other institutions. Interestingly enough, in its formative years, though Wurzweiler was one of America's smallest social work schools, it graduated one of the largest classes of group workers.[21]

School officials did not see Wurzweiler's intentions as parochial in the slightest. Though offered under the auspices of an Orthodox university, these "Jewish" courses were not designed or taught to make Jewish students better Jews (read Orthodox). Nor were these courses designed to proselytize Gentile students in the minority group's faith. These courses would be taught over the years by Orthodox, non-Orthodox, and even Gentile instructors, a practice which did not always sit well with some Orthodox students at Wurzweiler who saw these courses as "improvement as Jews" courses for others, but unnecessary for them.

At their most basic level, the objectives of the courses were to acquaint Jews and Gentiles planning to work with Jews and their institutions with the history, philosophy, present-day structure, and problems of that community. Implicit in this plan was the importance for Gentiles to know the basics about Jews and Judaism as a valuable aid to Jewish clients. There were more important and far-reaching reasons, however, for these courses.

Wurzweiler officials believed that obliging students, Jews and Gentiles alike, to confront their own ethnic identities and attitudes was essential preparation for social work careers of all kinds. Every social work school subscribed to the teaching that "any unresolved internal conflict on the student's part is bound to manifest itself and to intrude on his ability to render social work services." How well the future practitioner knew himself or herself was thus deemed a pivotal determinant of success in the field. Wurzweiler's point was that psychological and social self-awareness included one's under-standing his degrees of affinity for or alienation from ethnic pasts and identities. The ability to look inside one's ethnic self was as important for case workers dealing with individual or family emotional prob-lems as for the group worker concerned with developing Jewish com-munal activities. The ability "to tune in to the ethnic and cultural component of the client's background," it was strongly felt, changes "the student's perception of the client. He/she is educated to view the client not only from a systems perspective but from a perspective of his/her group's history values and beliefs." [22]

The social worker was educated by first seeing how Jews think and dream and how they organize and fought among them-selves and against outside threats in surviving as a community. Every effort was made to illuminate the idiosyncratic elements of the Jewish experience as well as what Jews have in common with other people. Gentile students were charged with drawing their own parallels to those of the "quintessential American ethnic group," even as all groups explored the history of Jewish-Gentile relations in this country.

But the spice of these courses was not cognitive but exper-iential. Students were constantly encouraged to publicly challenge the bases and implications of their colleague's ethnic beliefs and practices. Classroom encounters were often heated. One long-time instructor of these courses, proud of the process and the outcome, has written that

> the heterogeneity in the class composition forces the Jewish stu-dents from all walks of life to encounter differing ideologies. Many orthodox and non-orthodox students learn about each other's points

of view for the first time in the class and they invariably develop a
healthy respect for each other.[23]

A somewhat different agenda developed for Gentile students. Finding themselves for maybe the first time a minority within
another's large community—respected if sometimes kept apart from
Jewish interdenominational bloodletting—they learned firsthand what
life is like for a minority group in a free and generally accepting
society. They too, it was hoped, would take this valuable experience
into the field. Of course, the few black students who attended Wurzweiler did not have to learn that minority group lesson. But they too
had to deal with their own and with others' thoughts, beliefs, and
stereotypes.[24]

Dr. Belkin's threefold objective in university-building—service to the Jewish people, arguing the appropriateness of such concerns within the framework of an American university, and projecting
what he was doing at Yeshiva as a model for other universities to
follow consistent with the philosophy of cultural pluralism—was also
evident in the Jewish school's campaign to build a medical college.
The needs of the Jewish people here were not so much social as
political and occupational. As the postwar period opened, Jewish students still faced discriminatory admissions policies at this country's
medical schools. These quotas stymied and frustrated the youngsters
who applied. The persistence of prejudicial traditions served as an
unhappy reminder to all Jews of their minority status still in America.
The establishment of a medical school by Yeshiva would address one
of the residual problems imposed by the outside world, even as the
university looked sharply at the dilemmas wrought by the acceptance
of Jews in many other realms.

In this case, the appropriateness of Yeshiva acting for its
own was defended as part of the contribution made by Jews to the
broader American community. It was said that the bright and motivated Jewish physicians who would be produced would treat the ill
and find remedies for diseases that afflicted all. The model established here for other schools to emulate was that of a private medical
school, under denominational auspices, which would be totally nonsectarian and color-blind in its admissions policies. The best and most
committed of all groups would be allowed to take their places. In
fact, it would be argued, that out of this positive mixing of Jewish and

Gentile students would come not only a healthier America but a more egalitarian one as well.

Like so many of the causes Belkin successfully pursued, the idea of a medical college and the social rationale for its existence did not originate in his office. As early as 1930, at the very time that his predecessor, Dr. Revel, was fashioning a Jewish college, voices were already heard in the Jewish community calling upon Yeshiva to become a university, specifically to build a medical school. *"Numerus clausus* . . . difficulties for Jewish scholars to gain professorships," one editorial writer argued, "all have nurtured a readiness to welcome a Jewish university in America." The Jewish community was distressed, he reported, that most Jewish men who want medical training have to travel to Europe for their instruction. And the few who gain admission here "rarely come into contact with things Jewish." Clearly no allowances were made for Sabbath and holidays for Jewish physicians-in-training at schools that would gladly have done without any Semitic students.

Interestingly, the later, oft-expressed apologia that American health needs required that its medical schools open their gates for all who could qualify was also articulated early on. "The health of people," it was said, "dare not be sacrificed to prejudice or favoritism— the best student must be given due preference in preparation for medical career." In fact, the message that a nonsectarian Jewish medical school would ultimately send to this country's academy was outlined at the very beginning. It was stated in 1930 that "a Jewish medical college must be free from the narrowness and pettiness of those who come to the altar of learning with a pagan's hate. The Jew must ever be the beacon of civilization. He has played one of the greatest roles in the realm of medical history. He has still greater contributions to make to this vital field of human welfare." The success of this envisioned medical school would be judged by criteria beyond those apparent in the laboratory.

The only reservation these editorialists had about their projected initiative was whether American Jewry had sufficient funds to get a school like that started and still have resources to promote Jewish parochial institutions. As it turned out, Yeshiva's supporters at that moment had funds for neither. The idea of a "Jewish Medical College in America" was put off for another day.[25]

In the meantime, while Jews waited and struggled economically, Depression-era anti-Semitism continued and intensified further medical school discrimination. It was reported, for example, that the national medical school graduating class of 1940 (those who entered in 1936) had 477 Jewish students, a drop of some 48 percent over three years. These statistics were just the grossest reflection of a twenty-five-year trend which saw, between 1920 and 1945, the number of Jewish students at American medical schools decline by over 50 percent. Another glaring statistic was that three out of every four non-Jewish applying for physician training were accepted. Only one out of thirteen Jewish students found their way in.[26]

Most New York Jewish youngsters could hold out little hope of gaining medical school admission. If they went to CCNY in the 1930s—remember that Columbia College was itself well-nigh off-limits to them during that era—they would be attending the "Jewish" school that placed fewer than two out of every ten of its medical college aspirants in American schools. A generation earlier academic horizons had been much brighter. Then, six out of ten CCNY people with that desire made it to medical training. Students at Brooklyn and Queens Colleges faced similar discouraging realities.

Jewish students from religious homes faced obvious additional problems. How did one maintain one's traditions and observances in that time-demanding, unsympathetic world. Students from Yeshiva College confronted one additional, curricular problem. As structured, their college did not offer the requisite range of laboratory science courses to qualify for medical school admission. Summer school courses elsewhere would be an additional burden. All things considered, it is not surprising that at no time, from the start of the college to the end of World War II, did more that 7.5 percent of the students entering Yeshiva College consider what is now called "health science" as a career goal. These numbers included those realists who set their sights on dentistry and chiropractics. They could look ahead to schools that admitted more Jews with less hesitation.

The long-standing whispered, sometimes clearly articulated, reason for anti-Jewish policies was the opinion that while it was true that Jews had the brains to be scientists, they lacked the "character, personality traits, emotional balance and integrity to be effective physicians." This attack upon the very humanity of the Jews was wedded in the 1930s to economic considerations that further undermined Jewish enrollment. The Depression hurt the medical profession, as it did all other trades and occupations. Patients failed to pay their bills or simply went without medical attention. It was reported that doctors on average no longer earned their comfortable pre-Depression annual income of $11,000. Fearing that new doctors would cut into their dwindling income pool, the medical guild called for "drastic curtailing" of medical school programs. The number of places available at established medical schools were to be reduced and unnecessary schools closed entirely. The Council on Medical Education of the American Medical Association urged that the turning out of "4,800 doctors per year was too many for a national population of 125 million."[27]

The elite medical schools answered this plaintive call by cutting enrollment 5 percent. Meanwhile the medical establishment challenged the accreditation of those schools not in the "top 87." And although the A.M.A. never pointed to Jews as the ones to lose out when the best schools cut back, statistics show that they were among the first to be asked to abandon their quest for a place.

Ultimately it was more than just the Jewish student who suffered. The American people lost out on health care as bright minds looked elsewhere. In fact, it was estimated that by the close of World War II there was a shortage of some 35,000 physicians in this country, an approximate shortage of 19,000 after the complete demobilization of the armed forces. The President's Committee on Health Needs of the Nation projected a shortage of some 30,000 physicians in the United States by 1960.[28]

The medical establishment was unmoved by these dire statistics and predictions. They responded to charges that they were behaving more like members of a restrictive medieval guild than as affiliates of a modern health care society by asserting that their policies towards physician training in the 1930s had had precisely the opposite effect on national health. The raising of standards for admission and accreditation and the closing of some small, marginal schools, they argued, had eliminated medicine's future "quacks." All now could be reassured that those claiming an M.D. degree but "without a high school diploma" from "medical schools unworthy of the name" would no longer plague this land.[29]

But what about the charge that even if the medical community was truly more concerned with quality over quantity, it still excluded qualified Jewish students? To such charges at public hearings, the same tried and tired answers were offered. When not denying outright that discrimination took place—the burning by one dean of all prewar records helped mightily in this regard—they averred as always that "emotional stability and other things" were given strong consideration in admissions procedures. Those with the wrong religion, ethnicity, or even just a foreign sounding "mother's maiden name" were found to be less qualified.[30]

In addition, they found that what they had to say still found a receptive audience in significant segments of the population. When the *American Mercury* ran an investigatory piece blistering the A.M.A., a reader, himself a physician and typical of many, echoed long-standing sentiments when he described Jews as "excellent researchers and investigators but I doubt if by temperament they are really to be trusted with the responsibility of healing the sick minds and bodies of our society." This writer also had advice for those Jews who might protest his opinion or establishment policies: "Let them establish some Jewish universities of their own if they feel they are not getting a square deal in education. The democracy of America is based on the thesis that minorities might find it a haven, not a heaven."[31] For Jewish premedical students, stonewalling by postwar medical schools and the popular support it still evoked, chilled their dreams more than before. With the demise of the small schools and with European institutions in disarray the possibilities for admission seemed now even more remote unless something changed.

Jews of this period would, however, soon acknowledge the assistance of an invaluable new ally, the American government. Moved by real concern over an incipient health crisis, motivated by widespread—but clearly not universal—public revulsion against anti-Semitism in the first post-Holocaust years, and interested simply in helping out the former G.I. son of an immigrant, officials sought initially to verify the charges against the doctors and then to undercut their prejudice. In 1946, for example, the Council of the City of New York established a committee "to investigate the causes underlying the difficulties of graduates of city-maintained secondary schools and colleges in obtaining graduate and professional education." The deans of Columbia's College of Physicians and Surgeons and of Cornell Medical School were questioned and the committee's findings were widely publicized. To be sure, it would be a while before these elite schools moved away from their established practices, but the government's watchdog would be, from that point on, nipping at their heels. More importantly, there was a commitment within government to solve the medical crisis and end discrimination from without the existing old-line colleges. It was in this changing, more favorable sociopolitical climate that the movement was launched to build the school, later to be called the Albert Einstein College of Medicine of Yeshiva University (AECOM).[32]

Yeshiva's first goal in founding its own medical school was to serve qualified Jewish premedical students—and, for that matter, prospective Jewish medical school professors—suffering occupationally and spiritually from the persistence of discrimination. These building efforts, it was said, would bring meaning to the professional aspirations of many Jews. As important, from an Orthodox Jewish perspective, it would permit budding physicians to retain their religious commitments as they acquired their scientific skills. Dr. Elihu Katz believed that the "spiritual gain" from such a school for American Jewry would be almost incalculable. This president of the Society for the Establishment of a Medical School at Yeshiva University, a group born in 1947 to upgrade health science courses at YC—a first step towards the creation of a medical program—envisioned Jewish students afforded the opportunity to live in a Jewish environment during the years of their professional study. They would be able to carry on with their own religious principles and practices. They would not have to dwell in a new environment and live under conditions strange to them.[33]

But even as AECOM people expressed concern for the Jewish student, they were certain to emphasize that this school under Jewish auspices would not be solely or even predominantly for Jews. They would stand at the opposite pole from those "church or private groups (who built) medical colleges and then refused to turn them over to the education of non-contributors." The Yeshiva medical school application would require neither a photograph nor a statement of religious affiliation. The admissions committee would not inquire about national origins and would care little about maintaining a balanced geographical distribution in its classes. If its defiantly heterogeneous student body would soon make its mark in their profession, the contributions of AECOM graduates would end forever the tendentious allegations that Jewish doctors were not cut out to serve others. It would stop for all time the invidious carnard that Gentile minds and bodies cannot flourish through contact in the classroom, laboratory, or at the bedside with Jews. AECOM was thus presented as part of the solution to America's health care problems and as a certain aid to this country's spiritual and body politic. It would stand as a model of fairness, evidence to all that diversity was the spice of America's life.[34]

A successful AECOM would also do much, it was argued, to speed Jewish integration generally in America. Jews, proponents believed, would be shown to be not only "grateful guests in this country, but graceful hosts as well." This apologetic motif ran largely as follows: The non-Jews helped by AECOM practitioners would be grateful to those who trained that skilled physician. The Gentile graduates of AECOM would likewise feel a tremendous allegiance to their Jewish alma mater. After all, it was clearly understood that medical school tuition covered only one-quarter of the amount needed to produce a physician. Gentile "guests" served by Yeshiva would bring positive views of Jews and their institutions back to their own communities. There they would also speak of their experience of "getting along well" with Jewish colleagues and professors. Each of these encounters would "go a long way toward destroying racial and religious bigotry" in this country.[35]

This mixed message, service to their own youngsters and projecting a positive Jewish image to the outside world, proved immensely helpful in raising Jewish and Gentile moneys for this branch of the university. The depiction of Jews "as hosts and not as guests" was the leitmotif of AECOM's inaugural million-dollar campaign. Yeshiva's highly democratic approach also brought out the best in New York government officials, anxious to head off their own medical crisis. In 1950, not long after Yeshiva received its State Medical School charter, Mayor Vincent Impelliteri offered to establish "a professional training relationship" with Yeshiva through its Bronx Municipal Hospital Center in the East Bronx. With this pivotal educational-political relationship in place, it was just a matter of time and money before New York's first postwar medical school and American Jewry's first medical college opened its doors. September 1955 marked the official founding of AECOM on its campus in the Morris Park section of the Bronx.[36]

It would take a while for the AECOM approach to have a discernible impact on American medical education. And it is arguable how much good will AECOM guests spread about Jews and Judaism around the country. What is easily discernible is that the rise of AECOM had an immediate and dramatic effect upon its targeted constituency, American Jewish youngsters, most decidedly the men of Yeshiva College. During the years which spanned the granting of Yeshiva's Medical School charter and the graduation of AECOM's first physicians (roughly 1951–1959), premedicine moved from being an unpopular major to YC's most popular area of study. Registrar Morris Silverman was quick to note publicly this shift in career interests. In 1954 he announced that premedical and pre-dental majors constituted 12.4 percent of the student body, up from just 1.4 percent only four years earlier. This shift he attributed to "anticipation of the opening of the university's Albert Einstein College of Medicine." By 1958, he could count "nearly 40 percent of the total freshman class (as) enrolled in premedical and predental courses." Many of these science majors logically looked to Einstein for admission. There they could lead a full Jewish life in a rapidly developing school. Others would soon find places in other colleges—greater and lesser than AECOM—as doors to medical school swung wide in the 1960s. Some would be disappointed by Yeshiva and by the others. But, if they were rejected, it would be in most cases because of weak grades and not their religion.[37]

In any event, Yeshiva College's new-found and soon highly publicized commitment to premedical training provided mid-1950s students with a new rationale for attending that school. But aspiring premedical students would be but one of several new kinds of students who would change the face of the Orthodox Jewish college during Dr. Belkin's second decade of leadership.

Chapter 9

The Return to Tradition,
1950s Style

At the same time that Samuel Belkin was building a university to
serve the broadest possible Jewish constituency under Orthodoxy's
banner, ironically, his college was attracting, year by year, a nar-
rower and more religiously homogeneous range of students than ever
before. Between 1945 and 1955, the college community became increasingly like that of, say, Torah Vodaath, as many of the elements
others had previously and uncharitably called unhealthy or non-Orthodox left Washington Heights.

Every year fewer pupils with public high school diplomas
presented themselves to Yeshiva. At the time of Belkin's arrival, approximately 30 percent of the student body still came from the New
York and out-of-town public schools systems. Ten years into his administration, the percentage of boys applying from Boys High School,
James Madison, and the like hovered around 10 percent. In addition,
the vast majority of those public school youngsters had had some
yeshiva training on the day school level. Between 1940 and 1945
minimally two-thirds of Yeshiva College applicants had spent at least
their elementary school years in a Jewish parochial environment. A
five-year period ten years later (1950–55) witnessed the percentage
of Yeshiva applicants with such extensive training rise to between 78
percent–90 percent of the school, even as the size of the student
body itself increased dramatically.

Concomitant with the shift away from the public school was
the reality that, while in Belkin's early years roughly 20 percent of
the student body came from Hebrew high schools, by the 1950s the
percentage with that training diminished to something less than 10
percent in any given year. Altogether it was a student body that could
boast of more years of intensive Jewish study then the generation of
Washington Heights men that preceded it. During Revel's Yeshiva
College days, between six and eight out of every ten students presented themselves with claims of close to twelve years of Jewish

training. Ten years into Belkin's era, nine out of every ten students in some classes had that many years of extensive background. At the other end of the spectrum, in the early 1950s, less than 5 percent of those applying to Yeshiva had only four to six years of training. Those who were totally unlettered Jewishly, men with less than four years of religious education, had never sought out Yeshiva.[1]

Students coming from Torah Vodaath itself, Chaim Berlin, and their brother yeshivas, by then both in New York and elsewhere, more than filled the student ranks left open by the departure of public school youngsters. Secular career goals, dissatisfaction with the social or ideological environment of their old schools, or affinity for Yeshiva's unique approach to education and religion brought in these students.[2]

Very traditional fellows came from, for example, Baltimore's Ner Israel Yeshiva, an old-style European yeshiva brought to these shores in 1933 by Rabbi Yaacov Ruderman. They were joined in their New York classes by defectors from Cleveland's Telshe Yeshiva, a school miraculously transplanted from Russia during the early years of the Holocaust by its leaders Rabbis Elya Meir Bloch and Chaim Mordecai Katz. All of these youngsters were graduates only of their yeshiva's high school programs, set up as a second thought by their founders to provide boys with the basics of American education and culture. In coming to Yeshiva University, these youngsters were openly defying their school's view that college—particularly YC—was totally unnecessary.[3]

Interestingly enough, in 1955 the Telshe Yeshiva had only itself to blame when one of its boys went off to New York. In that year, to check on the quality of its general high school curriculum, the school arranged to have its students take a competitive Ohio state scholarship test. Three of the Telshe students did so well that they were offered academic stipends. For the father of one of these students, this was an offer one could not refuse. He packed his son off to Yeshiva, Orthodoxy's only university.[4]

In the meantime, Cleveland and Baltimore yeshiva administrators could, more generally, compare their unhappy notes with leaders of Lower Manhattan and Brooklyn-based schools that for more than a generation had watched many of their boys go off to Yeshiva. Beginning in the mid-1940s, officials of RIETS and YC's oldest competitor and long-time feeder school, the Yeshiva Rabbi Jacob Joseph, could commiserate with their confrères. Its high school, founded in 1940, steered students away from the Talmudical Academy, only to have some of the same boys choose the objectionable YC for their college years. Among the many young men who "checked out" of a Brooklyn Mesivta and rode uptown during this early postwar period was a chemistry major named Norman Lamm, who had a future far removed from the laboratory. He was destined to become, thirty years later, Yeshiva University's third president.[5]

The yeshiva-like profile of the college—at least on paper— was intensified further by the school's acceptance of foreign-born students, refugees, and survivors of Hitler's persecutions. In fact, in each of the first five years after the end of World War II, more than 5 percent of the students seeking places at Yeshiva came to the school without any prior training or education in the United States. There they joined the more than 10 percent to 15 percent of the applicants born overseas who had had either some or very extensive training in the United States.[6]

Some of these newcomers came to Yeshiva with remarkable stories to tell of their survival in war-torn Europe. One early 1950s applicant came to this country "in 1946 with the first boat of surviving D.P.s from Germany." He and his two older brothers, the "only survivors from the entire family in Poland, for almost two years . . . managed to hide in the woods, etc., until they escaped to the American zone in Germany." But that young man's tale was not any more amazing than that of the better known saga of Rabbi David Lifshitz, former chief rabbi of Suvalk, Lithuania, who was brought into the Yeshiva University family in 1946. "The last of the Kehillah to flee Suvalk," he traveled throughout wartime Eastern Europe, even staying for awhile in Persia, before being rescued by the Orthodox-led Vaad Ha-Hatzala. Rabbi Lifshitz was one of several important survivor-rabbis who would add luster to the Yeshiva's rabbinical program in the postwar college. He would also provide Dr. Belkin with an anchor among America's most traditional Jews as the university ideas took shape.[7]

Significantly, however, even as the students at Yeshiva seemed to come more and more from the same types of background, they continued to differ one from the other in what they studied and how they behaved on campus. The proportion of TI to RIETS students at YC during Revel's time—in most years a 40 percent to 60 percent ratio—did not change that much during Belkin's first decade. That meant that clearly not all the students from the different advanced yeshivas moved directly, or at all, into RIETS. The TI was not left without students with the departure of the public school cohorts. Of course, if the TI continued to be tarred as a hotbed of heresy and nonobservance, the onus now could be leveled only against boys from the same types of families as those who sat and learned in RIETS. In a word, the new era of TI "bums" were Orthodoxy's own "bums"; they came from yeshiva-affiliated homes and families.[8]

The narrowing of Yeshiva's community bespoke a more general and profound winnowing of American Orthodoxy underway in early postwar days. Until 1945 this small but heterogeneous lot, when it was large enough in the major cities to coalesce into a community, was made up of elements that held strongly to Orthodox traditions and those that did not. A typical Orthodox Hebrew school class in the 1930s—the place where the majority of youngsters from Orthodox families could be found—might include the rabbi's son or daughter. These children clearly came from homes where the Sabbath and kashruth laws were closely observed. But that class might also be home to students from families where lights and radios were turned on on the Sabbath or dietary laws not always followed outside the home. These people professed their Orthodoxy most consistently through their synagogual affiliation. Talmud Torahs might almost attract children of America's small band of Hebraicists, who observed much of Orthodoxy while questioning the bases of its traditions. These latter groups were in school because a parent, or possibly an East European grandparent at home, might have retained a strong affinity for the best of Orthodox traditions. To be sure, many of these Jews could relate to no other form of Jewish identification, unless it was Zionism, which in some neighborhoods, as we have shown, was often closely tied to the Orthodox community.[9]

At school their children joined the more observant youngsters and, like it or not, received a quality Jewish education. If they stayed in the best of these after-public schools they would be in class eight to ten hours a week, five days a week, forty or more weeks a year: a total of four hundred hours a year. They emerged from these schools able to communicate as Jews with the even more traditional element in their neighborhoods, the small minority of children who attended day schools and yeshiva high schools. And converse and interact they did, in the network of cultural and Zionist organizations which brought all types together in the after Hebrew school hours.[10]

Economics and anti-Semitism also combined with the neighborhood and school in keeping all elements of this variegated community in close contact. The intra-city migrations of the early 1920s came to an abrupt halt after 1929. The Great Depression made all—Jew and Gentile alike—stay where they were, in the 1920s neighborhoods originally of their choice. Those maintaining traditions and those slowly drifting away continued to live next door to each other through the generation of crises and then war.[11]

The difficulties of being a Jew in America, particularly for those seeing themselves as traditional, was also a source for common cause and experiences. One did not have to observe all the teachings of Orthodoxy to be concerned that those who wanted to live a Jewish life on a college campus would have great difficulty doing so. In this respect the best Talmud Torah students from the less than totally observant family would find that he and his people had much in common with his yeshiva-trained youth group leaders and their folks. Together they might go off to Yeshiva College, the son of the rabbi to RIETS, the son of the layman and the son of the Hebraicist to the Teachers Institute.

After World War II, the components that made up 1930s Orthodoxy split apart. To begin with, most observant youths left the public schools and Talmud Torahs for day schools and yeshiva high schools. In an America that was more culturally pluralistic, it was easier than before for a new generation of parents to argue that Jews had no social or patriotic obligations to expose their children to city systems, even as these once venerable and frightening temples of Americanization did all in their powers to respect and support the Jewishness of their children. To their more secure minds, whatever social benefits that could be derived from dealing daily through one's youth with children of all races and creeds were more than offset by the Jewish advantages provided by their own parochial schools. Soon it would be determined that the best 400-hour-a-year supplementary program could not compare with the day school's total immersion program, if the perpetuation of Judaism was one's highest goal. In addition, these parents believed that urban public schools were themselves no place for Orthodox or other Jewish youngsters.[12]

Significantly, these points could be made not only in New

York, where prewar Orthodoxy offered followers a choice of day school or Talmud Torah, but also in some seventy-three smaller communities where Jewish parochial schools were built in the first postwar decade. Under the auspices of Torah Umesorah (National Society for Hebrew Day Schools) concerted efforts were made to establish elementary level yeshivas whenever possible and to support their expansion beyond eighth grade whenever feasible. That meant that by the 1950s the local rabbis, and their most observant laymen from Atlanta to Harrisburg to Memphis to Louisville and many places in between, who had sent their sons to public school and enrolled them in their own synagogue's Talmud Torah, could now place their grandsons in the local Hebrew Academy. To be sure, when these young men reached their bar mitzvah, they would have to be sent out of town for more advanced Jewish education. But now, unlike twenty years earlier, there were many Talmudical Academies available to the boys. If New York seemed too far away or too frightening, there was always the Mesivta High School in Miami, Florida, or the old Talmudical Academy of Baltimore, now possessed of its own full-fledged general high school, or the less Talmud-intensive Ida Crown School in Chicago. There were twelve such institutions outside the metropolis. As far as homesickness was concerned, that still could be an individual problem, but loneliness could be shared with many other boys. Sending high school boys away had become a way of life among Orthodox Jews in America's smaller communities.[13]

All this important building activity meant that fewer and fewer Orthodox youngsters had to face the problems of public school life during their educational careers. Simply put, the son of the boy who had his hat handed to him by a cafeteria monitor at Baltimore City College would not feel the anxieties his father had experienced. In addition, he would not have to interact, unless he wanted to, with Jews different from himself all the way through college.

Meanwhile, the less observant elements in Orthodoxy's prewar coalition were doing their best to separate themselves from the "sons of rabbis." They too left the large communal Talmud Torahs behind, as well as the youth groups and Zionist organizations, when they left their old neighborhoods for suburbia.[14]

In countless numbers of families, the rootedness to Orthodox institutions, possibly maintained out of respect for an aging parent, ended with the demise of that elder. Kashruth and Sabbath traditions also came to be more honored in the breach as both became less important to a maturing next American generation. Jewish education, likewise, took a back seat to suburban social drives. The father, who had been forced to attend afternoon school four hundred hours a year, might implore his son or daughter to stay in a Hebrew or Sunday school, at least until bar mitzvah or confirmation. But the four to five hours a week twice a week over less than forty weeks (over two hundred hours a year) in an Orthodox or Conservative congregational school had to be fitted in with band practice, violin lessons, and gymnastics meets, activities all befitting the suburban Jewish life-style.[15]

Interestingly enough, these parents from Orthodox backgrounds were joined in suburban Talmud Torah PTAs by adults from families with much weaker ancestral ties to Jewish tradition. But they too wanted their children to attend the Hebrew school. In suburbia, it was good American teaching that youngsters should be instructed in their Americanized faith. But this religious education was not to be too extensive. Already by 1959 it was estimated that "80 percent of Jewish children attended one or another type of Jewish school . . . during the course of their elementary years, except that *they did not all attend at the same time nor stay long enough*" [sic]. A new community of marginally committed Jews was in the making. Soon it became clear that even the best of these Talmud Torah graduates would have little in common with those more committed Orthodox day school youngsters. They did not speak the same Jewish languages, see each other at school, or belong to the same teenage organizations. Their parents, too, had lost whatever they once had in common, including their apprehensions about their son' going to college.[16]

The suburban parent could reflect on how different his feelings were about having his child enrolled at the University of Michigan from those of his own more observant father about his enrollment at CCNY. He could muse that if he had done his job right and inculcated in his child, through Talmud Torah and synagogue activities, the desire to remain among other Jews, the collegian would find his way to the Hillel House on the campus. There he could participate in religious services, take a course or two dealing with Jewish culture, eat kosher meals at a Sabbath communal get-together, and meet Jewish girls on each occasion. All of this was available only if he wanted it.

The 1950s parent could also identify his son's college administration as a ally. One did not have to be moved by the decision made in the early 1950s New York's City University to officially mandate the Jewish high holidays as school observances. By then Michigan and many of the other less "Jewish" schools already had an honored tradition of looking the other way on those sacred Jewish days. In addition, Friday night classes were not the problem they used to be. A more permissive academic environment cared little about attendance sheets and one could always find someone to take notes.

The problem for concerned suburban parents was that relatively few students of this generation, even those raised in the best congregational school systems, cared much about Hillels. And Friday night classes were avoided because that was date night or football rally night, with or without a Jewish date. To be sure, if a son really wanted to be in a large Jewish academic environment, take in kosher meals when available, absorb Jewish studies courses and the like, and still feel that he was at a real general university, he could enroll in America's second university under Jewish auspices, Brandeis, founded in 1948 with former national Hillel director Abram L. Sachar as its president. Neither parent nor child would take a look at the other older Jewish school for rabbis on Washington Heights.[17]

Many day-school parents, on the other hand, looked directly to Yeshiva. Although they had to admit that Jewish life on other campuses was easier than before, they could still see that Orthodox Jewish college life did not really exist at other schools. The era of Yavneh Orthodox student organizations (post-1960) at secular schools had not yet begun, and the Young Israel Kosher Kitchen, founded in 1956 at Cornell was the only such luxury then offered at an Ivy League university. For such parents Yeshiva was not only an extension of their children's earlier education but a fitting projection of their own lives. Some of these adults were, of course, graduates of the College. In any event, they and their children were living lives quite different from those of their parents and fundamentally apart from those of their suburban non-Orthodox cousins.[18]

The great question before the Yeshiva community was whether it was comfortable with the growing dichotomy, call it a chasm, between its people, the less committed nominal Orthodox, and American Jewry in general. Not since the days before Bernard Revel's arrival had a confluence of demographic, sociological, and attitudinal concerns combined to draw Yeshiva's core constituency back toward its earlier moorings. It was not Torah Vodaath, the rabbis at the Brooklyn yeshiva would be sure to confirm that. As a school, Yeshiva still preached a mixture of tradition and modernity that it considered appropriate for all its fellow Jews. But as things stood, it was heard by only a select few.

Samuel Belkin, for one, was not content to see his Yeshiva speak only to the most committed. The whole thrust of his first decade of service had been to expand Orthodoxy's reach and to conquer communities against the forces of disaffection and liberal Judaism. To leave those with residual attachments to Orthodoxy at arms reach, untouched by intensive Jewish education, would contradict all that he had set out to accomplish through his university plans. Accordingly, in March 1956, Belkin announced "a new college admission policy . . . to prepare students lacking in sufficient background of Jewish knowledge for integration into RIETS or TI after a year or two of preparatory courses in Jewish studies." Soon this basic-level curriculum would stand on its own as the JSP (Jewish Studies Program, renamed in 1965 the James Striar School of General Jewish Studies) with its own director, a marvelous educator named Rabbi Morris Besdin, its own distinctive faculty, and its own religious academic guidance system.[19]

To be sure, there was, once again, a partial precedent from Dr. Revel's days for Belkin's departure. In 1934 it was announced in the Anglo-Jewish press that YC would begin offering courses "for students with no knowledge of Hebrew." These proposed studies, Revel claimed, were in response to the "many requests for the broadening of the College rules by Jewish organizations and by parents who seek for their sons an educational environment in which Jewish faith and culture remain a vital force in their training." The Yeshiva also canvassed for students on its own, in its own Mizrachi youth circles. The school even sent out feelers for applicants to rabbis trained by the JTS. By 1936 there was a large enough response to start a prototype program with none other than the aging Rabbi Drachman at its head. But this early endeavor—again like so many of Revel's ideas—was doomed from the outset by financial problems.[20]

Belkin's initiative differed from that of his predecessor in one very significant way. Revel reached out only halfway to the poorly trained student. He was to be allowed to attend only the Hebrew and

Jewish studies courses offered in the afternoon in the college division. He might take a Jewish history course for knowledge and for credit at the same time that a "regular" Yeshiva student in the same section was fulfilling his general history and language requirements. But the unlettered were not at the college in the morning, when religious studies were offered, and were thus set apart from the Yeshiva community. Belkin's plan was to open his Yeshiva completely to this new breed of students. Although they would ultimately be in their own division during the morning, they would thereafter be an integral part of the campus.[21]

The question was: how open did Belkin plan to make his Yeshiva? Precisely whom would Yeshiva attempt to recruit to the new school? How unlettered, and more importantly, how uncommitted could a youngster be and still find a place at Yeshiva? Early in the plan, harsh words were spoken in several quarters about the imminent decline of Yeshiva if the wrong boys were let in. The word had long been out that elements in the university were out to totally secularize the school. Very religious students, for example, were highly exercised over a remark in the 1956–58 YC catalog that compared the evolution of Yeshiva to that of Harvard, Yale, and Princeton. Each, it said, "started as theological seminaries and over the years broadened their scope." Student newspaper editors called upon Belkin to repudiate any efforts to make "Yeshiva reach the status of Harvard Divinity School." The announcement of the organizing of JSP redoubled fears that a radical shift in Yeshiva's orientation was afoot.[22]

School lore has it that a number of student leaders were so upset at what JSP might come to represent that they threatened to protest. As they saw it, even if more of the boys in the 1950s came from the most traditional of homes—and they were not privy to the statistics we have—there was still too much heterodoxy on campus to warrant opening it further to those with little grounding in the faith. In their view, boys from the best families often missed services, used safety razors in violation of Jewish law, and dated girls as other college students did. What could be expected of the unlettered? In essence, it was not only fear of what these newcomers would do to the spirit of a yeshiva, but also concern over whether the boys then in residence were themselves religious enough to provide this fledgling element with the appropriate models. Belkin reportedly had "to cut short a trip he had been taking to quell the fears" of his most traditional students. To them he reiterated what he had said earlier in public: "A student showing insincerity in his Jewish studies will be forced to leave. . . . The flooding of the College with any students who are not sincere in their quest for a religious education will never be permitted." Ultimately, Rabbi Besdin would come up with an even better preemptive formula to protect religious interests. The motto of his office would be: "All the noncommitted shall not be admitted." But still the question remained: what was to be the basic level of commitment necessary for admission?[23]

In its inaugural years, a debate over the religious pedigree of JSP students centered, strangely enough, around a small cadre of Jewish public school athletes, who, it was said, were taking quick advantage of the new curriculum but had no intention of becoming more Orthodox. Participants in the "Jewish Sports Program," as the JSP was sometimes derisively called, were depicted as "guys who came to shoot baskets, take the college courses, and go home." They were seen as having little affinity for the faith in their private and public lives. It was alleged that the only reason these players were at Yeshiva to begin with was because better "basketball schools" did not want them. More charitable critics might say that they wanted a quality secular education while still getting the chance to be a sports star.[24]

In truth, these youngsters were not Yeshiva's first athletes. Sports had been a minor but publicized part of the college's life as early as the mid-1930s. Those who went out for the team, regardless of backgrounds or personal commitments, had always run the risk of being labeled Yeshiva's foremost "bums." For sports, like few other activities on this college campus, underscored the difficulties YC always had in trying to be like other schools of higher education while at the same time retaining the atmosphere of a yeshiva.[25]

For some, the sight of a Yeshiva uniform represented another fulfillment of Revel's promise to bring the best of CCNY to Washington Heights. Now it would be possible for the boy with sporting inclinations to participate in this most all-American activity in a Jewish environment. Simply put, one could play intercollegiate sports and not have to violate the Sabbath. Yeshiva's games would never be held on Friday night. The Yeshiva team said one other important thing to its supporters. When this Jewish group competed, and sometimes even won, against Gentile clubs, they engendered a high degree of ethnic pride. Devotees of cultural pluralism could relate well to that.[26]

On the other hand, uniforms were unknown in the traditional yeshiva. In Eastern Europe pride in one's people had never been derived from competing physically with the outside world. Sports troubled its critics because it evoked an image of the ideal male different from that of tradition. The best of the Jews were always the sons of Jacob, those sallow youths who sat near the tents. American sportsmen were closer to the tribe of Esau, hunters removed from tradition. Yeshiva's European rabbis, for certain, had no affinity for these extracurricular pursuits.[27]

There were, moreover, practical objections to the sporting life. First, practice and games took the Torah student away from his studies. Although someone might evoke Maimonides as supporting the concept that a healthy body produced a healthy mind, no one would submit that that twelfth-century rabbi and philosopher would have approved of the modern emulation of Gentile ways. It was from the latter perspective that another objection was raised. Students playing and Yeshiva crowds observing these games were often seen as comporting themselves in an undignified manner, ill-fitting the men of Torah. In addition, these public representatives of a Torah community rarely wore yarmulkes when they played, another negative image.[28]

The basketball program's opponents could not claim with incontrovertible certainty that team participation had ruined the scholarly and religious potential of all members, although it was easy to say that TI players were among the most troublesome elements in the dormitory. After all, by the 1940s some good Orthodox rabbis had varsity letter sweaters hidden somewhere in their closets. Other former athletes went on to pursue Jewish educational and social work careers. As late as the early 1950s the school could point with pride to at least one Yeshiva sportsman who graduated from the College and the TI far more religious than when he entered. This young man had been an all-city basketball star at Dewitt Clinton High School in the Bronx and a standout on the still powerful freshman CCNY ball club before transferring to YC in 1951. That this student, possessed only of a Talmud Torah background and some extension courses from the Young Israel, found more than just basketball and a good college education at Yeshiva is evidenced by the fact that on graduation he and his young wife took jobs in a Jewish Center in Rock Island, Illinois. From this remote Jewish outpost, where he taught Hebrew school and engaged in youth work, he would write back to his mentor, Dr. Hyman Grinstein, at the TI:

> I have been doing some reading and studying in my spare time, which is quite a lot. I have been called upon to give some talks on Israel for the numerous Hadassah clubs. I'm learning quite a bit concerning administration and techniques. I would have preferred doing this work in New York, but I guess this is *what G-d would want* [emphasis mine].[29]

But could the Yeshiva community also be pleased with—or at least accepting of—a basketball player who graduated with merely a stronger identity as a Jew? Just that type of student-athlete graduated in 1957. Like our Clinton man, this Eastern District high schooler came to YC by way of CCNY. Equipped only with memories of a bar mitzvah in a Williamsburg, Brooklyn synagogue, he was enrolled along with one other student—a non-athlete—in a morning session Hebrew tutoring program, possibly a prototype of JSP. Unlike Dr. Grinstein's disciple, this young man did not apply himself religiously to his Hebrew studies. He often cut the morning sessions, reserving his energies for his YC philosophy major and the basketball court. But from his own recollections, he grew as a Jew from his exposure to the Orthodox environment.[30]

Bernard "Red" Sarachek, coach of both these young men, felt Yeshiva could take pride in each youngster's development. As he saw it, "if a fellow had a little Jewishness in him, he could find something that was everlasting at Yeshiva." For one, it might be strict Orthodox behavior. For the other, it might be respect for a tradition that said one did not belittle or publicly mock the religious values of one's home Orthodox educational institutions. Practically that meant that when the Eastern District boy was selected as a senior to tour for eighteen days with the world-famous Harlem Globetrotters as a member of an All-American college squad, he made sure not to play on the Jewish Sabbath. He had learned, or at least had come to understand, that whatever his own beliefs and practices, Friday night was not the time for some announcer in some arena in America to call out "representing Yeshiva University."

This all-star's coach believed, moreover, that even if the school did not succeed in moving his player in the "right" direction, surely the school did not lose its holiness from his presence in their midst. "If one was solid in his conception of Judaism," he would argue, "no one could teach you (the wrong ways). On the contrary, maybe you (the more observant one) could teach him something." In any event, it was his opinion that Yeshiva teachers should give students "as much as they can—including much that they could enjoy."[31]

So disposed, Saracheck had no second thoughts about recruiting athletes with minimal religious educational backgrounds to the new JSP. From the perspective of basketball, he knew that these highly skilled athletes who had played in competitive leagues, sometimes against the best Gentile clubs, could do more for his program than sheltered yeshiva-trained players. These students would mean more wins for the program and, not incidentally, more glory for the school. As he saw it, Sarachek's problem was rather how to convince budding basketball players that there was more to life than just the sport and more to his school than just "a place for rabbis."

Sarachek operated under the assumption that no one would, or should, come to Yeshiva just to play basketball. After all, he could not give scholarships. He could not even offer a home gymnasium for games and practice. Players had to travel downtown on the subway to the city's Central Needle Trades school after classes let out at 7:00 or 8:00 p.m. Sometimes Sarachek would begin practice on the subway with "skull sessions" to the amusement or astonishment of straphangers. What the coach could present to his potential players was the chance for a good education, the opportunity to grow as a Jew, and the unique privilege of representing the Jewish people. He would preach that "kids all over the country look at box scores for a Jewish name." These youngsters would also follow the exploits of a victorious Yeshiva and derive thereby a certain pride in their people's strength. As far as the commitment question was concerned, the coach believed that "if you are Jewish, you are committed. And anyway, how could one feel commitment, if he did not know anything." He asked only that his players "go to class" and remain open to what was taught.[32]

A group of four public school athletes heard either part or all of Sarachek's message and in 1956 enrolled as a full one-third of JSP's inaugural class. Of the four, only one had had any real prior contact with yeshiva education. He had attended the Talmudical

Academy's Brooklyn branch (BTA) for a number of semesters before transferring and emerging as a star on the Erasmus Hall public school team. The others had no more than the basic four years of Talmud Torah before their bar mitzvahs. None of them would have defined themselves as particularly religious or observant. Their arrival kept Yeshiva's streak of winning seasons, begun when the Clinton star arrived, going for three out of the next four years. During their tenure the Mighty Mites, as they were called, compiled a highly respectable .638 winning percentage. Their presence also touched off a lively debate in the school over whether their commitments and sports were appropriate for a yeshiva.[33]

One of the members of the ball-playing quartet, who transferred form Rutgers, remembers that some of his classmates actually "hero-worshipped" him and idolized his athletic skill. One RIETS student, he recalled, a second-generation son of a Yeshiva rabbi, brought "cymbals to the games and really stirred up the crowd." Many others were just thrilled by the winning record. However, a different element was "chagrined that *goyim* (Gentiles) were coming in to the hallowed halls of YC." This same student-athlete recalled being "ostracized," being given "the cold shoulder and the silent treatment" by students who did not "attempt to integrate" the athletes into the student community. This young man drew close to his three sports colleagues and those they found in the larger student body who were more tolerant of their backgrounds and position.

Coach Sarachek, for his part, did not feel as acutely the range of emotions his players faced on a daily basis. He remembered that even RIETS *semicha* students frequented his games. Saturday night at the Needle Trades was "date night," and sometimes hundreds of students packed the place. On the other hand, Sarachek did allow that it was possible that some of these people harbored mixed emotions during the week about the players' presence at Yeshiva.[34]

Among those more consistent in their feelings against the Yeshiva team were the individuals who damned "Red's boys" as "dumb jocks." More thoughtful critics argued that whatever value there was in Sarachek's Jewish approach—and remember that the coach himself was not a very observant Orthodox Jew—the boys he brought in, even when they were on their best behavior, did not contribute positively to the yeshiva atmosphere in the school. Moreover, whereas the 1954 star was a "one and only" outsider who could be ignored, now there was a group associated with the school, and those athletes clearly stood out physically at Yeshiva. And who knew, one contemporary remembered, "how big the (sports) program might become."[35]

Rabbi Besdin seemed to be of several minds over these earliest JSP recruits. Our JSP athlete believed that Besdin, "his first rebbe, loved us" and along with other faculty members "stuck his neck out on our behalf." Besdin himself, he thought, was also somewhat "ostracized" by RIETS faculty for his courageous stance. Coach Sarachek recalled a somewhat more ambivalent director. Clearly Besdin loved his boys and would even attend games to underscore his affinity for them. At the same time there were instances of tension between the two, as "some boys were allowed in, others were kept out because they did not have (in the rabbi's view) the right background or were not ready for Yeshiva." A third observer of Besdin's policies, himself a JSP athlete just a few years later, has suggested that when Besdin was more restrictive, for whatever reason, his approach had a chilling effect both on the number of ball players applying to the school and, equally important, on the number who after gaining admission felt at home in Yeshiva. The great advantages the class of 1956 had in making it at the school were that students came in together, stuck together, then found friends in the wider student body, and were often blithely ignorant of the opponents around them. Those who came in later, one at a time, found themselves to be increasingly different from even their fellow JSP students, who came in with more extensive religious backgrounds and more obvious positive commitments.[36]

These problems of acceptance and adjustment, when coupled with the objective reality that by the mid-1960s there were fewer Jewish public school athletes around to choose from, spelled doom for Sarachek's grand designs. He would have to rely on recruits from the YU-sponsored Metropolitan Jewish High School League which linked the then proliferating local yeshiva high schools. But many of the best of these more sallow youths did not choose to attend Yeshiva College. Yeshiva victories on the hardwood would soon become a rarity. In fact, a generation would pass before Yeshiva's flagship team, coached by one of Red's disciples and led by the smallest number of players with backgrounds and basketball abilities comparable to the 1950s stars, would bring the school back to athletic respectability.[37]

Jewish basketball players had Yeshiva's welcome mat more

or less pulled out from under their feet. Other types of Jews who, at first glance, had little or only marginal connections to Orthodoxy never approached the school to begin with. This 1950s-style Baal Teshuvah (return to traditional Judaism) campaign did look for its souls in suburbia and beyond. During the JSP's first generation of activity (1956–76), close to one out of every five students called New York's Queens, Nassau, and Suffolk counties their homes. And a most impressive four out of every ten students came from towns and communities smaller than American Jewry's twenty-five largest cities and boroughs. But it seems that in these corners, Yeshiva avoided youngsters possessed of only the most ephemeral ties to tradition. The JSP did not touch the boys of that Jew, whom we have followed religiously, from Delancey Street out toward Syosset. Large-scale missions to those rapidly on the way out of Judaism or most comfortable with non-Orthodox Jewish ways would be an agenda for other Orthodox groups of a later vintage.[38]

Among the groups who never saw Washington Heights were children from Reform Jewish families. Even those with the strongest ties to the wing of that movement now leaning toward more traditional behavior were never sought out or canvassed by Yeshiva. During the JSP's first generation no more than thirty-nine young men (only 1 percent of the student body) entered the program as veterans of the National Federation of Temple Youth (NFTY) chapters. They found ways on their own of expressing positive Judaism in a decidedly heterodox environment. Yeshiva's initiatives had no call upon them. Likewise, this basic-level Orthodox curriculum was never home in the 1950s–1970s to young men with the most limited of Jewish educations. A paltry 1 percent of JSPers, Reform Jews and other, arrived in town with only Sunday School training to their credit. In addition, during its first twenty years less than 5 percent of the new type of student came in with less than four years of Jewish training.[39]

The JSP's core constituency during its inaugural era was, rather, drawn from among those third-generation suburban Jewish families who had remained loyal to traditional ways and provided their boys with an adequate Jewish education through Hebrew schools. But it was the downgraded supplementary schools, those run by both Conservative and Orthodox congregations, that had failed their youngsters. It was as if the parents who had been sent to interwar Talmud Torahs and who later in their lives observed a modicum of traditions had the JSP children who wanted as collegians to become as Jewishly knowledgeable as their parents and decidely more observant.

It is statistically certain that close to half of 1950s–1970s JSP students had between seven and nine years of schooling and almost an equal percentage had up to twelve years of training. Largely, they were the best, most committed public school Talmud Torah students of their day. For these youngsters and for Yeshiva itself, their problem was not lack of motivation but lack of adequate prior training.

Rabbi Besdin was well aware of the personal outlook and educational deficiencies of his applicants. He interviewed personally every student who arrived at Yeshiva. (A relatively small number were admitted on the say-so of his Orthodox friends in remote American and Canadian communities.) Besdin took copious notes on the family life, character traits, educational backgrounds, present Hebrew achievements, and career goals of his boys. These reports are testimony to the life-style and orientation of that element once central to Orthodoxy that JSP seemingly was in business to recapture.[40]

Take, for example, the case of a 1968 entrant from Rochester, New York. This public school graduate was described by the director as "a *shomer shabbos* (Sabbath-observing) student from a very positive Jewish home." The family belonged to a local Orthodox synagogue which the father attended weekly before going off on Saturday afternoon, "compelled" by the need to make a living "to open his store." This youngster had attended his synagogue's Talmud Torah for five years, through his bar mitzvah. Clearly a dedicated student, he spent Sunday mornings during the next four years studying privately with the rabbi. He was Orthodox, his family was as Orthodox as it could be, and he was dedicated to his Torah studies. He was deficient only in his academic achievement. Rabbi Besdin's tests found that this public high school honor roll student's "knowledge of Hebrew and Bible is limited." He demonstrated, for example, an inability to read "Rashi script" (a printing style) without stumbling. Yeshiva welcomed this applicant "enthusiastically."[41]

The school was also happy with a future classmate from Pittsburgh, Pennsylvania. Another *shomer shabbos* public schooler "from a kosher but non-*shomer shabbos* home," this JSP entrant had eight years of Talmud Torah and Hebrew high school under his belt.

A somewhat more advanced student than the Rochesterite, he had spent his five hours a week in synagogue as a teenager (three hours on Sunday, two hours on Thursday night) studying the Prophets and Hebrew literature. When Rabbi Besdin interviewed him, it was determined that he had a "good background in Hebrew language but no Rashi (medieval Jewish commentator) or Mishnah."[42]

To be sure, not all of these new public school students were as strict Sabbath observers and careful about kashruth as were these two young men. The school, through Besdin, was highly tolerant and accepting of those boys whom the director might characterize as "respectful" or "mindful" of the Sabbath. These code words meant, as the documents reveal, that the youngsters would not travel on the Sabbath, do homework on the day of rest, or use electricity on that day. A more detailed study of the practices identified by this sensitive educator would suggest how varied indeed were the mixture of traditions observed and those not followed by Jews one step removed from Orthodoxy during this close-to-contemporary era.[43]

In a very large number of cases these students found out about Yeshiva and Yeshiva about them through Orthodox and Conservative youth group organizations. The most reliable feeder of students was clearly the Yeshiva University Synagogue Council Youth (YUSCY), its successor, the Orthodox Union's National Conference of Synagogue Youth (NCSY), and American Orthodoxy's elite youth corp, the Torah Leadership Seminar (TLS).

It is noteworthy that close to 30 percent of the JSP student body through the late 1970s had been touched either by YUSCY or NCSY. A solid 20 percent had attended TLS. They had met these organizations in the localities where they were needed most. A little more than eight out of every ten Yeshiva students with NCSY backgrounds came from communities outside New York City. If anything, a group like TLS, as others have pointed out, was brought into existence to deal with the same dilemmas that made JSP a reality. It was itself organized only one year before the college program. By its own statistics, it attracted the same cohorts that the Yeshiva recruited. It also did not touch the very marginal Jews whom Yeshiva too had no call upon. Each young man who moved from the experiential setup into Rabbi Besdin's world—Besdin himself had earlier been an instructor at TLS—was counted as a soul that had been saved.[44]

In looking back, in 1967, after thirteen years of activity,

Seminar leaders were quick to remind all of the crisis in Jewish education that the TLS had set out to meet. Their statistics have a familiar ring. While 75 percent of all American Jewish youngsters were receiving some religious training during their elementary years, only 4 percent of Talmud Torah graduates were then going on to Hebrew high school. Meanwhile, a full 75 percent of all youngsters who had attended Talmud Torah "for four years plus were unable to successfully pass a test in fundamentals based upon a minimum acquaintance with Jewish history, culture and religion." This group's other later internal statistics reveal that they also had reached out primarily to the best Talmud Torah students, although, it must be said, that they had always wanted to recruit more broadly if given the chance. Their study of participants over the period from 1955 through 1962 indicated that the preponderant percentage of "Seminarians" had between four and eight years of Talmud Torah training. Those with less than four years of schooling, those with day school training through the eighth grade, and those with yeshiva high school education were almost equally represented in the remaining one-third of the constituency. Comparably, a 1966 informal survey of just Canadian and East Coast-based TLS conclaves produced similar percentages. Close to two-thirds of the male participants had four to eight of Jewish training. Not surprisingly, a similar two-thirds majority of attendees had come from local orthodox youth groups.[45]

However, as befitting the stance of the division that spawned it, the geographical areas in which it operated and its university president's charge to conquer communities for orthodoxy, TLS could also note with pride the members of the United Synagogue Youth (USY), the Conservative youth movement, who came on board. And, once under Seminar influence, it was not a gigantic step to take to enroll for formal Orthodox training at their university.

Statistically, it seems that prior to the mid-1950s students with strong Conservative affiliations almost never landed on Washington Heights. Maybe here and there in the 1930s a random, Seminary TI high schooler would matriculate uptown in the TI, but he was not a product of any concerted effort to recruit such students. In the first half decade of the JSP's existence, however, close to fifty young men with USY backgrounds were admitted to Yeshiva. These numbers would more than double over the next half decade, with the vast majority of these people looking directly at JSS.[46]

Many were like our Pittsburgh youngster who may have received his adequate Hebrew training at Camp Ramah (the JTS summer camp) and at his local USY group. Others were like this 1966 entrant from Columbus, Ohio. A public high school graduate, he had had six years of Talmud Torah lessons, but tested as "almost not Hebrew-language knowledgeable." From a family that was "substantially but not entirely *shomer shabbos*—no electricity—kashruth," this young man, perceived by Rabbi Besdin as "quite observant," could also credit USY with providing him with a positive outlook on traditional observance.[47]

In a sense, these "Conservative" students brought the more than fifty-year relationship and struggle between Yeshiva and JTS full circle. From RIETS' earliest days, Yeshiva had always been a place which, for ideological or practical reasons, fellows left for the Seminary. Some of these men, upon ordination and much to the dismay of their first alma mater became leaders of Conservative congregations born out of insurgencies into existing American Orthodox synagogues. Other Yeshivamen left their movement after ordination from RIETS. In the post-1945 period at least twenty-five YU men became affiliated with the Conservative Rabbinical Assembly, even as Belkin and his troops were trying to hold and to gain ground for Orthodoxy. But now, simultaneously and seemingly through youth work and the JSP, Orthodoxy was making its first inroads into Conservative territory.

To be sure, these incursions could not have been undertaken without the cooperation of some of the very RA members who had defected from Orthodox ranks in that same generation. They were known to have welcomed Seminar people and, in at least a dozen cases, they sent their best USY boys, namely their sons, back to Yeshiva. There were even some cases, in the few years preceeding TLS, of Conservative rabbis sending the most traditionally observant prize members of their Training Leadership Fellowship youth groups to a career at Yeshiva.[48]

A smaller percentage of Conservative "affiliated" students found the JSP on their own. Rabbi Besdin was often moved to exclaim: "if only their numbers would increase in Israel" when boys like the one from Bellmore, Long Island, who arrived in 1968, presented themselves. This applicant told the director that he came from "a totally irreligious home" and "remembered little" of his six years of Conservative Talmud Torah training. However, while in high school he decided to "become more religious" and was now looking to Yeshiva for guidance. The school gladly absorbed this returnee to tradition into its midst, although it should be noted that, by the student's own account of his upbringing, he had not come to Judaism totally alone or new. His "irreligious" parents had had enough interest and pride in, or guilt over, their faith to send their son to Hebrew school for six years, considerably more training than many of his generation received. And there is no indication in Besdin's notes that his parents resisted their son's search for greater religiosity.[49]

Personal commitments were also clearly not an issue when the JSP welcomed back into the Yeshiva community boys from basically Orthodox homes who had not been afforded the full benefits of the expanding 1950s day school scene. In many ways, the Brooklynites who went to an Orthodox elementary school but did their high school work in a public school were true successors to the best of the 1930s TI crowd. Their homes and outlooks were kosher and a goodly number of them had kept in contact with the yeshiva's world while in high school through TLS activities. Some 15 percent of "Seminarians" had such backgrounds. Where they differed from interwar fellows was in the level of Jewish studies achievement. One applicant with seven years of combined day school, Talmud training, and TLS affiliation was characterized by Besdin having "a weak background."[50]

The same description applies to his 1968 Brooklyn neighbor who had only recently entered the yeshiva's orbit. A scion of a Sabbath-observing family, he had been sent, as a preteen, to public school and Talmud Torah. For some reason, he was enrolled in BTA for his high school years and clearly had a difficult time keeping up with his fellows, even as that yeshiva high school provided its own JSP-style catch-up program. In this case, the commitment was solid, but "textual ability (was) limited."[51]

Significantly, a goodly number of the more advanced JSP students—proficient due to background or advanced due to hard work in the program—did not stay forever in the general studies program. Some moved on to the Hebrew-intensive TI (in 1960 renamed the Erna Michael College of Hebraic Studies or EMC). Others, the greatest pride of the program, took a major step forward when they qualified for RIETS. By the mid-1960s, Yeshiva was already awarding *semicha* to former JSPers and the word was now out that Besdin's program was indeed producing some of the best Yeshiva men. Those who at first had more commitment than background were considered well-equipped to teach those with all the advantages of early Torah education the true meaning of dedication and enthusiasm for traditional learning. At the same time that the best JSPers were moving on, others in the program with equal or greater potential were content to stay where they were. In time, the lines of demarcation between the day school students in JSS and EMC would become extremely blurred.[52]

But no matter where they ended up, Besdin's committed admittees helped return significant portions of Orthodoxy's winnowed prewar constituency back into the Yeshiva orbit. By 1960 a full one-third of the student body was admitted with other than day school backgrounds. The percentage of youngsters with less than seven years of Jewish training returned to its pre-1945 level of approximately 25 percent. And those claiming Hebrew high school training often rose in the post-1955 era from 20 percent to 40 percent of the student body. In all, the religious public school students of the next generation had returned. These mixed elements would be on campus in the mid-1960s when the fabric of Yeshiva life would undergo change once more. This time the shift in atmosphere would be due not only to the type of student who came, but, as important, to the currents and crises in American civilization outside the institution that ultimately penetrated its walls, challenging other sets of Yeshiva assumptions. When Yeshiva students reacted they would speak not only with more than one voice but also several octaves higher. There were now women in Yeshiva's undergraduate life. They were the women of Stern College.[53]

Chapter 10

The Women of Stern College

Rabbi Moses Weinberger did not concern himself with women at all. He was intent on transplanting an East European religious civilization to America. The world he remembered had shown little interest in the systematic education of girls; in Hungary "the Jewish influence of the home" was counted upon "to teach the future mothers all the important customs and ceremonies and to develop within her the virtues of industry, thrift, modesty, chastity, and charity." If the girl was fortunate, her education at home would have included some rudiments of Yiddish and Hebrew reading and writing. This language arts training would have prepared her to read and impart to the next generation the messages of the Ze'enah u-Re'enah. This compilation of biblical stories, legends, and folklore was traditionally read aloud by Jewish women on Sabbath afternoons to their daughters. It was the pervasive, positive environment of the Jewish home doubled with negative perception of the Gentile world around them which kept Jewish girls close to their faith.[1]

Weinberger did not have to be reminded that back home only the *maskilim* argued the necessity of providing girls with formal schooling. These men, who were known to be less than scrupulous toward traditional teachings and mores, considered systematic Jewish education for girls as part of a wider curriculum for boys and girls. Their hope was to help integrate youngsters into what they prayed would ultimately be a more neutral Russian society. In Weinberger's opinion, modern schools like those set up in the 1860s in Moglin, Mir, and elsewhere by supporters of the Jewish Enlightenment were no place for religious girls.[2]

Weinberger had a simple, consistent answer to what he would have characterized as the "so-called problem" of educating Jewish girls in America. If pressed—and remember he did not deal with women at all in his book—he would have allowed that, if one could recreate European conditions on American soil, there would be no need to devise new systems to socialize daughters. If the atmosphere on Delancey Street could be made to approximate the one that had prevailed in Vilna and Volozhin, Jewish girls would be able to learn, as they always had, all they needed to know from their mothers. Indeed, for Weinberger to admit that mothers and families could not do the job against the pressures of Americanization which affected Jews of both genders, would have meant tacit abandonment of his unrealistic dreams. They very establishment of girls schools would have been an accommodation to the new environment that the rabbi would not and could not countenance.

These basic concerns over educational innovation did not even begin to address the hidden, knotty questions about exactly what these girls could study while remaining true to Jewish tradition. Weinberger was spared the logical next step in the debate: could girls study with or just like boys and what would formal Jewish training for women mean for Orthodox Jewry's gender roles.

The leaders of Etz Chaim's community likewise did not e-vince much interest in the education of their daughters. The same twenty-five to thirty families, who had labored against all odds to provide their sons with the most intensive Torah education possible in their country, took no discernible steps toward systematizing their daughters' Jewish training. Of course, they were acting precisely like the good transplanted East Europeans they were; they were teaching all their children just as they had and had not been taught in Russia. But they knew that conditions here were not like those in the Pale. All American children were obliged by the State to receive a general education. Those teachings and the lures of the streets were different from and inimical to the ways of the Jewish home. They could no longer count on atmosphere alone to insure Jewish continuity. Yet no efforts were expended to shield girls from the public schools. No organized plans were developed to offer them Jewish schooling as an answer to the world around them (on early educational policies of Etz Chaim see pp. 11–17).

Even those families most attuned to the new conditions did not move to protect or support their girls. Take, for example, the Andron family which had led the campaign to build the Rabbi Jacob Joseph School. By that family's own account, their drive to build a school sensitive both to Jewish learning and Jewish educational needs in America stemmed from the family crisis caused when a young Andron came home from public school and asked for money to attend a Christmas party. But their concern over what was wrong with the public schools' treatment of their children did not extend to their daughters. Well into the next generation, Andron women would continue to attend public school, even as their brothers and future husbands became more and more immersed in the Jewish parochial school system.

To be sure, this very Orthodox American family did not send their girls to public school without setting down strict rules of conduct while in the temples of Americanization. For example, Gentile friends were allowed to visit the Jewish child's home, but the girls were rarely permitted to be guests at their classmates' home. Of course, nothing could be done to offset what was inculcated in the classroom, save, it seems, to do at home what had worked in Europe. When it came to the girls' religious education, they were truer than ever to European traditions. The young Andron's sisters learned their Jewish lessons at home and were taught there to build their own loyal Jewish homes in the immigrant quarter.[3]

Had the senior Androns looked toward American Talmud Torah education for their daughters, they would have found that as late as World War I few schools offered classes to girls. In this regard, the more Americanized Orthodox families, who believed strongly in the possibility of co-existence between American and modernized Jewish supplementary education and who abhorred the studied separatism of the early Etz Chaim people, behaved very much like their European-looking counterparts. Important schools like the Downtown and Uptown Talmud Torahs remained afternoon and Sunday schools for boys only, even as they moved from being storefront school houses to large impressive bastions of American-style pedagogy. The Machzike Talmud Torah of East Broadway was alone among its major sister schools when, in 1894, it organized classes for girls under the influence of Harry Fischel. But the uniqueness of this departure is made clear by the fact that even when Fischel, more than a decade later, became president of the Uptown Talmud Torah, no effort was made there to introduce girls' classes, so strong was the disinterest in addressing the Jewish needs of the acculturating Jewish woman. As one early study of the problem determined: "The majority of parents have no desire at all for Hebrew studies for girls . . . whereas they at least send their sons to the *cheder*."[4]

It remained for elements on the fringe of the immigrant Orthodox community—the same group of Orthodox men of Hebrew letters who were later to build the Mizrachi TI—to take important strides on the women's behalf. In 1905 the Brooklyn National Hebrew School was established in that borough's Williamsburg section. Five years later, an East Side branch was organized on Madison Street. A. N. Perlberg, who would later teach Hebrew and pedagogy in the TI, began his educational career in the Brooklyn school and was the principal of the Manhattan school. In both places he was part of an institution which in its afternoon and Sunday sessions stressed Zionism and sought to provide students with basic Hebrew language skills and exposure to Hebrew literature and Jewish history.[5]

As with all their other activities and approaches, these Mizrachiites were themselves transplanting East European ideas. But their educational model was neither the home nor the yeshiva, rather a modern Jewish school, the so-called *heder metukkan.*

This educational departure grew, under Zionist influence, as a middle ground for modernizing Jews fundamentally different from both the still unchanged yeshiva and the new highly secularizing Jewish Enlightenment schools. Whereas the yeshiva abhorred secularization as a threat to Jewish continuity and the Haskalah schools prayed that "secularization will bring emancipation," the *heder metukkan* program aimed for "secularization plus nationalism" as the key to Jewish survival. Under that mandate, they offered what was later identified as the diversified Mizrachi Jewish curriculum along with general studies. Most critically, their sessions were for both boys and girls, and classes were sometimes coeducational. In some cases, by the turn of the century, classes were held in the late afternoon to accommodate those youngsters who were then attending Russian gymnasiums. It was thus quite simple for American Orthodox men of Hebrew letters to draw analogies from their recent European past in divining that American Jewry needed precisely this form of Jewish education for many of its boys and girls.[6]

Also in keeping with their European models, the National Hebrew schools, until World War I, offered classes only through the elementary grades. If a female graduate wanted more advanced training, she would most likely have to leave the specifically Orthodox educational fold. Benderly's Kehillah-sponsored "preparatory schools" welcomed the best of these girls, offered them a chance to be part of his great experiments in modern Jewish pedagogy, and, if they were willing, gave these sixth, seventh, and eighth graders their first push toward careers in Jewish education. The Marshaliah Hebrew High School system was the next step on the educational ladder. Beginning in 1918, girls would sit with boys in these most advanced supplementary schools. And, if they followed Benderly's plan completely, the final stop for New York's Orthodox girls was the Teachers Institute of the JTS. This coeducational institution always attracted more women than men and a goodly proportion of its elite cadre of students came from American Orthodox homes.[7]

In time, however, the Seminary would come to recognize the National Hebrew School group as a competitor for female students. In 1917 Perlberg and his Manhattan-based teachers took the first faltering steps toward creating an enduring high school program. Two years later, under a somewhat more secular Zionist poet named Moses Feinstein, the Herzliah Hebrew High School was established. And later, in the twenties, Herzliah structured its own teachers-training program for high school and college students. This institution, too, attracted some of the most committed Orthodox girls from the Lower East Side neighborhood to their co-educational classes.[8]

Significantly, the sight of the "sisters" of his RIETS' disciples taking advanced lessons at Schechter's Seminary did not seem to exercise Bernard Revel. Nor did the involvement of his own TI faculty members in both religious and secular Zionist training programs outside Yeshiva move the president to build his own solidly Orthodox competitive institution. Certainly there was no talk within Yeshiva of making the Teachers Institute coed. In fact, Revel's comprehensive plan for attuning Orthodoxy to this country's environment and making Yeshiva competitive with the Seminary did not address the changed social and educational needs of Jewish women. In this regard, the same man who argued that American yeshivas had to broaden their horizons, that teacher-training programs unknown in Eastern Europe had to be part of RIETS' world, and who developed the means of freeing Orthodox boys from public school and college problems, behaved much like those East European rabbis whose assumptions he roundly challenged. In turn, Revel was criticized by some of his most consistent supporters for this significant oversight. One outspoken editorialist called upon the RIETS community to "submerge our prejudiced views of former days . . . let us think of our children, girls as well as our boys—we regret that Dr. Revel seems to make no provision for the Jewish education of our girls." But these words had no discernible impact upon RIETS' Jewish educational policies.[9]

Revel also was apparently untroubled by the potential impact State-required public education and college training might have upon the distaff members of RIETS families. In truth, an Orthodox teenage girl could keep to herself in the public schools—as so many Orthodox boys were then doing out of town. And, if her family's Judaism was strong enough, she could be kept close to the traditions. But how could she, any less than her brother, lead a Jewish life on a college campus? That Gentile environment, it will be recalled, had played no small role in calling YC into existence. Was not Revel concerned with the survival of the young ladies' Jewish identity and commitment at that critical stage of their lives?

A combination of general American educational trends, broad Jewish communal attitudes, and specific Orthodox family objectives may have mitigated the problem somewhat. To begin with, it must be recognized that at no time in earlier American history had the majority of this country's youngsters attended college. In the decades that immediately preceded World War I, college was still for the elite minority. By one estimate, in 1916–1917, 2.2 out of every 1,000 American boys was enrolled in a college, and American girls at half that rate (1.1 per 1,000).

American Jews are, of course, legendary for their significant deviation from this model. Although, once again like Gentiles, the vast majority of Jewish youngsters did not go to college in the pre-World War I period, it was more likely that a Jewish boy would attend college (3.6 out of every 1,000) than his Christian neighbor. But here, it must be strongly noted that Jewish immigrants scrimped and saved almost exclusively on behalf of their sons. As late as World War I, a Jewish female was "going to college in only one-ninth the number of her brothers and in one-half the number of her Gentile sisters." Speaking of the then estimated only "1,000 Jewesses prolonging their education beyond the narrow reaches of high school," one observer remarked that "it takes 1,000 Jews to send to college .4 of a daughter."[10]

These general and Jewish enrollment trends did not change substantially during the interwar period. By the late 1930s "there were 1.33 men to every woman in college enrollment as a whole," while among Jews there were 1.93 men to every woman, even as the percentage of Jews in American colleges and universities rose to 9.1 percent of the population. To be sure, some 35,000 Jewish women could be found in college in 1934 to 1935. And in a school like New York's Hunter college, CCNY's all-women's sister school, Jewish students were the clear majority. Still, on balance, the Jewish girl with sheepskin in hand was a rare sight indeed in the group's community.[11]

Jewish parents simply did not see much economic or social value in having their daughters attend college. One contemporary observer remarked that, whereas immigrants might dream that their sons could come out of college as professional men with greater economic and social opportunities ahead of them, they harbored no such dreams for their daughters. The Jewish father "hasn't much faith in his daughter's ability to earn her own livelihood, he has less faith in the power of a college education to enhance her matrimonial chances." Accordingly, the Jewish girl was more often than not "kept safely at home by her well-meaning father and mother against the day of her marriage." Of course, she might be sent out to work in one of her ethnic group's industries, possibly to help raise money to send her brother to school.[12]

There are no extant figures on the percentage of Orthodox men and women attending college during Revel's years. But if what we know about American and general Jewish attitudes toward college could be our guide, we may reasonably assume that Orthodox women were less likely than their brothers and sister American Jewesses to look to higher education. The distaff applicant would have to put up with the same difficulties her brother had in being a religious Jew on campus and she probably would not have her family's and community's reassurance that a career was worth the effort. To be sure, a Jewish woman would not have all of her brother's scheduling problems. She would not have to balance Talmud classes with her college day, she could be bareheaded, and Jewish law did not oblige her to stop three times a day to pray. But did she, on the other hand, have to sit in class when unsympathetic professors sometimes pilloried Judaism's teachings if there was no clear career goal in sight?

These were precisely the sentiments of the Andron family whom we have followed since the days of their founding of the Rabbi Jacob Joseph School. In the 1920s, the granddaughter of Samuel Andron was prohibited by her father from "attending college to learn strange ideas." He was, rather, preparing her for "the college of marriage." This same family did not object, however, to her brother attending CCNY at night while learning by day at RIETS. And they warmly welcomed her brother-in-law, an accountant and a graduate of New York University, into the family. Study in college, if one had to make a living, it seemed, was one thing. Studying "strange ideas" for their own sake was another matter entirely.[13]

But even those Orthodox families less fearful of what college might teach their daughters did not rush to enroll them on campus. One religious Brooklyn mother sounded much like many American Jewish fathers when she warned her daughter that "overeducated college girls found it hard to get married." In her opinion, a position as a "private secretary" would be the ideal job for her young woman until "Mr. Right" came along. Significantly, this young women did not follow her mother's advice. She envisioned herself as an English and Hebrew school teacher and, in the early 1930s, looked to the then new Brooklyn College for her degrees. (Her brothers, by the way, went to Torah Vodaath by day and CCNY at night. And her future husband likewise was a Torah Vodaath man and a graduate of Brooklyn College's first class.)

Her experiences at school were somewhat reminiscent of those of the Yeshiva boys we looked at in the early 1920s who matriculated at CCNY's extension schools in the outer boroughs. Brooklyn College at that time had no real campus. Classes were held in office buildings. College social and organizational life was minimal. Religious young women drew upon the "survival skills" learned while in public school in dealing with those who were different from them. They were friendly with less-observant Jewish and Gentile classmates while in school, although the Orthodox women usually stuck together. But socializing did not extend to out-of-school hours and places. Besides, after college classes this young woman and some of her friends went to Hebrew classes to prepare them for their second, Jewish, career. To the extent that this young woman's experiences were typical while her parents' attitudes and those of stricter families still pervaded RIETS' orbit, it minimized for the school and its community the necessity to protect the souls of their women on campus.[14]

Interestingly enough, while Revel may have felt that college posed no widespread threat to his girls, others on the fringes of his community were on their own, addressing the large gap in Yeshiva's parochial school system: the absence of intensive Jewish education for women. First in 1928 and then a year later, Mizrachiites of several sorts took significant successful steps when they created the first day school programs for girls.

Joel Braverman, for one, founded the Yeshiva of Flatbush, America's first coeducational elementary day school in 1928. The *heder metukkan*, which Braverman himself had attended, was the European model for this Brooklyn initiative. In many regards, his work here in the 1920s and 1930s was to extend into the next generation the National Hebrew School approach and curriculum. This departure attracted a heterogeneous Orthodox student body—comparable in many respects to that of its neighboring all-male Etz Hayim Yeshiva. The one seemingly major difference between the male student bodies was that apparently fewer Flatbush boys continued their yeshiva education into the TA and YC. Public high school and some sort of supplementary training—Flatbush itself ran afternoon classes for just these boys—was the norm. Of course, even the most religious Flatbush girls had no TA to look toward.[15]

The all-girl Shulamith school, founded in 1929, was even closer to Etz Hayim's orientation. And, indeed, one might assume that it would have been the key "feeder school" into a girls' TA and a women's YC had such schools existed. Interestingly enough, the European model for this American Mizrachi endeavor was the Beth Jacob movement, sponsored first in Poland by the Religious Anti-Zionist, Agudat Israel party and organization.

Beginning in 1917, under the guidance initially of a truly revolutionary women named Sara Schenirer, some of Poland's most Orthodox Jews addressed the problem that even their most Americanized Orthodox rabbinic counterparts failed to confront: the growing dichotomy between the socialization of Jewish boys and girls. Schenirer and her followers recognized that the currents of modernization, even in Poland, were doing violence to the traditional Jewish family. To be sure, the young men might still be "safe," going off as they did to the yeshiva, although we know that already voices of secularization had penetrated there too. But the girls, bereft of a formal Jewish education and more widely and directly influenced by the culture around them—some attended Polish state schools—were drifting away from the traditions that once governed their lives. Schenirer capsulized the crisis of this changed environment when she wrote in her diary: "While the fathers of those girls are probably studying *Gemara* and the mothers poring over a *Ze'enah u-Re'enah*, leaders of a Polish Jewish girls' club were turning on lights on the Sabbath."[16]

The Beth Jacob answer to this dilemma was the creation of a Jewish educational system for Polish girls. Starting with a small school in Krakow in 1917, the movement gained supporters throughout Poland and Lithuania in the 1920s, so that by 1925 Beth Jacob could boast of forty-nine schools serving 6,500 students and, five years later, 162 schools served over 18,000 girls.

At its height, Beth Jacob offered a seven-year curriculum, teaching girls the prayers, the Bible, Jewish laws, customs, and history, all taught in Yiddish. The movement engaged its students in two different ways. After the state school, supplementary classes were offered in small towns in sessions running two hours a day, five days a week. In the larger cities, when possible, all-day schools were established where secular subjects were also taught as required and monitored by Polish law. To be sure, these separate Jewish educational centers were not "yeshivas" in the strictest sense of the word. The goals of the schools were not to produce great sages, but to intensify Jewish women's commitment to the old ways. Talmud, the core of the traditional yeshiva curriculum, was not taught at Beth Jacob schools in keeping with the Orthodox view that that world was an unnecessary, if not dangerous, discipline for Jewish girls.

Though these schools put distinct limits on what a student might study, few restrictions were placed on how long she could continue in that separate and unequal curriculum. By the mid-1920s, several Beth Jacob gymnasiums were extant. And in 1925, in Krakow, a Beth Jacob Teachers' Seminary was established. Through this system of pedagogy a new cadre of better educated Orthodox Jewish women was produced in interwar Poland.[17]

The American, Shulamith group held wholeheartedly to Schenirer's assumptions about the changed world around the Jewish girl and believed that in this even more secularized country, day school education was the key to Jewish survival. They differed, of course, in their conception of the Jewish ideological message to be offered by their school. As Mizrachiites tried and true, they emphasized Hebrew language skills, Jewish history, and love of Zion as essential training for girls. Not surprisingly, men like Samuel K. Mirsky and Pinkhos

Churgin of Yeshiva's TI fame played no small role in setting the directions for that school, which through the interwar period took girls up to the ninth grade.[18]

Almost concomitant with the founding of Shulamith, this same group of Mizrachiites, with assistance from the nascent Women's Division of the Orthodox Union but no discernible official help from Revel, ended the JTS and Herzliah's monopoly on advanced education for New York's Orthodox Jewish women. In 1928 Churgin was appointed principal of the new Hebrew Teachers Training School for Girls. A year later he relinquished that post to Rabbi Joseph Lookstein, who served through 1938 at the school housed next door to his Yorkville congregation. A limited number of public high school girls, the best of the Talmud Torah programs, or the new girl's parochial system were the natural constituency for the school. Characteristically, the forward-looking Lookstein felt, during these years, that Orthodox Jewish education should go one logical step further and sponsor a Hebrew College for Women. This school, he suggested would "get (us) off the educational double standard and offer to women the educational advantages that hitherto were only men's prerogatives" (at YC). It would thereby produce a "well-trained, culturally mature and thoroughly inspired Jewish woman." But that idea would not be picked up for another generation.[19]

In the meantime, the ideal American Jewish Orthodox woman—to YC families minds—was the one who took advantage of the best of supplementary Jewish education, under Orthodox auspices if possible, beyond the Shulamith school level. And if she went to college to become a more proficient teacher, she stuck to her friends and to her faith.

What has been said here about the limited educational opportunities available to two generations of Orthodox Jewish women in New York applies even more to their sisters in smaller Jewish communities. It may be that in towns where there were no early day schools in existence, Orthodox girls received primary Jewish education as they sat with boys in Talmud Torah classes. Small congregational and communal Talmud Torahs in Utica, New York; Portland, Oregon; and Houston, Texas, for example, always had such a limited pool of potential students that they could never stand on law or ceremony and restrict education to boys. One could surmise that the interested female might continue her lessons, as her brother did, with her father, the rabbi, or in some sort of secondary Talmud Torah program. But high school would be as far as she could go. Jewish teacher training school was a big city phenomenom. And in an era when many Americans and most Jews thought often before sending their daughters away to college, no one seriously considered sending their high school girl graduates to New York just to earn a diploma as a Jewish teacher.

Only those girls living in Boston, Philadelphia, Chicago, and Baltimore could have received as much training as their sisters in New York without total disruption of family life. Each of these cities was home to a nondenominational teacher training school. Gratz College operated in Philadelphia, the College of Jewish Studies was based in Chicago, which had the second largest American Jewish community. And Boston and Baltimore both had Hebrew Colleges.

At these schools the young Orthodox woman could build upon her Talmud Torah education and continue her Jewish education through her teen years. As in New York, she would be a disciple of one or another outstanding but unrecognized man of Hebrew letters, who saw in these youngsters from traditional homes a last opportunity to develop a Hebrew-speaking culture in this country. The most committed of these ladies might be moved to join her mentors in their pursuit or to consider Jewish education as a potential career. College-level courses would be the next step for the minority of the most inspired students. They would invariably complement substantive training with instruction in pedagogic methods at a local college or normal school. Here, once again, the typical interwar Orthodox Jewish woman's success story was the young lady who derived the maximum possible from after (public) school education, even though she was in a class with boys and girls less religious than she. That woman worked her way through a Gentile-run teacher training program with Jewish commitment intact, Jewish education as a goal, and a sheepskin in hand to allow her to teach during the day in a public school. Meanwhile, her brother might attend the local yeshiva as far as it went, study Talmud after high school, and, when opportunity came, go off to the great yeshiva in New York.[20]

The movement to provide Orthodox Jewish women with educational opportunities comparable to those offered to their brothers began after World War II. Here, finally, Yeshiva University, first through its assistance in the establishment in 1948 of the Central Yeshiva High

School for Girls, then through its absorption of the Hebrew Teachers' Training School in 1952 as its own Teachers Institute for Women (TIW), and ultimately through its institution of Stern College for Women (SCW), endowed by Yeshiva trustee Max Stern in memory of his parents in 1954, would make a profound contribution to Orthodox Jewish women's education. But its "separate and almost equal" approach to intensive, advanced schooling for young women was not the only plan then offered. Two other educational models would see light at approximately the same time. One was a product of the transplantation of a new breed of Orthodox Jews and institutions from Eastern Europe during and after the War. The other was an outgrowth of the concomitant efflorescence of coeducational day school education. Each of these programs would acknowledge, in different ways, the necessity to strengthen through continued schooling the Jewish identity of its women. Each would perforce address the trend—if not the aspiration—among Orthodox Jewish women to be part of a wider American educational and cultural scene.

It was the new transplanters, in the form of the Beth Jacob movement, who first tendered intensive—and fully separatist—secondary Jewish education to American girls. These Agudat Israel schools began reconstituting themselves outside of European lands of oppression in 1937 when Williamsburg became home to an elementary day school for girls. In keeping with its European traditions, it also offered after-school classes for Orthodox public school youngsters. And in 1946, it extended its reach into the high school years, when it organized supplementary classes ostensibly for both its day school graduates and its public school students. The American Beth Jacob movement came of age in 1948 when its all-day Parochial High School was set in place. There in Brooklyn and in its successor schools in Washington Heights and the Lower East Side, the European Orthodox women's curriculum was fully articulated. With Yiddish initially as its foremost language of instruction, girls were taught Bible, Jewish history, and their people's laws and customs. To be sure, Hebrew language skills were also cultivated, but Talmud, to their minds, the discipline that was religiously off limits to women, was not part of the curriculum.

Appropriately, Beth Jacob leaders also concerned themselves with their girls' educational futures beyond high school. As early as 1945, Beth Jacob set up its own seminary, modeled after the one destroyed during the war in Eastern Europe, and developed its own Hebrew teachers' training course. Its graduates would, by the early 1960s, run the some sixteen Beth Jacob elementary and secondary schools in New York and its two sister institutions outside the metropolis. But their teacher certification would not include a college degree. The whole thrust of their school's movement had been to provide them with the most solid Jewish education away from Gentile influences, while remaining, at least on paper, in conformity with State law. In their opinion, whatever might be gained by learning American ways of schoolteaching in college would not be worth the exposure to and immersion in American mores. And since a "safe" Gentile instructor could always be brought in to teach English subjects in their own elementary schools, their girls did not have to be sent out of their world to be trained in those disciplines.[21]

Shulamith School graduates and girls from the Crown Heights Yeshiva and the coeducational Flatbush Yeshiva, the three schools that fed most students into the Central Yeshiva High School for Girls, had significant difficulties with the assumptions and curriculum of the Beth Jacob movement. To begin with, their elementary education had emphasized a Mizrachi diversified course of study, not a girl's yeshiva training. That meant that all Jewish studies from bible to history to laws and customs and even to oral law, when the girls were advanced enough for it, were taught in Hebrew exclusively. Moreover, a conscious effort was made to instill in these young women a love of Zionism and the emerging State of Israel. Beth Jacob schools were clearly not committed to advancing these causes.

Nor did it seem that the Williamsburg group was much concerned with the "college-entrance" quality of its secular education. Beth Jacob girls were not encouraged to, and often were dissuaded from, going to college. Central Yeshiva graduates, the first phalanx of a new generation of Orthodox Jewish women with world views and career goals different from those of even their own mothers, looked directly at American higher education. In fact, every member of Central Yeshiva's first graduating class, sixteen girls in all, was accepted by a local municipal or private college. Finally, and equally important, Central's students were not comfortable with the social ambience at Beth Jacob schools. They saw themselves as truly Orthodox but highly American girls, just like their brothers at BTA. By the school's own admission, "girls (could) be found . . . between classes comparing notes on dates and the latest Mel Tormé recordings." And the school publicly proclaimed their "hair-ribboned and bobby-soxed girls . . . as representative of a unique school sponsored by Yeshiva University . . . the only high school where the Debka, Israeli version of the jitterbug, has more adherents than the mamba, and the latest Perry Como records take a back seat to the lively ballads of the 'challutzim' (Israeli pioneers)."[22]

Such American traits and mores were not officially countenanced at Beth Jacob. Students there, like their brothers at Torah Vodaath, as one contemporary observer linked them, did "without mixed bathing and dancing and limit(ed) dating," in keeping with a transplanted European Orthodox mentality. "Graduates of Baiss Yaakov (sic)," the same observer remarked, "would not only not protest but actually search for husbands who wanted them to wear a *Sheitel,* a burdensome wig, and who would insist on spending a few years of married life at one of the advanced Talmudic research institutions." The Central Yeshiva girls' horizons were obviously somewhat different.[23]

But, as suggested above, Beth Jacob and Central Yeshiva were not the only educational options open to Brooklyn Orthodox girls. Hebrew-intensive, diversified curricula for high school girls at schools that encouraged all to go on to college were available as early as 1945 at Manhattan's Ramaz School and by 1947 on Long Island at its Hebrew Institute (HILI). And, in 1950, just two years after Central opened, Flatbush Yeshiva expanded its program into the high school years. In both the Yorkville and Far Rockaway cases, the commutation problem made these schools logistically off limits to all but the most hardy subway adventurers, even before a family considered the appropriateness of sending their daughters to a coeducational institution. The latter concern—was it right for boys and girls to study together?—or, alternately, as one early graduate of Central put it, "the advantages . . . the freedom to express oneself without boys around that's typical of all all-girls schools" may have motivated Brooklyn parents after 1950 to prefer Central over Flatbush. It must be noted, however, that the Orthodox parents did not frown upon the healthy mixing of the sexes outside the classroom. Chaperoned parties and dances with BTA boys as guests and dates were part of that social scene in the 1950s.[24]

Understandably, Central Yeshiva High School graduates were

prime candidates for enrollment at Yeshiva's own women's college, Stern College for Women (SCW). In fact, one informal estimate five years after the school's beginning found that "almost 50 percent of the current (1959) graduating class" at Central Yeshiva were going on to Stern. Our own study of the first six classes entering SCW (1954–1960) indicates that somewhat less than one out of every three students was a Central graduate. And over the years, almost one-half of those Orthodox women raised in New York and attending SCW came with diplomas from Yeshiva University's High School for Girls. For these young women the logic of Stern's existence was inescapable. There they could remain for four more years in the homogeneously Orthodox and female educational environment they had always known, take their Jewish learning to the highest rung while earning a degree, perhaps as a Jewish or general studies teacher—the most popular major in the early years of the college. At the same time, as members of a larger Yeshiva University family, they were clearly not totally separated, outside the classroom, from Orthodox members of the opposite sex. The university did not disapprove of its men and women mixing at college-wide lectures, sporting events, Chanukah and Purim activities, and the like. In these regards, SCW people may have thought that they had the best of all possible worlds. They were continuing to learn to integrate an Orthodox Jewish life with the American world around them in a nurturing setting. At the same time they were not losing out on many of the youthful joys of campus life. Their YC brothers, at this process far longer than they, agreed, as they welcomed women into the world of Revel and now of Belkin.[25]

Still, the majority of New York's Orthodox young women—including most Central Yeshiva graduates—did not look to SCW for their higher education. The tuition-free and burgeoning municipal college system was, by the late 1950s, a highly viable alternative for graduates, male and female, from Yeshiva high schools. In retrospect, the first graduating classes from Central Yeshiva (1952–53) had, just a few years earlier, showed the way. They and their sisters wanted higher education and they were able to receive it at Brooklyn or Queens College without imperiling their Jewish identities. If teaching was their goal, these quality colleges provided more than adequate training in that discipline. And if coeds wanted something else, they were offered a wider range of subjects and majors to choose from than would be available at the fledgling Jewish women's school.

Moreover, faculty and administrators showed themselves more than sympathetic to such students' religious needs and obligations. No one was now penalized for missing classes to observe Sabbath and holidays. One had simply to get a note from one's rabbi attesting to one's religiosity to be officially excused.

As far as the college's social life was concerned, Central Yeshiva graduates found BTA men in their Brooklyn College classes. From there it was not a long stroll to tables in the cafeteria where youngsters could share their kosher sandwiches brought from home. If a Central woman had to or desired to work during the day and attend college at night, she might find, as classmates or snack-sharers, fellows from Torah Vodaath or Chaim Berlin. Women quickly became part of the now long-standing informal Orthodox life on city campuses after sundown.[26]

To be sure, the few Hebrew language and Jewish culture courses then offered on these campuses did not satisfy many of these Orthodox women's desires to continue the intense and advanced Jewish learning they previously had known. But on balance, for many Central graduates, it did not make sense to drag oneself from a Brooklyn home to SCW on Manhattan's 34th Street four and five days a week *just* to be more Jewishly learned. (In its early years, SCW provided dormitories only for out-of-town students.) A more reasonable approach to commutation and Jewish education was to attend Brooklyn College by day and then to satisfy oneself or one's parent's wishes by traveling into New York to Herzliah, JTS, or Yeshiva's own TIW one or two nights a week.[27]

College coed candidates, graduates of the Flatbush yeshiva and the Ramaz School, and, to a lesser extent, from HILI, could not have agreed more. The Brooklyn and Manhattan schools, in particular, rarely encouraged young women to go on to Stern or, for that matter, a young man to seek out YC. The ideal graduate of these schools was one who went on to the Ivy League or the Seven Sisters schools. Increasingly, the administration of these Jewish schools could be optimistic about their alumni/ae remaining observant in a wider Gentile world. The appearance of Yavneh at Columbia University in the early 1960s only anticipated an era when yarmulkes would be seen bobbing on heads in Harvard Yard. And if a youngster could not make it to the Ivy League, the City Colleges were considered respectable and Jewish enough for all concerned. SCW, on the other hand, clearly as Jewish as a college could be, was seen as an academically inferior institution. Moreover, these youngsters had been used to coeducational training. And all-women schools, except for Barnard, did not figure in their plans. One Flatbush graduate who did attend SCW, albeit for only one year, may have reflected the wider sensibilities of her peers when she recalled that "Stern was not a prestigious academic school. It had a library that was two by two . . . how could it compare to a Harvard, Yale, Columbia?" Moreover, she had dreams of becoming a physician. As she recalled, women were openly discouraged by a chemistry professor from becoming premeds. Early in her freshman year she started leafing through college catalogues as she made plans to transfer.[28]

By the same token, however, a Ramaz graduate of her generation more than stuck out the four years. She graduated with warm, positive memories of the institution. But, in fairness, she was not the typical Flatbush-Ramaz student of her time. Indeed, her experiences at school point up in a rather illuminating way the wide religious diversity of day school student bodies during her time.

All things being equal, this young woman's parents would have been happier had their daughter attended Central Yeshiva in Brooklyn. Their problem was that they lived in the Bronx and daily commutation to Bedford Street in Flatbush was deemed impossible. Had this girl had a brother he undoubtedly would have attended the convenient Manhattan Talmudical Academy. But in 1954, when she was ready for high school, Yeshiva had yet to build Central Yeshiva's Manhattan sister school. That branch was constructed in 1959. So, when this daughter finished the Yeshiva Rabbi Moses Soloveitchik, a Washington Heights elementary level yeshiva with classes for girls, Ramaz was identified as a reasonable and reachable alternative to either the geographically and ideologically remote Beth Jacob school on the Lower East Side or the local public high school.

Upon arrival at Ramaz, she and her five like-minded Soloveitchik female classmates found their families' definitions of appropriate public Orthodox behavior differed from that of most of their schoolmates. This difference manifested itself, for example, in the objection that these girls and their families had to their attending the then mandatory social dancing classes at an institution often described as an Orthodox "private school." Therefore, it was not surprising that three of these observant girls seriously considered Stern.

And since that young woman in particular, highly proficient and motivated in her religious studies, saw Jewish education as her future occupation, SCW was chosen logically over Hunter College. As far as the Jewish women's school's "inferior" academic reputation was concerned, she felt that "if one selected one's professors very carefully, good teachers could be found in many fields." Of course, she admitted that, in her opinion, the strongest professors were in Jewish studies, precisely her area of specialization. The major problem with Stern, she continued, was in the absence of a wide range of majors from which to choose. But that posed less of a problem for her than it might have, let us say, for a premed. Besides, coming as she did from the Jewish academically rich, if less religious, Ramaz, she possessed a better Hebrew background than many of her Central classmates and that made her a favorite of many teachers. Altogether she felt that that small school nurtured her talents and interests very well.[29]

The nurturing of individual student's abilities was, in fact, the strongest argument made by Stern officials to yeshiva high school girls who were looking at colleges other than Yeshiva. To the argument that Stern lacked facilities, style, and academic élan came the reply that "nowhere else but at SCW . . . would women find teachers who really care about you, who will go out for you and promote you. That's the beauty of Stern College. And from here you can go everywhere." But the success and favorable adjustment stories of Orthodox women at Brooklyn College represented an achievement which it was difficult to contest.[30]

Meanwhile, even as Flatbush and Ramaz families were denigrating Stern as less than a "real college," Beth Jacob officials and many of its families were defining Yeshiva's women's branch as too open and collegiate for their daughters. The advice tendered by Williamsburg teachers to graduates wanting training beyond high school was to stay within their own parochial system and prepare in their seminary, possibly for a teaching career in their own schools. However, if a girl, for whatever reason, truly desired to attend college, they directed her to Brooklyn College, preferably its evening session. They applied the principle first set down at Torah Vodaath in the 1930s. At a secular college, everyone clearly knows what is Jewish and holy and what belongs to the Gentile world that may be studied to advance one's career.

Yeshiva University, on the other hand, in this case SCW,

was decidedly the wrong place for their youngsters. There the lines of demarcation were hazy, and unreliable Jewish professors might be found. Moreover, Yeshiva did not discourage the academic or social integration of its men and women. That more open life-style, it was suggested, was not right for the truly religious girl. Significantly, Beth Jacob officials did more than just whisper against Yeshiva. In a number of cases, where a graduate evinced a desire to disregard their guidelines and apply to Stern, the high school refused to immediately release the girl's school records. One Beth Jacob student, who ultimately made it to Stern in the late 1950s, recalled that her father had to present himself in person in Brooklyn to demand that her grades be released.[31]

She was joined at SCW by several classmates whose parents had also made the trek to the principal's office. All of them were, in more than obvious ways, not "typical" Beth Jacob girls. They had finished only their secondary education in Brooklyn. For most of their prior schooling, they had attended Beth Jacob branches in the Bronx and in Spring Valley, New York, and Washington Heights for high school. Moreover, in the case of at least one family, enrolling their daughter in Washington Heights was a reflection less of their affinity for the philosophy of the school than of its convenience to their Bronx home. In another case, the Stern applicant attended Williamsburg's Beth Jacob for only one month after finishing its Upper Manhattan branch, found it too confining, and, following the fall Jewish holidays, appeared at Stern. Her records followed sometime later. For her parents and those of her classmates, it was apparent that "Yeshiva was better than a public college. Here you were with Jewish girls, rather than with other elements." But they were a minority within what was a less than monolithic Beth Jacob community: Williamsburg sent few girls and fewer records to SCW.

Ultimately, however, it would be neither the Beth Jacob, Flatbush, Ramaz, or even the Central Yeshiva girls' choosing Stern that would make it viable and its existence worthwhile. Ironically, during the first generation of its service (1954–1975), Stern more frequently than not attracted young women who, for one reason or another, had had less than the best prior opportunities for Jewish education. Many came from geographical areas where the Jewish atmosphere and constituency did not begin to approximate that which existed in Brooklyn. The arrival and persistence of these women at

Stern fit well with Dr. Belkin's agenda of extending the length of Yeshiva's reach in the first postwar decades.

Take, for example, the case of the 1971 graduate who came to Stern from the Newtown (public) High School of Queens. The daughter of recent immigrants to this country, she and her older brother began their education in elementary school yeshivas. She was enrolled in the Beth Jacob-Beth Miriam School in the Bronx. He was sent to an equally small boy's yeshiva, Zichron Moshe, in the same neighborhood. However, family finances soon dictated that funds were available only to see the boy through yeshiva. He ended up at the Rabbi Jacob Joseph High School and for college enrolled at YC. Our young lady, on the other hand, was taken out of yeshiva after the third grade and sent to public school. She continued her Jewish education in a local Talmud Torah. For high school, she went to Newtown and in the evening kept up with her supplementary training in the Central Hebrew High School of Queens. For her, enrollment at Stern was a second chance for her to gain "the yeshiva education . . . (she) had been cheated out of." Equally important, it provided her with a chance at a "normal social life at school with yeshiva kids." While at Newtown, she had very much wanted to be part of a student choir. But Friday night rehearsals and performances ruled out that activity for an Orthodox girl.[32]

Her experiences may well have been parallel, during her generation, to that of others of the 20 percent of Stern College students raised in New York City, who came to that school without a complete, comprehensive (twelve-year) day school education. A comparable full one-fifth of that same metropolitan area cohort approached Stern with at most Talmud Torah training to their credit. Altogether, a full one-quarter of New Yorkers who entered the college between 1954 and 1975 had less than seven years of Jewish training of any sort. These sisters provide evidence that Orthodox young men and women did not share equally in the efflorescence of day school education in the first postwar decades. For all the statements made by Beth Jacob, Flatbush, and Ramaz, each in its own way, the fact remained that many good Orthodox families, European-born and American-born parents alike, did not feel an overriding need to place their daughters in yeshivas. As maturing adults their daughters enrolled at Stern to fill a definite void in their social and educational lives.[33]

But they did not have to attend Stern to feel part of New York's Orthodox community. Their mothers had already proved this, and their friends from Central Yeshiva were showing daily that a 1950s-to-1960s woman could participate fully in their community's life—attend the right youth groups, be invited to the many Sabbath activities, meet many YC young men—without matriculating at Yeshiva's school. The same could not be said about Orthodox young women then being raised in America's smaller cities and remote Jewish communities. For them, and for that matter their brothers, there was no Jewish neighborhood to which they could naturally gravitate. They could learn the rudiments of Judaism at home and in the local Talmud Torah—even if they were the only really observant children in the class of their rabbi father. But for a real Orthodox Jewish environment and, not incidentally, the chance to meet eligible religious members of the opposite sex, the best place was New York. The question was what would be the most propitious time to leave home in the quest for, among other things, an advanced Jewish education?

Their fathers had left home for the great New York yeshiva after high school. Remember, there were then very few educational alternatives available. Their baby-boomer brothers, as customs changed, were being sent off after elementary school, some even earlier. To be sure, they were beginning to have a greater choice of towns, schools, and orientations from which to choose. But Orthodox families apparently thought many times before permitting their daughters, as young teenagers, to follow suit. The college years were the time for these daughters to seek a wider Orthodox world. And SCW was the place to be. There a New Britain, Connecticut, girl, for one, would no longer feel socially out of place, even as she was exposed to the advanced Jewish education that had been unavailable to her in her local Talmud Torah, while receiving the college education which she, like all her American Jewish sisters, increasingly desired.[34]

The young woman, the daughter of a rabbinic jack-of-all-trades—rabbi, ritual slaughterer, and Hebrew teacher—in that Connecticut town, had attended the local public schools. Her brother, typically, had been sent to a yeshiva in neighboring Hartford and eventually to the Talmudical Academy before matriculating at YC. Her Jewish education had consisted of training three hours a week in a congregational school and a few hours of "released time" as a high schooler. Her commitment to Orthodoxy stemmed primarily from the strictly religious environment at home. But that very Jewish life, of course, meant that she could not participate fully in the activities of an American teenager. "Boys," she recalled, "used to carry my books home from school. But I never dated socially . . . I was asked out but never went . . . I (stayed home and) read a lot of books."

She was already inured to this somewhat solitary life and to making the best of her situation when she graduated from high school and prepared to enroll at the nearby University of Connecticut. There she knew new challenges awaited her. How would she keep the Sabbath in her dormitory room? Possibly her Gentile roommate would accommodate her. And what about maintaining kosher laws on campus? A generation earlier, Orthodox Jewish women had not had to confront these issues. They did not attend college. How small-town Orthodox women of that generation found religiously observant husbands if they never left home is a different matter.

All these fears and anxieties were rendered moot when her father read in the *Morgen Zhurnal* about the founding of Stern College. A quick visit to New York and to Dr. Belkin's office confirmed the family's impression that Yeshiva was the answer for their daughter and she was enrolled in SCW's second entering class.[35]

Fifteen hundred miles away, an Orthodox woman at the University of Miami was feeling the same anxieties as the young woman in New Britain. Born in Augusta, Georgia, this student and her younger sister had been sent to that city's schools straight through high school and to a *heder* three days a week until age fifteen. The older sister's interest in a college education directed her to the University of Miami. But there a combination of "problems with kashruth" and the fact that there were "few Jewish fellows around" had made her disenchanted with university life. A transfer to Stern opened up for her—and for her sister who followed suit—a warmer Jewish world and, not incidentally, "the big New York City life" which enthralled her.[36]

And a few years later, from almost a continent away came a student whose selection of Stern grew out of observation of her own sister's difficulties at college. This young woman had been the beneficiary of the birth of day school education in her home town of Seattle, Washington. She attended that day school as far as it went—through seventh grade. Her sister, eight years older, had not had that opportunity, but had had to settle for Hebrew school. Both young women went to public high school, and the next step for the older girl had been the University of Washington. But her experiences, like her sister-in-spirit in Miami, had not been to her liking. At that public college, there was "no Jewish crowd, no religious circle . . . few chances to meet Jewish boys." The younger sister, schooled by these realities, looked to Stern, not so much to gain what she had lost due to the absence of higher Jewish training in her town, but simply to be "happy in college in a Jewish environment."[37]

This trilogy of student memoirs only begins to tell the story of SCW's "out-of-town girls," the clear majority of those enrolling at the school for, at least, its first generation. In the first five years of SCW's existence, when the school was just getting on its feet—and word about Stern was just getting out through the papers and rabbis, non-New Yorkers still constituted a good 60 percent of the student body. During the first generation (1954–1975), the out-of-town percentage was closer to 75 percent. And a full 35 percent of the entrants during the first generation came from cities and towns smaller and more remote than American Jewry's thirty largest communities. Hometowns like McKeesport, Pennsylvania; Fort Dix, New Jersey; Bangor, Maine; Sheboygan, Wisconsin; and Rockford, Illinois; all appeared at the top of applications during those years. It is also noteworthy as a contrast during this same period, two out of every three YC men in that much larger student body came from New York. And many of the others listed nearby and large Jewish communities as home. It is clearly a statistical certainty that young women from out of town in search of an intensive, warm Orthodox environment while in college and YC men, born in just that sort of Brooklyn-Yeshiva hub and planning to study Torah and science in that traditional academic setting, found each other in Dr. Belkin's world.[38]

Understandably, the young women brought to Stern a wide range of Jewish educational backgrounds, reflecting in part the geographical reach of day school education for girls in the 1950s to mid-1970s. Close to 40 percent of Stern out-of-towners were like the New Britain and Augusta girls. Either geography or parental disinterest had precluded their attendance at day school. Another 10 percent arrived at Stern with no formal Jewish training whatsoever. On the other hand, 48 percent of the student body may have had stories comparable to that of the Seattle youngster. For them secondary day-schooling was either unavailable or off limits. Four out of every ten Stern entrants were more fortunate. They lived "not too far" out of town in cities

like Chicago, which had a Jewish academy, or Boston with its Maimonides School.

These and other communities could see their girls through
a Jewish high school. For such girls, the question was how much
more Jewish education and what kind of Jewish environment could
SCW offer them. Significantly, only 7 percent of Stern's student body
between 1954 and 1975 was made up of Central Yeshiva graduates
born and raised outside New York, another indication of the reluctance of Orthodox parents to let their girls go at a tender age.[39]

Not all of these out-of-towners were daughters of rabbis or
even from completely Orthodox families. It must be remembered that
Stern was born just two years before the founding uptown of the JSP
and at the same time that NCSY-TLS and USY groups were having an
impact on Yeshiva. Not surprisingly, distaff counterparts of JSPers (although basketball players obviously did not appear at Stern) made up
a significant proportion of Stern's 1950s–1970s constituency.

A little more than one out of every five Stern College students in the school's first generation was touched in one way or another by NCSY or TLS. Not surprisingly, nine out of ten of these Seminarians and the like came from communities outside the New York
area. Understandably, these informal, experiential activities attracted
both the "classic" NCSY youngsters as well as women from the more
ritually observant homes who had been left behind when their brothers were sent off to a yeshiva. By the TLS' own determination, between 1955 and 1962, 57 percent of participants were female. Students were provided with the desired interaction with Jews of similar
interests and orientation, if not background. And, if properly motivated, the NCSY girl might go on to Stern. The already religious girl
had already chosen New York as her destination.[40]

A similar geographical pattern is true of the 113 USY youngsters who found their way to Stern during this time. Only six of these
"Conservative" youngsters had been raised in New York. Remarkably, the USY youngsters included some twenty-eight daughters of
Conservative rabbis, a number and percentage significantly greater
than that of sons of non-Orthodox rabbis then attending the divisions
of YC. But, as always, youngsters trained and motivated in the Reform
movement did not matriculate.[41]

Given the heterogeneity of Stern's student body—even more
diverse than the traditionally mixed YC crowd—it would be under-

standable if the intramural tensions that were part of uptown life might appear at Stern. But, from most indications, it seems that such was not the case. One possible explanation is that the open, accepting NCSY spirit may have permeated the new school more than the established men's campus. Another equally plausible explanation is that bubbling divisiveness may have been mitigated by the reality that the college, in its early years, was both a commuter school for New Yorkers and a dormitory school for out-of-towners. The Windemere, Prince George, Collingwood, and Executive Hotels were not equipped to hold every girl who wanted to live away from home. Stern's own dormitory was not bought until the late 1960s. Moreover, even if the "dormitories" had been open to New York women, many parents would have deemed "room and board" an unnecessary expense in addition to tuition.

The more Jewishly lettered, but not necessarily more religious, "Central" girls passed the out-of-towners on the way to their Group A (advanced) Jewish studies classes, while the NCSYers and daughters of country rabbis sat in their B-C-D lower level classes. Some have remembered girls passing with smiles and friendly greetings. Others remember less comradeship. Of course, all students mixed in the secular classes, always the great leveler. After school, it was off to the subways for the Brooklyn cohort and back to the dorm for the girl from New Britain and the other out-of-towners. To be sure, friendships did develop among schoolmates, most commonly when New Yorkers invited out-of-towners to their homes on the Sabbath. New York alumnae recall that such graciousness was a common occurrence. Their counterparts from out of town are not as certain. While New Yorkers perceived out-of-towners as privileged by virtue of the chance to live at college, dorm dwellers told a different tale.[42]

Night life on their concrete urban campus in midtown New York was closely monitored. Students were confronted with a seemingly endless series of house regulations, violation of which resulted in the assessment of demerits. Some students tried to make light of these penalties by plastering their demerit slips on dorm walls. Of course, such rules as those requiring girls to be in their rooms by 11 p.m. may have allayed the fears harbored by those parents who wondered if sending their daughters to New York was the right thing to do. How much would the metropolis change these young women? In this regard, Orthodox parents behaved about like their non-Orthodox Jewish counterparts who, a generation earlier, were described as "loath to permit their daughters to attend college at a distance . . . the parent fears, they learn habits of liberty and independence not at all compatible with a future of wifehood, motherhood, and domesticity.;"[43]

In any event, the girl from Miami and others of her kind seldom had any experience with the wide New York world. When she did, it was more often than not with a Yeshiva College date.

Yeshiva vs. CCNY, late 1950s

Yeshiva College student life, early 1950s

Women of Stern College, 1950s

Women of Stern College, 1980s

Men of Yeshiva College, 1980s

Dr. Norman Lamm confers upon President Ronald Reagan the honorary degree of Doctor of Laws in a White House ceremony. L to R: Dr. Norman Lamm, Hon. Herbert Tenzer, Mr. Jacob Burns, Mr. Sy Syms, President Ronald Reagan, Mr. Stanley Stern, Dr. Israel Miller, December 18, 1986

◀Dr. Norman Lamm, President, Yeshiva University (1976–   )

◀New York State and Yeshiva leadership celebrate Yeshiva University's completion of its debt restructuring campaign. L to R: Hon. Herbert Tenzer, Hon. Hugh Carey, Dr. Norman Lamm, Mr. Ludwig Jesselson, February 1, 1982

Centennial Semikhah Convocation, Rabbi Isaac Elchanan Theological Seminary, April 6, 1986

Chapter 11

Like All Other Universities?

The mid-1960s to early 1970s did not witness the incursion of new types of students into Yeshiva University. The decades that had broadened Dr. Belkin's community both within and without Washington Heights had come to an end. If anything, particularly in the men's school, there were some signs of a new homogeneity in at least the educational and family backgrounds of the youngsters. By the late 1960s, for example, the percentage of public school graduates attending YC hovered around 25 percent of the student body, down from the high of close to one-third reached at the beginning of that decade. This slow decline presaged a future, one decade later, when almost all students would be recruited to Yeshiva from one basic source: the burgeoning nationwide day school movement.[1]

To be sure, students from the same types of homes and families did not necessarily behave the same way or feel an equal commitment to Orthodox Judaism while on campus. The TI students were, as usual, seen by some classmates as the yeshiva's problem children. A semiscientific survey conducted by the college's student newspaper in 1972 must have been received by those concerned with the religious character and uniformity of the school with mixed emotions. On the one hand, it suggested that the JSS experiment was working and its integration had been achieved. JSS students reportedly "enjoy(ed) studying Jewish Studies at YU" even more than their RIETS counterparts. Likewise, they were depicted as close to RIETS' best men when it came to such questions as whether "they considered themselves a religious person" or whether "if I miss a davening (praying) I feel guilty." At the same time, it recorded that significant segments of the RIETS classes did not always toe the religious line. A full one-half of the RIETS men studied indicated that they did not "value religious studies more than secular studies." An almost equal number admitted that "there are certain laws that I just can't observe fully . . . N'giah (laws regarding sexual contact and intimacy) is one of them." In addition, more than a third of the RIETS students believed that "YU should be coed." Almost one-half of JSS youngsters agreed. Not surprisingly, TI fellows scored lower than RIETS and JSS counterparts in their religious commitments and higher in their secular drives and desires.[2]

Contemporary observers might have attributed the moods at the school, particularly the decline in religiosity at RIETS, in part to the presence on campus of 4D "draft dodgers," who were waiting out the end of the Vietnam War. It was an open secret at the school that, during this most unpopular of American wars, a number of YC students enrolled uptown primarily to receive the rarely questioned religious ministry deferment from military service. Their actions were not so very different from those of Jews and Gentiles at most colleges, who had to find more ingenious means of outwitting the Selective Service System. This was also the era which saw the rise of ephemeral, private "yeshivas," which ran "classes" and helped gain deferments for Orthodox students attending secular colleges all around the country. Clearly, the men sitting on Washington Heights until the coast was clear could not be counted among the most religiously committed elements in the school.[3]

Ultimately, however, the greatest and most exciting differences within Yeshiva's community during this turbulent era would not be found in the dorms or on dates, but in the streets and through the student newspapers. The last decade of Dr. Belkin's tenure at Yeshiva (1965–1975) saw a vocal minority of students express a wide variety of opinions about the direction their school and, more widely, American Orthodoxy should take. Probably not since the days of Dr. Revel's reorganization of Yeshiva some fifty years earlier, and certainly not since the founding of the college, by that time two generations ago, was so much said and written about the multiple missions of Yeshiva, the students and their school, and their relationship to the wider world around them.

Within the range of opinion, there could be found those who believed that the causes of general society had to be Yeshiva's, not only because those were what concerned other colleges and their students, but, more essentially, because such concerns were intrinsically a part of the agenda of Orthodox Judaism. Others perceived distinct philosophical and practical limitations for both the Jew and, most importantly, the man of Torah if he became involved in the world's social and political arenas. For a variety of reasons and at differents levels, it was believed that the Jew and the "Ben Torah" had other priorities.

Others saw those days as bringing, by virtue of legal and structural maneuvers by the university, a new era of creeping, if not galloping, secularization into Yeshiva itself, threatening the very soul of their institution. Within that contingent there were those who cried that while Yeshiva students, including some who sympathized with their fears, were out there legitimately sharing in their own way the commitments of other Americans, at home Yeshiva was losing its essential Judaism, becoming in fact like all other colleges. Limits had to be established to what was perceived to be the secular drift of the school. Others, harkening back to the oldest ideas at RIETS, saw threats of secularization in all corners and in all venues. But withal, in the maelstrom of the 1960s, the battle lines were not simply drawn and points of demarcation often overlapped. Some student spokesmen found themselves diametrically opposed to other articulate classmates. Others found common interests, intersection of philosophies, and even shared fears of authority, which drew them together even though they were committed to basically different causes. All perceived, from whatever perspective, that the stances taken by the school's leadership did not correspond to their ideas and needs, making Dr. Belkin's final years less than satisfying.

The troubled and turbulent mid-1960s provided both the general societal context and some role models for much of the debate and turmoil at Yeshiva. By 1965, even the most cloistered of Yeshiva's students could not help but notice that the optimism engendered by New Frontier rhetoric was rapidly dissipating with the increase in miscommunication at home and miscalculation abroad. True, by mid-decade, the drive on the domestic front for legal equality for blacks, supported—if haltingly—by the martyred President had been steered into law by his Texas successor. And Johnson's War on Poverty promised greater economic opportunities for America's most visible minority. But these pilot programs were either unknown, insufficient, or too slow in evolving for the masses of long suppressed ghetto dwellers who, during several long, hot summers, expressed their frustrations in urban riots. Concomitant with these riots and unfulfilled dreams was the rise of a new radical black leadership that challenged the voice and vision of the Rev. Dr. Martin Luther King, Jr.[4]

For Jews, the black revolution raised especially poignant

questions and dilemmas. When the Kennedy administration began, Jews were still seen as the most consistent supporters of black causes. That traditional stance was strengthened when Jews and blacks alike mourned the murder of three civil rights workers—two Jews and a black—in Philadelphia, Mississippi, in 1962. Half a decade later, that alliance was in danger of dissolving.

Using New York as our exemplar, the community Yeshiva students knew best, one could observe long-standing alliances and friendships being shattered by intergroup rivalries and misunder-standings. Jewish storekeepers in Harlem saw themselves as victims driven from the ghetto by the riots of 1964, even as the black inhab-itants thought they were being exploited by Jewish oppressors. Jewish school teachers in the Ocean-Hill Brownsville school decentraliza-tion struggle perceived Board of Education plans as threatening their tenure, while black parents and community leaders openly accused them of failing to provide their youngsters with a quality education. Jewish property owners in Forest Hills, Queens, rallied to keep low cost housing attractive to black families out of their neighborhood, connecting the incursion of blacks with the rise in crime rates. Every-where, Jewish leaders, thinkers, and people on the street questioned continued support for black causes at a time when many of its most outspoken young leaders were expressing defiantly anti-Israeli senti-ments as they identified with Third World ideologies.[5]

By the late 1960s, however, these urban-based conflicts were taking a back seat because of the problems caused by Johnson's for-eign policy. An alliance begun under the Eisenhower administration and maintained and slowly expanded under Kennedy became an all-out undeclared war in the first Johnson years. The Gulf of Tonkin incident of 1964 led to the expansion of U.S. military involvement in Southeast Asia. And the 1968 Tet offensive made clear to many Americans that the battle against the Vietcong would be long, expen-sive, and fruitless. Campuses erupted, moratoriums were held, and the 1968 Democratic national convention became the focal point for a street riot as police battled with protestors. Elsewhere, blue-collar hard hats saw no affinity with students; intellectuals of all kinds de-bated the morality of the war.[6]

American Jews, no less than their fellow citizens, were not of one mind on this question. To be sure, Jews—college students, rabbis, writers, and other communal leaders—played prominent roles

in the antiwar movements. Some even said that Jews played a dispro-
portionate role in the peace efforts. At the same time, there were
others whose profiles were equally high who supported Johnson's
policies. Backing for the President stemmed from belief in the the so-
called domino theory: If Vietnam fell, soon all of Southeast Asia would
come under Communism. Containment was the key. Others pledged
their allegiance to the administration on specifically Jewish political
grounds. It was suggested by friends and foes of Israel alike that it
was logically inconsistent to be a "hawk" when it came to support
for Israel and a "dove" on American Vietnam policy. Concern over
the ramifications of Jewish nonalignment with Johnson brought some
to the government's side.[7]

    This soul-searching in America posed new and important
questions for the men in "The House of God on the Hilltop." Although deep in the recesses of Yeshiva's memory there was the story,
almost the legend, of their own Dr. Revel's involvement as a young
European yeshiva student in "the movement for social betterment which
later turned to Leninism," the question of what role, if any, men of
Torah might play in affecting contemporary events and in highlight-
ing for other Jews the social justice issues of their times had rarely
been asked at Yeshiva. As we have noted, until the late 1960s the
most pressing questions which arose from Yeshiva's encounter with
America had centered around delineating the degree to which American secular culture would be permitted to permeate the holy institution. Now a new dimension was added to the dilemma of being a
traditional Jew attuned to the outside world. Can, and in what ways
should, Yeshiva people enter as a moral force into secular world crises?
To what degree were Orthodox Jews obliged to make the causes of
the great society their own?[8]

    For the student editorialist who in 1969 wrote "Black is
Beautiful or Sh'vart'ze," it was clear that Yeshiva men had to be in
the front lines of the social justice movement, reversing a pernicious
trend in their own community. The retreat in Jewish affinity for black
causes, he believed, was a development clearly to be mourned. In
his opinion, Jews were mistakenly equating "black equality . . . with
riots, black anti-Semitism, and terrorized Jewish merchants and
teachers." Jewish fears, he continued, were leading all too many Jews
to "dissociate" themselves from the "civil rights movement" and to
find kinship with the "Jewish Defense League which . . . fights might

with might." Other Jews, he noted, had simply become massively apathetic to the continuing legitimate struggles of blacks. Most importantly, he averred, YU and its students were among the most fearful, retreating, and apathetic American Jews; a position, as he saw it, totally inconsistent with the mission of the university. Accordingly, he was particularly exercised over "YU's gross insensitivity toward the death of Dr. King. While every elementary school, high school, and college in the country was closed for a day," Yeshiva remained open. "Isn't it sad," he wrote, "that the only university that has as a major portion of its curriculum the study of Torah is on record as having ignored the death of a man who died for many of the principles found in the Torah?"

To reverse this tragic trend, this critic urged that "distinguished black leaders . . . be invited to give lectures at YU, a religious tutoring program should be developed for Black Jews, roundtable discussion panels between black leaders and members of our faculty" should be held to deal "with issues such as black anti-Semitism and Jewish anti-Blackism," and a plaque honoring Dr. King should be erected at the school.[9]

The some sixty members of the Yeshiva University Neighborhood Youth Corp (YUNYC) were totally in agreement with their classmate. Moreover, as they perceived the challenge, it was not enough for Yeshiva men to become more aware and resensitized to the black man's plight. Yeshiva students had an obligation to go out in their own Washington Heights neighborhood and mend the fences around them. These activists certainly understood that more than a generation had passed since Jews and the Irish had lived somewhat peacefully in Upper Manhattan. Like so many other universities born into what were once solid middle-class neighborhoods, Yeshiva now found itself in the midst of a declining urban slum area. And an occasional mugging on or near the campus did little to engender friendly sentiments between Yeshiva students and the surrounding minority community.[10]

In their opinion, the fears of Yeshiva students had blinded them to the needs of the people of the Heights and, specifically, to the children who "die educationally year after year in the public schools." The Belkin administration, they protested, "is more interested in enclosing itself safely behind its new buildings than in getting involved in the community that lives in the old (buildings) around us."[11]

YUNYC members called upon their classmates to devote some of the time usually spent in the labs, classrooms, dorms, and, yes, the Talmud study halls to tutor neighborhood youngsters and to take the underprivileged on field trips to museums and stadiums. These efforts, they were convinced, would have the practical effect of reducing neighborhood tensions, strengthening the bonds of "mutual respect," and maybe slowing down the mugging rate. Most importantly, they argued, these activities were not only the wise and prudent things to do, they were also right and the most appropriate Jewish response to urban decay. One editorialist, highly sympathetic to YUNYC ideas, probably said it best when he began by noting that what YU should have been doing was already being undertaken by students at secular universities. He argued: "Where the legitimacy of Columbia's social responsibility may seem to be parliamentary or tenuous, only Yeshiva claims to represent a religious ethic. Only at Yeshiva College can we demand (by its very own definition) that Y.U. play an integral role in the social scheme of Washington Heights." To all who might say that he and his friends were acting outside the Jewish realm in their social activism, he declared, "The suggestions we propose were not campus plagiarisms but merely represent a request for consistency and religious imagination."[12]

Implicit in all of these activities and plans was the critique of Yeshiva's most important product: the "Ben-Torah." The student devoted to the study of the Torah to the exclusion of so many other things was depicted as all too narrow and parochial in his vision and his considerations of the role the Torah had educated him to play in the world. In a biting characterization, another student editorialist depicted such fellow students as Yeshiva's "Jews of Silence"; men who were so concerned with their own personal intellectual growth in Torah book learning and so overly concerned with monitoring the punctiliousness of observance within Yeshiva's home that they had lost sight of the great, if not greater, challenges Orthodox Jewry had to face outside the cloister:

> (he) doesn't get involved with any cause . . . looks on the world outside . . . Yeshiva as a Gehenna (Hell) populated by things which

aren't even human . . . He wears a black hat—or perhaps a large kipa (yarmulke). He's in the Beth HaMedrash every night. He complains because the cafeteria doesn't have glatt kosher meat . . . and bemoans the alleged lack of religiosity of his fellow Yeshiva University students. But is he religious? Can he have the audacity to call himself Shomer *Mitzvot* (observant of the commandments). What's his *heter* (dispensation) for ignoring *mitzvot bein adam l'chavero* (laws governing personal interaction). The Torah is unequalled as a document of social responsibility and social justice . . . All Jews are irrevocably bound together . . . (And) our responsibility does not end with Jews. Every non-Jew has his *Tzelem Elokim* (created in the image of the Almighty), the spark that separates us from the rest of creation. If we let that spark in the soul of a child in Washington Heights die, we are guilty of spiritual murder . . . When one Biafran child dies of starvation, we have not fulfilled our obligation to feed *B'nai Noach* (the children of Noah, i.e., mankind).[13]

In all these causes and through these expressions, Yeshiva social activists were clearly acting out the sentiments cogently articulated by a very popular history professor, Rabbi Irving Greenberg. In a 1966 interview granted by Greenberg to the college student newspaper, he outlined what one of his closest disciples would later characterize as "the central constitutional document for the test of whether Judaism was going to meet the test of modernity." When asked to describe the "primary problem facing today's Orthodox community," Greenberg was quick to respond that "Orthodoxy refuses to come out of the East European ghetto psychologically." To his dismay, he perceived his contemporaries as having "inherit(ed) the notion that Judaism entirely transcends the temporal, that Judaism should be independent of local culture." He asked whether a relationship with God required that one separate oneself from the world's problems.

In his opinion, it certainly did not. Those who "escap(ed) into the purely ritualistic realm of Halachah . . . homogenized Halachah and (have) made a virtue of it," he depicted as having done so based on the erroneous and rightened belief that "Torah cannot stand up to the challenges of contemporary civilization." As he saw it, Orthodox Judaism not only could have important things to say about the way the world was moving, but was obliged by Torah teachings to be involved. Focusing directly on the present issue, he declared that "it is our religious responsibility to participate in the current civil rights movement."

In judging how and in what way Orthodox Jews should be involved, Greenberg argued that there were two historical traditions for the committed to draw upon. There was "the prophetic messianic posture," wherein Jews were commanded to "pose a radical alternative to current behavior and warn of serious punishment if obedience does not follow." Alternately, Jews could identify with the Jewish "role . . . of healing and reconciliation . . . of embracing the qualities of goodness and value . . . in the status quo, of working soberly within the existing conditions for limited and gradual change." For him, the seriousness of contemporary problems ordained it as a time to act, not to console: "It is time," he wrote," to take up the prophetic theme again . . . (It) is requir(ed) that Jews possess a social consciousness and exercise it. . . . Jews are required to eliminate those conditions—physical or psychological—that humiliate people."

Practically that meant that Jews had "to stand for an increased war on poverty." It was our "religious duty to involve ourselves in politics and speak up for an increased poverty program." Most tragically, in his opinion, Yeshiva University was at present derelict in its failure to produce young men of Torah inculcated with this most fundamental religious teaching. And worse, the school was "turning out secularly oriented students," concerned with their own lives and professional development but not attuned to Orthodoxy's social justice agenda, "overlaid with an abundant practice of Orthodox ritual." In fact, he continued, many of the students who leave the Yeshiva without graduating are those who "are ethically and religiously more sensitive" than those who stay.[14]

There is no record of any response from Yeshiva's Office of Admissions to this outspoken challenge. But elsewhere at Yeshiva, both the assumptions and the practices of Greenberg and those who saw themselves as his disciples were closely scrutinized and ofttimes criticized. Not surprisingly, the Jewish Defense League branch at YU, established the same year as YUNYC, did not share their classmates' definitions of the urban crisis and of the Orthodox Jews' responsibilities to the wider society. This sociopolitical movement, born out of the tensions between Jews and blacks in declining Brooklyn neighborhoods and led by the highly charismatic Rabbi Meir Kahane, proclaimed defense of one's people against all enemies, foreign and domestic, as one of Judaism's highest religious obligations. In their opinion, at least in the early years of their operation, black militants and their supporters were among the clearest and most present dangers American Jews faced. Although JDL leaders at YU were quick to allow that there was nothing intrinsically wrong with Jews being concerned about the legitimate problems of their black neighbors—they certainly would have no problem with the vision of Yeshiva students out in the streets as they too were capitvated by the outside world's 1960s methodologies—the building of bridges could never be as important a priority as protecting Jewish people and businesses.[15]

Student "vigilantes" had no announced ideological beliefs or priorities for their activities. But it can be assumed that they agreed with the JDL. They viewed their neighbors with the greatest of suspicions and vowed to "retaliate" against what was widely admitted to be "frequent and furious" incidents of violence against Jews. They were clearly unmoved by YUNYC plans for "increased campus-community dialogue" and, if necessary, the organization of Yeshiva-police safety patrols in the vicinity.[16]

More moderate critics challenged, in their own subtle way, the agenda of YUNYC. Rather than suggesting that brickbats were more important than books in Washington Heights, they wondered whether student energies might not be better spent addressing the needs of their own Jewish city people than in helping others. Basing their view upon an old Jewish tradition, critics argued that "Yeshiva students would do better to use their spare time to tutor yeshiva students of the Soloveichik or Breuer (neighborhood) yeshivot." It was suggested that "by not availing (themselves) to the local *yeshivot ketanot* (elementary yeshivas), (they were) failing to live up to the unique character and purpose of the institution." The YUNYC's studied two-tiered rejoinder was that Yeshiva, like all other "urban colleges . . . cannot morally or practically afford to ghettoize itself from its immediate neighborhood . . . without leading to further polarization." Moreover, as the Jewish university, it had an implicit religious obligation to find time to address both their own and others' concerns.[17]

Meanwhile, in the Talmud study hall, trenchant questions were being raised about whether devoting time for both, or one or another form of student activism, was the most appropriate response of the student of the Torah to the problems, however defined, of Jews and the world around them. Clearly chafing under the implication that those who stayed with their books were either unaware of or unconcerned with the fate of Judaism and the universe, the *masmid* (he who studies Torah day and night) was counterposed as, in reality, the greatest fighter Jews had for their people and against social injustice. These scholars, it was reverently suggested, were the "pillars of the world . . . their devotion and dedication," arguably, "sustain the world." And through their study and prayer, "they perform a service (to the Jewish people) which certainly equals that of a picket." And who knows, one writer rhapsodized, "whether it was, in actuality, their *cavanah* (devotion) during *davening* (prayers) rather then demonstrations which has brought whatever relief has been realized" in world crises.

From this Jewish religious perspective, it was tactically wrong for scholars to spend their valuable time protesting. Unnamed Talmud scholars at the school were frequently quoted as having said that "to demand that they leave . . . and picket is like placing the Chiefs of Staff on the front lines or having neurosurgeons administer polio vaccinations all day." Another version had it that "it is loosely analogous to asking a team of cancer researchers to do routine medical work."

Taking the medical analogy one step further, it was noted that the specialist had to leave his laboratory only when faced "with epidemic conditions." Even then he had to judge whether his actual hands-on work would make the ultimate difference. So it was with the student of Torah. In each instance, it had to be determined whether it was, as they would put it, an *et laasot* (a religiously ordained time to act). And here an additional important distinction was made between patently Jewish causes, like freedom for Soviet Jewry or support for Israel, and general society's pressing concerns. On the latter "momentous problems," it was divined that their resolution ultimately did not "depend on the involvement of the yeshiva community."

Finally and most pointedly, they concluded that to project other ways of behavior as more appropriate for a yeshiva man would constitute a tacit reduction of the "Yeshiva to the level of all other secular schools." In their view, Yeshiva University would be totally on its mark if and when it recognized that "the traditional yeshiva has as its ideal the temporary physical detachment from normal participation in society" (while) the contemporary college has "come to regard full-fledged involvement in the problems of society as essential."[18]

It remained, however, for another young and immensely popular Talmudic scholar and professor, Rabbi Aaron Lichtenstein, to offer the most far-reaching alternate view of Yeshiva's, and Orthodoxy's relationship to the world around it. In a wide-ranging rejoinder to Greenberg's manifesto—Greenberg, in truth, had spoken about more than just Orthodox activism; he had offered views on Orthodoxy's attitudes toward Conservatism, Vietnam, and even a modern Orthodox sex ethic, and Lichtenstein had replied in kind—Lichtenstein turned his attention to Orthodoxy and the demands of social justice.

As Lichtenstein saw it, there was certainly room within the Yeshiva student's life for social activism as YUNYC men or their mentor might have defined it, even as he was quick to assert that the reclusive scholar, with whom Greenberg had great difficulties, personified "a genuine path to *avodat ha Shem* (service of God) which despite its lack of sophistication I prize most highly." If pressed Lichtenstein might have agreed that one could not easily make a clear distinction between supposed primary, Jewish and secondary, universal social causes. After all, he himself had once left his Talmud classroom to rail publicly against the then emerging human tragedy in Biafra. Discussions of that gross calamity in no wise constituted, in his opinion, a *bitul torah* (unnecessary break from Torah study). Indeed, he would write in his open letter to Greenberg that the latter's "appeal for more intensive and extensive application of Halacha to the social and political realm is very much in place . . . I also think that your diagnosis of the current state of YU is generally sound."

At the same time, Lichtenstein had serious reservations about some of Greenberg's assumptions and solutions. He did not accept his colleague's characterization of Orthodoxy's slowness to respond to contemporary issues as indicative of "ghettoization, spiritual paralysis or what-have-you. Rather it stemmed from a superior sense of responsibility, to *Z'hiruth* (caution) in the best sense of the word." And this caution, for him, quite clearly grew out of the recognition that the Torah's path in remedying social ills was a complicated one. And there were finite limits to the Jew's participation in great crusades. "I suspect," he wrote that "you greatly overestimate the extent to which the right liberal solutions could be arrived at by increased

Halachic effort and that you correspondingly underestimate the possible real conflict between traditional and modern values."

Referring pointedly to matters of "tactics and emphasis," Lichtenstein contended that, while he concurred on the necessity of placing "greater stress upon the social and political application of Halacha especially in regard to *Eretz Yisrael* (Israel), I do not think that we should immerse ourselves in American society to the extent you advocate." Here he may have been thinking of the multitude of strange bedfellows one might encounter in the political maelstrom whose ultimate goals might be quite different from, if not inimical to, those of the Jews. Or, as one of his own students put it, "As worthy as certain social and political objectives may be, the moral duplicity adhering to the methods and organizations advocating these goals may prevent the active involvement of committed Jews."

Ultimately Lichtenstein decided that in picking and limiting one's commitments, paramount interest "must be the more selfish (goal) . . . yes, selfish, one of surviving as a viable tradition and I cannot buy your thesis that this can be done in American political life." Surely he was also thinking what his student wrote: "(if) fulfillment of our covenant rests upon applying revealed values to the general culture and specific problem situations of the contemporary culture . . . it could only result in a most destructive paradox, one in which the relevance of Torah would ultimately depend on the ability of the host culture to provide suitable outlets for Torah values." For Rabbi Lichtenstein and those of his school, "the concept of priorities and of an axiological hierarchy must be our guiding principle." [19]

Some of these same Orthodox thinkers debated the issues of priorities, Jewish values as opposed to those of general society, as part of the even more complicated question of what position, if any, Yeshiva and its students should take in response to the Vietnam War. [20]

For those students who would ultimately spearhead the YU Vietnam Moratorium Committee, protest against administration foreign policy constituted, as more than one leader recalled, "the Jewish experience of our lifetimes." It said so much to them about "how you define yourself as a Jew." In their view, "Judaic morality was being played out in Vietnam." Their belief that the American incursion into Southeast Asia was, in Jewish terms, an "unjust war," meant that they deemed it a religious obligation to speak out, regardless of the consequences. To do otherwise, one student said, to "exist in a religious community with each other knowing that our indifference and our overconcern for personal and social convenience have caused the death of so many," would be tantamount to "enslavement to an almost idolatrous culture." Or, as one of his teachers put it, "As a religious Jew, one cannot divorce himself from the problem. If war is wrong, there is a moral obligation to speak against it." Moreover, confirmed as they were in the rightness of their Torah position, they felt a missionary zeal to make their point of view known not only in Yeshiva's world but also in the streets. For some of them it was paradoxical that, in an antiwar movement that attracted so many Jews possessed of the most limited contact with their religious heritage to a great moral crusade, the most Jewish of Jews, Yeshiva people so attuned to the "Jewish view" of Vietnam, should remain on the sidelines.[21]

Once again, student activists were influenced in no small measure by the persuasive Greenberg. He was among the first Yeshiva professors to speak out publicly against the Johnson-Nixon policies. In the 1966 interview discussed above, Greenberg argued that not only were Orthodox Jews bound by tradition to investigate fully and challenge, if need be, the immoral actions of the government, but as American citizens "in the spirit of the democratic society . . . suggest that others accept our attitude and follow our actions." And for Greenberg, once again, the arena for this action was not only Yeshiva, but "the political marketplace" to which Jews had "to descend . . . and demand the specific policies of our government which best preserve the dignity and life of the Vietnamese." Fully confident of his stance and aware of the disapproval such arrogation of leadership would receive, he argued that no one "need fear the results (of activism). It is the mark of the security and commitment to the democratic society that only it could allow such dissent."[22]

So influenced, student activists set out, beginning in the fall of 1969, both to raise consciousness on the Yeshiva campus about the tragedy of Vietnam and to make their unique statements within the wider Vietnam protest movement. Though what they would do clearly paled in comparison to what was done on other campuses— no sit-ins took place, no labs were destroyed, there was no ROTC to drive off campus—for Yeshiva, their attitudes and approaches were indeed most radical. Never before in Yeshiva's history had students and faculty members, as citizens of the United States, openly challenged the actions of the government. Indeed, another new dimension in that traditional group's encounter and integration with wider society here unfolded as Yeshiva students, following the lead of colleagues on secular campuses, demanded that their university suspend school attendance requirements, albeit only for the secular classes, and end "business as usual" to permit them to express Jewish reservations about Vietnam policies.

Protests over American military involvement—or maybe better said, spirited discussion of several opinions—were first publicly aired at Yeshiva in October 1969. Seeking to be part of a nationwide "effort to demonstrate the growing public opposition to the war in Vietnam," a YC moratorium was held in the afternoon of October 15 following a regular morning of religious studies classes. At that meeting, strong words were heard about the obligation facing American Jewry "to actively voice opinion against any further needless sacrifice of life." Interestingly enough, and significantly, as this saga unfolded, other speakers, strongly supportive of Nixon's policies, were also heard. Most notably, one professor expressed a feeling common at Yeshiva at that time which many paused to consider: "American commitment to insure Israel's territorial integrity," he argued, "would be weakened should the United States withdraw from Vietnam."[23]

Several weeks later, antiwar activists may have felt further frustrated when the November 1 Vietnam moratorium was not officially observed at Yeshiva. The school remained in session all day. Those who were committed had to find kindred spirits off-campus. But activists may have been moved by the respect shown for their personal beliefs by school administrators. Allowances were made for students to be excused from classes to attend rallies at other institutions.[24]

In fact, it was off-campus that the Yeshiva moratorium people made their most profound early statements. During the weekend of Friday, November 14, and Saturday, November 15, 1969, some thirty-five Yeshiva and Stern students joined 250,000 other college students in the, until that time, largest antiwar march on Washington. Like many others, Yeshiva students experienced serious logistical problems in getting to the Capitol. The bus they ordered was cancelled at the last moment; some unsympathetic bus drivers refused to carry the dissidents. Students had to make other plans. Some took regularly scheduled Greyhound buses. Others, interestingly, crowded onto the bus carrying JTS students. In additional, Yeshiva, and for that matter many JTS students, had the problem of observing the Sabbath and maintaining kashruth while on the protest road. Food from home, a Torah commandered from a Yeshiva synagogue, and assistance from the B'nai B'rith Hillel in Washington solved those problems. Significantly, it was important for these young people, from a Jewish perspective, to be able to endure these difficulties, to make their statement as Orthodox Jews, within the larger protest movement. Not surprisingly, Greenberg joined his students in Washington and spoke at an Oneg Shabbat open to all Jewish students. For one young man who was there, this confluence of making a moral appeal, informing others about Judaism's point of view, showing that Orthodox Jews cared while remaining true to the limitations on action prescribed by the Sabbath made that "Shabbat . . . the most beautiful I can remember . . . spent sleeping on a floor and participating in a march. What endowed this Shabbat with such beauty was that I, at least temporarily, synthesized the values most significant to me." [25]

This November march was, for Yeshiva students as it was for other collegians, but a foretaste of the even larger-scale protest that ensued the following May. When Nixon expanded the war into Cambodia, campuses exploded all over the country. And when four students were gunned down by National Guard troops at Kent State University, confidence in the American government and respect for this country's system reached a new low in the hearts and minds of many college students. Appalled by what they deemed as the needless shedding of blood everywhere, YU moratorium people felt that all Yeshiva people had to stand shoulder to shoulder with others around the country. Business could not continue as usual. They demanded that college attendance requirements be overlooked for the duration of the semester to permit students "compelled to direct . . . efforts to activities other than the daily educational process." Attendance at religious studies classes would continue as usual. *Bitul Torah* of that magnitude was never entertained, even by the students most involved. [26]

In mounting this crucial protest, as in all prior demonstrations, Yeshiva moratorium people were faced with, sometimes to a greater degree, many of the same problems student activists confronted elsewhere. Student apathy was one source of sadness, even disillusionment. Even at radical campuses, New York's CCNY for example, significant proportions of the student body did not follow closely the unfolding of events. It was said that when convocations were held at that school's Great Hall a better venue for having students hear about war protests might be Jones Beach, where so many were beginning their summer vacations early. At Yeshiva, it was clear that for all the heartfelt statements about religious and moral issues, student apathy was even greater. To be sure, as at CCNY, when the moratorium's overriding question, should students be excused from college classes, was discussed and brought up for a vote, hundreds of students turned out. They dutifully voted overwhelmingly to permit students to withdraw from classes and to take an incomplete grade or qualitative letter grade "if work justified it." But it was also clear that many were more concerned about the end of the school year than the end of the war. Probably student leaders should have known better. As early as the October debates, school newspaper reporters were writing that "most students were indifferent to the issues. Those interested were a handful of activists . . . Most students saw it as an opportunity to get a day off."

One skeptical student editorialist directly tied the high level of Yeshiva apathy to the insularity from the real world of military service available to "ministry students." Somehow, he observed, "antiwar protest did not seem to fit in. Perhaps the security of the 4D deterrent discouraged most students from attending the seminars and removed them from taking a stand on a grave moral issue."[27]

This student apathy may have affected the attitude of the college dean toward proposals that class attendance be made optional. Though student activists were, in retrospect, quick to credit Dr. Isaac Bacon with having respect for the sincerity of their feelings, even as he opposed the moratorium's proposal, it is also clear that Bacon, like many college deans nationwide, took the position that the pursuit of academic excellence should go on even during times of crisis. Student activists strongly but conscientiously disagreed. But they would have been hard-pressed to offset the impression that, excluding themselves and a limited group of followers, they stood alone in their commitments.[28]

Then there were, at Yeshiva as at CCNY or Columbia, elements in the student body and faculty who did not accept the antiwar analyses of the military-political scene in Southeast Asia. And, since this was Yeshiva, they cast what they said in another version of Judaism's definition of right and wrong.

A man like Aaron Lichtenstein, an influential voice on campus, was thoughtfully unconvinced that there was but one clear moral path for Jews to take in responding to this nation's nightmare war. The faith, he argued, placed the highest premium upon preventing the needless spilling of blood. But, at the same time, Jewish values were not necessarily in opposition to those of his colleagues who were domino theorists. Was it just, he wondered, for Jews and others to stand by and abandon a country to Communism, knowing how Communists have treated both their own people and their opponents? Moreover, in understanding the contemporary American scene, he was not prepared to cast the administration as an unprincipled evil villain. In his opinion, government officials could be legitimately criticized only as passive lovers of peace, not active pursuers of peace.[29]

It was also an open secret that Dr. Lichtenstein's father-in-law, the venerable Rabbi Soloveitchik, was himself unquestionably in agreement with the administration's stance on foreign affairs. One student editorialist, who had written strongly about Judaism's mission to oppose United States policy, could confirm that. During a chance meeting with the Rov, his teacher had made it clear in no uncertain terms that while he respected the young man's integrity and sincerity, he felt that he and his fellows were tragically naive about the evils of Communism. He also remarked that if students, however misguided, felt a moral imperative to speak out, then they should do so, fearlessly, but with the utmost dignity befitting men of Torah.[30]

A Yeshiva moratorium committee leader remembered that the Rov expressed these precise sentiments at a more decisive meeting when, in May 1970, plans to suspend normal operation of the school were nearing their completion. Called to an audience with the revered teacher, he found the Rov as convinced as ever that the student's perceptions of the war were incorrect. That night, however, his ultimate concerns were not with instructing the collegian on the domino theory but with ascertaining the directions and limits protest might take in a House of Torah. He wanted clear reassurance that nothing would be done that would undermine the ongoing study of Torah; the regular religious studies classes had to remain inviolable. Second, he wanted to be certain that students would be sincere in their convictions. He demanded that "a signed statement by students be required in order to prevent them from taking an early summer vacation." But, probably most important, he wanted the leaders' words that when they went out of Yeshiva into the political world they would be eternally cognizant of the limits to which protest might be taken without desecrating God's name. Yeshiva boys, he prayed, would not come into association with radicals whose values were anathema to Judaism's world. Once again, the question of limits on Jewish social action were raised at Yeshiva as the Rov demanded and the moratorium people agreed to word the text of their resolution "to limit (protest) to (Vietnam) in order to prevent students from becoming involved with Black Panthers and New Left protest movements." Under these conditions, the Rov, in spite of misgivings, stood aside and did not publicly condemn the moratorium or its leaders. Criticism from that high source, all agreed, would have doomed public debate on the subject and would have rendered those who continued outlaws within the Yeshiva.[31]

Yeshiva activists were clearly moved by what they perceived to be the sensitivity and responsiveness of the Rov. In a way, Yeshiva could here stand as a model for other universities. Its religious academic leadership had tacitly legitimized the right of free speech and dealt rationally with the needs of the time, even as they pledged themselves to be responsible in moving the debate toward the streets, keeping in mind the multiple missions of their school and faith. At the same time, they must have known that the Rov's authoritative tacit approbation notwithstanding, his was not the only strictly religious voice on campus. There were those who not only disagreed with the activist's definition of the world's problems, but, even more troubling, questioned whether the methods of their expression were appropriate at a yeshiva.

The ongoing 1960s debate over whether and how yeshiva men might address worldly concerns was joined anew as significant segments of the school's religious community wondered whether their students and classmates were, in protesting, acting faithfully to their high calling as men of Torah or rather were simply taking cues from their friends "from NYU or Columbia." In their opinion, moratorium people had frequently lost sight of the fact that Judaism's ordained response to moral crisis or impending or existing tragedy began in the synagogue and house of study. The traditional teachings of "penitence, prayer, and charity" (as counteracting the evil decree), one critic cried, "should have been taken to heart by the demonstrators at Yeshiva." Instead, student activists were seen as intent on saying, "let us be like the rest of college students and prove we're real men."

High on their list of proofs that those leading the demonstrations were not truly yeshiva men was that, at first glance, Yeshiva rallies were "fascimiles of actions at Columbia or NYU." It was reported that "the songs were the songs they sing on all campuses, the dress was the dress . . . the shouts were the shouts" heard elsewhere. One rabbi was particularly exercised by the sight and sound of bongo drums beating out the chants rising from the classroom building. This emulation of the Gentiles, it was felt, led to unconscionable desecrations of God's name. Opponents of public protest were quick to point to the shouting match that took place during a student-run moratorium meeting. Late in an evening of debate, some students requested that discussions be suspended temporarily to allow for the recitation of the evening prayers at their most appropriate time. Other students objected, arguing that Cambodia was "the more pressing issue . . . and let Minyan and Prayer be suspended during this night of crisis." In this and other instances, it was alleged that students "preferred to look upon themselves exclusively as college students and human beings . . . and place their religious commitments in the background."

It may have been, conservative voices continued, that moratorium leaders had gone astray and were leading others down that path because they had not sought out the advice of the most appropriate authorities. It was noteworthy, critics observed, with more than a touch of hyperbole, that the "moral leaders of protest were drawn from YC and Belfer (the Science Center) who knew nothing of Jewish approaches to ethics and behavior." Indeed, had they known about the students' meetings with Rabbi Soloveitchik, they could have pointed out that it was not the protestors who sought out the Rov for approval, but the senior rabbi himself who engaged the youngsters. The right approach would have been to seek out the wisdom of the rabbis. In that world view, scholars of Torah, by virtue of their closeness to the traditions, were the acknowledged authorities on all human activities, including issues which, at first glance, seemed totally within the secular realm.[32]

These were attacks with which moratorium people ultimately had to live. For themselves, they seemed secure and resolute
in their definition of appropriate Jewish behavior. Moreover, to have
accepted this highly authoritarian and wide latitudinal view of rabbinic authority would have run counter both to the liberal traditions
in which they had been schooled and the spirit of the times of which
they clearly were a part. At least one spokesman questioned "whether
most of the rabbis were capable or sufficiently informed to discuss
the Vietnam issue intelligently even within the confines of halacha."
There was another type of Jewish criticism, both from within and
without the yeshiva, which gave moratorium people greater cause for
pause. That was the suggestion, noted briefly above, that profound
limits had to be placed upon the high profile of Jewish activists because of the possible deleterious impact on the American government's attitude toward the State of Israel.[33]

When all was said and done, it was argued once again, the
Orthodox Jewish activist's greatest responsibility was not to some
ephemeral—or even concrete—social justice cause, but rather to the
real and present needs of the Jewish people. One had to think "first
as a Jew"—defining Judaism here in more parochial terms than would
others—in determining whether and how to speak out against the
American government. For, as those concerned critics saw the national scene in 1970, "President Nixon even more than President
Johnson will rebuke the Jews for urging activism in the Middle East
and opposing it in the Far East." Several years later, this spokesman
would allow further that, in his opinion, having Jews out in the streets
for all causes threatened to limit their effectiveness when they had to
protest on behalf of their own people: "Our position was that it (Vietnam) was not a Jewish issue. There were many more important issues
more relevant to Jews. If we demonstrated for every issue, important
and unimportant, then it became meaningless."[34]

Some antiwar people on campus were appalled by this stance.
Not only did it speak volumes about placing the potential needs of
Jews above the real tragic demands of humankind, but it also said
much about the acceptance by Jews of a minority status within this
free country. One articulate professor of French literature could not
countenance this self-effacing viewpoint. He called upon colleagues
to "discard their ghetto mentality . . . We should not consider what

will non-Jews think" in addressing moral issues. Interestingly enough, Rabbi Soloveitchik seemed to agree with this view of Jewish activism, even as he supported the Johnson-Nixon efforts. He made clear to student protestors that they should stick to their views. To do otherwise, he said, "would be to adopt a slavish mentality." [35]

Other moratorium people said less about the values of the "Israel First" mentality. They were more inclined to try to undercut the supposed political sagacity of their opponents. For one, Greenberg offered his own Jewish "strategic analysis." He argued that, if one looked closely at the U.S. Congress, one would recognize the support of most "hawks" for Israel was far from definite, while most "doves" consistently backed the Jewish State. To be sure, he recognized that Jewish antiwar activities could provoke a resurgence of anti-Semitism, but he was too sanguine about America's promise to believe that. He would rather place his faith in the reservoir of "admiration for Israel" discernible in the land. [36]

Still, for a few moratorium people, the "Jewish stake in Vietnam" position could neither be passionately nor practically dismissed. One of Greenberg's students, for example, the young man who had been with his teacher in Washington, D.C., and who had spoken so eloquently about the beauties of observing Shabbat while demonstrating felt keenly the confrontation between "Jewish self-interest and universal moral concerns." It was a dilemma not easily dismissed or resolved. He spoke of his ambivalent feelings when he wondered "can one be a religiously whole personality, if he accepts, condones, and thus helps perpetuate non-Jewish suffering as a legitimate price for the stability of the Jewish position?" At the same time, he feared that if "Israel were to be destroyed due to America's refusal to get involved (because of an isolationist policy engendered by prior opposition to Vietnam), could I avoid suffering a trauma of permanent guilt for aiding in its destruction." His conclusion may touch the very heart of this 1960s debate over the essence of Orthodox Jewish life both in the yeshiva and in America: "to be a conscious human being in galut (Diaspora) and also a conscious Jew does not always allow for synthesis." [37]

At the same time that these social action students were defining for themselves—with the help of friends, critics, and opponents—the limits of Orthodox Jewish participation in the wider American secular world, other classmates were raising anew Yeshiva's oldest and most complex question: To what extent may the secular be permitted to pervade the halls of their own institution? Interestingly enough, as once again a small hard core of committed students advanced their cause, they found as allies—at least temporarily—a few of the moratorium's leaders. Whether it was the latter's natural 1960s anti-authoritarism bent, their perception of the emerging legal and moral issues on campus, or the influence of their own teachers, moratorium people found themselves designing, if not actually helping to carry, the placards of the Concerned Students Coalition (CSC) as they too took to the streets in the turbulent spring of 1970.

For some future CSC spokesmen, the battle to save Yeshiva's soul—to preserve its essential religious character—was well underway by the mid-1960s. They first saw Yeshiva losing its way when in 1966 plans were announced to construct a 15 million dollar science center on the Washington Heights campus. To be sure, the Belfer Graduate School of Science had been at Yeshiva since the late 1940s when it was launched as the Institute of Mathematics and was housed initially in quonset huts. Rabbinical students, desirous of scientific training while they learned Talmud by day, were among the first students. But now it seemed that this division "devoted exclusively to secular education" was being moved into the center stage of university life. The delicate balance first set generations earlier defining what Orthodox Jews could and could not study in a yeshiva environment and from whom one could and could not learn the secular was now perceived as tilting the wrong way.[38]

Black-hatted Cassandras foresaw "bareheaded" scientists untouched and unmoved by Orthodox traditions dining in the school's cafeteria and influencing, by deed if not by word, impressionable segments of the Yeshiva community. It was feared that the role models to whom students "who have little Jewish background" might turn "will no longer be religious Jews, many of them might not even be Jews," in that avowedly nonsectarian branch of the university. It was predicted that before long these scientists would demand that the laboratories remain open on the Sabbath to permit continuous monitoring of expensive research materials. And even if neither of these calamities were realized, the sight of Belfer sixteen stories high on Washington Heights would be seen as an unfortunate image—under Dr. Belkin science and not Torah was the university's most important product.[39]

The administration's defense, that even as experiments continued the oldest priorities would remain intact, was not readily accepted. Critics did admit that a graduate school of science under Orthodox auspices could help YC and SCW graduates continue their
education "without encountering the obstacles to *shmirat shabbat*
(Sabbath observance) and kashruth that are prevalent on other campuses." And something had to be said for the propinquity of the house
of study to the laboratory enabling "the more dedicated YC student
. . . to remain in contact with the *beis medrash* (sic) while pursuing
an advanced degree." Moreover, it could be claimed that the undergraduate science program would benefit from the quality of instructors brought in—so long as they restricted their teachings to their own
disciplines. And who knew? Maybe the scientist's encounter with Orthodox life might move some in the "right" direction. Still there was
the impression that Dr. Belkin, in pursuit of federal funding—and
money was then available for scientific research—was inadvertently,
or possibly purposefully, charting a new, nonreligious course for the
House of Torah.[40]

In this regard, much was made of the administration's public relations dispatches that seemed to prove to critical minds that
Yeshiva was being cast in precisely this wrong direction. A 1969 student polemic claimed that upstairs every effort was being made "to
divest Yeshiva University of an overly religious appearance and por-
tray it as an institution of liberalism." These efforts, it claimed, not
only have succeeded in "alienating and embittering many segments
of the Jewish community," but more importantly "often militate towards self-fulfillment." To dramatize that point, they recalled a speech
made by John F. Kennedy, a 1957 university award recipient, who,
they claimed, "gaug(ed) the plans of his audience with great accu-
racy." Kennedy had stated:

> I am a graduate and a member of the Board of Overseers of another
> great American university which started as a theological seminary
> and gradually broadened its scope of educational activity to be-
> come one of the foremost university's of our time. Yeshiva seems
> certain to follow the story of Harvard.

This oldest of fears, that Yeshiva would become like all other schools
was, to some minds, close at hand.[41]

Dissenters' demands that the university control the explosion of Belfer were very much to the point. Science facilities could never be opened on the Sabbath. No Belfer students were to be housed on the uptown campus. A separate dining hall was to be created for the outsiders. And preferential treatment should be accorded YC-SCW graduates seeking admission to that graduate school. But beyond these specifics, they wanted President Belkin to strongly reassert the centrality of Torah study as Yeshiva's essential mission in all its divisions. Tragically, in their opinion, while Dr. Belkin was out building and innovating, his leadership was lacking at home in responding to what they saw as a widespread religious malaise. Students were seen simply as not as religious as they once were.[42]

Concomitant with the growth of Belfer, one concerned religious editorialist decried a classmate's published opinion that "even in such matters as teaching Talmud, our *roshei ha-yeshiva* (talmud instructors) are simply out of touch with the time. (The RIETS curriculum) is a hand-me-down from prewar Lithuania . . . largely oblivious of the new society." Another critic spoke sadly of the three types of student at Yeshiva, only one of whom he could respect. Understandably, he admired the Ben Torah, "whose devotion and total commitment to Torah and Yiddishkeit (Judaism) is unquestionable." But he questioned the place at the Yeshiva of his generation of "bums," those students whose "complete immersion into secularism and cynicism have unfortunately given many people in Orthodox circles a false picture . . . of Yeshiva." He also did not mince words in upbraiding the "middle group . . . the by-products of synthesis," a concept with which he personally was all too uncomfortable. In his opinion, many basically observant and knowledgeable fellows had the wrong priorities. Their "aspirations were geared towards graduate school and not to the intensive learning of Torah." Their dormitory rooms, he pictured as "marked by bookcases bursting with paperbacks and textbooks while a dilapidated Sefer (religious book) or two is crushed into the forsaken corner of some shelf."[43]

Significantly, a third spokesman against the perceived status quo related the troubles at the college directly to the plans to push Belfer and determined that the time was simply not ripe for experimentation: "YC is in enough trouble," he noted, trying to create an authentic religious atmosphere "without the additional hindrance of a 'nondenominational institution which not only intrudes on campus but . . . represents the triumph of the secular over the holy."[44]

As always at Yeshiva, the doomsayers were not without their own set of critics. It seems that overall those who were so put off were in the minority. Focusing only on those who engaged in the debate over these issues—remember, like the Vietnam question, a very large segment of the student body went merrily about its business—there were those who defined the "Belfer case (as) a test case for Modern Orthodoxy." Could the school, they asked, establish a first-rate graduate school and still conform to Jewish law? Far more optimistic about the "ramifications" of the experiment than those whom they called "fundamentalists," student supporters of the administration spoke proudly of "what is being tried and tested at Belfer—the very survival of Orthodoxy in the modern world." As far as the issue of general religiosity on campus was concerned, those with historical perspective could remind all that in a heterogeneous school like Yeshiva, there are always those who are more and those who are less committed to Torah study. Certainly few then on campus felt that the conflict over Belfer and the issue of religious diversity had yet reached a crisis stage. Still, the debate simmered until the close of the 1960s.[45]

Then, in the winter of 1969–1970, alarms went off when a university restructuring effort convinced a significant minority of students that their worst fears about the future of their yeshiva were becoming reality. To qualify for state funding under the Bundy Law of 1968, which granted aid to non-sectarian institutions based on the number of advanced degrees awarded yearly, Yeshiva had to reconstitute itself as formally "nonsectarian" in order to comply with the Blaine Amendment's provision that public money not be used "to aid schools under the control and direction of any religious denomination or in which any denominational tenet is taught." Failure to satisfy Blaine, one administration spokesman emphasized, would bring to reality Yeshiva's recurring nightmare: extinction due to lack of funds. Practically, these new laws meant that RIETS, Yeshiva's senior extant branch, had to be officially divorced from the university. It would now be only "an affiliate" of YU, albeit with its own Board of Directors, but dependent upon the university from which it was now separated for its financial survival.[46]

For "religiously sensitive students," including those already troubled by the paths Belkin allegedly was taking, the subjugation of the soul of Yeshiva, if only on paper, to meet state strictures for a university was a slap in the face of all that was holy. And that, in their opinion, was only half the problem. Other aspects of the plan, potentially more troubling and frightening, stirred them to action and brought others to their side. As reconstituted, YC and SCW were now "nonsectarian" institutions. Gone from the new catalogs, published apparently to put Yeshiva in the best possible light in Albany, was the requirement—impossible under Blaine—that "no student may attend YC unless he is simultaneously attending one of the following: RIETS, EMC, or JSS." It was thus conceivable that irreligious Jews, or even non-Jews, might show up on campus in search solely of Yeshiva's quality secular education. Interestingly enough, Dr. Revel long ago had theoretically welcomed Gentiles to Yeshiva. But he wanted them to study Jewish culture. This was not the type of outsider 1960s dissenters feared. Rather, they envisioned youngsters who "openly flaunt religious values and opt out of taking . . . Jewish studies." Here all along, the most religious students had complained that even in an environment where religiosity could be "enforced"—wake-up calls for services, for example—not enough had been done to keep those who wavered on the straight and narrow. Now the doors were being swung wide open, never to be closed again.[47]

    Administration attempts to quell fears were initially of little avail. If anything, explanations brought additional support to the opposition's side, including, at that stage, some of the Vietnam War moratorium people. The reality was, or so officials asserted, that no substantive changes were being made in Yeshiva's admissions policies or in its approach to student life. In an early meeting with student leaders, Dr. Belkin reassured them that no student would be accepted unless he attended one of the Jewish Studies divisions. The loopholes created by the new catalog existed "merely on paper" to insure eligibility for badly needed funds. Yeshiva would never be in danger of being overrun by hordes of Gentiles and irreligious Jews. Nor was the institution without power and the means of insuring that, come what may, the school would remain Orthodox, notwithstanding the rhetoric of "nonsectarianism." Moreover, the administration asserted that Albany was well aware of the legal fictions being created and certainly was "not being fooled by the college." Students were counseled to behave like the committed yeshiva students they purported to be, to have faith in the intelligence, vision, and, above all, the integrity of the head of their yeshiva, who would see them through the real financial crisis and their own spiritual crises.[48]

But faith in the prescience, perspicacity, and perceptions of administration officials was then a rare commodity among Yeshiva student protesters. The core of the CSC, with all due respect to the president, could not share his optimism about the limited ramifications of his acts. One loyal opponent cried: "But are all these merely changes on paper? Can we be so schizophrenic as to represent ourselves in one way to the outside world, while remaining inwardly true?" His position was shared by those who deemed Dr. Belkin's position tragically naive and legally untenable. They shuddered at the vision of a rebellious student taking Yeshiva to court for forcing him to observe religious teachings in a "nonsectarian" college. That point of view found common cause with others, including some of the Vietnam War protestors, who challenged not so much the foresightedness of the school but the ethics in composing legal fictions.

That minority opinion included those who wondered whether Yeshiva had indeed told the whole truth to Albany and, if not, would ultimately have to pay the price. Finally, there were those who trusted both Dr. Belkin's motives and insight and yet still had fears to express about the future after his presidency. Without structural guarantees, without the strength or the commitment to the oral laws that still governed Yeshiva's daily life, it might be possible, over the course of time—and no one knew how long Belkin would continue at Yeshiva's helm—that a "Brandeization" of their yeshiva might be effected. It was thus a very loose coalition of those who questioned Belkin's leadership and the directions Yeshiva had long been taking, along with those who loved and respected Dr. Belkin while considering him misguided, those who did not support him at all, and those who realized that he was not immortal, who joined in mounting strident opposition to Yeshiva's charter revision plans.[49]

Interestingly enough, like the Vietnam War protesters, CSC people were immediately caught up in the problem of getting their position across to an apathetic, sometimes even antagonistic, student body. There were those, to begin with, who simply could not see what the fuss was all about. One pro-administration student argued, after several months of the new system, that "from an objective nonemotional stance, one must surely admit that no demonstrable effect has occurred in the day to day life of students." In his opinion, whatever religious heterogeneity could be found on campus, was "not directly attributable to the nonsectarian definition." A minority went even further, suggesting that nonsectarianism might even be welcomed at Yeshiva. It would truly give students freedom of choice, thereby bringing to the school a freshness and openness, even as it would, he predicted, remain Orthodox.

On the other hand, others were concerned with the possible long-range effects of the move. They were worried about what public debate over Yeshiva's status would do to its reputation and to the image of its graduates. One student tried to alert others: "It appears that Yeshiva is truly in an inextricable crisis and complaining only tends to aggravate it. The future of Yeshiva is not at stake by changing a few words in a catalogue . . . Reason dictates that students think twice before they bury Yeshiva." As far as the suggested disingenuousness was concerned, one Vietnam moratorium leader who found himself arm in arm with the CSC remembered, that among his friends, the feeling was that the greater danger on campus could be found in the cells of the CSC than in the administration. For these students the furor over charter revision was a smoke screen created by some of their fundamentalist classmates to discredit their institution and to undermine the mission of the university. For them, the battle over nonsectarianism was part of a plan to desecularize Yeshiva.[50]

There was apparently some truth to that last allegation. It showed as the CSC dealt with the nagging problem inherent in all protest groups: maintaining unity of purpose and tactics among disparate interests and constituencies. Although all seemed to agree that a student protest against their administration was not an inappropriate act for yeshiva students, an *et laasot* had been reached. The question was: how far could they go in their actions without "desecrating God's name"? This question, as already noted, had been on the agenda during policy meetings of Yeshiva's Vietnam protesters. For CSC people, the problem took on much greater significance. After all, many of them were champions against secularization: they could never countenance appearing to behave like all other college students!

Interestingly and paradoxically enough, some of the elements least sympathetic to the long-standing policies of the Belkin administration, the out-and-out critics of Yeshiva's outlook within the institution, suggested the most un-Yeshivalike methods. There was talk, during the winter of 1970, of student strikes and of sit-ins on campus. Ultimately cooler heads prevailed, even though the administration seemed unyielding in its plans for charter revision. The com-

promise plan that ultimately emerged was that a public demonstration, respectful but strong, would be mounted against the
administration's policies—but not against Dr. Belkin himself—during
the rabbinic ordination celebrations of April 1970 unless of course,
the administration showed real signs of changing its course.[51]

For the most responsible student protestors, even this well-
tempered approach was cause for some intensive soul-searching. All
their lives they had been taught to respect religious authority. And
Dr. Belkin was "their Rosh Yeshiva." They could not see themselves
questioning his prerogatives. Still, voices told them that this great leader
was ultimately wrong. As one activist of those times remembered it:
"the spirit of the times was for demonstrating," if those who led did
not respond adequately. But the ambivalence did not end with that.
Many did not know how to manage a protest, even as they took notes
on what went on "at Columbia" while swearing that their statements
would not be like all the others. Their demonstration would be one
"for Torah."

To be sure, the CSC fellows were buoyed significantly by
the sometimes active, ofttimes tacit support given them by their rabbinical teachers. Some of these instructors, like the students they inspired and influenced, expressed their long-standing disapproval of
the "secular" ways of Yeshiva. For them, charter revision was no
surprise. Others, most notably here again Rabbi Aaron Lichtenstein,
were concerned with the limits and ethics of the issue. He and his
colleagues were not of the view that Yeshiva had already lost its way.
But they were concerned with Belkin's apparent myopia about the
negative potential of the plan. And they were worried about Yeshiva's
relationship with Albany. Ultimately, however, the most thoughtful
CSC people realized that, to insure the viability of their protests both
personally and tactically, they needed the approval of Rabbi Soloveitchik.[52]

The Rov's approval would grant their acts the legitimacy
they so badly needed. They also knew that if the Rov firmly opposed
their views or methods, his censure would effectively end their activities. Neither they, nor anyone else at Yeshiva, would deign to even
contemplate ignoring the words of the man who ultimately set the
limit for American Orthodox behavior. On the other hand, a strong
definitive statement from that leader of leaders would not only bring
significant numbers of apathetic and wavering students to their side

but would also make the strongest possible statement to the Yeshiva administration.

The feeling on campus as the days before the ordination celebration approached was that the Rov's sympathies were basically with the dissenters. On the other hand, it was also clear that throughout the conflict, the Rov retained his longtime, high regard both for his president and his work. He, too, it seemed, did not want Yeshiva's clock turned back. Nor could he conceive that his friend, Dr. Belkin, was disingenuous in his acts. What concerned Rabbi Soloveitchik most were questions pertaining to the future: the fate of his yeshiva in a post-Belkin era. Still it pained him to think that his students might take to the streets, even in the most responsible manner, and thereby endanger, even if inadvertently, the good name of Yeshiva.[53]

Ultimately the Rov, on the very day of the ceremony, decided that the charter revisions would have to be called back, but that a public demonstration, even in support of what was right and just, was wrong at Yeshiva. He informed his disciples—some of whom were the leaders of the CSC—that he would champion their cause, but that street action would have to be called off. He decided that he would speak strongly from the heart for them, when called upon to speak during that afternoon's convocation.

The students in the Rov's classes—his immediate and closest disciples—out of respect for their teacher, followed his orders. But unknown to Rabbi Soloveitchik, the protest was "too far along" to be canceled at the last moment. With the word still out that the Rov was behind the demonstration, an estimated crowd of some two hundred Yeshiva and Stern students, placards in hand, marched in the streets as the Rov ascended the rostrum upstairs.

In a tension filled room, the Rov spoke in a hushed voice of the "skeletons or ghosts" of nonsectarianism within the walls of the beloved Yeshiva. He then announced that the concerns of the CSC were his—particularly what would happen after Dr. Belkin, even as he asserted that he had called off the protest. At that moment he was interrupted by a voice from the back of the hall. One of his students shouted, "Rebbe, there are hundreds of students in the streets," leaving a surprised but unshaken Rabbi Soloveitchik to admit, "It is a demonstration for Torah, my heart is with them."[54]

This unambiguous statement by the Rov seemed, at first glance, to be the break CSC people needed. Subsequent to that day's dramatic events, a meeting of minds was reached between the Rov and Dr. Belkin. The demands of the CSC were to be taken seriously. Mechanisms were to be developed to insure both that the university not appear ambiguous in its intentions and that its religious character would always be maintained. It was agreed that Rabbi Soloveitchik would play an essential role in insuring the latter. In addition, many of the peripheral issues of the CSC would be placed under advisement and ultimately implemented. A new spiritual advisor would be appointed to counsel Yeshiva students and upgrade the tone of Jewish life on campus. An improved religious studies curriculum would be adopted at SCW. Teachers of Talmud, the very souls of the institution, would be accorded higher salaries. And the concerns of those earliest involved in the secularization question would be addressed. The Belfer Graduate School and its building would be totally shut during the Sabbath and holidays.[55]

But in the late spring and summer of 1970 Yeshiva moved ever so slowly in implementing those reforms, which, for the next generation of Yeshiva students, would be an unquestioned part of their campus existence. In this respect, the Belkin administration was acting very much like its old-line downtown yeshiva antecedent. And Yeshiva University was also performing like so many good colleges at the time. One could ask Vietnam War protesters around the country about the slowness with which their home academic institutions moved on agreements reached with students and faculty before the summer break. Back at Yeshiva, failing to fulfill immediately the mandate of April, the Belkin administration once again asked for time, trust, and latitude. Rabbi Soloveitchik seemed to agree. He would not confront Dr. Belkin publicly again. The most responsible leaders of the CSC followed suit. One former CSC member said that he took to heart the advice given him by one of Dr. Belkin's right-hand men. The young graduate was told that if he truly wanted to see Yeshiva maintain its traditions, he was obliged, as a loyal alumnus, regardless of what a catalog might say, to monitor from within and without the character of his alma mater. That was the message he needed to hear. Besides, by that time his energies had been dissipated by the close of the semester. And the next fall he was off on other pursuits.[56]

In the end, only a small minority of protesters, including some who had feared Dr. Belkin's motives and plans long before the charter revision began, continued the fight. By all accounts, the battle turned ugly and personal. Dr. Belkin was reported to be pained that he and all he had sought to build were being held up to scorn by irresponsible critics who cared little for his or Yeshiva's good name. It remained for the students themselves to demand that this nihilistic crusade end. In a strongly worded, front-page editorial in the student newspaper, almost two years after others had given up the fight—or regained their trust in their school—the student body was called upon "to unite . . . to finally end the destructive influence that (has been) exerted on this school." Students themselves, it was continued, "must make it clear" that attacks against Dr. Belkin "will no longer be tolerated." "After two years of accepting, for the sake of fair play," unconscionable acts, "the time has finally come to demand action." This last statement of loyalty from students may have served as partial consolation for the rapidly aging President as he led Yeshiva through the final years of his administration.[57]

Chapter 12

Toward a Second Century

In September 1975, an ailing Dr. Samuel Belkin asked the Yeshiva Board of Trustees to relieve him of his duties as president of the university. At the trustees' request, he accepted the largely honorary post of Chancellor, from which he pledged "to serve the university in a less demanding way," while returning to his first love of "research and scholarship." Belkin was, however, destined to live but another eight months. He died on April 18, 1976.[1]

During the 1975–1976 academic year, the daily life of the university was managed by an Executive Committee for University Affairs composed of the school's four vice presidents as a fifty-member university-wide Presidential Search Committee looked for a successor. In August 1976, the committee announced that Yeshiva had selected one of its own, forty-nine-year-old American-born Dr. Norman Lamm, the 1949 YC valedictorian and a 1951 ordainee of RIETS, as the university's third president.[2]

A self-defined disciple of Rabbis Soloveitchik and Belkin, Lamm was widely seen as one of American Orthodoxy's brightest young men. A philosopher by academic training, the recipient of a Ph.D. from Yeshiva's own Bernard Revel Graduate School, he had already addressed, through his works and writings, many of the almost century-old dilemmas and promises wrought by Orthodoxy's encounter with modern America. He had been the founder and first editor of *Tradition,* an Orthodox philosophical journal, where colleagues and opponents both within and without Yeshiva University addressed many of the issues that had energized and perplexed his community. It was, thus, understood that Lamm would stand foursquare for those teachings most dear to his predecessors.[3]

Dr. Lamm's connections to YU proper were twofold and of no small import. He was the rabbi of the Jewish Center, that leading West Side New York congregation whose leading members from the days of the Lamports, Gottesmans, and Mazers through the era of Max Stern had long backed the school. Not incidentally, he had also

been, fresh out of rabbinical school, an assistant rabbi under Lookstein at Kehilath Jeshurun, Ramaz' old synagogue, another Yeshiva
financial stronghold. Equally important, he had been, for two decades, a professor of philosophy in several of Yeshiva's divisions.

During his relatively brief administration to date, he has occasionally spoken of his continued optimism for the possibility of Orthodoxy living with modernity. A quick perusal of published statements made by Dr. Lamm to Yeshiva rabbis and lay leaders would
find him sounding much like Belkin of the 1950s when he urged
Yeshivamen "to broaden our horizons beyond our immediate needs
and the concerns of our narrow constituency to embrace all of the
Jewish community throughout the world." And he could have been
borrowing a page from Revel's book when he argued that:

> we are committed to secular studies, including all the risks that this
> implies not only because of social and vocational reasons, but be-
> cause we consider that it is the will of God that there would be a
> world in which Torah is effective; that all wisdom issues ultimately
> from the Creator and therefore it is the Almighty who legitimizes all
> knowledge.

It is too early to judge how strongly his voice will be heard within
the American Orthodox seminary and yeshiva that he champions.[4]

It may also be somewhat premature to evaluate how successful Lamm will be seen as manager, executive, and fund-raiser for
the university over which he presides. To be sure, a great part of the
first decade of his leadership has not been devoted to making lofty
philosophical statements but rather to the nitty-gritty work of a contemporary university president at a small liberal arts college and a
professional university during the 1970s and 1980s. He came into
office with Dr. Belkin's last great building project, the Benjamin N.
Cardozo School of Law, off the drawing board but not yet in place.
He would greet the first class at Cardozo just a month after his election to the presidency and describe both himself and the budding
attorneys as Yeshiva's latest newcomers. Over the next ten years, he
would receive with pride reports that Cardozo had received its legal
and state accreditation as it took its place among the city's law schools
and its graduates began to find their way into law firms and the government.[5]

However, at least two other legacies from Belkin's administration were cause for profound sadness, even fear. Historically and economically intertwined, Yeshiva's 1970s–1980s battles over faculty unionization and against financial default received wide-scale publicity and some notoriety. Part of those days of stress was the closing of Belfer in 1977 because, as the University put it, "of increasing ongoing deficits and declining enrollments" and the movement of Wurzweiler for financial reasons from its Greenwich Village home back to Washington Heights, where it had begun. Each move fueled long-existing angers and tensions. Fortunately, said one high Yeshiva administration official in 1985, although "a residue of tension" remains at the school, "the tension is restricted to a small number of people." To be sure, one of the leaders of the Yeshiva Faculty Association did not agree. For him, by that late date, there was rather a more "vulcanized faculty" brought together by an unbent administration. Having asked himself, after a decade or more of struggle, "are things different now?" he replied; "vis-à-vis the administration, no. Vis-à-vis the faculty yes." Clearly, the question of whether the internal fires that spread into the Lamm era have ended or have simply been banked remains to be seen.[6]

What can be said with a certain degree of assurance is that whatever Dr. Lamm and his generation achieve—by 1985 he was already being hailed for his economic revitalization of the school—will be done in an Orthodox Jewish and American world very different from the one his predecessors knew. The rules and tenor of Orthodoxy's encounter with the larger society have changed dramatically in the few years of his administration. It is to this changed relationship that we now turn our attention.

By the mid-1980s one could conclude that Orthodox behavior patterns and social attitudes, if not theological teachings, were tolerated if not approved of more than ever before in American history. Meanwhile, Orthodox Jews in many ways have attempted to achieve a new degree of insularity from the host culture that accepts them. One has only to look at the social-cultural conflict that has occupied us—the relationship between the Orthodox Jews and the citadels of secular learning—to see how much times have changed from Revel's and even Belkin's days, raising in turn new crucial questions about Yeshiva's reasons for existence.

Dr. Revel's Yeshiva College had been born during an era when colleges severely tested the religious loyalties and sensibilities of Orthodox young people. To attend an American college meant encountering a new universe of a different people and of philosophies and sciences that were often inimical to Jewish teachings. Moreover, campuses made no accommodation for the maintenance of religious observances and practices. Orthodox youngsters were seen by sympathetic observers as afflicted by a "mental dualism," on their own for the first time in the foreign world of academe. It took great survival skills—in picking classes, times, and instructors—for young Orthodox Jews to make it in a totally Gentile world while remaining true to their ancestral traditions. During that era Yeshiva was an extraordinarily important collegiate option (see chapter 6).

Dr. Belkin's Yeshiva University evolved during a time when American universities were beginning to put their intolerance toward Jews behind them. For Orthodox Jews, that meant that they seldom had to deal with antagonistic school administrators who had in the past refused to allow student absences to observe the Sabbath or holidays. As we have noted, by the 1950s, at some "Jewish" schools like CCNY, Jewish high holidays were officially days off from college. Elsewhere, school officials looked the other way. At the same time, other vexing social and philosophical problems endured. Orthodox Jews still felt alone, somewhat alienated from, and decidedly non-integrated with, their college community. That isolation began to be mitigated with the growth of Yavneh, the Orthodox Jewish students organization and Young Israel Kosher Kitchens in the 1960s. But they were not comfortably integrated with the ivy-covered world. In addition, there was for some Orthodox students, the issue of confrontation with the new college universe, when those behind the lectern might denigrate their adherence to outdated practices and beliefs. For one or both of these reasons, Yeshiva and Stern Colleges were reassuring alternatives (see chapters 8 and 9).

Today, after a decade of Dr. Lamm's administration, Orthodox students at secular institutions experience no "mental dualism" and may not always face social and philosophical dilemmas. They live in an era when college admission officers not only understand the value of placing the best and brightest on campus regardless of their confession—and Jewish day school students do well on exams—but Deans of Students take pride in the heterogeneity of campus life-styles. In this atmosphere, scheduling problems are a thing of the past. Moreover, in many instances the nature of college curricular regulations have been so changed and liberalized, that Orthodox students who may be troubled by the new universe can work their way around troubling areas. Indeed, in some schools, admissions officers, desirous that yeshiva youngsters enroll, help them overcome such obstacles.

Take, for example, the experiences of a group of Orthodox young women—day school products—who attended Barnard College in the late 1970s. One study has shown how simple it was for them to receive the benefits of a Columbia education while avoiding philosophical pitfalls and social dilemmas. Upon arrival on campus, they made every effort to seek out other Orthodox youths. The omnipresent day school grapevine may have been useful in this regard. Of course, if they had been men, the networking process would have been even easier. The only Jewish women wearing yarmulkes on campus were potential Reform and Conservative rabbinical school students. Still, Hebrew name pendants or mezuzah necklaces proved to be an adequate substitute in finding their sisters.

Their conscious efforts to stay with their own kind were highly successful. In 1977, close to 80 percent of the group reported that "all the people (they) were living with were Jews." Almost all noted that the majority of their friends at college were Jews. Moreover, almost nine out of ten stated that most of their friends were Orthodox Jews. This clustering together, it must be emphasized, reflected not only their desire to be with those who shared their commitments but also their "apprehensions in relating to non-Orthodox students," lest they challenge their religiosity.

To be sure, the moments of tension between them and less religious Jews—and, for that matter, Gentiles—were limited by the Orthodox youngster's relatively low level of participation in general, or even general Jewish, activities on campus. Look, for example, at the life on campus of this typical Orthodox Barnard woman.

This day school graduate spent a year in an Israeli women's yeshiva before going to Barnard. A significant portion of her out-of-classroom time was spent learning in an off-campus Orthodox women's teachers' institute. She and her tightly knit band of Orthodox roommates "rarely mixed with other people." She "seldom attended Jewish events on campus, but did participate in off-campus (Orthodox?) Jewish groups." It may be assumed that when she did participate on campus, it was to attend a traditional Orthodox study group provided by the chaplain's office of Columbia University. Three times a week, a local yeshiva sent in a teacher for collegians. These non-credit courses supplemented the wide range of Jewish studies courses offered by a number of college departments.

Barnard's administration also played no small role in facilitating and maintaining this happy self-isolation. Every year the college's housing authorities set aside a number of dormitory suites for students who maintained Jewish dietary laws. If there were not enough suites to go around, provisions were made to make kosher foods available "along the lines of a college cafeteria." This college, which a generation or so earlier had made life very uncomfortable for all Jewish girls, now asked no hard questions about Jewish holidays. Indeed, one student reported that in a particular class where "there were maybe four or five of us . . . (who) missed about four days because of the holidays, (the professor) would sit down with us each time and give us a makeup lecture."

Equally significant, in this era of heightened sensitivity to traditional religious behavior, few Barnard faculty members made the Orthodox woman's life in the classroom a theological and philosophical trial. Even when professors attacked religion in general, they did so cautiously and with circumspection. One cannot imagine a 1930s Columbia professor saying what a 1970s Orthodox student heard in her philosophy class: "I don't mean to offend anybody and if you want to get up and walk out of the room you can . . . (but) all religion that is based on faith is just humanistic nonsense." And if the students were offended and never wanted to return to that class, there would have been no penalty. Barnard's curriculum did not require that all student take the humanities courses where these troubling issues might be raised.[7]

At New York's City University the ability of Orthodox students, if they desire to attend college without encountering the troubling new universe that higher education once implied, has become part of an unwritten social contract between that area's Orthodox community and City University officials. In an era of declining enrollment, of the flight of white and Jewish middle-class students from the now fully integrated city system, and of the rise of the policy of granting credit for "life experience," school officials anxious to attract Orthodox students have been willing to give college credits for yeshiva studies. It is now possible to fulfill one's humanities distribution at Queens College by applying post-high school Talmud studies to one's transcript. After all, does not the Talmud include philosophical, historical, literary, and linguistic elements? Practically, it means that a Torah Vodaath High School graduate could attend Brooklyn College at night while earning "college credits" by day in his advanced yeshiva, and graduate with his degree, let us say, in computer science and never have to encounter heretical foreign studies. It means that today most students have less practical need than ever to attend Yeshiva College. They can earn the B.A. quicker in Brooklyn than on Washington Heights. The same would also be true for the Talmudical Academy boy who spends his "freshman" year at an Israeli yeshiva and returns with two semesters of "credit" in hand, gaining him advanced credit at a City University branch. Transfer of credits is not as simple at his "home" institution, Yeshiva University, where for ideological and practical reasons more careful distinctions are made between the sacred and the profane. And if pressure is placed on him by parents and friends to continue learning Torah beyond his Israel year, he does not have to do it only at Yeshiva University. He can study days or evenings at a yeshiva while attending Queens College.[8]

A similar relationship between yeshiva and the secular university exists in Baltimore. There students at the Ner Israel Yeshiva have for a number of years received credits at a Catholic college, Loyola of Baltimore. Familiarity with Maimonides earns them philosophy credits, knowledge of responsa counts as history, and their Talmudic studies in general are regarded as theology credits. For those yeshiva students in search of a "secular" degree there is no need to travel to New York.[9]

But generally, Orthodox life away from the metropolis is not so simple, and the policy of exchanging yeshiva for college credit is rare. All students have to face the secular in class. Although scheduling is no longer a problem, isolation and social discomfort often remain. Still, Orthodox Jewish life is increasingly possible on college campuses from coast to coast. Yavneh has its community at some colleges and there are some ninety-eight colleges in twenty-four states (including New York State, but excluding New York City) where kosher meals are readily available to those who want them, in Young Israel and Hillel houses and in cafeterias on campus. Noteworthy in this regard is the presence on the Princeton University campus, since 1971, of "Kosher Stevenson" dining hall, operated at a university until recently notorious for its descrimination and anti-Semitism. Now it has become a popular school for some of the nation's best day school students who can complement their secular studies with a Talmud class or two in their Yavneh House or in neighboring Elizabeth, New Jersey. For them, like their brothers at Yeshiva, it is truly possible to live in two cultures.[10]

For Yeshiva officials, this ever-widening acceptance of the Orthodox Jew on his own terms on the college campus poses a new challenge to their school's mission and survival. Indeed, it might be suggested that if the teachings of cultural pluralism once provided a rationale for YC's coming into existence, that doctrine's wide acceptance today by the secular university might render Yeshiva well-nigh obsolete. If Princeton now accepts the best young Orthodox intellectuals—and enough of them to make them feel at home—challenges their minds to explore new worlds while respecting the will to believe in and practice the old and hallowed, it would seem that the TA and Central Yeshiva's leading youthful lights would not have to look to Yeshiva for advanced training. And if Queens College says, both to the best and to the others of this generation, that a college education is available at low tuition, without requiring the Orthodox youngster to come to grips with secular humanism, students unwilling to confront Yeshiva's commitment to "Torah U' Mada" have now an accommodating option. Morever, if they too can find friends, dates, and colleagues, if not in kosher dining halls at least at a kosher fast-food outlet, then Yeshiva's warm friendship network may also prove to be no real inducement to enroll. It would seem that Yeshiva's constituency is destined to be limited to the chosen few who want the intensity and extensiveness of its Jewish studies programs, apparently the only speciality Yeshiva still has to offer.

And yet Yeshiva's supporters would argue that their school's long-standing approach to comprehending secular culture and integrating it with religious life remains unique and viable. They might agree that today almost everywhere an Orthodox student goes, he can feel at home, and, if he plans well, can be with his friends. Moreover, if he succeeds at Princeton, he can compartmentalize his study of the great books as a discipline apart from his continued learning of the Greatest Book. If Queens is his choice, he can work around the controversial and the study of the new, even as he earns a college diploma. "Only at Yeshiva University," as the contemporary slogan puts it, must an Orthodox student, as Dr. Revel planned, consciously integrate the two worlds, with the holy and secular meeting and influencing each other. The school's supporters are quick to suggest that even beyond what the students learn in their classes, it is their campus' "clean cut," moral, and "bucolic" atmosphere that makes it special. Yeshiva officials are sanguine that illicit drugs and other such social problems are rare at their colleges, making them unique among their neighboring schools. If their system works and their environment can be maintained, it is hoped that Yeshiva men, more than their Princetonian brothers and Queens sisters, are destined to play leading roles in what Dr. Lamm began to call in the early 1980s "Centrist Orthodoxy."[11]

But having said all that, Yeshiva leaders would have to admit that, their faith in Dr. Revel's commitment notwithstanding, at home, within their institutional walls, the debate over whether, and how much of, the secular may be part of a yeshiva remains alive. The school's oldest and most enduring question resurfaced in 1985 when the YC undergraduate student newspaper published a symposium addressing the question of "why do (Yeshivamen) attend college." In proposing the debate, the editor noted that "one might expect that in a university such as ours, where Torah U'Mada is the proclaimed guiding ideal, these issues would be easily resolved. On a practical level, however, Yeshiva's motto does not offer a simple solution to this complex issue." To the surprise of no one who has followed Yeshiva's history during these one hundred years, one American-born Talmudic scholar responded with opinions that were frequently heard before and during Dr. Revel's time but articulated less during Dr. Belkin's. Going to college, "pursuing secular studies for livelihood purposes" is fine, albeit one should be careful that "that pursuit does not engage one in an area where he is exposed to *kephirah* (unbelief)." When problems do arise, one should be certain to work through the issues with one's rabbi. To be sure, he perceived no Torah hierarchy of secular occupations one might consider nor a universally approved date to start seeking a career, so long as one had personal priorities and perspectives in order.

The rabbi also agreed that, in theory, secular sciences could be helpful in advancing one's knowledge of the Torah. The problem with studying sciences or, for that matter, foreign matters in general beyond practical professional objectives, is that rather than being "an aid in developing one's self Jewishly," such study may become "dominant" in one's world outlook. Thus, "to say that the study of Chinese Art will aid one's development is questionable." And to the opinion that "English Literature can help one understand Jewish philosophical ideas better," he responded flatly that that discipline may promote unbelief. And more importantly, its extensive study supposes that it contains great wisdom comparable to that of the Torah. Along these same lines, he made it abundantly clear that the ultimate study of "secular pursuits *lishmah* (for their own sake) is dangerous on many grounds."

At the root of his dissent from the university with which his theological seminary (RIETS) is affilitated was his belief in the ultimate incompatibility of Torah U'Mada. As he saw it, he who studied the secular overmuch or overlong for its own sake involved himself "in two worlds which usually are not complementary . . . leading to "a tremendous philosophical clash." And even if one is able to maintain one's religious posture, the person will still be battered." He foresaw the danger that the student "will lose his religious *weltanschauung* in the process." And what of the "psychological battering" caused by "the constant pull and tension that exists?" To the view that "tension is helpful and productive because it forces one to develop better insights and get keener understandings of things," he submitted that one must never lose sight of "all the dangers that are involved." "Even though sometimes the worlds will not clash, basically they are clashing worlds and this I find highly objectionable."

Practically, all this meant was that in his opinion "Y.C. should focus on the professional areas and on the ways it can be helpful in Torah," while looking upon "the view that the secular should be studied for its own sake" with jaundiced eyes.[12]

Rabbi Moses Weinberger would have agreed fundamentally with these views. He also would have been moved by the miracle that a rabbi born in this ungodly country could articulate sentiments so close to his East European heart. Dr. Lamm undoubtedly was not surprised to read that such opinions exist in his university. He probably harbors the greatest respect for the sincerity and Jewish commitment of the speaker. His dilemma might be described as the problem of convincing those like his Rosh Yeshiva that his university's more accommodating, accepting, and challenging approach to modernity has at least equal legitimacy. And so the dialogue continues!

Notes

1. STUDENTS AT YESHIVA COLLEGE, 1984

1. Yeshiva University, Office of the Executive Vice President. "Why You: Survey of Freshmen and Sophomores at Yeshiva College, May 16, 1984." See also Office of Admissions, Yeshiva College, "Statistics 1981–1985," for information on the geographical distribution and school background of those classes.

2. See, as examples of the abundance of YC-SCW marriages, "Who's Whose," *Comm.*, December 3, 1984, p. 2; April 3, 1985, p. 2.

3. "Yeshiva University President Urges Orthodox Community to Broaden Its Horizons," undated press release, Union of Orthodox Jewish Congregations of America.

4. In the fall of 1984, a similar study entitled "Freshman and Sophomore Survey—Stern College for Women" was conducted at that school. When those data are combined with other Office of Admissions material, it becomes apparent that the Stern College student is not that different in background and orientation from her YC brother. For example, in 1984, among those enrollng somewhat less than one-half came from the tri-state area. Among the boys, a little more than one-half came from the tri-state. As we will see in chapter 10, Stern College always seems to have attracted larger numbers of out-of-New-York-area students than Yeshiva College. The fathers of SCW enrollees, in eight out of ten cases, are college graduates. Mothers have sheepskins in six out of ten cases; both statistics are like those of YC parents. The proportion of SCW students with Yeshiva alumni parents—approximately three out of ten—is similar to that of YC students.

Eight out of ten SCW women have parents who own their own homes, a figure quite comparable to that of YC students. A somewhat higher percentage of Stern women work part-time, less than eight hours a week. It has been suggested that this difference might be due in part to parents placing greater pressure on boys, as opposed to girls, to devote all their time to their books.

Philosophically, close to four out of ten SCW women, approximating YC numbers, were "most positive" or "very positive" toward Yeshiva's approach to Jewish and secular education. Obviously, it is difficult to draw comparisons between YC and SCW when it comes to career goals, since the rabbinate is not an option for SCW people. But as far as teaching and Jewish communal service is concerned, the numbers are still revealing. Eleven percent saw teaching, university teaching included and not differentiating between Jewish and other teaching, as their prime choice. Only 5 percent were looking at Jewish communal work.

5. The major quantitative sources that inform this study—particularly chapters 6, 9, 10, and 12—are the files of some 9,500 students (9,504 to be precise) who attended, from 1928 (the founding date of Yeshiva College) to the present, YC or Stern College for Women and/or its varying Jewish studies divisions exclusively. Some stu-

dents, for example, particularly in the late 1970s, applied to the Jewish Studies Program, renamed in 1965 the James Striar School (JSP) for basic Jewish training after they had completed their undergraduate training with the expectation (in some cases) of going on to RIETS. They did not attend YC.

We examined year by year the age, nativity, and hometown of the students, their parents' occupations, the students' primary and secondary Jewish education, their years of Hebrew training, whether they attended private public school or yeshivas of varying kinds before approaching the campus, their social affiliations and career goals among some thirty or more questions put to their files. The results of our findings are integrated within the discussions in the several chapters and help explain why students have chosen Yeshiva over the last fifty or more years.

There are, however, some limitations to this source material that should be noted immediately. For none of the years under study do we have a complete set of files. Particularly in the early years of YC files were not preserved as well as they would later be. Thus, for example, in 1928 nonquantitative sources indicate that 31 students entered the school's first year. We have complete data on 23 (roughly 75 percent) of that limited early student body. This problem exists to a lesser or greater degree for all subsequent years. Thus, when statements are made about the composition of the student body for any given time period, it is obvious that the findings are on *observable* members of the student body. Of course, in those limited cases where the mathematical equations and logic indicated that the numbers and proportions emerging were inaccurate and misleading, those statistics were simply not used. These sources are designated in the notes as Yeshiva Men and Women (YUMW). The raw data have been stored in perpetuity at the Yeshiva University Computer Center at the Albert Einstein College of Medicine and the printed summaries have been deposited in the Yeshiva University Archive and are available to other scholarly investigations.

In addition to these quantitative sources, the student files for the years 1930–1945 often contain student essays. For one generation, applicants were obliged to write three essays—a writing sample if you will—as part of the admissions process. They discussed why they wanted to attend Yeshiva College, what a typical weekend was like in their home, and their unassigned readings the prior summer. These essays often yield important historical data about the backgrounds and orientations of the students. When quotations are used from these essays, they are noted as "student files" with a number appended. These numbers identify the authors in the registrar's archive while preserving their anonymity. These essays, too, can be examined by simply following the numbering system established in the files. Comparable background information was appended to the files of JSP students (1956 to present) by its late director, Rabbi Morris Besdin. See chapter 9.

2. THE ROOT OF A TRANSPLANTED ORTHODOX COMMUNITY

1. Weinberger's original work "ha-Yehudim veha-Yahadut be-Nuyork" has been translated into English: M. Weinberger, *People Walk on their Heads: Moses Weinberger's "Jews and Judaism in New York"*, Jonathan D. Sarna, tr. (New York: Holmes and Meier, 1982). The following bits of Weinberger's extensive observations are derived from this text.

2. The introductory section to Judah David Willowski's *Sefer Nimukei Ridbaz Perush al ha-Torah* (Chicago: n.p., 1903) addresses many of the same issues which continued to haunt the religious immigrants almost a generation after Weinberger. See also on this subject Aaron Rothkoff, "The American Sojourns of Ridbaz: Religious Problems Within the Immigrant Community," *AJHQ* (June 1968), pp. 557–572.

3. Lillian Wald, *The House on Henry Street* (New York; Holt, 1915), pp. 99 and *passim*; Charles S. Bernheimer, *The Russian Jew in the U.S.* (Philadelphia: Winston, 1905), pp. 186–189, 408; Hutchins Hapgood, *The Spirit of the Ghetto* (New York: 1902; repr. Schocken Books, 1962), pp. 28–29. On the Jewish immigrants attitudes toward the public school, see Diane Ravitch and Ronald H. Goodenow, *Educating an Urban People: The New York City Experience* (New York; Teachers College Press, 1981) and Selma Cantor Berrol, *Immigrants at School: New York City, 1898–1914* (New York: Ayer, 1978). On Jewish problems with the teachings in the public schools, see Leonard Bloom, "A Successful Jewish Boycott of the New York City Public Schools," *AJH* (December 1980); pp. 180–188.

4. Alexander Dushkin, *Jewish Education in New York City* (New York: Bureau of Jewish Education, 1918), particularly pp. 63–99.

5. Weinberger, *People Walk on Their Heads*, p. 39. The term "submerged scholars" was used by Hapgood to describe teachers who labored in the mire of early Jewish education. See Hapgood, *Spirit of the Ghetto*, pp. 55–57. Willowski made the famous "treif land" remark.

6. Weinberger, p. 55. For the description of the school's curriculum see the text of the "Constitution of the Society Machzeki Jesibath Etz Chaiem Organized 5646 (1886)" which appears in Gilbert Klaperman, *The Story of Yeshiva University: The First Jewish University in America* (New York and London: MacMillan, 1969), p. 237. Notice the variant spelling of the institution's name.

7. Stephan F. Blumberg. "Going to America, Going to School: The Immigrant Public School Encounter in Turn-of-the-Century-New York City," *AJA* (November 1984), pp. 114–115.

8. The names of the leaders of Etz Chaim were derived from Klaperman, *Story of Yeshiva University*, p. 21. Klaperman notes that Rothstein was part of both the school and the Chief Rabbi experiment. A comparison of Klaperman's list with names appearing in Abraham J. Karp's important early study "New York Chooses a Chief Rabbi," *AJHQ* (March 1955), pp. 129–198, indicates that the more famous Sarasohn and Eisenstein were also involved in both endeavors. On Eisenstein as the earliest historian of downtown Orthodoxy see his "The History of the First Russian-American Jewish Congregation: The Beth Hamedrash Hagadol," *PAJHS* (1901), pp. 63–74.

9. See Klaperman, *Story of Yeshiva University*, pp. 23–29, for discussions of primitive fund-raising procedures at Etz Chaim. See also the Constitution of Etz Chaim in Klaperman, p. 239, for a description of honors granted benefactors.

10. The rise of a new elite of East European philanthropists within and without the Lower East Side is part of the evolution of the yeshiva. See more on this in chapter 3.

11. Karp, "New York Chooses." pp. 163–164.

12. This estimate of the yeshiva's student body was derived by Klaperman from Eisenstein's article "Yeshibah" in *JE*, 11:600.

13. Leon Stein, P. Conan, and Lynn Davison, trs. *The Education of Abraham Cahan* (Philadelphia: Jewish Publication Society of America, 1969), pp. 371–372. This work is a translation of the first two volumes of Cahan's own Yiddish autobiography, *Bleter fun Mein Leben* (New York: Forward 1926).

14. Stein, Conan, and Davison, pp. 373–374. There was, at least during the year 1896, a second downtown all-day Orthodox Jewish educational institution that devoted little attention to secular educational concerns. Rabbi Moses Weinberger seems to have been the dean of a school called Yeshiva Ohr Torah located at 306 2d Street on the Lower East Side. Reportedly, it was a school with five distinct classes and was home to elementary and advanced students. The goals of the school, besides the bringing of more European learning to these shores, were ultimately to train "rabbis and teachers in Israel." Our one source indicates that some 20 students were enrolled in the advanced class and up to 80 students were in all classes. The curriculum and the assumptions of the school were similar to those of Etz Chaim. Possibly learning from and along with Etz Chaim's example, the society that supported the school, the Hebra Marbezei Torah ve-Yeshivas Ohr Torah, recognized the unavoidable desire of American students to learn about the society around them. Accordingly, they provided exposure to secular subjects so long as these teachings did not conflict with the traditions and obliged the religious heads of the school to make sure that the nonessential secular subjects not become too essential. See, on this ephemeral institution, *Organization and Constitution of the Jewish Rabbinical High School Association* (New York: Held and Kestenbaum 1896), n.p.

15. On the founding of the Rabbi Jacob Joseph School, see Dushkin, *Jewish Education*, pp. 75–77; Ruchama Shain, *All for the Boss* (New York: Feldheim 1984), pp. 47–48; *JF* (1922), 10(10):450.

16. *YT*, November 3, 1904, p. 26; noted in Klaperman, *Story of Yeshiva University*, p. 31.

3. AN EAST EUROPEAN YESHIVA IN AMERICAN SOIL

1. For a brief biographical sketch of Matlin's career, see *Sefer ha-Yovel shel Agudat ha-Rabbanim ha-Orthodoksim de-Artsot ha-Brit ve-Canada* (New York: Arias Press 1928), p. 146. See also Gilbert Klaperman's biographical description in *The Story of Yeshiva University: The First Jewish University in America* (New York and London: Macmillan, 1969), p. 50.

2. *YG*, January 15, 1897, quoted in Klaperman, p. 49. Hayim R. Rabinowitz, "60 Shana le-Shvitot be-Yeshivat Rabbeinu Yitzchok Elchanan," *Hadoar*, June 14, 1968, p. 552.

3. See "Certificate of Incorporation, Rabbi Isaac Elchanan Theological Seminary Association," in Klaperman, pp. 244–245. See also on the earliest raison d'être for RIETS, Jacob I. Hartstein, "A Half-Century of Torah in America," in *Hedenu: Jubilee Publication of the Students of the Rabbi Isaac Elchanan Theological Seminary and Yeshiva College* (New York: RIETS, 1936), pp. 22–23. See below for discussions of the nature of Torah learning in East European yeshivas at this time.

4. See Klaperman, *Story of Yeshiva University*, pp. 56–57, 63, 64, for discussions of the nature of the school in its earliest days. See also Klaperman, pp. 65–69, for discussions of early fund-raising methods.

5. For an organizational account of its founding see *Sefer ha-Yovel*, pp. 13–24. See also my discussion of the Union's founding in "Resisters and Accommodators: Varieties of Orthodox Rabbis in America, 1886–1983," *AJA* (November 1983), pp. 110–111.

6. *AJYB* (1903), p. 160, *YT*, August 28, 1903, p. 2b; August 1, 1904, pp. 5d, 6a, noted in Klaperman, p. 70. See below for more complete discussions of the nature of rabbinic training in Eastern Europe.

7. See "Constitution of the Union of Orthodox Rabbis of America," in Aaron Rakeffet-Rothkoff, *The Silver Era in American Jewish Orthodoxy: Rabbi Eliezer Silver and His Generation* (Jerusalem and New York: 1981), p. 319; Ephraim Lisitzky, *In the Grip of Crosscurrents* (New York: Bloch, Yeshiva University Press/Feldheim 1950), pp. 90–94.

8. Lisitzky, pp. 92–93. On the processes and goals of the yeshiva in Eastern Europe, see Gedalyahu Alon, "The Lithuanian Yeshiva," Sid Z. Leiman, tr. in Judah Goldin, ed., *The Jewish Experience* (New York: Bantam Books 1970), pp. 450–452.

9. See *HS*, January 18, 1901, p. 4; *AH*, February 3, 1901, p. 379; April 5, 1901, p. 596.

10. Lisitzky, *In the Grip*, pp. 91–92.

11. Lisitzky, *In the Grip*, p. 94; Klaperman, *Story of Yeshiva University*, pp. 64, 84–86.

12. Lisitzky, *In the Grip*, p. 94.

13. The student strike manifestos were published in *YT*, January 18, 1906, pp. 4a–6, and *YG*, January 26, 1906; see translation in Klaperman, pp. 95–96.

14. *AH*, January 4, 1901, p. 231; July 8, 1904, p. 204; July 30, 1904, p. 282; Eugene Markovitz, "Henry Pereira Mendes: Architect of the Union of Orthodox Jewish Congregations of America," *AJHQ* (March 1966); pp. 380–381; Gurock, "Resisters and Accommodators, pp. 112, 168.

15. Bernard Drachman, *The Unfailing Light: Memoirs of an American Rabbi* (New York: Rabbinical Council of America, 1948), pp. 152–153, 167, 177; *AH*, June 10, 1908, p. 172.

16. Drachman, pp. 177–182; Gurock, "Resisters and Accommodaters," pp. 100–106, 160–163; Moshe Davis, *The Emergence of Conservative Judaism: The Historical School in 19th Century America* (Philadelphia: Jewish Publication Society of America, 1963); p. 237; Cyrus Adler, "Semi-Centennial Address," in Cyrus Adler, ed., *The Jewish Theological Seminary of America: Semi-Centenniel Volume* (New York: JTS, 1939), pp. 5–7.

17. *AH*, December 6, 1901, p. 118; February 7, 1902, p. 375; May 2, 1902, p. 725; December 25, 1903, p. 205.

18. *AH*, September 30, 1904, p. 516; *HS*, October 7, 1904, p. 7; *AH*, January 16, 1903, p. 295; Karp, "The Conservative Rabbi: 'Dissatisfied but not Unhappy' " *AJA* (November 1983), pp. 203–211.

19. Herbert Parzen, *Architects of Conservative Judaism* (New York: Jonathan David, 1964), pp. 196–198; Klaperman, *Story of Yeshiva University*, pp. 95–96, 102; Rabinowitz, p. 552.

20. For a statistical analysis of the background of the East European leaders in the OU see Gurock, "Why Albert Lucas Did Not Serve in the New York Kehillah," *PAAJR* (1983), 51:55–56; Klaperman, *Story of Yeshiva University*, pp. 58–59.

21. Herbert S. Goldstein, ed., *Forty Years of Struggle for a Principle: The Autobiography of Harry Fischel* (New York: Bloch, 1928), pp. 52–54 and passim.

22. Isaac Unna, "Ezriel (Israel) Hildesheimer," in Leo Jung, ed., *Jewish Leaders 1750–1940*, (New York: Bloch, 1953), pp. 219–227; Samuel K. Mirsky, ed., *Mosdot Torah be-Eiropah be-vinyanam uve-hurbanam* (New York: Egen 1956), pp. 689–713.

23. *AH*, January 4, 1905, p. 235; First Hungarian Congregation Ohab Zedek, *Golden Jubilee Volume* (New York: Congregation Ohab Zedek 1923), passim; Drachman, *The Unfailing Light*, p. 280.

24. *AH*, January 4, 1905, p. 235; *AJYB* (1904–05), p. 152: Zvi Hirsch Masliansky, *Masliansky's Memoirs: Forty Years of Life and Struggle* (New York: Hebrew Publishing Co., 1924), passim; *YT*, May 5, 1904, p. 8; April 4, 1905, p. 8. Though it is true that Solomon Schechter and some of his professors, most notably at that time Louis Ginzburg, were identified with the "Higher Criticism," it remains to be determined to what extent these views were part of the Bible curriculum of the Seminary. On Ginzburg's ideas, see Mel Scult, "Controversial Beginnings: Kaplan's First Congregation," *The Reconstructionist (July/August 1985)*, pp. 23–24.

25. See *EJ*, 11:960, and *AJYB* (1903–1904), p. 79, for basic biographical information on Ramaz. See also Gurock, "Resisters and Accommodators," pp. 121–122.

26. For Ramaz' pulpit career and an in-house look at his relationship with Kaplan pre-1910, see Joseph H. Lookstein, "Seventy-Five Yesteryears: A Historical Sketch of Kehilath Jeshurun," *Congregaton Kehilath Jeshurun, Diamond Jubilee Year Book, 1946* (New York: Congregation Kehilath Jeshurun 1946), pp. 17–26.

27. Klaperman, *Story of Yeshiva University*, pp. 98–99.

28. Rabinowitz, pp. 553–554. See Klaperman, *Story of Yeshiva University*, p. 101, for a text from the *Tageblatt's* coverage of the 1908 strike.

29. *MZ*, May 14, 1908, pp. 1f–g; *YT*, May 13, 1908, p. 1c; noted in Klaperman, p. 107.

30. *AJYB* (1903–04), p. 74; Naomi W. Cohen, *Not Free to Desist: The American Jewish Committee, 1906–1966* (Philadelphia: Jewish Publication Society of America, 1972), p. 563; Alex Goldman, "Bernard L. Levinthal: Nestor of the American Orthodox Rabbinate," in *Giants of Faith: Great American Rabbis* (New York: Citadel, 1964), pp. 160–176. On Levinthal's being RIETS' "Solomon Schechter," see *MZ*, June 24, 1908, p. 1d, noted in Klaperman, *Story of Yeshiva University*, p. 109. See also Klaperman, pp. 102, 107.

31. *Sefer ha-Yovel*, p. 18; *AH*, July 8, 1904, p. 204; Rakeffet-Rothkoff, *The Silver Era*, p. 319; Gurock, "Resisters and Accommodators, pp. 112–114; Klaperman, p. 108.

32. See A. S. Sachs, *Worlds That Passed* (Philadelphia: Ayer, 1928) p. 251; first quoted in Arnold Edward Rothkoff, Vision and Realization: Bernard Revel and His Era" (D.H.L. dissertation, Yeshiva University, 1967), p. 33, for a discussion of the impact of the Haskalah upon the yeshiva world. On Reines' ideas and the yeshiva he created, see Alon, "The Lithuanian Yeshiva," p. 450; Hayyim Z. Reines, "Isaac Jacob Reines," in Jung, ed., *Jewish Leaders*, pp. 279–289. See also William Helmreich, *The World of the Yeshiva* (New York: Free Press, 1982), p. 13.

33. See Gurock, "Resisters and Accomodators," p. 166, for a discussion of

the Agudath ha-Rabbanim's affinity for Mizrachi even as they opposed Americanization.

34. Students left the yeshiva for the Seminary before the 1906 strike, during
that year's altercations, and also in 1908. See, on this phenomenon, Rabinowitz, p.
553; Klaperman, *Story of Yeshiva University*, pp. 89–91, 219. One such 1908 defec-
tor, Solomon Goldman, became an outstanding Conservative Rabbi; Jacob I. Wein-
stein, *Solomon Goldman: A Rabbi's Rabbi* (New York, KTAV 1973), pp. 4–5. On the
state of RIETS facilities, see Ephraim Deinard, *Koheleth Amerika* (St. Louis; Moinester
Printing Co. 1926), p. 3.

35. Drachman, *The Unfailing Light*, pp. 197–200, 252–259. On Schechter's
approach to producing a united American traditional Judaism, see Herbert Rosenblum,
"The Founding of the United Synagogue of America, 1913" (Ph.D. dissertation, Brandeis University, 1971).

36. *YT*, July 11, 1904, p. 8; *AH*, July 1, 1904, p. 180; noted in Klaperman,
Story of Yeshiva University, pp. 70, 220. *Sefer ha-Yovel*, pp. 18, 52a. It is interesting
to note that Levinthal, who proposed the condemnation of the Seminary, had a son
who attended that institution. See chapter 4 for more on that paradox.

37. Rabinowitz, p. 553.

38. Rabinowitz, p. 553–554; *YG*, January 29, 1909, p. 16d; noted in Klaperman, *Story of Yeshiva University*, p. 118.

39. Rabinowtiz, pp. 553–554.

40. Rabinowitz, pp. 553–554.

41. Klaperman, pp. 121, 124–129.

4. BERNARD REVEL AND AN IDENTITY FOR AMERICAN ORTHODOXY

1. *MZ*, June 9, 1912, p. 4e; quoted in Gilbert Klaperman, *The Story of Yeshiva University: The First Jewish University in America* (New York and London: Macmillan, 1969), p. 131.

2. This short description of Revel's early life is derived from Aaron Rothkoff,
Bernard Revel: Builder of American Jewish Orthodoxy (Philadelphia: Jewish Publica-
tion Society of America, 1972), pp. 27–34, which in turn comes from, inter alia, "Rabbi
Dr. Bernard Revel," *Eidenu: Memorial Publication in Honor of Rabbi Dr. Bernard
Revel* (New York; RIETS 1942), pp. 15ff.

3. See Aaron Rothkoff, *Bernard Revel*, pp. 225–241 for a list and discussion
of Revel's contributions to rabbinics.

4. In eulogizing his father, Hirschel Revel offers us the only source on why
Revel joined the Bund. Hirschel Revel suggested that his father's "multi-faceted personality and profound grasp of historical events" led him to contribute to the ideology
of the Bund. See Rothkoff, *Bernard Revel*, p. 33. See also Rothkoff, p. 31, for his
impressions of what Revel studied of the Haskalah while in Europe.

5. See Bernard Revel, "Inquiry in the Source of Karaite Halakah," *JQR* (April
1912), 2(4:) 518–519, for his remarks about Geiger's scholarship as part of his arcane
researches into Karaism. For more on Revel's student academic days, see Aaron Rothkoff, pp. 38–39.

6. For the family tradition about Revel's early married life in the Southwest
as an oil tycoon and independent Jewish scholar, see Aaron Rothkoff pp. 41–42.

7. *YT*, July 13, 1915, p. 7c; quoted in Klaperman, *Story of Yeshiva University*, p. 139. Bernard Revel to David Rackman, March 6, 1908, quoted in Klaperman, p. 140. See also the original Hebrew source in David Rackman, *Kiryat Chana David*, Judah Rubinstein, ed. (New York: n.p., 1967), pp. 244–246.

8. The Revel-Maslinansky correspondence was published in Hayim R. Rabinowitz, "60 Shana le-Shvitot be-Yeshiva Rabbeinu Yitzchok Elchanan," *Hadoar*, June 14, 1968, p. 554.

9. For a brief biography of Levine, see his *Sefer Yad Ha-Levi* (Bridgeport; n.p. 1906), n.p. On Rabbi Aronowitz, see Ben Zion Eisenstadt, *Doros Ha-Aharonim* (New York; A. H. Rosenberg 1913), p. 44. In 1956, Rabbi Gerstenfeld filled out his own "Biographical Record Form" for the Yeshiva University Public Relations Department. Information on Gerstenfeld was derived from that source.

10. Moses Seidel, *Hikre Mikrah* (Jerusalem; Mosad Ha-Rav Kook 1978), p. 7; Abraham Isaac Kook, *Iggerot ha-Re'ayah* (Jerusalem; Mosad Ha-Rav Kook 1943), 131–132.

11. *JE*, 11: 410.

12. *EJ*, 16: 975–976; Zalman Shazar, *Morning Stars* (Philadelphia: Jewish Publication Society of America, 1967), pp. 173–182.

13. *JF*, February 20, 1920, p. 71.

14. Bernard Drachman, *The Unfailing Light: Memoirs of an American Rabbi* (New York: Rabbinical Council of America, 1948), pp. 260–261.

15. Joseph H. Lookstein, "Dr. Revel and the Homiletics," in *Hedenu: Jubilee Publication of the Students of the Rabbi Isaac Elchanan Theological Seminary and Yeshiva College* (New York: RIETS 1936), pp. 61–62.

16. *Alumni Association Talmudical Academy Register* (New York; TA, 1930), passim; *The Rabbi Isaac Elchanan Theological Seminary Register* (New York: RIETS, 1924–25) pp. 11–13.

17. Alvin Irwin Schiff, *The Jewish Day School in America* (New York: Jewish Education Committee of New York, 1966), pp. 33–34.

18. Ira Robinson, "Cyrus Alder, Bernard Revel and the Prehistory of Organized Jewish Scholarship in the United States," *AJH* (June 1980), pp. 497–505.

19. Jacob I. Hartstein, "Dr. Bernard Revel—An Appreciation" in *Eidenu; Memorial Publication in Honor of Rabbi Dr. Bernard Revel* (New York: RIETS 1942), p. 22; Samuel Belkin, "Statement of Appreciation," in *Eidenu*, p. 31.

20. These statistics are derived from *The Rabbinical College of America Register 5678 (1917–1918)*, published in Klaperman, *Story of Yeshiva University*, pp. 262–263.

21. *The Rabbi Isaac Elchanan Theological Seminary Register*, p. 14.

22. Interview with Rabbi David Silver, November 21, 1984. Arnold Rothkoff identified Zeitlin and Seidel as primary objects of rabbinic scorn based upon his interviews with Zeitlin and Mrs. Sarah Revel some twenty years ago. Rothkoff recorded the results of his interview; "Vision and Realization," p. 66. Unfortunately neither the audio tape nor Rothkoff's original notes are extant for detailing the opposition. See Leo Jung, "Bernard Revel," in *Eidenu*, pp. 9–10, for Revel's reaction to these critiques.

23. Aaron Rothkoff, *Bernard Revel*, pp. 138–139.

24. Arnold Rothkoff, "Vision and Realization" pp. 129–133. See also *MZ*,

August 6, 1924, p. 1; H. L. Gordon, "Rabbi Solomon Polachek-Ha-Illui me-Meitshet," *Ha-Doar*, March 5, 1965, pp. 286–287.

25. See Aaron Shurin, *Keshet Giborim* (Jeruselem; Mosad Ha-Rav Kook 1964), pp. 200–206, for a biographical sketch of Moses Soloveitchik. In the interregnum between Polachek's death and Soloveitchik's arrival, RIETS' Talmud department was strengthened by the presence of Rabbi Shimon Shkop, a famous scholar later of the yeshivas in Mir and Volozhin. See Arnold Rothkoff, "Vision and Realization" p. 134–135.

26. For Selig's question and Revel's responsum, see Aaron Rothkoff, pp. 225–226. On sex differentiations at social events in the East European shtetl, see Mark Zborowski and Elizabeth Herzog, *Life Is with People: The Culture of the Shtetl* (New York: Schocken Books, 1962), pp. 136–137.

27. See *Congregation Kehilath Jeshurun Diamond Jubilee, Year Book, 1946* (New York: Congregation Kehilath Jeshurun, 1946) pp. 26–28, 99, for evidence of these interesting lay-rabbinic, rabbinic-rabbinic relationships.

28. Hyamson to Rabbi Isadore Goodman, April 12, 1926; to be found in the Yeshiva University Archive, published in Aaron Rothkoff, *Bernard Revel*, pp. 163–164.

29. See Klaperman, *Story of Yeshiva University*, pp. 70, 122, 220, for Levinthal's critique of JTS and his colleague's response. See also Aaron Rakeffet-Rothkoff, "The Attempt to Merge the Jewish Theological Seminary and Yeshiva College, 1926–27," *Michael: On the History of the Jews in the Diaspora vol. 3* (1975), pp. 256–257. On the senior Levinthal sharing his son's Conservative pulpit, see the recollections of Rabbi Herschel Schacter who witnessed it as a young man; interview with Herschel Schacter, August 27, 1985.

30. Documentary evidence of this merger discussion was published by Rakeffet-Rothkoff in "The Attempt," pp. 254–279.

31. The essay "Seminary and Yeshiva" is a manuscript in the Yeshiva archives, written in the hand of Dr. Revel. It seems clear, as Rothkoff first noted, that this article was designed as an apologia to RIETS board members to set the record straight on the JTS-RIETS issue. See the text of that document in Aaron Rothkoff, *Bernard Revel*, pp. 268–275. Finally, it should be noted that in his earlier treatment of this issue Rothkoff suggested that Louis Marshall supported the merger as a way of stopping RIETS' plans to build what would become Yeshiva College. Though it is true that Marshall opposed Yeshiva College and backed the merger, there is no hard evidence to suggest that scenario. Marshall's involvement against the college clearly postdated the Seminary issue; See Morton Rosenstock, ed., *Louis Marshall: Champion of Jewish Rights* (Detroit; Wayne State University Press, 1965), pp. 888–889.

5. THE TEACHERS INSTITUTE AND THE TRIALS OF ORTHODOX MEN OF HEBREW LETTERS

1. Aaron Rothkoff, *Bernard Revel: Builder of American Jewish Orthodoxy* (Philadelphia, Jewish Publ. Society of America, 1972), pp. 269–271.

2. On the founding of the Mizrachi see Samuel Rosenblatt, *The History of the Mizrachi Movement* (New York: Mizrachi Organization of America 1951), pp. 5–33; Meyer Waxman, *The Mizrachi: Its Aims and Purposes* (New York: Mizrachi Bu-

reau 1916), p. 20–24; Pinkhos Churgin and Leon Gellman, *Mizrachi: Jubilee Publi-cation of the Mizrachi Organization of America (1911–1936)* (New York: n.p. 1936), passim.

3. Jacob Levinson, "On the 25th Anniversary of the Teachers Institute," *The Teachers Institute of Yeshiva College 25th Anniversary* (New York: N. P. 1944), p. 100; *Ha-Ibri,* June 6, 1916, p. 26; quoted in Isidor Margolis, *Jewish Teacher Training Schools in the United States* (New York; National Council for Torah Education, 1964), pp. 138–139.

4. Hyman B. Grinstein, "The History of the Teachers Institute of Yeshiva University," in Moshe Carmilly and Hayim Leaf, eds., *Samuel Belkin Memorial Vol-ume* (New York; 1981), pp. 257–258; Margolis, pp. 139–142.

5. Jacob Kabakoff, "Hebrew Sources of American Jewish History," Bertram W. Korn, ed., *A Bicentennial Festschrift for Jacob Rader Marcus* (Waltham, Mass. and New York: American Jewish Historical Society and KTAV, 1976), pp. 219–235; Mi-chael Gary Brown, "All All Alone: The Hebrew Press in America, 1914–1924," *AJHQ* (December 1969), pp. 139–175; Martin Feinstein, *American Zionism, 1884–1904* (New York: Herzl Press, 1965), p. 23

6. Yizhak Raphael ed. *Entsiklopediyah shel ha-tsiyonut ha-datit* (Jerusalem; Mosad Ha-Rav Kook 1965), 3:147; Grinstein, "History of the Teachers' Institute," p. 257; Macy Nulman, ed., *Concise Encyclopedia of Jewish Music* (New York; McGraw-Hill, 1975), pp. 28–29.

7. *EJ,* 16:368; Leah Mishkin, "The Writings of Dr. Meyer Waxman," in *Sefer ha-Yovel Meir Vaksman* (Chicago and Jerusalem: Ha-Midrasha le-Limudei ha-Yahadut, 1966), pp. 9–11.

8. *Jewish Theological Seminary Student Annual* (1916), 3:192.

9. *Who's Who In American Jewry* (New York: Jewish Biographical Bureau, 1928), p. 773; *Jewish Theological Seminary Student Annual* (1914), 1:54.

10. Meyer Waxman, "Some Recollections on the First Period of the Teach-ers' Institute," *Teachers Institute,* p. 108; Grinstein, "History of the Teachers' Institute," p. 264.

11. On the Kehillah's plans for Jewish education, see Arthur Goren, *New York Jews and the Quest for Community: The Kehillah Experiment 1908–1922* (New York: Columbia University Press, 1970), pp. 96–110. On new elite participation in the educational program see Gurock, "Why Albert Lucas Did Not Serve in the New York Kehillah," *PAAJR,* 51:55–72. On Ramaz and the Kehillah plans see Gurock, "Resisters and Accommodators: Varieties of Orthodox Rabbis in America, 1886–1983," *AJA* (November 1983), pp. 120–124; See also Gurock, *When Harlem Was Jewish, 1870–1930* (New York: Columbia University Press, 1979), pp. 100–109. On Samson Bend-erly and his boys see Nathan H. Winter, *Jewish Education in a Pluralist Society: Sam-son Benderly and Jewish Education in the United States* (New York: New York Uni-versity Press 1966) passim. On JTS and TI comparative approaches see Margolis, p. 74; Grinstein, p. 260.

12. Boza Shahevitch and Menachem Perry, *Sefer ha-Yovel le-Shimon Halkin* (Jerusalem: Alpha Press, 1975), pp. 44–48; *EJ,* 7; 1,191–1,193.

13. An examination of the early careers of the first four years of Talmudical Academy graduates substantiates the fact that Hebrew teaching was not a highly de-sired calling among these students. Of the 72 students then graduated from the Tal-

mudical Academy only 3 were Hebrew school teachers in the mid-1920s. Twenty-one were rabbis, 15 were lawyers, 11 were businessmen, 8 were public school teachers; the four most popular callings. See *Alumni Association Talmudical Academy Register, March 30, 1930,* passim. See also Gilbert Klaperman's transacribed notes of an interview with Pinkhos Churgin conducted by Hyman B. Grinstein, March 25, 1955, hereafter noted as Churgin interview.

14. Churgin interview; interview with Isidor Meyer, October 25, 1984; "List of Graduates," *The Teachers Institute,* p. 13.

15. Norman B. Abrams, "Bet Medrash Le-Morim," *Nir: Student Publication of the Teachers Institute* (New York: Student Organization of the Teachers Institute, 1926), pp. 26–33; Grinstein, "History of the Teachers' Institute,", p. 258; Margolis, *Jewish Teacher Training Schools,* p. 142. The original agreement drafted between Revel and Mizrachi then extant in the Yeshiva University archives is quoted by Arnold Rothkoff, "Vision and Realization-Bernard Revel and His Era," (Ph.D. dissertation, Yeshiva University, 1967); p. 69. According to Churgin in his 1955 interview, Revel had heard of him from articles he had written in the Hebrew and Yiddish press. On Churgin's background see Hayim Leaf, "The Literary and Ideological Activities of Dr. Pinkhos Churgin" (D.H.L. dissertation, Yeshiva University, 1968); see also *EJ,* 5:557. It is not surprising that Berlin found a sympathetic ear in Revel. In 1917 Revel himself convened the first conference of yeshivas in an effort to organize them for the improvement of standards. See *Teachers Institute,* n. p.

16. Churgin interview; Margolis, *Jewish Teacher Training Schools* pp. 149–150; Abrams, "Bet Medrash Le-Morim," pp. 26–33.

17. Arnold Rothkoff, "Vision & Realization" pp. 68–72. Most of the issues discussed by Rothkoff come from the letters and notes between the Tulsa-based Revel and the New York-based Sar.

18. Aaron Rothkoff, *Bernard Revel,* pp. 65–70. The tone of the deputations and the nature of Revel's new agreement with the trustees suggest that Revel left in 1919 and in 1921 not only because of Travis' problems but also because of residual difficulties with trustees unhappy with his rapid reorganization of RIETS. When he returned he was given full power and authority to manage all the affairs of the yeshiva.

19. Interview with Pinkhos Churgin quoted in Sidney Z. Lieberman, "A Historical Study of the Development of the Yeshiva High School Curriculum in New York City" (Ph.D. dissertation, Yeshiva University, 1959), p. 90.

20. Grinstein, "History of the Teachers' Institute," p. 260.

21. Margolis, Jewish Teacher Training Schools, p. 158; Arnold Rothkoff, *Bernard Revel,* p. 70, quotes Churgin from his 1955 interview as saying that in the opinion of some the TI was a "strange branch."

22. On the enrollment criteria, see *The Rabbi Isaac Elchanan Theological Seminary Register,* p. 8; on Samuel Mirsky's background, see Gersion Appel, ed., *Samuel Mirsky Memorial Volume: Studies in Jewish Law, Philosophy, and Literature* (New York and Jerusalem: Ha-Machon le-Mechkar Sura 1970), pp. 287–290. See *Ha-Doar,* May 14, 1954, pp. 528–529, for a biographical sketch of Gandz. For information on Klotz, see Guido Kisch, ed., *Das Breslauer Seminar: Judisch-Theologisches Seminar (Franenckelscher Stiftung) in Breslau, 1854–1938* (Tübingen: J.C.B. Mohr 1963), p. 423. Other staff members new to the yeshiva were Shabbatai Turboff, Abraham Soyer, P. Seidman, and Professor Gilden; see Grinstein, "History," p. 259.

6. THE MEN OF "THE HOUSE OF GOD ON THE HILLTOP"

1. *JF*, June 1925, pp. 241–242; October 1920, p. 357; July 1928, p. 358.

2. On Jews' problems in the public schools, including Christianity in the classroom, see Leonard Bloom, "A Successful Jewish boycott of the New York City Public Schools," *AJH* (December 1980), pp. 180–188. More importantly, see Deborah Dash Moore's "Ethnic Identity in the Neighborhood School," in her *At Home in America: Second Generation New York Jews* (New York: Columbia University Press, 1981), particularly pp. 89–107, for an excellent account of the relationship between immigrant and second-generation Jews and the public schools. Hurwitz and Safir apparently went through the public school system unscathed. In opting for the public schools, it is suggested, general Jewish assumptions applied to them too. On the disinterest American Jews showed toward the yeshivas for their children, see Alvin J. Schiff, *The Jewish Day School in America* (New York: , 1966), p. 35.

3. Harry Fischel once pointed to the dilemma of the poverty of Jewish education among the children of the new Jewish rich. These Jewish patricians apparently did not want their offspring to associate with the poor. See *MZ*, August 11, 1913, p. 5; October 12, 1913, p. 4; and *HS*, October 3, 1913, p. 10; discussed in Gurock, *When Harlem Was Jewish, 1870–1930* (New York: Columbia University Press, 1979), p. 106. Harry Fischel personally could not be accused of declaring yeshivas off limits to his children since he was the father of four daughters and no sons. On Stern College and Jewish women's education, see chapter 10. On the other hand, many of his friends at Kehilath Jeshurun and the Jewish Center sent their children either to Dalton or Fieldston.

4. For names and statistics about the early elementary and secondary yeshivas in America and some information about their educational orientations see Schiff, *The Jewish Day School,* pp. 37–39. See also the essay from student file #2630.

5. *JF*, June 1922, p. 194; May 1928, p. 237.

6. On the Jewish constituency at CCNY, NYU, Hunter, and elsewhere, see *AJYB* (1917–1918), pp. 400–409. On the problems Jews faced at schools other than CCNY and NYU, see the contemporary account, Heywood Broun and George Britt, *Christians Only: A Study in Prejudice* (New York: Da Capo, 1931).

7. A. L. Shands, "The Cheder on the Hill," *The Menorah Journal* (March 1929), pp. 266–267; interview with Jacob I. Hartstein, August 14, 1985.

8. *JF*, June 1928, pp. 291, 294; Jacob I. Hartstein, "A Half-Century of Torah in America," *Hedenu: Jubilee Publication of the Students of the Rabbi Isaac Elchanan Theological Seminary and Yeshiva College* (New York: RIETS, 1936), pp. 26–27; *JF*, August 1932, p. 263; David B. Hollander, "What Does the Yeshiva Mean to Me," *Hedenu*, p. 92.

9. Interview with Israel Upbin, August 7, 1985. See Shands, p. 266, for a discussion of the number of Jewish teachers at CCNY by day as opposed to night school.

10. Interview with Upbin; Shelley Safire to Arnold Rothkoff, see Arnold Rothkoff, "Vision and Realization: Bernard Revel and His Era," (Ph.D. dissertation, Yeshiva University, 1967), p. 94.

11. These statistics were derived from a directory of graduates published by the Talmudical Academy Alumni Association in 1930. It should be noted that for 76 of the 280 graduates there was no mention of their post-high-school affiliations and

activities. Clearly they have to be seen as somewhat apart from their alma mater for the school to know nothing about them. See also *JF*, August 1932, p. 263; Hollander, "What Does the Yeshiva Mean," p. 92.

12. *Alumni Association Talmudical Academy Register*, passim.

13. *Hedenu*, p. 17.

14. For Revel's term "The House of God on the Hilltop," see Aaron Rothkoff, *Bernard Revel: Builder of American Jewish Orthodoxy* (Philadelphia-Jewish Publication Society, 1972), p. 92. On Yeshiva's building plans see "Building Plans for $5,000,000 Yeshiva of America Announced," YPR, 1926. See also *Reform Jewish Advocate*, December 8, 1923.

15. "Former YU English Teacher Recalls Birth of University," *Friends of YU Views and News* (Summer 1985), pp. 4, 8; Arnold Rothkoff, "Vision and Realization" p. 95.

16. *EJ*, 7:582; 9:42.

17. "Appointments to Yeshiva College Faculty Announced," YPR, October 19, 1928. For an example of a faculty letter of inquiry noting personal anti-Semitic encounters, see "Application for Faculty Position, 1925–34," file #8/2 (YA); Nathan Davidson "Enter: The Yeshiva College," YPR, October 19, 1928.

18. On the famous December 1924 fund-raiser, see Aaron Rothkoff, *Bernard Revel*, pp. 74, 76, 77; *New York Times*, December 20, 1924, p. 15. On the context of exclusionary anti-Semitism see Bernard Revel to Samuel Levy, May 1, 1926, in Arnold Rothkoff, "Vision and Realization," p. 93, and comments by YU benefactor Gustavus Rogers, in Arnold Rothkoff, "Vision and Realization," p. 92. Goldstein's remarks were widely reported in the Anglo-Jewish press. See, as an example, *Reform Jewish Advocate*, December 8, 1923, n.p., Reznikoff, p. 893, *The American Israelite*, December 13, 1923, p. 23.

19. On collegiate social anti-Semitism and Anglo-Saxon conformity, see Harold S. Wechsler, *The Qualified Student: A History of Selective College Admission in America* (New York: 1977), and Marcia Graham Synott, *The Half-Opened Door: Discrimination and Admissions at Harvard, Yale, and Princeton* (Westport, Conn.: Greenwood, 1979).

20. Morton Rosenstock, *Louis Marshall: Defender of Jewish Rights*. (Detroit: Wayne State University Press, 1963), pps. 245–255.

21. *JF*, June 1925, pp. 241–242; May 1928, pp. 253–254.

22. Interestingly enough, some funds for Yeshiva filtered in from Reform Jewish circles, causing talmud instructors some discomfort. A question was raised about the propriety of accepting moneys and then rewarding, through elevation to the honorific Board of Trustees, men identified with a movement "destroying what we most desire to maintain." But to the Yeshiva treasurer's dismay, Revel's responsum limiting Board membership to those not affiliated with Reform was then more theoretical than addressing a real situation. Aaron Rothkoff, pp. 226–227.

23. Fifteen of the 23 students identified in 1928 came from the T.A. By 1936, nine years into the school's existence, 155 of 296 students (52.3 percent) were TA graduates. The figures for 1928–1940 are 271 of 557 or 48.7 percent. During Revel's lifetime, the TA constituency dropped only twice to below 40 percent. That low proportion would not occur again until 1956, corresponding possibly to the founding of the JSP. See chapter 9. For the statistics on TA men choosing YC as opposed to other

schools, see *Alumni Association Talmudical Academy Register*. See also interview with Israel Upbin, August 17, 1985.

24. Aaron Rothkoff, *Bernard Revel* p. 81.

25. Student files #257, #389, #584. Of the 557 identified students who attended YC between 1928 and 1940 108 came from these smaller Jewish communities (YUMW).

26. There were some 52—approximately 10 percent of the students—children of *klai kodesh* (religious functionaries) at the Yeshiva during Revel's administration. Many of them from outside the New York area. Add to these numbers the 66 rabbis and 10 Hebrew teacher parents and we have approximately one-fourth of the student body from clerical families. These figures would remain constant until well into the 1950s (YUMW). For statistics on the placement of Agudat ha-Rabbanim functionaries during this time period, see Gurock, "Resisters and Accommodators; Varieties of Orthodox Rabbis in America, 1886–1983," *AJA*, (November 1983), pp. 173–174.

27. Student file #3205. See also S. Joshua Kohn, *The Jewish Community of Utica, 1847–1948* (New York; American Jewish Historical Society, 1959), pp. 57–58, 114–116.

28. Other communities did the same. In 1938, a TI student from Cincinnati was given a scholarship from his local school to attend the TA and ultimately YC. See student files #2705, #2499.

29. Student file #584.

30. Y. S. Soker, "On Hebrew Education in Baltimore," *Sheviley Ha-Hinukh* (February 1926), pp. 82–83; Schiff, *The Jewish Day School*, pp. 41–42.

31. Interview with Israel Miller, August 22, 1985.

32. Nathan H. Winter, *Jewish Education in a Pluralist Society: Samson Benderly and Jewish Education in the United States* (New York: 1966), pp. 112–118, 131–137.

33. One of the instructors at the Pre Eitz Chaim School was a Seminary rabbinical student. Interview with Oscar Fleishaker, August 17, 1985.

34. Helmreich, "Old Wine in New Bottles: Advanced Yeshivot in the United States," *AJH* (December 1979) p. 243.

35. Winter, *Jewish Education*, pp. 162–164, 178–179.

36. As early as the late 1920s, the Seminary's TI program was subdivided among preparatory, academic, and teacher-training departments. All students as freshman and sophomores studied in the preparatory department. These classes were held on Sundays and on weekday evenings. In the junior year those training for teaching posts attended classes in the morning and a program (begun in 1929) which led to a B.S. from Columbia University Teachers' College and a BJP from the Seminary. The majority of TI students—like the YCTI men—who did not plan on teaching careers continued on Sundays and weekday evenings. See Isidor Margolis, *Jewish Teacher Training Schools in the United States* (New York: National Council for Torah Education, 1964), pp. 88, 89, 102; Winter, p. 179.

37. Student file #252.

38. Hyman B. Grinstein, "The History of the Teachers' Institute of Yeshiva University," in Moshe Carmilly and Haylm Leaf, eds., *Samuel Belkin Memorial Volume* (New York: Erna Michael College, Yeshiva University 1981), p. 260.

39. Of the 528 students on whom we have information about their years of

Hebrew training between 1928 and 1940, some 384 had 10–12 years of training, 121 went to Hebrew schools for 7–9 years, 20 had 4–6 years of training, and only one entered with less than 3 years of Jewish education and two came in with more than 12 years of training (YUMW).

40. Winter, *Jewish Education*, pp. 124–129; Moore, "Ethnic Identity," pp. 89–122.

41. Student files #190, #211, #375, #526

42. See, for example, student files #2643, #2632.

43. Moses I. Shulman, "The Yeshivah Etz Hayim Hebrew Institute of Boro Park," *Jewish Education* (Fall 1948), pp. 47–48; Noah Nardi, "A Survey of Jewish Day Schools in America," *Jewish Education* (September 1944), pp. 22–25; Schiff, *Jewish Day School*, pp. 40, 75.

44. Shulman, p. 47; Nardi, p. 24; interview with Jacob I. Hartstein, August 27, 1985.

45. Nardi, p. 25. On the growth of a uniquely American form of Zionism before and during this period see Melvin I. Urofsky, *American Zionism from Herzl to the Holocaust* (Garden City, N.Y.: Doubleday, 1975), and Yonathan Shapiro, *Leadership of American Zionist Organization, 1897–1930* (Urbana; University of Illinois Press, 1971). These works survey national trends. Clearly more needs to be known about the local community's response. In any event, to the extent that Zionism flourished in the 1920s and 1930s, Brooklyn was a hotbed of activity.

46. Interview with Hyman Pomerantz, August 30, 1985. Afternoon yeshiva-style classes for Brooklyn public high school boys were also held at the Yeshiva of Bensonhurst and the Yeshiva of Crown Heights in addition to Etz Chaim and Flatbush. It also should be noted that the Seminary, as early as the 1930s, ran afternoon high school classes attracting some of these students, facilitating their move into that institution of higher Jewish learning. Thus you could have a student with a resumé of day school, public high school, high school classes at the Seminary, CCNY, and Seminary TI college classes. Classmates with more secularized Jewish cultural horizons could have looked to the Herzliah Teachers Institute for high level supplementary Jewish education as they attended public school. Some of the Herzeliah boys moved on to the Seminary, others came to Yeshiva. It also should be noted here that numbers of Yeshiva TI men from out of town came through Jewish teacher training institute high school classes in other cities. Philadelphia's Gratz College and Boston's Hebrew Teachers College were but two of these schools which led young men to the New York higher institutions during interwar days. See, Margolis, *Jewish Teacher Training Schools in the United States* (New York: National Council for Torah Education, 1969), pp. 6–53, 189–239, 242–262.

47. Interview with Moses Feuerstein, November 7, 1985; Joseph Kaminetsky, October 29, 1985; Israel Miller, August 22, 1985. It should also be noted that the practice of removing one's yarmulke and wearing no hat after leaving Yeshiva's precincts was not limited to TI fellows; interview with Benjamin Kreitman, October 24, 1985.

48. Interview with Israel Miller, August 22, 1985; Jacob I. Hartstein, August 14, 1985; Moses Feuerstein, November 7, 1985.

49. See discussion in chapter 5 *Sefer Kenesseth Ha-Rabbanim* (New York: Dov Aryeh Switer, 1924), 2:44–45.

50. During the first eight years of YC's existence, some 37 students (or 12.5 percent of the student body) came from secondary yeshivas other than the TA. The figures for 1928–1940 are 97 students out of 557 or 17.4 percent from other yeshivas. Most of the students were Brooklyn-born and raised, but some came from out of town to the Brooklyn Mesivta. Thus, the student body of YC during these dozen years may be broken down in the following way: 48 percent came from the TA, 17 percent came from other yeshivas, and 33 percent came from public high schools; the remaining 2–3 percent came either directly from Europe or some other geographical or ideological direction (YUMW).

51. Sidney Z. Lieberman, "A Historical Study of the Yeshiva High School Curriculum in New York City," Ph.D. dissertation, Yeshiva University, 1959, pp. 80–81; Schiff, *The Jewish Day School*, pp. 40–41; William Helmreich, *The World of Yeshiva: An Intimate Portrait of Orthodox Jewry* (New York: Free Press, 1982), pp. 26ff; Sylvia Fuchs, "And Now a Word from *Our* Fathers," *Jewish Observer* (January 1978), pp. 18–20.

52. Alexander Gross and Joseph Kaminetsky, "Shraga Feivel Mendlowitz," in Leo Jung, ed., *Men of the Spirit* (New York: Feldheim, 1964), pp. 557–563; George Kranzler, *Williamsburg: A Jewish Community in Transition* (New York: Feldheim 1961), pp. 16–18.

53. Kranzler, pp. 142–143; Fuchs, "And Now a Word," pp. 18–20.

54. Helmreich, *The Word* pp. 26 ff; interview with Herschel Schacter, August 27, 1985. Early in its history, for at least a number of years, Torah Vodaath students attended TA's secular classes in the afternoons. They simply took the subway from Williamsburg to the Lower East Side. One student from those days suggested that Revel pressured these boys to transfer to his yeshiva. Interview with Joseph Kaminetsky, October 29, 1985; Moses Fensterheim, November 10, 1985.

55. Lieberman, "A Historical Study," p. 250; Kranzler, *Williamsburg*, pp. 213–219; interview with Moses Fensterheim, November 10, 1985.

56. Interview with Herschel Schacter and Morris Charner, September 23, 1985. Charner was a student at the Yeshiva Chofetz Chaim during the 1930s and attended CCNY at night. Chofetz Chaim, which in reality was a breakaway yeshiva from Torah Vodaath, is not discussed in detail here because our statistics indicate that no students from that school went on to YC. However, that school's opinion about YC is valuable to our study.

57. Interview with Morris Charner, September 23, 1985.

58. Helmreich, "Old Wine," pp. 30–31; Schiff, *The Jewish Day School*, pp. 46, 53.

59. Helmreich, p. 27.

60. Interview with Herschel Schacter, student file #2049

61. Student file #3112

62. Nineteen of the 557 entering YC in Revel's era fit that category. See also Leon Stitskin, "Dr. Samuel Belkin as Scholar and Educator," in Leon Stitskin, ed., *Studies in Judaica in Honor of Dr. Samuel Belkin as Scholar and Educator,* (New York: Ktav, 1974), pp. 3–18, and Hayim Leaf, "Dr. Samuel Belkin: Scholar, Educator and Community Leader" (Hebrew), in *Samuel Belkin Memorial Volume* Moshe Carmilly and Hayim Leaf, eds. (New York: Erna Michael College, Yeshiva University 1981), pp. ix–xx.

63. Interviews with Jacob I. Hartstein, August 22, 1985; Joseph Kaminetsky, October 29, 1985. Kaminetsky recalled that he "tutored" the renowned talmudist Rabbi Chaim Zimmerman when this "illui" came from Russia. Kaminetsky also noted that a number of men destined to play important roles in Orthodoxy, which questioned the assumptions of Yeshiva, began their American careers on Washington Heights; among them were Rabbi Mordecai Gifter of the Telshe Yeshiva transplant in America, Rabbi Nosson Wachtfogel of Lakewood, and Rabbi Avigdor Miller.

64. Interview with Israel Miller, August 22, 1985.

65. From 1932–1935, more than 70 percent of YC students came from the Bronx, Manhattan, and Brooklyn. In 1935, 41.2 percent of the students came from Brooklyn alone (YUMW).

66. January 10, 1913, p. 303; *HS*, January 12, 1913, p. 9; *MZ*, January 10, 1913, p. 4; *HS*, September 29, 1929, p. 11; January 18, 1918, p. 9; *Young Israel: Its Aims and Activities* (New York; 1935?).

67. Interview with Hyman Pomerantz, August 30, 1985; Kranzler, *Williamsburg*, p. 167.

68. Student file #2049. At least 90 out of the 557 students enrolling at YC during the Revel years were self-designating Young Israelites (YUMW).

69. Student file #2493; interview with Eugene Nelson, August 27, 1985.

70. Ninety-seven students, mostly New Yorkers, were Mizrachiites, a figure similar to that of the Young Israel constituency. Many belonged to both organizations (YUMW).

71. On Mizrachi activities in Brooklyn during that time see Kranzler, *Williamsburg*, p. 169. On Mizrachi ideology, see Pinchos Churgin and Leon Gellman, *The Mizrachi: Its Aims and Purposes* (New York: 1916), pp. 3–17, and S. Y. Yavetz, "The Goals of the Movement" (Hebrew), in Y. L. Fishman, ed., *Sefer ha-Mizrachi* (Jerusalem: 1946), pp. 182–193.

72. See, as examples of student concern over Yeshiva's religiosity, *Comm.*, April 8, 1935, p. 1; May 20, 1935, pp. 1–2; May 6, 1935, pp. 1–2. This issue was raised during deliberations over Revel's successor. See chapter 7.

73. A very incomplete list of defectors from Yeshiva College during Revel's day who were destined to play major roles in the more liberal expressions of Judaism would include Alvin Reines, Benjamin Kreitman, Robert Gordis, Eugene Mihaly, Israel Moshowitz, Simon Noveck, Meyer Abramowitz, and Sidney Greenberg.

7. INTERREGNUM

1. *Eidenu, Memorial Publication in Honor of Rabbi Dr. Bernard Revel* (New York: RIETS 1942), pp. 3–4.

2. In 1917–18, the *Rabbinical College of America Register* listed 17 alumni of that institution. The 1924–25 RIETS *Register* counts 33 graduates since "the reorganized Seminary" came into existence. Of the 17 pre-1918 alumni, 7 were noted as having positions in New York or Brooklyn synagogues or schools. Four others found pulpits in the Baltimore-Boston areas and an additional 3 resided in western Pennsylvania or upper New York State. Omaha, Seattle, and Canton were home to the remaining 3 rabbis. Of the 33 pre-1925 graduates, 24 found jobs in New York-Brooklyn synagogues and schools. The Baltimore-Boston axis attracted 2 others and western

Pennsylvania and upstate New York became home for 4 others. The remaining 3 rabbis lived in Savannah, Georgia; Omaha, Nebraska; and Ottawa, Canada.

3. Aaron Rakeffet-Rothkoff, *The Silver Era in American Jewish Orthodoxy: Rabbi Eliezer Silver and His Generation* (Jerusalem and New York: Yeshiva University Press Feldheim Publ., 1981), pp. 107, 171.

4. Gurock, "Resisters and Accommodators; Varieties of Orthodox Rabbis in America, 1866–1983," *AJA* (November 1983), p. 141.

5. Rakeffet-Rothkoff, *The Silver Era*, pp. 105–06.

6. Aaron Rothkoff, *Bernard Revel: Builder of American Jewish Orthodoxy* (Philadelphia: Jewish Publication Society, 1972) p. 169.

7. Aaron Rothkoff, *Bernard Revel* pp. 166–178. On the Agudat ha-Rabbanim's problems with the height of *mechitzas* versus Revel's concerns with losing congregations to the Conservatives, see Rakeffet-Rothkoff, *The Silver Era,* pp. 105–107.

8. Gurock, "Resisters and Accommodators," pp. 37–142.

9. "Rabbinical Association of Yeshiva" (circa March 29, 1932), "Records," 8/2, "Application for Faculty" (YA). Interview with David Finkelstein, November 7, 1985.

10. Gilbert Klaperman, *The Story of Yeshiva University: The First Jewish University in America* (New York and London: Macmillan, 1969), p. 168, Aaron Rothkoff, *Bernard Revel,* p. 191.

11. Klaperman, *The Story of Yeshiva University,* p. 168; interview with Klaperman, August 13, 1985.

12. YUMW.

13. Shelly Safir to parent of YC student (1935), student file #2475

14. Shelly Safir to parent of YC student (1935), student file #2475; Aaron Rothkoff, *Bernard Revel* pp. 140–142.

15. Interview with Morris Charner, September 23, 1985; Aaron Rothkoff, *Bernard Revel,* pp. 139, 154–157.

16. *Eidenu,* pp. 3–4

17. The Agudat ha-Rabbanim's move on Yeshiva was part of a five-year program to limit the influence of the RCA rabbis and their modernist tendencies. See also interview with Joseph H. Lookstein and Alexander Rosenberg, referred to by Louis Bernstein in *Challenge and Mission: The Emergence of the English-Speaking Orthodox Rabbinate* (New York: Shengold, 1982), p. 11. See also Rakeffet-Rothkoff, *The Silver Era,* pp. 263–266.

18. The tendency to move may have reflected personal ambition, the better organization and financial picture on Morningside Heights, or personal theological affinity for Conservatism or a combination of these factors. In any event, of the 69 Rabbis ordained by JTS between 1940 and 1944, 19 (27.5 percent) were YC men. Six of the 13 men who were ordained in 1942 (almost 50 percent) were from Yeshiva; the highest percentage during those years. See interview with Benjamin Kreitman. For these statistics, see *The Jewish Theological Seminary Register,* 1939–40, 1940–41, 1942–43, 1943–44, 1944–45.

19. RIETS-YC Bd., February 25, 1941 (*JHLP*).

20. I. Wohlgelernter, "Ha-Rav Hayim Heller . . ." *Ha-Pardes* (May 1930), p. 26; Oscar Z. Rand, *Toldot Anshe Shem* (New York: Chevrat Toldot Anshe Shem, 1950), 1:36–38; Hillel Seidman, "R' Hayim Heller" in Shimon Federbush, *Hochkmat*

Yisrael be-Ma'arev Eropah (Jerusalem: M. Neiman 1963), pp. 101–102; Klaperman, *Story of Yeshiva University*, p. 152.

21. For close to ten years Heller taught in New York while occasionally traveling to Berlin and elsewhere before settling in the United States.

22. RIETS-YC Bd., February 25, 1941 *(JHLP)*.

23. RIETS-YC Bd., March 27, 1941 *(JHLP)*; Aaron Lichtenstein, "R. Joseph Soloveitchik," in Simon Noveck, ed. and introd. *Great Jewish Thinkers of the Twentieth Century* (Clinton, Mass.: Talpinger, 1963), pp. 282–285.

24. RIETS-YC Bd., February 25, 1941, March 27, 1941, Rakeffet-Rothkoff, *The Silver Era*, pp. 267–272.

25. RIETS-YC Bd. March 27, 1941; April 23, 1941 *(JHLP)*.

26. Lichtenstein, "Soloveitchik," pp. 282.

27. Bernstein, *Challenge and Mission*, pp. 49, 59, and passim. See also Dr. Soloveitchik's influence evaluated in Gurock, "Resisters and Accommodators," pp. 143–146.

28. RIETS-YC Bd., June 26, 1941 *(JHLP)*.

29. *Ibid.*

30. RIETS-YC Bd., June 26, 1941 *(JHLP)*; "Report of the Executive Board of the Yeshiva and Yeshiva College and Recommendations for Action by the Board of Directors of the Yeshiva and Yeshiva College, October 1941 *(JHLP)*; "Copy of Report read by Rabbi Lookstein for Executive Board" *(JHLP)*.

31. RIETS-YC Bd., April 23, 1941 *(JHLP)*; *JF*, January 1941, p. 2; interview with Moses Feuerstein; copy of report read by Rabbi Lookstein for the Executive Board, June 24, 1943 *(JHLP)*; RIETS-YC Bd. June 24, 1943 *(JHLP)*.

32. Copy of report read by Rabbi Lookstein, June 24, 1943.

33. Interview with Max J. Etra, October 22, 1985.

34. Interview with Max J. Etra, October 22, 1985, and with Moses Feuerstein, November 7, 1985. On Jung's activities within and on behalf of Yeshiva, see his autobiography, *The Path of a Pioneer: The Autobiography of Leo Jung* (London and New York: Soncino Press 1980), pp. 105–123. For more on Jung's Yeshiva connections, see interview with Leo Jung.

35. RIETS-YC Bd., June 24, 1943 *(JHLP)*; interview with Max J. Etra, October 22, 1985.

36. RIETS-YC Bd., June 24, 1943 *(JHLP)*.

37. Alumni Association discontent with the election process was expressed in a "Memorandum to the Board of Directors of Yeshiva and Yeshiva College from the Executive Board of the Yeshiva College Alumni Association, June ?, 1943" *(JHLP)*.

38. Interview with Moses Feuerstein, November 7, 1985; Joseph Kaminetsky, October 29, 1985.

39. RIETS-YC Bd., June 24, 1943 *(JHLP)*.

8. SAMUEL BELKIN AND THE MISSION OF AN AMERICAN JEWISH UNIVERSITY

1. See chapters 5 and 7; "Yeshiva Synagogue Council," YPR, March 5, 1945; *OU*, August 1933, p. 5; December 1933, p. 6; July 1937, p. 2; December 1942, p. 5.

2. *JF*, September 1935, p. 223, *OU*, April 1943, p. 5; February 1945, p. 11.

3. Gurock, "The Winnowing of American Orthodoxy," *Approaches to Modern Judaism* (1984), 2:41–54.

4. Marshall Sklare and Joseph Greenblum, *Jewish Identity on the Suburban Frontier: A Study of Group Survival in an Open Society* (2d ed.; Chicago: University of Chicago Press, 1979). On the general nature of suburban living see Herbert J. Gans, *The Levittowners: Ways of Life and Politics in a New Suburban Community* (New York: Columbia University Press, 1982); and Kenneth T. Jackson's recent *The Crabgrass Frontier: The Suburbanization of the United States* (New York: Oxford University Press, 1985).

5. Nathan C. Belth, Harold Braverman, and Morton Puner, eds., *Barriers: Patterns of Discrimination Against Jews* (New York: Friendly House, 1958), charts the decline of social anti-Semitism in the immediate post-World War II decade.

6. Marshall Sklare, *Conservative Judaism: An American Religious Movement* (New York: Irvington, 1982), pp. 15–82.

7. Sefton Temkin, "A Century of Reform Judaism in America," *AJYB* (1973), pp. 59–62; Lawrence Siegel, "Reflections on Neo-Reform in the Central Conference of American Rabbis," *AJA* (April 1968), pp. 63–84.

8. "Community Service Bureau," YUPR, December 24, 1944; interview with Victor Geller, December 30, 1985. The growth of the Bureau and its ultimate emergence as a division in 1954 went through a number of phases. These phases were related to the changing relationship between Yeshiva and the Orthodox Union and the attempt of Belkin to project the university as the spokesman for American Orthodoxy.

9. Interview with Victor Geller, December 30, 1985.

10. Sklare, *Conservative Judaism*, pp. 83–129.

11. Interview with Abraham Stern, December 24, 1985.

12. Interview with Victor Geller, December 30, 1985. For a thoughtful defense of Orthodox practice during this era by a future president of Yeshiva University, see Norman Lamm, "Separate Pews in the Synagogue: A Social and Psychological Approach," *Tradition* (Spring 1959), pp. 1–2.

13. Interview with Victor Geller, December 30, 1985. Division people were most distressed with the RIETS graduates who went over to the Conservative Rabbinical Assembly in the 1950s and then brought their synagogues with them into the liberal orbit. This practice of finishing at Yeshiva, gaining ordination, and then going over to the Conservatives continued into the 1960s.

14. *Hazedek,* (April 1945), 2(1):9.

15. "Dr. Samuel Belkin Discloses Plan to Make Yeshiva a University," YPR, May 7, 1945; "Yeshiva University to Open New School of Education and Community Administration in September, 1948," YUPR, January 14, 1948.

16. Walter A. Lurie, "Present Programs of Training for Jewish Communal Service," *Jewish Social Service Quarterly* (September 1949), pp. 131–141.

17. "Yeshiva Now a University," YUPR, December 3, 1945.

18. Solomon H. Green and Eli S. Levy, "Ethnicity and the Social Work Curriculum: Professional Education for Jewish Communal Service," *JSWF* (Spring 1977), pp. 6–7.

19. Morton I. Teicher, "The Wurzweiler School of Social Work: An Historical Overview," *JSWF* (Spring 1975), pp. 1–2; interview with Solomon Green, December 24, 1985.

20. "Yeshiva University Establishes Two New Graduate Schools," YUPR, July 29, 1957.

21. Teicher, "The Wurzweiler School," p. 1

22. Charles Levy, "The Special Purpose of the Jewish School of Social Work," JSWF (Fall 1963), pp. 7–14; Norman Linzer, "The Jewish Dimension of the Wurzweiler School of Social Work," in "Appendixes to a Self-Study Report" (typescript, Wurzweiler School of Social Work), Spring 1979, pp. 9–11; Green and Levy, "Ethnicity and the Social Work Curriculum," pp. 1–9.

23. Linzer, "The Jewish Dimension," p. 14.

24. School of Social Work, Yeshiva University, "Application for Reaffirmation of Original Accreditation," May 1, 1962, pp. 14–15.

25. JF, August 1930, p. 282.

26. Frank Kingdon, "Discrimination in Medical Colleges," American Mercury, October 1945, pp. 391–395.

27. Kingdon, p. 393; Lawrence Bloomingdale, "Medical School Quotas and National Health," Commentary (January 1953), pp. 30–31; YUMW.

28. Bloomingdale, p. 31; Kingdon, p. 394.

29. "Doctors Dilemma," Newsweek, January 23, 1950, p. 76.

30. Walter R. Hart, "Anti-Semitism in New York Medical Schools," American Mercury, July 1947, pp. 55–63.

31. "Discrimination in Colleges," American Mercury, March 1946, pp. 380–381.

32. Hart, pp. 53–63; "Discrimination in Medical Colleges," American Mercury, December 1945, pp. 758–759; "The Open Forum," American Mercury, January 1946, p. 124.

33. Elihu Katz, "A Medical School Under Jewish Auspices," YUPR, September 13, 1948, pp. 104.

34. "The Open Forum," American Mercury, January 1946, p. 124; "Medical School Proposed at Yeshiva," YUPR, November 22, 1948.

35. Katz, "A Medical School Under Jewish Auspices," pp. 1–4; and "A Medical School at Yeshiva," YUPR [1951?].

36. Tina Levitan, "The Albert Einstein College of Medicine," JF, September 1956, p. 118.

37. "Yeshiva Frosh Favor Science 3 to 1," YUPR, February 2, 1958; "Report on Majors," YUPR, May 5, 1954; April 10, 1955.

9. THE RETURN TO TRADITION, 1950s STYLE

1. During the first decade of Belkin's administration, the percentage of students entering the school with between ten and twelve years of Jewish training ranged from 77 percent to 93 percent, with only two years witnessing the percentage dipping to under 80 percent. During the 1930s the range of this elite group was between 66 percent and 80 percent of the student body. These statistics and those appearing in the text are derived from YUMW.

2. During the years 1945–1950, the percentage of students in YC from yeshivas other than the Talmudical Academy and its brother school, the Brooklyn Talmudical Academy (BTA) established in 1945, ranged from 27 percent to 39 percent. In the

next decade the percentage would range from between 15 percent and 34 percent of the student body (YUMW).

3. On the history of the transplantation of Telshe and the organization of Ner Israel, see Chaim Dov Keller's hagiographical sketch of Rabbi Bloch, "He Brought Telshe to Cleveland," in Nisson Wolpin, ed., *The Torah World: A Treasury of Biographical Sketches* (New York: Mesorah Publications 1982), pp. 262–276, and William Helmreich, *The World of Yeshiva, An Intimate Portrait of Orthodox Jewry* (New York: Free Press, 1982), p. 33. To be sure, there were other yeshivas of these types established in the 1940–1955 period. But schools like the Beth Medrash Govoha of Lakewood (1943), Brooklyn's Mirrer Yeshiva (1946), or the Talmudical Academy of Philadelphia either did not operate high schools in this early period or their youngsters did not defect to Yeshiva University. For more on the history of the growth of these advanced level yeshivas, see Helreich, pp. 37–49, and Alvin J. Schiff, *The Jewish Day School in America* (New York: Jewish Education Committee of New York, 1966), p. 147. See also Charles S. Liebman, "Orthodoxy in American Jewish Life," *AJYB* (1965), PP. 93–99.

4. Interview with Shulamith K. Goldstein, January 28, 1986.

5. See Schiff, *The Jewish Day School*, pp. 58–59, on the growth of the Yeshiva Rabbi Jacob Joseph. On Dr. Lamm's background, see "Norman Lamm," *Current Biography* (1978), pp. 27–30. It should be noted that in 1946 Torah Vodaath and Chaim Berlin attempted to deal with the problem of their boys going to Brooklyn College and Yeshiva College by making plans to establish their own American Hebrew Theological University. The school never did open and, as Helmreich points out, "quite a few students from the Brooklyn school attended the Manhattan school" (*The World of the Yeshiva*, pp. 47–50).

6. YUMW. Interestingly enough, Yeshiva never did attract many students from its Washington Heights neighboring community, the Breuer group, which came to the United States during and after World War II. See Liebman, "Orthodoxy," p. 71.

7. See an undated letter to the Yeshiva registrar which seems to have been written in 1948 in student file #1497 (YUMW). On Rabbi Lifshitz, see Noah Goldstein, "Ha Rav Dovid Lifshitz, Shlita," in the RIETS Rabbinical Alumni *Chavrusa* (April 1982), p. 4.

8. Between 1940 and 1955, the percentage range of TI to RIETS students was between 35 percent and 51 percent of the total student body. Most years, the percentage was around 44 percent (YUMW). On the perception of TI students as "bums" in the 1950s, see *JF*, January 1954, p. 2, and telephone interview with Shulamith Goldstein and Joel Rosenshein, January 27, 1986.

9. On the socioreligious character of the communal talmud torah constituency in the 1920s and 1930s, see Judah Pilch, "From the Early Forties to the Mid-Sixties," in Judah Pilch, ed., *A History of Jewish Education in America* (New York: American Association for Jewish Education, 1969), pp. 128–129, 131. See also the discussions in chapter 6 and in Gurock, "The Winnowing of American Orthodoxy," *Approaches to Modern Judaism* (1984), 2:41–54.

10. Pilch, pp. 122, 128–129.

11. C. Morris Horowitz and Lawrence J. Kaplan, *The Estimated Jewish Population of the New York Area, 1900–1975* (New York: Federation of Jewish Philanthropies of New York, 1975), pp. 1–25.

12. Doniel Zvi Kramer, *The Day Schools and Torah Umesorah* (New York: Yeshiva University Press, 1984), pp. 17–24. See also Schiff, *The Jewish Day School,* pp. 75–85, and Pilch, pp. 140–143.

13. Kramer, p. 38. See also *Directory of Day Schools in the United States and Canada* (New York: Torah Umesorah, National Society for Hebrew Day Schools, 1981–1983), passim.

14. One indication of the late arrival of *shomer shabbos* Jews in suburbia is the date of the establishment of suburban day schools. Schiff, in *The Jewish Day School,* shows that the first date for such a day school is 1951. He points out that there was a seven-fold increase in such enrollments between 1951–1964. But as late as 1964, only 8.3 percent of all day school children were attending schools in suburbia.

15. Pilch, "From the Early Forties," pp. 121–122, 128–131.

16. Pilch, "From the Early Forties," p. 121. Will Herberg, *Protestant-Catholic-Jew* (Garden City, N.Y.: Doubleday, 1955), pp. 192–193.

17. On the history of Hillel, see Deborah Dash Moore, *B'nai B'rith and the Challenge of Ethnic Leadership* (Albany, N.Y.: SUNY, 1981), pp. 135–151, and Harry Kaplan, "The B'nai B'rith Hillel Foundations—A Survey of the First Quarter of a Century," in *The Central Conference of American Rabbis 59th Annual Convention* (1949), pp. 231–237. On the founding of Brandeis and its orientation as a Jewish-funded university but not a "Jewish university," see Abram Leon Sachar, *A Host at Last* (Boston and Toronto: Little, Brown, 1976), pp. 243–258. It was not always easy to be an Orthodox Jew on the Brandeis campus. In June 1950, commencement exercises at Brandeis were held on the Sabbath. The *Jewish Forum* excoriated "Brandeis University (as) Neither Jewish nor American." See *JF,* July 1950, p. 120.

18. On Yavneh's organization and early constituency see Liebman, "Orthodoxy," p. 57. See also the typescript "News from the National Council of Young Israel," January 23, 1986, which notes the thirtieth anniversary of the founding of the Cornell Kosher Dining Club.

19. *Ha-Melitz,* March 1, 1956, pp. 1–4. It has been suggested that not only was YC's constituency then homogeneous, but that it was also one with limited growth potential. One of the supposed reasons for the new program was to broaden the numerical and financial basis of the then still small yeshiva. See interview with Yosef Blau, January 30, 1986.

20. *OU,* April 1934, p. 1; *Comm.,* November 18, 1936, p. 2. Interview with Jacob I. Hartstein, August 15, 1985; Aaron Rothkoff, *Bernard Revel: Builder of American Jewish Orthodoxy* (Philadelphia: Jewish Publication Society, 1972), p. 198.

21. See Revel's description of the proposed course of study in Aaron Rothkoff, *Bernard Revel,* pp. 198–199. In the 1936–37 *YC Catalog* there is some mention of Jewish studies courses in YC "for students whose knowledge of Hebrew is not sufficient." A year later there is a comparable reference: "specific preparatory courses are provided (in YC) for students with inadequate preparation in Jewish studies." YC catalogs are thereafter silent on unprepared students until 1948 when reference is made to an admissions category for students "who are not registered in either of the above schools" (TI or RIETS). Mention of this seemingly nameless prototype is made a year later when three categories of students are mentioned as in the "Yeshiva College of Liberal Arts and Sciences." Four years later the catalog noted in parenthesis that "students not registered in either the Theological Seminary or the Teachers Institute can

therefore be admitted only with the special permission of the President of the University." There were students in this unnamed JSP prototype. See below for information on one basketball player who was, it seems, admitted under this program. Another student who went through this program recalls taking twelve hours per week of Jewish studies in the morning. This student had come in with a Talmud Torah and public high school background. He also had had early Jewish training at the Crown Heights yeshiva. Telephone interview with Steven Jaffe, January 30, 1986. Interview with Label Dulitz, February 6, 1986. The JSP clearly was the most organized and visible of these initiatives. See *Yeshiva College Catalog,* 1936–37, p. 16; 1937–38, p. 21; 1948–49, p. 12; 1953–55, p. 12; *Yeshiva University Bulletin,* January 1946, p. 8.

22. *Ha-Melitz,* May 14, 1956, p. 2.

23. *Ha-Melitz,* March 1, 1956, pp. 1–4; Joseph Walter Eichenbaum, ed., *The James Striar School of General Jewish Studies Bar-Mitzvah Journal* (New York: n.p. 1969), pp. 8–9. Yosef Blau pointed out that the activities and remarks must also be seen in the context of the effloresence of Yeshiva as a university in the mid-1950s. The building of AECOM and the social work school provided a basis for fears that the yeshiva was losing its way. See interview with Yosef Blau, January 30, 1986; Goldstein in telephone interview with Rosenshein, January 27, 1986; interview with Label Dulitz, February 6, 1986; Aaron Rothkoff, April 3, 1985.

24. Interview with Sandy Ader, November 5, 1985; Yosef Blau, January 30, 1986.

25. Interview with Hyman Pomerantz, August 30, 1985.

26. See the pro-sports editorial in the *Boston Jewish Advocate* of 1934, quoted in Aaron Rothkoff, *Bernard Revel,* p. 137.

27. Aaron Rothkoff, *Bernard Revel,* p. 138; *JF,* April 1954, p. 55.

28. See *Comm.,* April 15, 1948, p. 2, for complaints about unbecoming behavior at basketball games. The issue of no *kipot* was also raised. Coach Bernard Sarachek claimed there was a tacit agreement with Dr. Belkin that when Yeshiva played in Madison Square Garden the boys would wear *kipot* on the bench. On the court, it was a question of personal safety, which the rabbi understood. Interview with Bernard Sarachek, January 26, 1986.

29. Interview with Hyman Pomerantz, August 30, 1986. Among the rabbis who went through the Yeshiva basketball program were two requiring special mention. Abraham Avrech, destined to play an important role in CSD, was instrumental in founding the Yeshiva high school league. Irving Koslowe was a student coach of the Yeshiva team in 1930–1939. The letter to Dr. Grinstein can be found in student file #1758.

30. Interview with Irwin Blumenreich, January 26, 1986.

31. Interview with Bernard Sarachek, January 26, 1986.

32. On subway "skull sessions" see *New York Times,* November 25, 1955. Interview with Sarachek, January 26, 1986.

33. Interview with Sandy Ader, November 8, 1985; *YU Athletic Program (1985–86),* n.p., is the source for Yeshiva's basketball statistics.

34. Interviews with Sandy Ader, November 5, 1986; Bernard Sarachek, January 26, 1986; Yosef Blau, January 30, 1986.

35. Interview with Yosef Blau, January 30, 1986.

36. Interviews with Sandy Ader, November 6, 1985; Bernard Sarachek, January 26, 1986; Yosef Blau, January 30, 1986; Sam Stern, March 17, 1986. It has also

been suggested that, although Rabbi Besdin clearly loved the 1956 team members, it was not he who admitted them. Apparently he was appointed director after the first admissions had been made. Subsequent to that initial class, more careful screening took place.

37. To be sure, the debate over the place of basketball players at Yeshiva did not end with the graduation of the first JSP players. In the winter of 1964 a controversy developed over a plan to hold a "homecoming weekend honoring the basketball team and the alumni." Proponents of the plan argued that basketball players, Saracheck's men, had made significant contributions to Yeshiva's life and reputation. It was they who had "given of (themselves) so that the Yeshiva name would be respected." Initially their plan was approved by the student council, but after growing opposition became manifest, permission was rescinded. One opponent argued that while extracurricular activities could play a role in the Yeshiva's life and "members of a team may be serving a useful and even necessary function," they would "hesitate to call their contribution a noble one." For these critics, Yeshiva had to be "recognized" and "respected" as a "House of Torah." See *Comm.*, December 10, 1964, p. 11; December 31, 1964, p. 7, *Hame.* (Shevat 5725), p. 3. On the contemporary basketball scene, circa 1986, see *YU Athletic Program* and *Outreach* (1985) a pamphlet published by the Yeshiva University Public Relations Office which profiles one of the new era basketball stars.

38. During JSPs first generation approximately 8.7 percent of its students came from Queens and 9 percent from Nassau and Suffolk counties as against 15.4 percent from Brooklyn, Manhattan, and the Bronx. Thirty-nine percent of the students came from the smaller Jewish communities (YUMW).

39. The breakdown of "years of Jewish training" for JSP's first generation and beyond was 4.2 percent with less than 4 years, 23.8 percent with 4–6 years, 44 percent with 7–9 years, and 27.3 percent with 10–12 years (YUMW).

40. Rabbi Besdin's records indicate the religious training and outlook of parents, provide the results of his personal testing system, and also give glimpses into the personality of each applicant. In addition, Besdin's own enthusiasm for his students comes through in his exhortations and declamations recorded in his notes.

41. Student file #867.

42. Student file #868.

43. See, for example, students files #663, #684. Through these interviews one derives a sense of the multiplicity of levels of observance and non-observance of the Sabbath held by 1950–1970s American Jews with links to the Orthodox synagogue.

44. For the 1950–1970 period, a total of 707 students entered YC claiming affiliation with either NCSY, TLS, or both. Of this total, some 534 or roughly 75 percent were enrolled in JSS. And 82 percent of NCSY-TLS youngsters who entered YC came from outside New York City (YUMW). The TLS' own study, based in part on an interview with the late Rabbi Besdin, suggests that 20 percent of his JSP students were influenced by TLS. See Susan Schaalman, ed., *Torah Leadership Seminar Bar Mitzvah Yearbook 1955–1967* (printed by the Youth Bureau, Community Service Bureau, Yeshiva University, 1967), p. 27.

45. Abraham Stern, "The Evolution of the Seminar Idea," in Schaalman, ed., p. 3. See Elliot Lissman, "Seminarians' Backgrounds," in *ibid.*, pp. 56–58. See also

Chana Lazarus, "Eight Years of Service, 1955–1962," in *ibid.*, pp. 61–66. To be sure, if the male students were factored out of the latter study there might be a larger percentage of day school and yeshiva students included, but certainly not a larger number with the most minimal of educations.

   46. Eichenbaum, ed., *The James Striar School*, p. 22. Prior to 1956 only fourteen students in YC's twenty-eight years of existence came from identifiable Conservative groups. Between 1956 and 1960, 44 USY members entered YC; between 1960 and 1965 some 98 did likewise. A total of 303 such students chose Yeshiva between 1956 and 1979, 237 in JSS. Ninety percent of the USY youngsters came from outside the New York area.

   47. Student files #868, #1404; see also student files #663 and #852.

   48. On RIETS graduates in Rabbinical Assembly pulpits in the post-1945 period, see Lawrence S. Zieler, "Orthodox Musmachim and their Membership in the Rabbinical Assembly" (seminar paper, Bernard Revel Graduate School, Yeshiva University, Fall 1983). Letters to and from Dr. Hyman Grinstein and Samuel L. Sar in student file #2775.

   49. Student file #1282.

   50. Student file #685; see also Lissman, "Seminarians' Backgrounds," pp. 65–66.

   51. Student file #680.

   52. Eichenbaum, ed., *The James Striar School*, pp. 19–20; Schaalman, ed., *Torah Leadership Seminar*, pp. 27–28. For more on the lines of JSS-TI demarcation issue, see chapter 11.

   53. Two years into the JSP program, the percentage of students with primary yeshiva education had dropped to 63 percent. It rose to 66 percent a year later; a figure that would long remain constant. The percentages on Hebrew high school students noted in the text were comparable to those during Dr. Revel's days (YUMW).

10. THE WOMEN OF STERN COLLEGE

   1. Sarna, in his introduction to his translation of Weinberger's work, discussed how religious problems in the home affected sons of immigrants, but "the book ignores daughters." See Weinberger, *People Walk on Their Heads: Moses Weinberger's "Jews and Judaism in New York*," Jonathan D. Sarna, tr.," (New York: Holmes and Meier, 1982), p. 20. On the nature of Jewish education for girls in Eastern Europe, see Emanuel Gamoran, *Changing Conceptions in Jewish Education* (New York: Macmillan, 1925), 1:120–121.

   2. On those new programs for Jewish and secular education for girls in late nineteenth-century Eastern Europe, see Gamoran, *Changing Conceptions*, pp. 193–194. See also Zevi H. Harris, "A Study of Trends in Jewish Education for Girls in New York City" (Ph.D. dissertation, Yeshiva University, 1956), pp. 120–121.

   3. Shain, *All for the Boss* (New York: Feldheim, 1984), pp. 30–31, 42, and passim.

   4. Alexander Dushkin, *Jewish Education in New York City* (New York: Bureau of Jewish Education, 1918), pp. 64, 74, 240–241; JCR, pp. 367–393; Herbert S. Goldstein, ed, *Forty Years of Struggle for a Principle: The Biography of Harry Fischel*

(New York: Bloch, 1928), pp. 38–39; Israel Konovitz, *A Brief Survey of 31 Conferences Held by Talmud Torah Principals in New York City* (New York: Bureau of Jewish Education, 1912), p. 22. Dushkin noted, in 1917, that of the approximately 31,500 boys and girls receiving formal supplementary Jewish education at NYU, only 10,500 or one-third were girls. And these girls were overly represented in "namby pamby, goody goody" Sunday Schools, not in the more intensive day and Sunday communal and congregational schools.

5. Dushkin, *Jewish Education*, pp. 81–84; Hyman B. Grinstein, "The History of the Teachers Institute of Yeshiva University," in Moshe Carmilly and Hayim Leaf, eds., *Samuel Belkin Memorial Volume* (New York: Erna Michael College, Yeshiva University, 1981), p. 259.

6. Gamoran, *Changing Conceptions*, pp. 196–200.

7. Initially the preparatory schools were designed to be coeducational, but opposition from the Orthodox talmud torahs changed Benderly's mind and the schools became for girls only. See Arthur Goren, *New York Jews and the Quest for Community: The Kehillah Experiment, 1908–1922* (New York: Columbia University Press, 1970), p. 111; Harris, "A Study of Trends," pp. 54–55.

8. Harris, "A Study of Trends," pp. 156, 246; Isidor Margolis, *Jewish Teacher Training Schools in the United States* (New York: National Council for Torah Education, 1964), pp. 244–247.

9. *JF*, June 1925, p. 234.

10. Jacob Rader Marcus, ed., *The American Jewish Woman: A Documentary History* (New York and Cincinnati: Ktav, 1981), pp. 701–705.

11. *UJE*, 10: 370–371.

12. Marcus, *The American Jewish Woman*, p. 705.

13. Shain, *All for the Boss*, pp. 92, 97, 194, 198, 385–387.

14. Shulamith Goldstein interview with Sylvia Fuchs, February 15, 1986. See also, on other exceptions to the rule, Shulamith Goldstein interviews with Sadie Klavan and Elizabeth Isaacs, February 15, 1986. The latter interviewee attended Barnard between 1919 and 1923, during which time she found possibly 20 observant Jewish young women in the entire student body. Interestingly, she suggested that the proportions of women from her upper middle class peer group attending college were higher than the average. See also interview with Esther Zuroff, March 10, 1986.

15. On the Flatbush Yeshiva's approach to Jewish education and its student body, see Sidney Z. Lieberman, "A Historical Study of the Yeshiva High School Curriculum in New York City (Ph.D. dissertation, Yeshiva University, 1959), pp. 162–165; Moses I. Shulman, "The Yeshiva Etz Hayim Institute of Boro Park," *Jewish Education* (Fall 1948), pp. 47–49. See interview with Hyman Pomerantz, August 30, 1985, on afternoon classes at Flatbush.

16. Harris, "A Study of Trends," pp. 28, 30; Joseph Friedenson, "The Mother of Generations," in Nisson Wolpin, ed., *The Torah World: A Treasury of Biographical Sketches* (Brooklyn, N.Y.; Mesorah Publications, 1982), pp. 162–174; Judith Grunfeld, "The Story of Beth Jacob," in *Jubilee Book Agudas Israel Organization* (London: n.p. 1942), pp. 36–39.

17. Harris, "A Study of Trends," p. 30. On the knotty issue of appropriate Jewish curriculum, including the question of women studying Talmud, see the recent

discussions of Warren Zev Harvey, "The Obligation of Talmud on Women According to Maimonides," *Tradition* (Summer 1981), pp. 122–129; Arthur M. Silver, "May Women Be Taught Bible, Mishnah, and Talmud?" *Tradition* (Summer 1978), pp. 74–84.

18. Harris, "A Study of Trends," pp. 128ff. In 1938 the school set up its Midrasha Shulamith, a four-year evening high school for graduates who were then at public school during the day.

19. *OU,* September 1933, p. 6; February 1938, p. 4.

20. *OU,* December 1943, p. 14; Margolis, *Jewish Teacher Training Schools,* pp. 32–53, 195–228, 291–327. See also interview with Israel Miller, August 27, 1985.

21. Harris, "A Study of Trends," pp. 136, 156, 177.

22. "Sixteen to Graduate from the First Jewish High School for Girls," YUPR, May 17, 1951. Telephone interviews with Sylvia Klaperman Tuchman, March 14, 1986; Selma Rosenman Nadboy, March 19, 1986; Miriam Scheiner Krischer, March 15, 1986; Yospa Goldberg Werner, March 17, 1986; interview with Samuel Levine, March 26, 1986.

23. George Kranzler, *Williamsburg: A Jewish Community in Transition* (New York: Feldheim, 1961), p. 146.

24. Harris, "A Study of Trends," pp. 160–162; interview with Esther Zuroff, March 10, 1986; telephone interviews with Sylvia Klaperman Tuchman, March 14, 1986; Selma Rosenman Nadboy, March 15, 1986. To be sure, when dances were held in Central's precincts in the early 1950s, a committee of parents protested the school's policies and the activity was ultimately abolished. See also interview with Samuel Levine, March 26, 1986.

25. Lieberman, "A Historical Study," p. 248. Between 1955 and 1960 some 31 percent of SCW enrollees came out of Central, as opposed to 5 percent from Beth Jacob Schools, New York based and otherwise (a goodly proportion of the small Beth Jacob group came from its Baltimore affiliate). Another 18 percent of the student body came from day schools both in and out of New York. Between 1954 and 1975, 49 percent of the entrants from New York came from Central, its Brooklyn, and later its Manhattan branches. General elementary and secondary education and Jewish education were the most popular career goals for almost the entire generation between 1954 and 1975. (YUMW). Telephone interview with Marsha Brickman Hirt, March 12, 1986; Judith Jacobs Leifer, March 9, 1986.

26. Telephone interviews with Selma Rosenman Nadboy, March 15, 1986; Yospe Goldberg Werner, March 17, 1986; interview with Esther Zuroff, March 10, 1986. It also should be noted that the free tuition policies at City University played an important role in college decision making at that time.

27. Untitled YUPR dealing with Yeshiva's creation of its TIW, September 28, 1953. Jack H. Doueck, "Jewish Education for Women and the Teachers Institute for Women" (seminar paper, Bernard Revel Graduate School Yeshiva University, 1985, pp. 14–21).

28. *AJYB* (1962), 63:511; telephone interview with Sheila Siegel Tanenbaum, March 12, 1986. Interview with Esther Zuroff, March 10, 1986.

29. Telephone interview with Marsha Brickman Hirt, March 12, 1986.

30. Interview with Esther Sar Zuroff, March 10, 1986.

31. Interviews with Paula Kestenbaum Fuchs, Miriam Weintraub Reiss, and Helen Berger Laufer, March 11, 1986.

32. Interview with Paula Goldstein, March 25, 1986.

33. For the years 1954–1975, 72.9 percent of the women entering Stern from New York homes had attended primary level day schools (through eighth grade) as opposed to 20.5 percent who had attended a Talmud Torah or Sunday School; 18.4 percent of the New York Stern enrollees did not attend Yeshiva High School; 49 percent of New Yorkers attending Stern came from Central as opposed to just 7 percent from Beth Jacob schools of all sorts and 24.2 percent from day schools. Of the enrollees from New York 10.6 percent had less than three years of Jewish education and 8.7 percent had between four and six years of training (YUMW). An informal estimate of the Jewish educational background of SCW's second graduating class indicated that "25 percent knew no Hebrew, 25 percent had a scanty talmud torah education, 25 percent attended the Yeshiva ketanah, while 25 percent went all the way through the high school." See *JF*, June 1959, p. 90.

34. Interviews with Rita Markowitz Siff and Genia Prager Socol, March 9, 1986.

35. Interview with Genia Prager Socol, March 9, 1986.

36. Interview with Beverly Tanenbaum, March 9, 1986.

37. Interview with Miriam Schreiber, March 9, 1986.

38. For the first five years of SCW 40 percent of the students were New Yorkers, but during the first generation (1954–1975) the percentage dropped to 24 percent. In the first five years 22 percent came from smaller communities and the percentage increased to 35.2 percent during the first generation. For the same period approximately two-thirds of the YC student body came from New York (YUMW).

39. Thirty-six percent of the students entering SCW from outside New York in the 1954–1975 period had only talmud torah backgrounds as opposed to 56 percent who had primary day school training. Thirty-eight percent of SCW people from out of town had day school educations through the twelfth grade as opposed to 48 percent who did not. And over 10 percent of the out-of-towners came with no formal training at all (YUMW).

40. Of the students entering SCW 21.8 percent noted their NCSY-TLS connection and more than 91 percent were from outside the New York community. The remaining people, the New Yorkers, may have been "advisers" to their less learned colleagues (YUMW). See also Chana Lazarus, "Eight Years of Service, 1955–62," in Susan Schaalman, ed., *Torah Leadership Seminar Bar Mitzvah Yearbook 1955–67* (printed by the Youth Bureau, Community Service Bureau, Yeshiva University, 1967), p. 61.

41. Although the 113 students were only 2 percent of the total SCW enrollment, they constituted in both numbers and percentile a more significant group than their counterparts on the uptown campus. The NFTY contingent was less than one-half of 1 percent of the student body (YUMW).

42. Interviews with Genia Prager Socol, Ethel Pelcowitz Gottlieb, Rita Markowitz Siff, and Roslyn Koenigsburg, March 9, 1986; and with Shulamith Goldstein, March 22, 1986.

43. Marcus, *The American Jewish Woman*, p. 702; Stern College memorabilia in the possession of Genia P. Socol, made available to me in March 1986.

11. LIKE ALL OTHER UNIVERSITIES?

1. We have estimated that by 1960 a full one-third of the Yeshiva student body came in with other than day school backgrounds. Documents from the files of the Yeshiva University Office of Admissions indicate that in the early 1960s (1960–1964), the percentage of public school youngsters entering YC ranged from between 24–33 percent of the total. By 1967–68 the percentage had dropped to 18 percent and from then through the 1970s the percentage never exceeded 25 percent in any given year. By 1981 the percentage had dropped to approximately 12 percent of the total. In 1984 it hit an all-time low of 7 percent.

2. In 1964 the TI student council president upbraided the critics of his classmates for creating a "religious curtain" at the school. See *Hame.*, (Sivan 5724), June 1964, p. 2. For the full report on the survey of religious attitudes, see *Comm.*, May 23, 1972, p. 4.

3. On the 4D dilemma at YC, see *Pulse*, September 18, 1969, p. 1; February 27, 1969, p. 2; January 3, 1969, pp. 1–2. On the multitude of draft dodges used in the 1960s and 1970s, see Lawrence M. Baskir and William A. Strauss, *Chance and Circumstance: The Draft, the War and the Vietnam Generation* (New York: Random House, 1978), pp. 6–7, 19–25, 27–32, 36, 64–65. On the experiences of one Orthodox student in a yeshiva draft school, see interview with N. D. Gurock, June 1, 1986.

4. Thomas Powers, *The War at Home: Vietnam and the American People* (New York: Grossman, 1973), pp. 138–163; Stokely Carmichael and Charles V. Hamilton, *Black Power: The Politics of Liberation in America* (New York: Random House, 1967), pp. 34–56, 161; Alexander Kendrick, *The Wound Within* (Boston and Toronto: Little, Brown, 1974), pp. 206–207, 224–225, 239–240.

5. Nat Hentoff, ed., *Black Anti-Semitism and Jewish Racism* (New York: Schocken, 1969); Louis Harris and Bert E. Swanson, *Black-Jewish Relations in New York City* (New York: Praeger 1971); Gary T. Marx, *Protest and Prejudice: A Study of Belief in the Black Community* (Westport, Conn: Greenwood, 1979).

6. Among recent histories of America's long nightmare in Vietnam, see Stanley Karnow, *Vietnam: A History* (New York: Viking Press, 1983), especially, pp. 22, 189–191, 195, 318; Kendrick, *The Wound Within*, p. 250, 523–545.

7. On Jewish responses to the crisis of Vietnam, see the range of opinions in *Judaism* (Winter 1969), pp. 17–29; *The Reconstructionist*, December 12, 1969, pp. 4–5; *Jewish Life* (September-October 1969), pp. 22–29; *Jewish Observer*, May 8, 1970, pp. 8–9.

8. On Dr. Revel and his "Bundism," see chapter 4.

9. *Pulse*, October 24, 1968, p. 2.

10. *Pulse*, September 26, 1968, p. 1; October 17, 1968, p. 2; March 6, 1969, p. 3. On early, sometimes turbulent Jewish-Irish relations in that neighborhood, see Ronald Bayor, *Neighbors in Conflict: The Irish, Germans, Jews and Italians of New York City, 1929–1941* (Baltimore: Johns Hopkins University Press, 1968, pp. 150–153. On the problem of muggings in Washington Heights in the late 1960s, see *Comm.*, November 14, 1968, p. 1.

11. *Pulse*, October 17, 1968, p. 2.

12. *Pulse*, September 26, 1968, p. 1.

13. *Pulse*, May 27, 1969, p. 2. On social activist criticism of Yeshiva's in-

action in response to the Biafra crisis, see *Pulse*, December 5, 1968, p. 1; September 18, 1968, p. 1; October 17, 1968, p. 2.

14. *Comm.*, April 28, 1966, p. 6. See also *Comm.*, May 21, 1966, for Greenberg's response to criticism of his original article.

15. *Pulse*, November 7, 1968, p. 1. For the JDL's own authorized version of their early history see Meir Kahane, *The History of the Jewish Defense League* (Radnor, Pa.; Chilton, 1974).

16. *Pulse*, November 14, 1968, p. 2.

17. *Comm.*, December 6, 1972, p. 2.

18. *Hame.*, December 1969, p. 3. See also, *Pulse*, May 27, 1969, p. 2.

19. *Comm.*, June 2, 1966, p. 7.

20. In truth, the Yeshiva campus was first caught up in the question of Vietnam about 1967 when the issue of chaplaincy was first raised. Few students were ready to enter military service as rabbis. For Yeshiva officials, this reluctance was a touchy moral and patriotic question. Here scholars were receiving pre-ministry deferments (4Ds), but were unwilling to pay Uncle Sam back. Accordingly, they instituted a semi-official draft lottery for chaplains. Of course, students questioned the policy, reflecting not only their opinions of the war but also the question of how to be a *ben-torah* away from shul, friends, and colleagues in this secularized environment. See, on this issue, *Hame.*, March 9, 1967, pp. 5, 6, 8; November 1, 1967, p. 1.

21. *Hame.*, (Teveth 5730), January 1970; *Comm.*, November 26, 1969, p. 5; interview with Steven Bayme, April 7, 1986.

22. *Comm.*, April 28, 1966, p. 6.

23. *Comm.*, October 30, 1969, pp. 1, 6.

24. *Comm.*, November 13, 1969, p. 1.

25. *Comm.*, November 26, 1969, pp. 3, 5, 7; see also *Comm.*, December 24, 1969, for a discussion of antiwar activities at SCW. Some SCW women were as active as their YC brothers on this issue, and a few traveled to Washington for the November demonstration.

26. *Comm.*, May 27, 1970, pp. 1, 8.

27. *Comm.*, November 26, 1969, p. 5; May 21, 1975, p. 8; October 30, 1969, p. 7.

28. Interview with Steven Bayme, April 7, 1986; interview with Gary Rubin, April 10, 1986.

29. *Comm.*, October 30, 1969, p. 6; interview with Shalom Carmy, April 7, 1986.

30. Interview with Shalom Carmy, April 7, 1986.

31. *Comm.*, May 27, 1970; *Hame.*, (Iyar, 5730), May 1970, p. 3; interview with Gary Rubin, April 7, 1986.

32. *Hame.*, (Iyar 5730), May 1970, p. 4; *Comm.*, May 27, 1970, p. 8.

33. *Comm.*, October 30, 1969, p. 7.

34. *Comm.*, May 27, 1970, p. 8. See also *Hame.*, December 28, 1967, pp. 1, 3, 9, 10; (Nissan, 5730), April 1970, p. 6.

35. *Comm.*, May 27, 1970, p. 7; interviews with Shalom Carmy, April 7, 1986; Gary Rubin, April 10, 1986.

36. *Comm.*, September 29, 1970, pp. 1, 8, see also *Hame.*, December 28, 1967, pp. 1, 3, 9, 10; (Nissan, 5730), April 1970, p. 6.

37. *Comm.,* October 30, 1969, pp. 3, 7.

38. *Hame.* (January 1966), p. 2; flyers of the Negotiating Committee of the Concerned Students Coalition, April 17, 1970, in the possession of Heshie Billet.

39. *Comm.,* November 11, 1969, pp. 1, 6; *Hame.,* September 30, 1968, p. 4; interview with Mordecai Feuerstein, May 20, 1986; David Ribner, April 9, 1986.

40. *Comm.,* November 11, 1969, pp. 1, 6; *Hame.,* January 1966, p. 2; *Pulse,* October 31, 1968, p. 1.

41. *JSS Report: Part II,* May 1969, pp. 1, 2.

42. *Hame.,* January 1966, p. 2; flyers of the Negotiating Committee.

43. *Hame.,* December 28, 1967, p. 2; October 10, 1966, pp. 4, 6.

44. *Hame.,* September 30, 1968, p. 5.

45. *Comm.,* November 11, 1969, pp. 1, 6; interviews with Heshie Billet, May 8, 1986; Mordecai Feuerstein, May 20, 1986; and David Ribner, April 9, 1986.

46. *Comm.,* February 19, 1970, pp. 1, 5; see also *Hame,* December 1969, p. 2.

47. *Hame.,* December 1969, pp. 1, 2; *Comm.,* February 19, 1970, p. 8; March 5, 1970, p. 1; *Hame.,* March 1970, p. 2.

48. "Report of a Meeting at Dr. Belkin's House," March 5, 1970, typescript copy of minutes of meeting between student representatives and administration representatives in the possession of Heshie Billet; *Comm.,* May 5, 1970, pp. 1, 4; February 19, 1970, pp. 1, 5.

49. *Hame.,* December 1969, pp. 1, 2; *Comm.,* December 24, 1969, p. 2; *Hame.,* March 1970, p. 2; *Comm.,* March 5, 1970, pp. 1, 5; interviews with Heshie Billet, May 8, 1986; David Ribner, April 9, 1986; Mordecai Feuerstein, May 20, 1986; and Eliezer Diamond, May 26, 1986.

50. *Comm.,* February 19, 1970, pp. 1, 5; December 24, 1969, p. 2; May 15, 1970, p. 5. Interviews with Mordecai Feuerstein, May 20, 1986; David Ribner, and Gary Rubin, April 10, 1986. The CSC, as noted, was led by Semicha students with significant support from undergraduate RIETS fellows. The presidents of the JSS, EMC, and SCW student councils seem also to have supported the efforts. But it also appears that the YC student council leadership and the editorial board of the *Commentator* were far from totally sympathetic. In fact, one might speak of *Commentator* as supporting the Belkin administration while *Hamevaser* backed the dissenters.

51. *Hame.,* March 1970, p. 2; *Comm.,* March 5, 1970, pp. 1, 5; interviews with Eliezer Diamond, May 26, 1986; and Mordecai Feuerstein, May 20, 1986.

52. Interviews with Heshie Billet, Mary 8, 1986; David Ribner, April 9, 1986; and Mordecai Feuerstein, May 20, 1986.

53. *Comm.,* April 15, 1970, pp. 1, 5; interview with Mordecai Feuerstein, May 20, 1986.

54. *Comm.,* April 15, 1970, pp. 1, 5; *Hame.,* April 1970, p. 2; interviews with David Ribner, April 9, 1986; Heshie Billet, May 8, 1986; and Mordecai Feuerstein, May 20, 1986.

55. Flyer of the Negotiating Committee; *Hame.,* May 1970, pp. 1, 6.

56. Interviews with David Ribner, April 9, 1986, and Mordecai Feuerstein, May 20, 1986. Some of the more responsible members of the CSC did, in fact, participate in a review of Yeshiva's policies with State officials in the fall of 1970; see *Comm.,* September 29, 1970, p. 1; November 18, 1970, pp. 1, 5.

57. *Comm.,* December 16, 1970, pp. 1, 6; March 22, 1972, pp. 1, 6. These protestors adopted a subtle name change. They now called themselves alternately "The New Students Coalition" or the "Semicha Students Coalition." They published and distributed broadsides against Dr. Belkin at a variety of public functions. See, as an example of these documents, the undated flyer "Did You See the Belfer Dedication, Sunday?"

12. TOWARD A SECOND CENTURY

1. "Dr. Samuel Belkin Named Chancellor of Yeshiva University"; undated YUPR, September 1975?; *New York Times,* April 19, 1976.

2. "Dr. Samuel Belkin" undated YUPR; "Dr. Norman Lamm, Author, Philosopher and Teacher," undated YUPR (August 1976). Yeshiva press reports have it that fifty candidates were considered during the six-month process.

3. "Norman Lamm," *Current Biography* (1978), pp. 27–30; "Dr. Lamm, Author," undated YUPR.

4. "Yeshiva University President Urges Orthodox Community," undated press release, Union of Orthodox Jewish Congregations of America; Norman Lamm, "Modern Orthodox Identity Crisis," *Jewish Life,* May-June 1969, p. 7, quoted in William Helreich, *The World of Yeshiva: An Intimate Portrait of Orthodox Jewry* (New York: Free Press, 1982), p. 230.

5. "New York's Newest School, Benjamin N. Cardozo School of Law Opens September 8," YUPR, September 3, 1976; Benjamin N. Cardozo School of Law Opens with 303 Students," YUPR, September 13, 1976; *Benjamin N. Cardozo School of Law-Yeshiva University,* undated pamphlet (1980?).

6. *New York Daily News,* February 2, 1982, "What the High Court's 'Yeshiva Decision Has Meant to Yeshiva University Itself'"; *The Chronicle of Higher Education,* February 20, 1985; "Yeshiva University," undated YUPR fact sheet on its schools, p. 13. An additional component in the Yeshiva University faculty labor difficulties may arise because of the differences between a *rebbe* and a college professor. It may be argued that those who opposed unionization pictured the Yeshiva instructor as a religious teacher, albeit one who is Americanized and even secularized, while union forces had as their basic frame of reference the situation at other colleges.

7. Linda Yellin Fisch, "Patterns of Religious and Feminist Socialization Among Jewish-College Women" (Ed.D. dissertation, Columbia University Teachers College, 1983), pp. 40, 42, 48, 70, 80–82.

8. Interview with Judy Paikin, June 4, 1986; Helmreich, *The World of Yeshiva,* pp. 227–228. Interestingly, the battlegrounds for student recruitment involving Yeshiva admissions officers are often Israeli yeshivas that offer one-year programs for American high school graduates. After that year, the question is whether the study of Torah will continue at Yeshiva or at another yeshiva which deemphasizes the secular, or will the year constitute the end of intensive Jewish study, and off to Queens College or Columbia.

9. Helmreich, *The World of Yeshiva,* p. 228.

10. Marianne R. Sauna, "The Beginning of Our Redemption: Stages in the Development of Jewish Life at Princeton University" (seminar paper, Jewish Theological Seminary of America, 1985). Statistics on kosher food on campus are derived from

Ivan L. Tillem, ed., *The Jewish Directory and Almanac* (New York: Pacific Press 1984), pp. 388–400.

11. *The Jewish Week.* September 26, 1986, pp. 4, 52; for early statements by Dr. Lamm on "Centrist Orthodoxy," see *The Jewish Week-American Examiner,* October 4, 1981, p. 4; *Jewish Times* (Baltimore), July 16, 1982.

12. *Comm.,* May 9, 1985, pp. 7, 9.

Index

Abraham Lincoln High School (New York City), 103
Abramowitz, Aaron, 18
Abramowitz, David, 18
Abramowitz, Meyer, 273n73
Abrams, Norman, 88
Adass Israel (congregation, Berlin), 30
Adler, Cyrus, 54, 63, 100
After-school education, 16, 99; *see also* Supplementary Jewish education
Agudat ha-Rabbanim (Union of Orthodox Rabbis of the United States and Canada), 20, 21, 22, 23, 24, 25-26, 28, 30-31, 32, 33, 34, 40, 56, 61; and JTS, 39; membership, 95, and Orthodox Union, 25-26; RIETS and, 35-37, 44, 48, 51, 57, 62; selection of Belkin, 129, 131-32, 135, 136, 139, 140; support for and conflicts with Revel, 122-26; and YC, 93-94
Albert Einstein College of Medicine of Yeshiva University (AECOM), 160-62; post-World War II context for, 156-59
Alexandrian Halakah in Apologetic Literature, The (Belkin), 137
Alperstein, Rabbi, 21
American Academy for Jewish Research, 55
American Hebrew Theological University (proposed), 278n5
Americanization, 10, 20, 21, 167; and education of girls, 187; resistance to, 12, 14, 109, 142; RIETS and, 43, 44, 47, 52, 58-60; of seminary training, 29-31, 32, 33-35, 37, 38-42; *see also* Assimilation
American Medical Association, Council on Medical Education, 158, 159

American Mercury, 159
American Orthodoxy, 117; battle with Conservatives after World War II, 146-48; direction of, in 1960, 214-15; ideological shift in, 1950s, 148-49; ideology for response to postwar American society, 142-45; methodology in meeting educational needs, 89; as movement, 51, 78, 117; Revel's articulation of, 43-66, 121; social characteristics, 1980s, 1-5; and Talmud Torah system, 99-100; winnowing of, 166-69, 185; YC students as leaders in, 7, 120
Andron family, 187-88, 192-93
Andron, Jacob, 16
Andron, Samuel Y., 16, 19
Anti-Semitism, 90, 91, 167, 234, 253; decline in, 144; in higher education, 155-60; social, 143
Anti-Vietnam War movement, 217, 225-31, 241
Aronowitz, Benjamin, 48, 49, 134
Assimilation, 10, 27, 93, 120; resistance to, 13, 142-45, 150; through public schools, 83, 102
Association of American Orthodox Congregations, 12, 29
Avrech, Abraham, 280n29
A-Z Lewin-Epstein, 34

Bacon, Isaac, 229
Baltimore, Md., 197, 252; Jewish education in, 84, 97-98
Baltimore City College, 97
Barash, David Harry, 24
Barnard College, 203, 250-51, 283n14
Baron, Nachum Dan, 23, 41, 52